The Persistence of Reality I

Pragmatism without Foundations

The Persistence of Reality
JOSEPH MARGOLIS

The Persistence of Reality

Pragmatism Without Foundations

Reconciling Realism and Relativism

JOSEPH MARGOLIS

Basil Blackwell

©Joseph Margolis 1986

First published 1986

Basil Blackwell Ltd
108 Cowley Road, Oxford OX4 1JF, UK

Basil Blackwell Inc.
432 Park Avenue South, Suite 1503,
New York, NY 10016, USA

British Library Cataloguing in Publication Data

Margolis, Joseph
      The persistence of reality.
      1: Pragmatism without foundations:
      reconciling realism and relativism
      1. Reality   2. Perception
      I. Title
      153.7   BD331

      ISBN 0–631–15034–X

Library of Congress Cataloging in Publication Data

Margolis, Joseph Zalman, 1924–
            (The persistence of reality; 1)
            Includes index.
            1. Realism. 2. Relativity. I. Title. II. Series:
Margolis, Joseph Zalman, 1924–   . Persistence of
reality; 1.
B835.M34   1986   149′.2   86–10755
ISBN 0–631–15034–X

Typeset by Photo·Graphics, Honiton, Devon, UK
Printed in Great Britain by The Camelot Press Ltd, Southampton

For my very dear friends, who have strung the space between the Aaland Islands and the island of Hönö and a little beyond with a fine affection: Mats Furberg, Ingrid Björkman, Sven Linnér, Gören Hermerén, and Johan Wrede in particular.

Contents

Preface

I have no wish to hide my pleasure at having completed this essay. It's the first sustained new effort I have been able to make since a longish illness that now, happily, is behind me. I mention it primarily to give point to the sense I have of something very much like a second life. No need of course to pursue the theme, except perhaps to say that discontinuities in life, rather like Kuhnian discontinuities in science, sometimes usher in small revolutions.

Time has been on my side, I think. The intervening years have enabled me to try my notions a little more patiently than I might have done. In the interval, a number of opportunities have come my way to test these in that dialectical spirit philosophy requires. I single them out for special mention. They have brought me new friends and have imposed responsibilities of a professional sort without which this book could not have become whatever it now is.

In 1982–3, I was awarded a Senior Fellowship from the Center for Dewey Studies, which gave me time to formulate what I now regard as a distinctive option for a disciplined pragmatism. It is somewhat on the heterodox side, so I am particularly grateful to the Center for unconditional support. In 1980, I directed a National Endowment for the Humanities summer seminar on the concept of culture, which I believe shaped my sense of, first, the hopelessness of ignoring the need to reconcile Anglo-American and Continental European philosophical currents, and, second, the inescapability of conceding the full import of the fact that science is a cultural achievement. These are themes only grudgingly acknowledged among the exemplars of analytic philosophy. I trained myself in that mode of philosophy more than I can say I was trained in it. But I suppose I have always had a sense that its rigor – and its rigor is admirable – has simply been wantonly spent without much regard for answering those ulterior questions on which its own confidence should have depended. It seems patent, now, that that confidence is simply unearned – I don't say, misguided.

In 1983–4, I was designated Distinguished Professor at my home university, Temple University, and was able, during that year's release from ordinary teaching-duties, to draft the core essays of this volume – through a series of public lectures and a series of faculty seminars. The principal emphasis of that year's work was the recovery, within the conceptual orientation and idiom of the Anglo-American world, of the neglected issues of the most important Continental European currents of the twentieth century. It was then that I persuaded myself of the extraordinarily detailed convergence between the two traditions, largely ignored on both sides of the Atlantic despite developing mutual curiosity. Also in 1984, I was designated Senior Lecturer for the Council for International Exchange of Scholars (the Fulbright Program), and spent a marvelously rich few months in Scandinavia, lecturing and conferring at nearly all the principal universities in Sweden and a surprisingly large number in Britain, Norway, Denmark, and Finland. That proved a whirlwind visit. I believe I gave thirty lectures in sixty days and met a great many of the ablest philosophers of Scandinavia. As I review that visit, I find the main theme I was refining was in fact the theme of this volume: the interrelationships among the notions of relativism, realism, and pragmatism. I now see that each of these four benefits has been, in its own way, decisive for the order in which my work has cast itself. And, in saying that, I have of course failed to give more than the slightest hint of the freshness and charm of the entire adventure. No doubt it's inappropriate in a professional exercise to rhapsodize about such things. But memory cannot fail to.

Finally, in the last several years, the Greater Philadelphia Philosophy Consortium has regularized its activities. I had a hand in its inception and am most pleased to see it begin its fifth season, with the same professional camaraderie with which it first took life. Under its auspices, I met fortnightly with a group of professionals exploring the linkage between relativism and rationality and put my own theories to the test of the very best sort of contest. There is no real substitute for that. In fact, in both a professional and a personal regard, to be without it is simply to be deprived. The regulars of that group will appreciate my debt to them.

I must add a word of thanks, as on so many other occasions, to Grace Stuart, who once again has put mountainous manuscript into final form.

Philadelphia, Pennsylvania   J. M.
October 1985

Acknowledgements

The following papers have been incorporated, with alterations, into the present volume: "The Nature and Strategies of Relativism," *Mind*, XCII (1983); "Relativism, History and Objectivity in the Human Studies," *Journal for the Theory of Social Behaviour*, XIV (1984); "Historicism, Universalism, and the Threat of Relativism," *The Monist*, LXVII (1984); "Obectivism and Relativism," *The Aristotelian Society Proceedings*, LXXXV (1984–85); "Pragmatism without Foundations," *American Philosophical Quarterly*, XXI (1984); "A Sense of *Rapprochement* between Analytic and Continental Philosophy," *History of Philosophy Quarterly*, II (1985); "Cognitive Issues in the Realist/Idealist Dispute," in Peter A. French et al. (eds), *Midwest Studies in Philosophy*, vol. 5: *Studies in Epistemology* (University of Minnesota Press, 1980); "Skepticism, Foundationalism, and Pragmatism," *American Philosophical Quarterly*, XIV (1977); "Scientific Realism as a Transcendental Issue," *Manuscrito*, IX (1985–6).

Prologue: A Sense of the Issue

Prologues are a form of magic, mixing bias with tact. How to begin what is already finished? How not to answer what has not yet been asked?

A Homeric voice would surely elude the trap of silence: "I sing the reconciliation of realism and relativism!" But the song is a rather complicated one, possibly not even apt for singing. It must soon descend to prosy puzzles

All relativism is divided into three parts: two, known and much maligned; the third, relatively unknown but not malign. Its most ancient form still struggles against the charge of self-contradiction. It is said to claim that whatever is affirmed is at once both true and false. The doctrine is usually labeled *Protagoreanism*. It is derided nearly everywhere – though it still survives and denies the charge. In our contemporary world, relativism is thought rather to be a form of skepticism, in particular that doctrine that fans out in a variety of graded versions of so-called *incommensurability*: the thesis that, for given inquiries, there is no common conceptual ground in terms of which to adjudicate pertinently opposed claims – as of compared meanings, truth values, merit, power. Its opponents hold it to be incoherent or, more moderately (if that's the term), anarchical or irrational. But, again, it survives and alarms its enemies by its undoubted vigor. The third part is a new parcel meant to fulfill the promise of the other two, while not so readily vulnerable to similar suspicions. It provides a sense in which judgments that, on a standard model of truth values, would yield incompatible or contradictory claims need nevertheless not be so construed; and that they may, at the same time, be managed in a way that is tolerant of indeterminately many diverging conceptual orientations, without insisting on radical incommensurability. Is it possible to formulate such a relativism, and would it be at all convincing or useful?

The answer has to do with its bearing on realism, in particular with its bearing on what would count as a reasonable theory of the cognitive powers of our science. Minimally, by *realism* one signifies that, one way or another, the capacity of humans to sustain and discipline an investigation into what they take to be the real world – and, doing that, to state what is true about the world – is a capacity justifiably affirmed. In an obvious, perhaps even trivial, sense, we are all realists – no matter how strenuously we protest. But it is possible both to put this minimal notion into question and to whittle away at the credentials of any less guarded version of that very notion. For instance, one might claim that realism signifies that there are formulable or intelligible truths about the world (truths that we ourselves perhaps could formulate) the confirmation of which requires the cognitive powers of titans or gods who exceed our own such powers. In the current idiom, this doctrine has been labeled *metaphysical realism*, sometimes just realism; and it is often said to be incoherent in much the same spirit as the incommensurability thesis. But it survives. On the other hand, it is clear that both Protagoreanism and incommensurabilist claims call into question the comfortable platitude of our minimal realism. It is in this sense that realism and relativism are thought to be opposed. The third sort of relativism, the favorite of the argument that follows, is meant of course to convey and vindicate our Homeric theme.

There is no way to appreciate the intellectual drama of such an effort without attention to the history of famous quarrels. In fact, the *agon* of our song is just that; since the ancient Protagorean quarrel, many things have changed – so much in fact that, at the present moment, it makes very good sense to attempt once again to reconcile realism and relativism. Now, however, the pertinent quarrel lies between the incommensurabilist version of relativism and the third kind, which we have only barely identified. Both try to come to terms with the most powerful philosophical currents of our contemporary world, and both mean (in rather different ways, of course) to accommodate whatever is salvageable of our minimal realism. Sometimes, the champions of incommensurability – or near-incommensurability – resist characterizing themselves as realists. Certainly, their opponents charge them with being anti-realists of some sort. But that is an extravagance on both sides, perhaps uttered with the seriousness of partisans who insist on remaining recognizably distinct and opposed; for there can be no question that the most challenging versions of the incommensurabilist claim are advanced by warriors notably informed about, and concerned to make sense of, the history of our sciences.

We may, however, for the sake of convenience (and in the spirit of honest bias), distinguish the incommensurabilist and the champion of the third variety as "external" and "internal" relativists. Our intended story, then, is that the historical movement of Western philosophy – of both the Anglo-American and the Continental European sorts – has effectively obliged us, by reason of its largest and least resistible developments, to reconsider the relationship between realism and relativism; and that, with those developments in mind, a fine case can be made to support the claim that realism and *internal* relativism are compatible and, indeed, that a relativistic reading of realism may well be the best that we can afford and the one best suited to the largest conceptual constraints that the converging history of Western thought appears to have recognized. (The epithet "Western" is here meant as an admission of illiteracy in a certain planetary sense.)

Philosophy has been undergoing a revolution. What is perhaps not usually acknowledged in making such pronouncements is that, *if* philosophy is undergoing a revolution (or is not), then all the principal intellectual pursuits of man are undergoing a revolution as well (or are not), even if at somewhat different paces. For philosophy is profoundly parasitic, in examining the conceptual structure and would-be legitimacy of more-or-less regularized inquiries of *other* sorts – although in doing that it inexorably returns to consider its own credentials. It is also a strange conceptual chameleon, since, in examining the conceptual structure of other disciplines, it is colored by those disciplines and, one may even say, becomes an indissoluble part of each. It is a standard claim of our time that there is no principled demarcation between a science and the history or practice of that science; it is just as reasonable to hold that there is no principled demarcation between a science and the (philosophical) theory of that science. Both claims have quite radical implications. At any rate, the shifting themes and doctrines of contemporary philosophy are very strongly opposed to what, for a very long time, used to be regarded as the comparatively settled canons of the discipline: hence, on the claims just mentioned, we must expect that the various sciences and the other disciplines of inquiry are profoundly affected by the bearing of those changes on their own undertakings.

What for our present purpose is particularly salient concerns the gradual "preparation" of the various sciences (inadvertent, of course) for a reconcilation of realism and relativism. Claims of intellectual revolution are often dubious – and myopic. But that is a risk conviction cannot avoid. We may in fact make a rough tally of the constituent themes and leave the ultimate finding with the argument that follows – and its reader. We can only identify them here; they will figure, some more prominently than others, in the detailed disputes that are to come. But there can be little doubt that their converging import is not unreasonably focused in terms of the tenability of external and internal relativism and of their respective fit with regard to the developing theory of the various sciences and of rational inquiry in general. Thus seen, the argument to be advanced is itself meant to encourage the developing revolution – along certain lines rather than along others. But that is the *agon* promised. Also, it should be said, if our thesis proves reasonable, then we may surely expect, on its own terms, that it cannot have exclusive sway. On the relativist view, there are bound to be competing (and otherwise incompatible) accounts that, though weighted in comparative terms in different ways, need not be so opposed dialectically that vindicating some one account entails precluding the defensibility of all others incompatible with itself. Clearly, much of the force of the intended argument lies with the effectiveness of contrasting the two sorts of relativism and with providing, in addition, a sense of rigor sufficient to insure something more interesting than the merely vacuous claims that might otherwise threaten.

What then are the principal currents that compose our revolution? They are largely but not entirely occupied with retreating from more sanguine positions that now seem either hopeless to sustain or very nearly so, and with pursuing eligible versions of the classic questions of philosophy under these seriously qualified admissions. It is certainly possible (one concedes, without the least glimmer of conviction) that these retreats will prove to be quite temporary. If they do, then we may expect the currently developing interest in relativism to reverse itself. In the meantime, we may take note of the following.

First of all, there is nowadays a very widespread rejection of what may be titled the *transparency* thesis – so marked, by a term of art, for the sake of putting the point in as global a way as possible. By the transparency thesis is meant all doctrines, however attenuated or variable, by which one holds that there is a determinate match or adequation between the cognizable properties of the real world and the cognizing powers of the human mind such that the *distributed* truths of science or of other disciplined inquiries may be assured that the inquiring mind does not, by its very effort, distort or alter or fail to grasp the world's independent (cognizable) structure: the world, or key parts of it, are in this sense cognitively transparent to the mind. There are an enormous number of versions of the transparency thesis that have been championed throughout the history of philosophy, and they are all on the run at the present time. The most familiar targets are currently labeled representationalism, the correspondence theory, foundationalism, positivism, naturalism, cognitivism, rationalism, objectivism, scientism, essentialism, universalism, logocentrism, ontotheology, structuralism, totalization, the epistemological model, the mirror image – and even include realism itself.

The wholesale retreat of these and similar movements generates uncertainty about *how* the realism of science may be recovered. Relativism is particularly heartened by this retreat. What we have called external relativism is tempted by it (at least) to dismiss the would-be competence of philosophy itself – on the grounds that there can be no philosophy that does not adhere to the transparency thesis. But, on an argument suggested a moment ago, if science and philosophy cannot be demarcated in principle, then such extreme versions of incommensurability (or of a very strongly diffused pluralism that masquerades as incommensurabilism) risks all science as well, which it hardly wishes to do. What we have called internal relativism enters the breach and attempts to reconcile the realism of science – under the constraint of rejecting transparency – with a logically weakened model of truth-like values. Seen from this point of view, the extreme form of external relativism just mentioned may well be motivated by a wish to avoid a strong internal relativism, once transparency is lost. But, even as the point is made, we realize that we must resist at this introductory moment any attempt at actually sustaining an argument.

There are, in addition, a great many retreats from positions that have been championed in the most strenuous ways by the defenders of those historical movements known as positivism and the unity-of-science program. The undertakings of these movements are still vigorous and vigorously supported, it should be said; but their theoretical defense, or legitimation as we may say, is decidedly attenuated or largely abandoned at the present time even by those who are committed to them. For example, there is a wholesale retreat from the attempt to construct a comprehensive theory of meaning or linguistic meaning, of verification, of the methodology of science itself, of the very question of drawing a principled demarcation between questions of meaning and questions of belief. Along these lines, there are certainly very serious doubts and challenges – offered, however, with the greatest respect for the achievements of the movements in question – regarding formal models of scientific explanation, inductivism, extensionalism, physicalism, the theory of reference, the status of theoretical entities and of natural laws, and the like. Again, all of this, by default at least, encourages the prospects of relativism of both sorts. And, although these questions have understandably acquired their modern form only within the last century, it is reasonably clear that they have important theoretical affinities with the principal commitments of the entire early history of philosophy.

On the more positive side, two major themes that have become increasingly prominent in Western philosophy since the nineteenth century, and that were once closely linked with one another *and* linked with the retreats just collected, have proved responsible for generating what we have ventured to identify as a philosophical revolution. These are, first of all, the priority of *praxis* with respect to human speculation: that is, that theory, science, cognition itself are guided by the largely tacit, biologically grounded activities of human societies seeking to survive and reproduce their numbers, always in accord with the contingent pattern of life of particular cultures; and, secondly, the deep *historicity* of human existence and inquiry: that is, that man is, uniquely, a being whose existence is historicized (or, simply, that human history and "natural history" are not the same thing), that man is in some profound sense formed by, a creature of and embodying, an historical language and culture, and that therefore his cognitive and praxical concerns are oriented and limited by the historical horizon of his own particular culture. It is surely but a simple step to grasp that, given these prevailing intellectual currents, both external and internal relativism should thrive and compete with one another – and that the recovery of realism promises (or threatens) to require a reconciliation between realism and relativism.

One important countermove may be mentioned here, since it will prove a prominent antagonist of the argument that follows. It is easy to see that one might theorize that history itself conveys a strong sense of a tradition in which regularities, near-universalities, near-essences, near-necessities resembling what versions of the transparency thesis would more directly have championed may still be justified or legitimated. Such a theory might hope to snatch a strongly convergent sense of objectivity, of directed consensus, of a clear disposition of an inquiring community toward uniquely favored findings and claims, from the disadvantages of a cognizable order of things in which transparency is denied. Call the thesis (for want of an established name) *traditionalism*. On this reading, traditionalism seeks to recover as much of what the transparency thesis would otherwise yield – given the loss of transparency itself – by reference and appeal to the inherent cognitive directionality of the historical traditions in which humans are forever embedded. Traditionalism, therefore, like external and internal relativism, accommodates both the notion of *praxis* and the notion of historicity. Hence, the disputes that we must sort out, in supporting our thesis, involve both the contest

between the two sorts of relativism and that between traditionalism and
either of the two relativisms.

There you have the *agon*. In effect, the isolation of our theme misleadingly suggests a manageable topic. Plainly, it is only a strategic
banner under which to march through the whole of philosophical Gaul.

Introduction

We cannot seriously believe that science utterly misrepresents the way the world is; and we cannot accurately determine the fit between the two. Surely these are among the most stable intuitions we are likely to entertain about the human condition and the prospects of human inquiry. They are not altogether irresistible, as the intellectual record attests: at the very least, skepticism and the correspondence theory have had their impressive innings. The trouble is the human being intrudes too much: if only we could check to see how he distorts what meets his eye, how his experiments and labor and inventions produce apparent effects that deflect us from the true regularities of nature, how his native speculation spontaneously alters what he sees and how he acts and induces him to attribute too much reality to his fancies! Of course, the agent then responsible for the implied corrections would be the agent responsible for the original errors: ourselves. So the puzzle is perennial, part of the "problematic" of man, drawn with equal plausibility from every channel of his reflection.

The history of philosophy is largely a chronicle testing the limits of these intuitions. That is as fair and instructive a way of fixing the theme of human understanding as any that could be stated in a single line. Can we escape their implied constraints? Can we attenuate the cognitive insecurities they identify? Can we preserve a safe haven for science within their limits? Such questions mark the inevitable optimism of human life itself: for even a negative answer signifies a certain confidence of discovery. If we persist in our simplified reflections, we can hardly fail to accumulate other simplifed profundities. We could for example tabulate the principal sources of *escape* or *reconciliation*: say, privilege, practice, and salience. These would be meant as terms of art, of course, but they would be meant to catch up the usual sources of natural cognitive optimism. Thus, privilege would be the way of escape, the affirmation that one way or another the world is transparent to the human mind, or that the mind reliably discerns its own world or worlds, or that world and mind are so mutually attuned as to entail the disclosure of the first to the second. Here, privilege is meant to signify not only a global fit between mind and world but quite detailed assurances about particular claims. ("Practice" and "salience" are less obvious and require more preparation to be made clear.)

By and large, Western theorizing has rejected privilege. It cannot do so entirely, because *any* assurance that the race is actually capable of knowing the way the world is – in however qualified (or global) a way – requires some legitimation of the sources of that assurance. The weakest recovery we could make would be to deny the "direct" privilege of any of our cognitive powers (the privilege of perception or reason or the like – what might be called first-order privilege) and to affirm, only *en bloc*, not distributively, for reasons drawn from what we suppose the survival function of cognition to be, the attenuated privilege of our usual cognitive powers (what might be called second-order privilege). Of course, the effectiveness and validity of such second-order arguments would, in their turn, need to be scrutinized and confirmed as well. However we maneuvered, the essential trick would oblige us to enlist some version of privilege in the interest of reconciliation instead of escape. In the light of our initial intuitions, this would mean that, however drawn, the grounds of "privilege" could not themselves be cognitively privileged: the (first-order) privilege that would have signified escape must be traded in for the characteristic sources of optimism suited to reconciliation.

This is a madly simple summary of the drift of two thousand years of speculations about our ability to know what we purport to know. It is, as one glibly says, intended heuristically. But we surely believe that there is no point to heuristic instruction that is not governed by what we suppose to be the true state of affairs.

Honesty forbids any premature assurance that relevant speculations must converge ideally on any single account. And yet, only a moment before in the long history of such reflection, Charles Sanders Peirce *had* supposed such a convergence "in the long run." In this – to risk a premature conclusion – Peirce naively restored a kind of first-order privilege by way of a second-order argument intended to repudiate all forms of first-order privilege. And so he became one of the great modern *Denkmäler*, to warn us of what we might favor but should avoid – within the strategy of reconciliation. Only a half-moment after in that history, placed between Peirce and ourselves, Martin Heidegger announced that the entire Western tradition of philosophy was hopelessly and inextricably committed to privilege. But in saying so he obviously exempted his own complaint, formulated as it was in the idiom he took to be inseparable from that same disorder; and he increasingly reserved for himself novel glimpses of the REALITY ordinary science and philosophy had only pretended to capture by pieces. There you have the paradox, however floridly displayed, of the attempt to deny privilege altogether. And so Heidegger as well – at least in the mortal vision here intended – counts as one of the attractive stones of thought by which to orient our account of the powers of human inquiry.

One could have selected any number of other philosophers to furnish clues for one or another picture of the whole of the human effort to understand the world: what man honors first as his science and philosophy. But, in the bias of this particular account, our age belongs to Peirce and Heidegger – and to Wittgenstein; and, primarily through these, to others – for instance, to Marx and Nietzsche (without at all intending to rank the merit of their doctrines). These penny sketches, then, form the briefest introduction to what motivates the sequence of the questions and answers that follow.

If, to go on, reconciliation cannot fail to have a touch of privilege (on pain of incoherence), its principal sources – somewhat obscurely dubbed a moment ago as practice and salience – cannot fail to be placed within the setting of a second-order confidence about deprivileged first-order powers. All the *best* clues about the nature of inquiry acknowledge that our science must be continuous with, perhaps a tolerably reasonable idealization of, the modes of life and activity by which that currently viable species, man, survives. (Of course, to say so is to collect in a few prefatory remarks the conclusions that will require the intervening argument that follows.) There is a double consideration here: first, human science and inquiry – which (to self-inquisitive man) may identify no more than the most arresting features of the tacit survival powers of the stock – do seem in principle to endorse a (second-order) sense of privilege in so far as the viability of the species rests on cognition; secondly, the theories of science that, in cognitive terms, form the idealization of those powers are most obviously fitted to certain preferred practices drawn by way of comparison from among the extraordinary variety of the forms of life the human species supports – changing, subtly interrelated, differentially skilled, contingent, but always *sub*-species-wide. In a word, *if* we favor reconciliation rather than privilege, we must see how difficult it is to deny "generally" (that is, without first-order privilege) the cognitive power of collective practices of actually surviving peoples. This is the heart of Ludwig Wittgenstein's theme (of the *Investigations* primarily): that individual behavior and thought are improvisational variants consensually tolerated within a society whose essential practices men have mastered merely by growing up in it; and that every such natural society is a free variation among the resemblant forms of life man has favored elsewhere.

This is not only Wittgenstein's theme. Peirce collects it optimistically, in terms of what he calls the "logical socialism" of rational inquiry, within a biologized cosmos in which man mythically becomes the cognizing organ of nature. Heidegger collects it pessimistically, in terms of what he sees as man's fatal inclination to turn himself into a mere thing, an object of his own technologized capacity to discover, within the viable practices of social life, what he fatuously represents as the fixed properties of the real world. Nietzsche collects it ironically, in terms of man's absorbing need to reinterpret an alien world and his place in that world, congruently with the changing history of the subterranean interests that dominate his horizon. Marx collects it prophetically, in terms of a continuous history within which, as they become more intelligible, the social conditions for the production and reproduction of human life are judged capable of being brought (and therefore are committed to being brought) under fully rational control.

They are partisans, of course, as are we all. But each has a small glimpse of the elephant through his own spectacles – possibly even against his own conviction. Peirce fastens on the tacit or biological function of social inquiry and, thus construed, on its essentially consensual nature. Heidegger stresses its ineluctable historicity, hence its preconditional partiality, its finitude and provisionality. Nietzsche emphasizes the peculiarly artifactual, even disruptively metaphoric, nature of human inquiry, how it must be irretrievably skewed in plural ways to fit the perspectives of different communities rising and falling without their full discovery of their own prejudice and appetite. Marx argues that our theoretical understanding of ourselves and nature flowers, under the suspicious eye of self-criticism, within the limiting and enabling horizon of the organized forms of productive labor that, for a time, insure our transient survival and our search for human freedom. And Wittgenstein shows how conceptually disastrous it would be to deny the natural mastery of the practices of a society on the part of its own apt members.

But all confirm the sense in which the supposed work of science and philosophy rests on the cognitively focused natural practices of a viable society. This is the convergent theme of Peirce, Heidegger, Nietzsche, Marx, and Wittgenstein – with respect to every strategy of reconciliation. And this of course is why one treats them as the spirits of the age. We privilege *praxis*, therefore, in a second-order privileging of our cognitive powers; and we do this without any pretense that particular truths are perennially privileged. So the method of reconciliation begins to fall into place: we deny first-order privilege; we find we cannot deny the viability of the species and its reliance on our powers of inquiry; so we provide an attenuated second-order privilege for our deprivileged cognitive powers, taking them globally or *en bloc* only in terms of a deeper, noncognitive function; we therefore privilege natural practices in a second-order way.

The next step is plain: within the context of natural practice, we concede the cognitive saliences of our collective experience – perceptually, reflectively, argumentatively, interpretively, experimentally, inventively, behaviorally, affectively, devotionally, intentionally. The fear of nuclear holocaust, for instance, is a currently irresistible and spreading preoccupation of all contemporary societies. How such a theme might give shape to a vision of human science is a matter tha only a collective history could provide. But there are lesser saliences that an emerging community of investigators find they cannot or will not ignore: possibly the odd behavior of the divining-rod or the colors of the Northern Lights or the remarkable predictive success of a Mendeleev. The point about salience is that there can be no privileging of practice without the recognition of salient phenomena within the life of a particular practice: for that signifies the collective recognition of certain detailed features of an experienced world that, however affected by our diachronic effort to understand and influence the nature of things, are (provisionally) so robust that theory cannot ignore them and cannot erase them (as yet) as mere artifacts of itself. Such cognitive stubbornness, of course, may fix on conceptual orientations as readily as on perceptual phenomena. Here, in terms of first-order salience, we recover what an older age was inclined to enshrine in terms of first-order privilege. The maneuver is as reasonable as it is obvious. In this respect, we are all realists. But whether that means that, acknowledging the clever disputes of the philosophical tradition, we may also rightly claim to be scientific realists or anti-realists or idealists or instrumentalists or anything of that kind is quite unclear.

Saliences change – and in many ways; and no salience provides a confirmation of any particular claim. Salience marks only the compelling core of a society's experience, within which detailed judgments and inquiries seek out the various sources of consensual support – which they affect in turn. Practices, which are the natural home of every promising inquiry, are themselves plural, risked by shifts of contingent fortune, historically open-ended. The inventions of a society – whether theories or gadgets – are bound to generate in their own wake their own local salience. They also have dialectical connections with one another and therefore affect the import of what a society has already posted as salient. At the level of theory, then, we cannot ignore the usual threats to objectivity: the claims of skepticism, incommensurability, relativism at least. This returns us to the project of reconciliation.

In the account that follows, again by way of a term of art, we shall treat any affirmative theory of objectivity – what (tendentiously) may now be called scientific realism – as an expression of the ascendent program of *pragmatism*. Our purpose, by a sort of frank colonial abuse of labels, is to identify the remarkable convergence of the principal currents of contemporary Western philosophy – in terms of its seemingly best prospects. (It could, of course, have been labeled in other ways.)

There is, however, no point to ruminations of this sort that fail to risk sketching the central puzzles of our time. In fact, on the theory barely aired, there is no other way to proceed. We draw out the largest limits of our speculation – our boundary intuitions; we specify the imaginative minds that give the best sense of focus within that space – the spirits of our age; we identify the principal strategies that have been or could be adopted *vis-à-vis* the central puzzles – privilege and reconciliation; and we provide an open sense of how we mean to proceed – as pragmatists. Others will prefer another vision. That is as it is, possibly as it ought to be, possibly even as it could not fail to be. But, within our enterprise, we can hardly fail to acknowledge that the problematic of our time concerns at least the reconciliation of realism and relativism within the changing contexts of history. That, at any rate, is the theme of what follows.

Part One

The Defense and Application of Relativism

1

The Nature and Strategies of Relativism

I

Opponents of relativism often charge that it is and must be incoherent. But there is good reason to think that they fail to distinguish important varieties of relativism. They may also trivialize or weaken the doctrine in such a way that it is no longer interesting to defend – or much less interesting than it would otherwise be. Their arguments are sometimes cast in general terms, without regard to particular domains of inquiry, and sometimes they are focused on the puzzles of particular inquiries where the obvious inference of a pointed claim adds spice to the issue. For the purpose of fixing our own initial bearings, such differences may be safely ignored. Thus: they may

1 construe relativism as a form of extreme skepticism against the possibility of rationally assessing pertinent claims within a given domain;

2 confuse it with advocating probabilizing or "plausibilizing" truth claims relative to available evidence;[1]

3 construe it as utterly segregating apparently conflicting claims within the scope of independent conventions or conventionally specified domains (relative to which such conflicts are disallowed);[2]

4 construe it as a form of subjectivism, as in holding that moral judgments ultimately rest on feelings of approval and disapproval that vary from person to person (regarding which, however, judgments are objectively true or false);[3]

5 construe it in a noncognitivist way, as in holding that pertinent judgments are no more than expressions of feelings and psychological attitudes that vary and conflict (regarding which, questions

of truth and falsity do not even obtain);[4]

6   construe it as confirming only the empirical and conceptual possibility that different agents may (given some competent criterion of justification) justifiably subscribe to some judgments or maxims of action or the like that, universalized, are incompatible;[5]

7   simply confuse it with the empirical reality of divergent or conflicting social practices (what is often now called cultural relativity or cultural relativism);[6]

8   conflate it with versions of social policy that, in principle, tolerate divergent, potentially conflicting social practices of historically well-entrenched sorts (what, in effect, comes to social or political or legal pluralism).

Understandably, the most widely debated forms of relativism have been formulated with regard to the logic of value judgments and the conditions of validity or rationality of personal conduct. But there is no reason to restrict the discussion of relativism in this way: particularly in our own time, the problem has been brought to bear on the methodology of science, on the reidentification of referents within diachronically changing scientific theories, on the prospects of essentialism and of fixing a uniquely valid ontology, on the status of cognitive claims if foundationalism is untenable, on the problematic status of determining empirical truth, on the implications of challenging criteria demarcating the analytic and synthetic, on the implications of the realist–idealist controversy, on the nature of hermeneutic puzzles within human history. Opposition to relativism, therefore, may be temperately construed as requiring the formulation of a thesis that is

(i)   internally coherent;
(ii)   intended to account for assigning truth values or otherwise justifying in cognitive terms well-entrenched practices and forms of behavior;
(iii) at least moderately congruent with the tradition of such practices and behavior;
(iv)   responsive to well-known and otherwise reasonable conceptual challenges;
(v)   set within the framework of an articulated philosophical strategy; and
(vi)   dialectically pitted against its own opponents.

These are entirely fair constraints – not by any means suited to relativism alone. But, if we take up the question in this spirit, then it seems entirely possible to maintain that a reasonably powerful form of relativism *is* viable, applicable to a very wide range of cognitive inquiry, resilient in competition with opposing theories, and, given widely held philosophical views, probably ineliminable at the present time. One could hardly deny that an argument of this sort is not generally conceded or familiar.

These preliminary remarks afford a convenient economy. For the most interesting versions of relativism are bound to avoid all forms 1–8. There is no need to dispute whether theories of those sorts are genuine forms of relativism; they may be, but they will not satisfy our sense of a genuinely forceful theory. Hence, overviews of relativism that maintain only that all versions either are or must be internally incoherent or else reduce to one of forms 1–8 are either tendentious or premature if there remains a strategy that meets conditions (i)–(vi) in a relatively powerful way. It is hard to understand the sense in which the philosophical opponents of relativism could, merely by advancing a candidate theory intended to stand in for all alternatives, hope to make overviews of the sort mentioned effective. We may satisfy ourselves on this point by considering two well-known accounts, each adjusted to a quite restricted domain of value judgments.

In an overview of ethical theory that he has to a considerable extent now replaced, Richard Brandt has argued that what he termed the Qualified Attitude Method appears to be consistent with relativism on the basis of "ordinary thinking", that "the Qualified Attitude Method represents the practice of many or most thoughtful people in testing ethical judgements," *and* "that there are good reasons for using the method, for accepting and following the rule ['Assert an ethical proposition if and only if it satisfies the conditions of the Qualified Attitude Method!]."[7] In short, he favored the Method as providing a reasonably objective canon, "a unique rational method for answering ethical questions," roughly analogous with the role of induction in empirical science.[8] The details of the Method are not terribly important here (and the presumption of an uncontroversial inductive canon is somewhat naive). The details involve deciding "particular problems both by appeal to principles that we already have more or less explicitly in mind and by appeal to our preferences, feelings of obligations, and so forth," corrected by discounting attitudes that fail to be suitably impartial or are uninformed or are due to an abnormal state of mind or that lead to certain inconsistencies and the like.[9] What is important, however, is Brandt's view that

> if we are to be consistent relativists, we must not only have a specific understanding of the Qualified Attitude Method . . . but also a particular understanding of the quasi-naturalist definition

[of such terms as "desirable" and "good"]. We must specify this definition in a relativist direction. . . . We can say, to take "desirable" as an example, that "*x* is desirable" means "Desire for *x on my part* satisfies all the conditions that would be set . . ." (and so on), with the understanding that the "set conditions" may be such that desire for *x* on the part of one person may meet them, and desire for non-*x* on the part of some other person may also meet them. . . . If we are not prepared to understand the quasi-naturalist definition in some such manner, we must in consistency reject relativism."[10]

Brandt sees the adjustment as tantamount to equating the "quasi-naturalist definition" and its "noncognitivist counterpart."[11] To that extent, Brandt's conception of relativism hovers between versions 4 and 5, already marked as among the less interesting varieties; it is also perhaps rather similar to version 3. Brandt fails, therefore, to consider that there may be a viable relativism that, first, need not relativize the *meaning* of pertinent predicates, if the conditions for their application independently insure relativism (which seems entirely possible, logically); second, is not restricted to predicates designating subjective feelings and attitudes (which, again, seems entirely possible and worth exploring); and, third, is not bound, in so far as it admits predicates involving feelings and attitudes, to treat one's own subjective feelings and attitudes as criteria for correctly applying such predicates (which, once again, seems quite possible and worth exploring). In spite of these obvious restrictions, Brandt's view probably represents the most generally accepted overview of ethical relativism in the analytic tradition.[12] Also, since the context of ethical dispute has almost casually been taken to provide an adequate and fair setting within which to explore the prospects of relativism in general, Brandt's standard maneuver pretty well suggests how relativism has come to be treated in domains quite different from the ethical.

Monroe Beardsley has, in a well-known account, examined "the possibility of *criticism as knowledge*" – that is, of the description, interpretation, and evaluation of artworks (particularly, literature).[13] More narrowly, with respect to literary interpretation, Beardsley says, "I do not see how an interpretation could be reasonable unless reasons can be given to show its superiority to some alternatives; and I do not see how the reasons could count unless they are reasons for thinking it true."[14] He adds, "I hold that *all* of the literary interpretations that deserve the name obey the principle of 'the Intolerability of Incompatibles,' i.e., if two of them are logically incompatible, they cannot both be true."[15]

It is, in context, reasonably clear that Beardsley regards relativism as committed to supporting contradictories, hence as untenable in the strongest sense possible.[16] But the odd thing is that Beardsley himself concedes that "there might be reasons for making a certain judgment that are not reasons for saying it is true, if it should be the case that judgments cannot be true or false." He offers this opinion in the same context in which he says, more characteristically, that "Reasons in what I think we can call the 'ordinary' sense are reasons that have a bearing on the *truth* of the [critic's] judgments. And the relevance of such reasons presupposes that the judgments can be true or false. This is indeed my view."[17] Beardsley does not intend his concession to be a strong one, for he means (as in discussing verdictives, in J. L. Austin's sense) to hold that, although verdictives, estimates, and the like are not normally termed true, "an estimate surely involves a claim to truth, which may be allowed or disallowed."[18] Clearly, Beardsley believes that questions of truth and falsity always obtain where cognitive claims are at stake – even if particular judgments are normally not said to be true or false. But he has actually not shown that this is so, and the example of estimates hardly touches the essential issue. At any rate, Brandt's and Beardsley's views illustrate the strategic weakness of standard objections to the tenability of relativism: the first by restricting relevant versions to uninteresting varieties; the second, by charging or implying, without evidence, that relativism must be logically incoherent.

Let us now turn to countermeasures. It is absurdly easy, on formal grounds alone, to introduce, by fiat, a set of claims and judgments that are taken to be open to cognitive support (by supplying evidence or reasons), that are denied the truth values "true" or "false" (or at least "true," assuming these values are not to be treated symmetrically), and that are assigned truth values or truth-like values logically weaker than the bipolar pair "true" or "false." There is no formal reason why such a system should be logically incoherent or yield contradictory judgments. Hence, there is no purely formal reason on which Beardsley, for instance, can make good his charge that the mere fact that judgments invite supporting reasons entails that those judgments "can be true or false." Nor is his *caveat* regarding estimates to the point: for it is not merely that the judgments in question need not (or cannot) take the values "true" and "false" once we favor idiomatic usage; it is rather that, by logical fiat alone, we may exclude the eligibility of whatever values we please. Of course, it will always be legitimate to ask whether any such restriction has a significant use – and the substantive defense of relativism requires an affirmative answer. Nevertheless, it is an essential part of that defense to grasp that the mere cognitive status of claims and judgments hardly entails that they *must* take the specific values "true" and "false".

However elementary it may be, this charge is surprisingly powerful. It is often quite confidently affirmed that we simply cannot consistently acknowledge a given utterance to be a cognitive claim if, at the same time, we deny that it *can* take the bipolar values "true" and "false". Notice that the point at stake here is rather different from that favored by so-called intuitionists, by Michael Dummett for example, although it is capable of being neatly reconciled with the *project* at least of the so-called anti-realist position, without actually supporting it. (In any case, the intuitionist or constructivist interpretation of anti-realism is hardly the only – or even the most perspicuous – version of anti-realism proper to the larger context in which our present issue is still to be located.) Dummett holds that

> We are entitled to say that a statement *P* must be either true or false, that there must be something in virtue of which either it is true or it is false, only when *P* is a statement of such a kind that we could in a finite time bring ourselves into a position in which we were justified either in asserting or in denying *P*; that is, when *P* is an effectively decidable statement.[19]

(Intuitionism is of course very different from old-line positivism, although it is committed to its own form of verificationism.) The essential motivation is directed against the "platonist" or "realist" or "meta-physician" who would treat statements (initially mathematical, but now extended to "ordinary statements") as being assigned "meanings such as to render them all determinately either true or false independently of our knowledge."[20] (The positivist, by contrast, is primarily concerned with developing a theory of meaning itself.) *Our* issue, however, concerns the question whether, and why, we *should* concede, on *either* "realist" *or* "anti-realist" grounds, that cognitive claims *must* take bipolar truth values if they take any truth-like values at all. After all, even on the extended intuitionistic thesis (once we move from mathematics to "ordinary statements," statements about the empirical world), whether we hold a particular statement to be true or false is a function of our being in a suitable position to decide it; hence, there could be a constructivist account of relativistic truth values – whether Dummett would favor such a position or not. In any case, there is an obvious lacuna in both the "realist" and "anti-realist" lines of argument. To put the point in the form of a paradox, Dummett's anti-realist challenge to his

opponent (the so-called "platonist" or "metaphysician") disallows construing statements as either true or false unless and until they are decidable in a finite undertaking; but Dummett himself appears to favor the
"metaphysician" or "realist" to the extent that (like his opponent) he,
too, is committed, *in advance* of formulating distributed decision procedures, to the assured outcome that cognitively pertinent statements
will invariably take bipolar values (the doctrine of *tertium non datur*).
On the relativist proposal here being developed, this restriction might
itself be viewed as a violation of the anti-realism intended – although
relativism need not as such entail Dummett's form of anti-realism. Also,
of course, the argument so far formulated is entirely general and formal –
addressed only to local possibilities.

To return: a rather radical application of the restrictive sort of relativism here intended is provided by Nelson Goodman, who quite
recently has described his own view as "a radical relativism under rigorous restraints."[21] Pressing his well-known account of the problem of
induction, Goodman declares,

> On the question what distinguishes right inductive categories from
> others, I can only indicate the nature of a tentative reply   A
> primary factor in projectibility is habit; where otherwise equally
> well-qualified hypotheses conflict, the decision normally goes to
> the one with the better entrenched predicates. Obviously there
> must be leeway for progress, for the introduction of novel organ-
> izations that make, or take account of, newly important con-
> nections and distinctions. . . . Argument for the categorization,
> the scheme, suggested could not be for its truth, since it has no
> truth-value, but for its efficacy in worldmaking and under-
> standing.[22]

Here Goodman has managed to advance a view (and something of a
rationale for it) in which judgments are clearly capable of being cognitively supported, challenged, and compared; are assigned truth-like
values other than "true" and "false" and characterized as *incapable* of
taking the latter values; and are so specified as to be hardly restricted
to, or even primarily concerned with, subjective feelings and attitudes
functioning as epistemic criteria. Despite the opposition between their
respective views, W. V. Quine's account of ontological relativity is at least
superficially similar to Goodman's (without invoking worldmaking); it
similarly restricts the applicability of "true" and "false" without precluding cognitive concerns (though for reasons quite different from
Goodman's). So Quine says,

Ontological relativity is not to be clarified by any distinction between kinds of universal predication – unfactual and factual, external and internal. . . . When questions regarding the ontology of a theory are meaningless absolutely, and become meaningful relative to a background theory, this is not in general because the background theory has a wider universe. . . . What makes ontological questions meaningless when taken absolutely is not universality but circularity . . . paraphrase in some antecedently familiar vocabulary, then, is our only recourse, and such is onto-logical relativity. . . . Identity is thus of a piece with ontology. Accordingly it is involved in the same relativity. . . .[23]

Our own concern for the moment is the bare coherence of accounts in which pertinent judgments and claims are precluded (for cause) from the straightforward application of the values "true" and "false." Good-man takes "true" to be a species of "right," and expressly denies that, in proposing useful (inductive) categories with respect to which truth claims properly arise, decisions selecting one such system of categories over another can, coherently, be judged in terms of truth at all. And Quine argues in effect that, if we use "true" and "false" with respect to the ontology of a theory, we are committed to a (benign) conceptual regress and cannot take these terms in an "absolute" sense – that is, in a sense that presupposes some accessible form of the correspondence theory of truth (essentialism or foundationalism or the like). Goodman and Quine, therefore, have provided at least part of a reasoned defense for restricting the use, or our sense of the use, of "true" and "false." We are not bound to accept their rationales, but their programs are potential specimens of uses of relativism quite different from, and much more powerful than, those considered by Brandt and Beardsley. We shall want to consider what defensible minimal grounds there are for restricting truth values in the way favored by relativism.

We are, at the moment, trying to orient ourselves with regard to the options a relativist might claim for himself. We began with more or less formal restrictions. But, in the company of Brandt and Beardsley and Dummett and Goodman and Quine, we are already beginning to get a sense not only of interesting and uninteresting varieties of formal restric-tion on cognitive claims, but also of the need to link explicitly the selection of a formal thesis about truth-like values and its bearing on the would-be features of particular sectors of inquiry. This line of exam-ination, then, already yields provisional gains that, doubtless, will have to be tested more strenuously again and again.

Any coherent relativism that does not reduce to any of the less interesting of versions 1–8 must, we may say, specify a range of judgments that take truth values or truth-like values logically weaker than "true" and "false" (or, admitting a more than two-valued system in which "true" and "false" do not behave symmetrically, truth values logically weaker than "true"). The reason is that a cognitively interesting variety of relativism must provide for the defense, severally (that is, jointly but not conjunctively), of judgments that, on a model of truth and falsity, would count as contradictories or incompatible judgments. In a relativistic system, such paired judgments are *not* contradictories or incompatibles, because the eligible truth values assigned are logically weaker than the exclusive and exhaustive pair (truth and falsity). So stated, this condition is easy to meet even in nonrelativistic ways. For example, relative to evidence available at time t, it is conceivable that the claims *Nixon knew about Watergate in advance* and *Nixon did not know about Watergate in advance* have, respectively, the probabilities (of being true) p_1 and p_2. (The probability of their conjunction, of course, is zero; but, without contradiction, one could jointly affirm the probability of each.) Now, ordinarily, to affirm the probability of a statement is to acknowledge that that statement could, in principle, also be true or false (in the standard sense). So, although probabilizing claims (or "plausibilizing," in the same respect) relativizes assessments to evidence at t, the practice need not, and characteristically does not, treat truth claims relativistically. More is needed. In fact, it is most reasonable to treat such probabilized contexts so that statements such as those just instanced are not detachable from their evidentiary clauses, wherever they function within a deductive argument or are examined for entailments.[24] Seen in this way, relativistic systems similarly treat statements as not detachable from pertinent evidentiary clauses, but only under the additional constraint that such statements be assigned *only* truth values weaker than "true" and "false." Hence, relativistic systems (of the interesting sort) provide for *incongruent* judgments – that is, for judgments that

(a)   are epistemically eligible within the same context of inquiry;
(b)   would, on a model of truth and falsity, be contradictories or incompatible, but do not now so function;
(c)   are only assigned truth values weaker than "true" and "false"; and
(d)   are not detachable in the evidentiary sense.

There is no formal reason why these conditions cannot be met by simple fiat; and none of the uninteresting varieties 1–8 is addressed to satisfying the set of these or similar conditions – most are incompatible with the set. *We may, then, take (a)–(d) as the necessary and sufficient formal conditions of any "interesting" variety of relativism.*

Notice that the admission of probabilized judgments does *not* preclude the relevance of consistency and coherence constraints even with respect to such judgments. For instance, it will, within probabilized contexts, normally make sense to hold that, relative to evidence E, the probability that Nixon knew about Watergate is p_1 and the probability that Nixon did not know about Watergate is p_2; *and* that *Nixon probably knew about Watergate entails that Nixon probably did not know about Watergate* is self-contradictory. Obviously, considerations of relevance bear on the issue. But, if these obtain in probabilized contexts, there need be no fear that formal consistency must be abandoned in relativized contexts. This shows, incidentally, the need to reconcile the assignment of relativistic values with the assignment of bipolar values.

It needs to be emphasized that condition (c) is to be construed in some epistemically operational way – that is, as permitting, on the basis of suitable evidence or grounds, the ascription of truth values (of some sort) weaker than "true" and "false". Once we appreciate this, two further qualifications are in order: first, the formal conditions of relativism do not preclude the range of affected judgments from *depending*, in epistemically relevant ways, on judgments that do not behave relativistically; and, second, whether or not operational criteria are available for ascribing (in the standard sense) "true" and "false" to any set of judgments – in particular, to those on which relativistic judgments epistemically depend – there is (so far) no reason why a relativistic account (an epistemically operational one) cannot avail itself of a (non-relativistic) *theory* or conception of truth. For one thing, the usual large theories – correspondence, coherence, pragmatist theories – normally have no operational import at all; and, for another, there are strong reasons for thinking that, in empirical disciplines at least, the operational use of "true" and "false" provides (and must provide) for revisions of given ascriptions in ways incapable of being construed as clearly and exclusively favoring the conception of truth advanced by any of those large theories. In particular, provision must be made for real-time bets or conjectures about what to *take* as true, subject to review in the light of subsequent considerations. (Nevertheless, there is a constraint, which we shall shortly consider, that all such theories impose.)

II

It seems possible, then, to adopt a theoretical stance regarding relativism that is not as radical as the acounts either Goodman or Quine (but particularly Goodman) advances. In any case, relativism can be made formally compatible with the admission of the standard use of "true" and "false," provided only that the set of judgments that take the values "true" and "false" be segregated from those that take the weaker values. Any such system, in which the ascription of the weaker values presupposes a domain to which the stronger values apply and depends upon the application to that domain of the stronger values, may be termed a robust relativism.[25] For example, *if*, in accord with Quine's famous remark, "manuals for translating one language into another can be set up in divergent ways, all compatible with the totality of speech dispositions, yet incompatible with one another"[26] – that is, if (in some admittedly difficult sense) ontology can be segregated from a certain minimal range of empirical findings about behavioral responses to "nonverbal stimulations" – then, *to that extent*, ontology can be treated relativistically, relative to a body of empirical knowledge or science that is *not* construed relativistically. Of course, Quine wishes to radicalize truth in science even further, but his notion of "indeterminacy of translation" (confined in the manner just noted) may be fairly construed as a robust relativism. There is good reason to think that Quine's theory is ultimately untenable – even incoherent; but that is not because of its relativism, but because of the way Quine relates indeterminacy to the rest of his theory.[27]

A somewhat simpler example of a robust relativism may be drawn from the practice of art criticism. Briefly, if the *description* of an artwork takes the values "true" and "false" because, on a favorable theory, it identifies the determinate properties that the artwork *has*, and if the *interpretation* of that artwork depends on such a description but can only *impute* to the work, and not rightly claim that it *has*, certain further purposive structures (as, say, in construing Kafka's "A Hunger Artist" as an image of Christ's passion), then conditions (a)–(d) are satisfied in just that way in which a robust relativism obtains. The justification might go this way: stories sometimes appear to lack a unity and closure of form assignable solely on the basis of clearly describable features – in spite of the fact that normal reading invites or requires some such unity and closure; informed readers and critics tend, with due respect to the disciplined practice of reading, to improvise an interpretation or interpretations conceded to go well beyond what the merely describable features could be said to entail or (in some attenuated sense) to indicate. On this hypothesis, the limitation is a function of the *nature* of stories, not merely of the ignorance of readers: the provision of a reasonable interpretation will (on that basis) hardly be said to preclude other, incongruent interpretations. The argument is obviously coherent and worth debating; and formal analogues justified on entirely different grounds may be claimed in other domains (for instance, Quine's regarding indeterminacy).

Goodman, of course, is more extreme than Quine. It is possible that a *theory* of truth cannot, conceptually, be avoided – in the sense that, from *any* cognitively coherent stance (conceding the intelligibility of competing and divergent claims and interests), the very notion of empirical truth signifies that all pertinent truth claims address the (one) real world and that what is true of it must, ideally, form one internally consistent system. *If* this is the one legitimate constraint common to the principal theories of truth, then Goodman's account – what he calls a *radical relativism* – is incoherent; for Goodman relativizes not only *truth claims* but the *concept of truth* itself. The very point of a theory of truth seems, however, to be to acknowledge the conceptual need for a single system of coherence for all truth claims, no matter how generated. (*How* could there be more than one such system, intelligible to the same agent?)

Since, however, "even reality is relative" for Goodman, it very much looks as if Goodman cannot (and will not) provide for a single such system. So he says, "We are not speaking in terms of multiple possible alternatives to a single actual world. . . . Here . . . we turn from describing or depicting 'the world' to talking of descriptions and depictions, but now without even the consolation of intertranslatability among *or any evident organization of the several systems in question.*"[28] Yet he also says that "We can have words without a world but no world without words or other symbols";[29] and he explicitly declares, regarding appraising truth, that "differences between true versions [of the world] cannot be firmly distinguished from differences between worlds [which are construed by the use of words]."[30] The difficulty of his position is patent once we see that, as a consequence of Goodman's thesis, the cognitive agent himself – who presumably understands these alternatives – must also be such that we cannot "firmly distinguish" between versions of *his* cognitive role and a congeries of different agents in putatively different worlds. In fact, unaccountably (though inexorably), Goodman is prepared to speak of "right world-versions"; but it would seem as if "rightness" must, on his own thesis, be relativised as radically as "truth." Without the conceptual advantage of a single, common world – addressed cognitively – we would not even have an inkling of what it means to gauge (never mind, of how to gauge) the rightness of the indefinitely many "worlds" that would be generated. Quine's opposition, of course, is motivated not merely by such considerations but also (perhaps more protectively) by his own commitment, within relativistic concessions, to the adequacy of a Leibnizian strategy for securing the extensional discernibility of all numerically distinct particulars: say, by uniquely satisfied predicates (for instance, "pegasizing") fitted to the one and only world we share.[31] This is the point of the fundamental contrast between Quine and Goodman, and between robust and radical relativism. If the difficulty be conceded, then every viable (and interesting) relativism must be of the robust, not of the radical, sort. *Radical relativism*, then, fails to make provision for nonrelativistic truth claims (even if nonrelativized truth claims are relativised to evidence, context of inquiry and the like, provisionally or in principle – as, in the latter case, in the familiar fallibilist views of Peirce, Popper, and Dewey). Quine's theory, unlike Goodman's, is *not* a radical relativism: it merely attenuates our theory of science as far as possible, once such doctrines as the correspondence theory of truth, foundationalism, essentialism, the demarcation of the analytic–synthetic distinction, and the like are rejected. It may be incoherent, as suggested, but that is not because it has overstepped the conditions of a coherent relativism.

To see this, one must recall that, normally, probabilizing or "plausibilizing" truth claims (or relativizing truth claims even in the pragmatist's manner, in terms of warranted assertibility) does not, in principle, eliminate reference to a single system of truth and falsity. On the contrary, the point of such relativization *is* to preserve, without risking contradiction, the use of paired statements that, on a model of truth and falsity, could not but be contradictories or incompatible. Radical relativism fails to preserve this constraint, whereas theories such as Quine's merely deny that there is an operational sense in which the two-valued model can actually function *in an evidentially detached way*.[32] This is simply the result, one way or another, of resolving the so-called realist–idealist controversy and of favoring pragmatism.

Put very simply, the point is that relativizing truth claims to evidence so that they are not detachable in an evidentiary sense is *not*, in itself, a relativistic commitment. For example, the resolution of ambiguity is normally managed by what may be termed the "plausibilizing" of alternative construals in a nonrelativistic way – without precluding, of course, the possibility of a relativistic account. This is the reason why Quine's view of "background theories" against which changes in scientific theory are to be understood is not as such a relativistic theory, even though Quine himself is attracted to relativist accounts of all sorts. The upshot is that a viable theory of any form of cognitive inquiry pursued under real-time conditions – relativistic or not relativistic – *must provide for some set of truth claims that are not detachable in the evidentiary sense but are still suitably constrained by logical and methodological conditions associated with a model of truth and falsity (that permits or affords a conception of detached claims, in the standard sense).* This is another way of saying that, in a nonrelativistic system, probabilized (or otherwise similarly encumbered) claims are, in principle, ideally capable of being true or false, even if there is now (or in real-time terms) no epistemically operational way in which to apply the values "true" and "false" *simpliciter.* So seen, a robust relativism provides for *another,* alethically and (therefore) epistemically, *dependent* range of claims to which truth values weaker than "true" and "false" alone apply; hence, although they are also not detachable, such claims are denied truth values (or truth-like values) like those that nonrelativistic systems provide, where the latter are conceptually linked to the standard two-valued model. The profound novelty of this way of conceiving relativism is straightforward enough: it is *not* necessary to hold that, if *some* domain of inquiry behaves relativistically, then *every* domain does as well. Standard versions of relativism, whether defended or attacked, seem to have been taken to favor global and comprehensive rather than "distributed" claims.[33] But this is an avoidable extravagance, given that radical relativism is logically incoherent.

Let us be clear about the charge – provisional though it must be at this early point in the argument. The classic objection to relativism is that it is self-contradictory, in maintaining (so-called Protagoreanism) that a statement may be both true and false in the standard sense of those terms. The suppler view we have very briefly sampled in Goodman's recent theory cannot be accused of that sort of incoherence; and perhaps a fuller account would show that it is not incoherent on any grounds. But at the very least it threatens to succumb to a distinct form of incoherence, since, in avoiding the older disorder by making it impossible to identify a common world relative to which pertinently opposed claims may even be suitably compared, it risks being unable to admit and to make sense of a common conceptual framework within which one and the same agent may actually entertain the "construction" of alternative worlds. What is more important, Goodman's thesis is very strongly akin to, even if it does not actually instantiate, the notorious incommensurability doctrine, which in recent philosophy has become the principal version of relativism under attack. To approach these two views in this way helps enormously in the attempt to identify a third line of relativistic orientation, one that may escape the weakness of the others at the very point of accommodating their best perceptions. That is precisely the project intended in advancing the formal characterization of what we have called incongruent judgments. But the supporting reasons are still some distance away.

To return to Beardsley for a moment, it is, on a relativistic account, quite possible to defend literary interpretations that, *on a model of truth and falsity*, would be contradictories or incompatible (the famous alternative interpretations of one of Wordsworth's Lucy poems, for instance); but it would *not* be possible to do so (in the same sense) on a nonrelativistic account, in spite of the fact that the relevant claims would also not be detachable in an evidentiary way. The reason is that, relativistically, *incongruent* claims, assigned values no stronger than "plausible" or "apt" or the like, *need never be judged in terms of the two-valued model*; hence, it hardly matters whether we treat them as detachable or not. But, nonrelativistically, such claims are always, in principle, provisional (perhaps permanently), precisely because, on a model of truth and falsity, they *are* incompatible; this is just what is captured by their nondetachability. Schematically, we should say that, on a relativistic account, such claims *are* "apt" or "plausible" or the like, but cannot in principle be true; whereas, on a nonrelativistic account, such claims are "probable" or the like only *relative to the evidence offered*, but cannot be jointly true where incompatible. Hence, that relativistic claims would, on a model of truth and falsity, be incompatible (1) does not affect the truth values or truth-like values they are said to *have* (on the relativistic model); and (2) does not render such truth values provisional in any sense linked to the possibility of assessing them *as* true or false – as (in principle) evidentially detached. Relativistic claims are never evidentially detached; but, since they are also alethically restricted so that the detachable values "true" and "false" (the exhaustive and exclusive pair) are not assignable in principle (quite apart from operational possibilities), there is nothing tentative or provisional about *incongruent* claims as such. But, precisely because *non*relativistic claims are (operationally) treated in an evidentially nondetachable way (on pragmatist or idealist grounds, for instance, or merely because of the paucity of decisive evidence – without reference, that is, to any larger theory of truth and the real world), probabilized or plausibilized claims *are* inherently provisional because (on the model of truth and falsity to which they subscribe) they may yield contradictories or incompatible judgments. In short, the *incongruent* interpretations of Wordsworth's Lucy poem need not be tentative or provisional as such, but merely *probabilized* (*non*relativistic) interpretations cannot but be tentative. Here we see how competing theories of truth affect the epistemic standing of otherwise operationally indistinguishable claims.

Clearly, the rationale for introducing such distinctions rests with substantive views about the actual properties of different domains of inquiry. A (nonrelativistic) probabilized model is normally restricted to contingent epistemic or cognitive limitations affecting agents of inquiry, regardless of the domain under scrutiny; whereas a relativistic model (of the sort here favored) could hardly be convincing unless it rested on arguments regarding *the properties of the domain in question*. In this sense, a robust relativism links inquiry and reality – epistemology and metaphysics – in a more fundamental way than is usual in probabilistic accounts; although, as in current disputes about quantum physics, probabilized values need not be construed in epistemic terms alone.

But, at least on formal grounds, it is obviously easy to introduce in a relativistic manner such many-valued truth-like predicates as "plausible," "apt," "compatible," and the like.[34] It should of course be noted that the truth-like predicates in question are not here fully characterized – are, therefore, not prematurely restricted in any particular way, may be taken more or less in terms of familar usage, are entirely amenable to discipline in accord with any particular practice of professional inquiry (literary criticism, political history, or speculative cosmology, for instance), and are not to be construed in terms of the exercise of mere tastes or personal feeling. Furthermore, it is very important to take note of the fact that *both* relativistic truth values and the (nondetachable) truth values of nonrelativistic systems provide for comparing and appraising the relative strength of competing claims. It is often said that relativistic accounts of science – Thomas Kuhn's, say – are quite implausible because they cannot provide for the obvious evidence of irreversible scientific progress with respect to particular competing theories.[35] But there is no formal reason why robust relativism (as opposed to radical relativism) should be precluded from reasonably firm assessments of the comparative and even ranking sort; and, *if* foundationalism, essentialism, and related doctines are untenable, then even *non*relativistic theories cannot insure more than the provisional reliability of such assessments. In any case, the burden of proof rests with those who would deny that relativism is compatible with comparative assessments as such or (more strongly) with comparative assessments congruent with actual scientific practice (or even with the particular assessments favored by nonrelativistic accounts). Relativism is a theory about the alethic properties of certain judgments in certain domains – not a theory (necessarily) about all judgments, and not a theory that "anything goes" among truth claims or that truth and falsity can be reversed at will.

III

Now, the defense of relativism has two foci: one, formal considerations in virtue of which relativism can be shown to be internally coherent and viable; the other, substantive considerations in virtue of which relativism can be shown to be particularly pertinent to the inquiries of given domains. Regarding the latter, we must confine ourselves here to sampling the general strategy, for particular arguments are bound to be occupied with the special features of this inquiry or that – as for instance, in Quine's or Goodman's or Kuhn's account. Nevertheless, there are some telling grounds on which we are likely to find domains predictably hospitable to relativism. Thus, it is no accident that relativism seems quite reasonable wherever *evaluative*, *appreciative*, and *interpretive* undertakings are involved. This is not to say that such undertakings cannot but be relativistic in principle, only that the conditions on which they are best construed nonrelativistically are noticeably difficult to defend or make convincing. For example, regarding such moral issues as the defense of abortion, suicide, capital punishment, homosexuality, euthanasia, and war, it seems too thin a theory to construe favorable and unfavorable stands in terms of consistency with a mere social convention itself not thought to be morally supportable on independent grounds.[36] Furthermore, such a conventionalism is not an interesting variety of relativism, in the sense already supplied. Quite the contrary. On the other hand, if moral essentialism is untenable (that is, the theory that what is good for human persons is derivable from an examination of their nature), or if moral cognitivism in general is untenable (that is, the theory that we may directly exercise native cognitive powers, such as perception or intuition, in order to discern the moral qualities of things), then, very probably, given the full range of cultural relativity, it would be very difficult to preclude, or defeat, pertinent forms of robust relativism (though moral relativism is not derivable from cultural relativity). If this is true with respect to persons, then, at least, since artworks are artifacts, it is bound to be true as well of aesthetic evaluation. The corresponding argument regarding interpretation – whether of artworks, actions, history, linguistic utterances, or the like – depends rather more on the important fact that we lack a clear consensus about the correct criteria for demarcating the internal or intrinsic or describable features of the relevant phenomena and those features merely imputed to them (however reasonably); *and* we can hardly suppose that our critical interest in those phenomena is confined to whatever may be taken to be "in," or merely internal to, them. Consider an example.

With respect to literature, Beardsley had advanced the bold postulate "that literary works exist as individuals and can be distinguished from other things"; also, the corollary "that literary works are self-sufficient entities whose properties are decisive in checking interpretations and judgments."[37] Nevertheless, in pursuing the issue of interpreting a poem,

Beardsley quite candidly (and reasonably) concedes that

> Some things are definitely said in the poem and cannot be over-
> looked; others are suggested, as we find on careful reading; others
> are gently hinted, and *whatever methods of literary interpretation
> we use, we can never establish them̄ decisively as "in" or "out."
> Therefore whatever comes from without, but yet can be taken as
> an interesting extension of what is surely in, may be admissible.* It
> merely makes a larger whole.[38]

But, then, Beardsley's argument, intended to obviate and even to defeat
relativism, actually turns out to provide the solid foundation for a
pertinent form of robust relativism. Literary works simply do not present
themselves to readers in such a way that their "meanings" can be straightforwardly found "in" them: the analogy with boundaried, well-demar-
cated physical and perceptual objects (which Beardsley favors) is completely unhelpful. And the only alternative (to the New Critical theory
to which Beardsley subscribes) that has had any prospect of sustaining
a nonrelativistic defense of critical interpretation is the one offered by
what is generally known as romantic hermeneutics – that is, the theory
that the meaning of literary texts (and, by extension, of other artifacts
of human history) is exclusively, adequately, and accessibly determined
by determining original authorial intent. Beardsley himself opposed that
theory (reasonably); it is demonstrably untenable on internal grounds;
and later hermeneutic theories, impressed with the historical problem of
recovering even authorial intent, have had to face the persistent threat
of relativism much more directly.[39]

It is not difficult to see that counterpart arguments can be easily
mounted regarding the interpretation of language and history and human
conduct. The point, here, is not to establish a relativistic account of any
of these concerns, only to demonstrate the reasonableness of putting
one forward. In general, cultural phenomena, involving as they must
intensionally qualified intentional features, *cannot*, in any way comparable to what may be said regarding the "boundaries" of physical
objects (to the extent that we may so speak of the latter), support a clear
demarcation between what is "in" and what "out" of the relevant entities
or phenomena.[40] Furthermore, the complicated intentional features of
cultural phenomena may, not unreasonably, be said to be a function *of
subsequent historical interpretation.* If this were conceded, then it would
be extremely difficult to avoid a relativistic theory. At any rate, it would
surely be an attractive and viable option. In literary theory, the thesis
is very close to what is now called "intertextuality" – that is, that the

meaning of any text is a function of the context of antecedent texts into which it is born *and* of the unpredictable subsequent texts still to be produced (against the background of which a particular text is justifiably reinterpreted).[41] Clearly, the interpretation of human history cannot fail to show strong similarities (in a methodological sense) to the interpretation of literary texts. More generally, there is much to be said for the (nonrelativistic) thesis that the apt speakers of natural languages cannot have internalized all the rules of the language they speak; that the meaning of what they utter is a function at least of consensual interpretations of their own linguistic communities; that the regularities of their language yield only diachronically shifting, alternative, idealized rules; and that linguistic meaning is itself a function of the changing non-linguistic experience of particular communities.[42] For widely different reasons, this is pretty well the suspicion (more than the suspicion) of both Anglo-American and Continental European views of language. But this is just what a robust relativism would prefer.

Finally, if there is no convincing way in which to provide a theory of knowledge and inquiry in which inquiry itself is completely transparent, facilitates our discovery of "what there is" independent of such inquiry, or can be reliably corrected with respect to any potential distortion – that is, if there is no convincing way in which to justify our adherence to the sort of (direct) realism presupposed by the correspondence theory of truth, or to the familiar forms of foundationalism, essentialism, and related doctrines – then, globally, there is no way to demarcate the realist and idealist elements of human knowledge. We should then have to concede a hermeneutic dimension to all human science, including the physical sciences, which in principle are addressed to phenomena whose existence does not even depend on the existence, mode of activity, and inquiry of human beings. (Put more perspicuously, this would mean that physics, for instance, was as much concerned with the ability of human inquirers to fathom the physical world as with the properties of the world thus fathomed; or that physics presupposed the conceptual inseparability of the two orientations.) By such considerations, different for different domains, grounds may be laid for bringing into question the ubiquitous adequacy of insisting on the bipolar model in genuine inquiry. Given the apparently insuperable underdetermination of high-level theories in physics, for instance, by anything that could be regarded as observational data, there could be no *a priori* objection to the mere eligibility of a relativistic account of such theories. Once admitted, of course, such an account would have to make its way disputatiously, as every philosopher's claim must.

Whatever relativistic concessions would have to be made for reflexive human studies – anthropology, linguistics, literary criticism – would have to be made for all forms of human inquiry.[43] Here we return to the radical doctrines espoused by Quine; for this is just the upshot of his rejection of the analytic–synthetic distinction and of his having relativized (to background theories) all questions of identity, reference, ontology, and even predication itself. The result is that, without subscribing to Quine's particular theories, *there remains no form of cognitive claim or inquiry that is not open to being construed, responsibly and coherently, in relativistic terms*. Here one can only stop to invite rebuttal. Relativism has been so much maligned that the mere demonstration of its viability *and* pertinence and potential power may well come as a small surprise. In pressing the advantage, we must not suppose, of course, that the required considerations have actually been supplied: the gain lies largely with recognizing how the argument should proceed – and why.

But let us at least collect the argument succinctly: (1) relativism *can* be formulated in an internally consistent way; (2) this can be done on purely formal grounds, without regard to any substantive application; and (3) there *are* substantive grounds on which its application is reasonably favored in a very wide range of particular inquiries. On formal grounds alone, we must distinguish between (i) nonrelativistic judgments relativized only in an evidentiary sense – logically encumbered as not to be detachable, in the context of argument or entailment, from the very evidence in accord with which they are assigned their truth-like values; and (ii) relativistic judgments that, apart from restrictions similar to those of (i), are assignable only truth-like values logically weaker than truth and falsity (in the two-valued sense). The justification for relativistic restrictions must be specified for particular domains; but their eligibility is in general enhanced by the defeat of essentialism, foundationalism, epistemically operative versions of the correspondence theory of truth, the systematic demarcation of realist and idealist components in human cognition. Relevant strategies are bound to be applicable to the physical sciences as well as to the human and cultural studies. In fact, the contrast between the two becomes increasingly difficult to maintain in cognitively operative terms. But, precisely in the human and cultural disciplines, the phenomena in question all exhibit intensional complexities, regarding which the fixity of reference, the boundaries of objects, diachronic shifts in background theory, the contrast between actual and imputed properties and between description and interpretation become decidedly problematic – in such a way, in fact, that systematic relativization cannot but be pertinently eligible. So at least the most global considerations are entirely favorable. Beyond them, we must turn to particular quarrels.

IV

There is perhaps a need for a final observation. One senses a deeper objection against relativism, involving the choice of quite general philosophical strategies. Thus far, the position here adopted is Aristotelian, in the mild sense that formal canons of argument are taken to be best construed as abstractions or idealizations drawn from and empirically fitted to paradigm arguments within the living practice of a society. It is misleading, therefore, to treat formal canons or logical rules – for example, the law of excluded middle – as inviolate *a priori* or, better, as uniformly applicable in all interpreted domains without reference to constraints relevant to their interpretation. Whatever their force, formal constraints apply as such to uninterpreted formulae; or, in interpreted domains, only within executive bounds of sense or decidability or the like. For example, in the well-known Gettier counterinstances to the so-called "justified true belief" conception of knowledge, the logical force of the test cases presupposes (dubiously) that modal (epistemic) contexts of argument behave logically in just the same way as standard non-modal contexts do;[44] and yet it is obvious that the *epistemically interpreted* counterinstances exhibit a decided logical impoverishment of information already hypothesized for each instance, in which (by permitting disjunction or existential generalization) an inference is drawn that on higher-order considerations of relevance might reasonably have been blocked. Gettier-like cases invariably permit one to make ascriptions of knowledge to agents holding certain beliefs – on the basis of inference rules standardly admissible but epistemically paradoxical and irrelevant. Similarly, discourse about fictional entities (say, about Sherlock Holmes) is sometimes said to be logically improper because it violates the law of excluded middle (say, because Sherlock Holmes neither has nor lacks a mole on his back);[45] and yet, of course, one could always vacuously (and pointlessly) satisfy the would-be law by acknowledging that the complement of what is denied is true, but not (alas) pertinently specific *in the interpreted context*; or, one could distinguish between the formal law itself and its interpreted (or interpretively restricted) application, and one way or another *ad hoc* devices could be supplied in order to display the practice of prediction in fictional contexts as formally consistent with the law in question (though interpretively constrained). Or, sometimes, relevance constraints or interpretations of logic itself bid us abandon a would-be logical theorem (double negation, for instances, or disjunction) – or even excluded middle.[46] And sometimes, particularly regarding the vexed matter of so-called quantum logic, it is quite unclear

how to distinguish satisfactorily between formal and empirical (or interpreted) features of what may be affirmed, or how to reconcile the
apparent (logical) anomalies of the described domain with the assumed
"laws of thought" of more standard domains.[47]

All in all, *if* formal canons are abstractions or idealizations drawn
from actual argumentative practices, then it is hopeless to deny that their
range and mode of application are governed by the higher-order concerns
of the living practices from which they are drawn or to which they are
bound. In this sense, the liberalization here advocated is quite modest;
consonant with general doubts about the invariance or universal applicability of well-known formal rules; not at all disposed to generate
unusual or unnecessary paradoxes; and motivated well within the spirit
of received theories of the very nature of logical rules. It must be said
that to see matters this way is to be very strongly disposed to construe
all programs of extensional regimentation or reduction as conceptually
responsible and subservient to intensionally (or interpretively) provided
distinctions. That in itself is simply another way of expressing the
Aristotelian theme already mentioned. It is also not in any essential way
intended prejudicially – for instance, so as to disqualify *ab initio* strong
extensionalist projects. But it is true that perceived dangers along these
lines sometimes encourage the opponents of relativism to imagine that
the best defense is to attack the apparent logical novelties before the
substantive arguments are even mounted. That is what I have been at
pains to offset. The more profound import of the strategy adopted is
that we must remain open to whatever in the actual contexts of human
judgment and behavior appears most salient. In this sense, the defense
of relativism is only a sortie of quite limited scope – but it is also a sign
of potentially more fundamental conceptual changes that may be needed.

Notes

1   These alternatives are offered by Richard Brandt in his overview of ethical
    relativism: see Richard B. Brandt, *Ethical Theory* Englewood Cliffs, NJ:
    Prentice-Hall, 1959), ch. 11. Brandt rejects the first ("methodological rela-
    tivism") but he seems to construe the second as a fair account (p. 274). For
    a rather comprehensive survey of alternative versions of relativism – both
    "cognitive" and "moral," see Jack W. Meiland and Michael Krausz (eds),
    Relativism Cognitive and Moral (Notre Dame, Ind.: University of Notre
    Dame Press, 1982).
2   Gilbert Harman identifies himself as a relativist of this sort: see Gilbert
    Harman, *The Nature of Morality* (New York: Oxford University Press,

1977), pp. 45–6 (ch. 9); cf. Philippa Foot, *Moral Relativism* (Lawrence: University of Kansas Press, 1979).

3   This is the view notoriously advanced by Edward Westermarck: see Edward A. Westermarck, *Ethical Relativity* (New York: Harcourt, Brace, 1932). Westermarck, of course, does not speak as a critic of relativism.

4   This might be a fair reading of C. L. Stevenson's thesis, in *Ethics and Language* (New Haven, Conn.: Yale University Press, 1944), particularly ch. 7. But see his *Facts and Values* (New Haven, Conn.: Yale University Press, 1963), ch. 5.

5   This is Brandt's relativistic gloss on Kant's treatment of would-be moral maxims: cf. Brandt, *Ethical Theory*, pp. 31–3. Brandt notes the same concession in R. M. Hare's *The Language of Morals* (Oxford: Clarendon Press, 1952); cf. Brandt, *Ethical Theory*, p. 224. Brandt favors this much of relativism, though he clearly believes that such alternative "systems" will severally satisfy the same higher-order criteria of rational choice: see Richard B. Brandt, *A Theory of the Good and the Right* (Oxford: Clarendon Press, 1979), p. 192 (ch. 11).

6   See Ruth Benedict, "Anthropology and the Abnormal," *Journal of General Psychology*, X (1934).

7   Brandt, *Ethical Theory*, pp. 280, 251–2.

8   Ibid., p. 278.

9   Ibid., pp. 249–50.

10 Ibid., pp. 280–1.

11 Ibid., pp. 280f.

12 See entry "Ethical relativism," (prepared by Brandt) in Paul Edwards (ed.), *The Encyclopaedia of Philosophy*, vol. III (New York: Macmillan and Free Press, 1967), pp. 75–8.

13 Monroe C. Beardsley, *The Possibility of Criticism* (Detroit: Wayne State University Press, 1970), p. 13.

14 Ibid., p. 42.

15 Ibid., p. 44. I discuss Beardsley's view in *Art and Philosophy* (Atlantic Highlands, NJ: Humanities Press, 1980), chs 6–7.

16 Beardsley: *The Possibility of Criticism*, p. 87; *Aesthetics* (New York: Harcourt, Brace, 1958), p. 48. Later, in *Aesthetics*, Beardsley explicitly considers relativistic conceptions of "good" and other concepts in terms restricted to versions like 4 and 5 above; cf. pp. 478–89, which really tend to favor version 3.

17 Beardsley, *The Possibility of Criticism*, p. 71. The context involves P. H. Nowell-Smith's and J. L. Austin's views, though Beardsley does not really explore the issue systematically.

18 Ibid.

19 Michael Dummett, "Truth," *Truth and Other Enigmas* (Cambridge, Mass.: Harvard University Press, 1978), p. 16f.

20 Ibid., p. 17 and Preface, p. xxviii.

21 Nelson Goodman, *Ways of Worldmaking* (Indianapolis: Hackett, 1978), p. x.

22   Ibid, pp. 128–9. Goodman's point, it may be remarked, is a reasonable one quite independent of the quarrelsome thesis (which he favors) that worlds are made, that "reality in a world . . . is largely a matter of habit," that "even reality is relative" (p. 20) – which many, notably Quine, have found preposterous. Cf. Israel Scheffler, "The Wonderful Worlds of Goodman," *Synthese*, XLV (1980).

23   W. V. Quine, "Ontological Relativity," *Ontological Relativity and Other Essays* (New York: Columbia University Press, 1969), pp. 53–5.

24   See C. G. Hempel, "Inductive Inconsistencies," *Aspects of Scientific Explanation* (New York: Free Press, 1965).

25   Cf. Maurice Mandelbaum, "Subjective, Objective, and Conceptual Relativisms," *The Monist*, LXII (1979).

26   W. V. Quine, *Word and Object* (Cambridge, Mass.: MIT Press, 1960, p. 27.

27   Cf. Joseph Margolis: "Behaviorism and Alien Languages," *Philosophia*, III (1973); "The Locus of Coherence," *Linguistics and Philosophy*, VII (1984).

28   Goodman, *Ways of Worldmaking*, pp. 2–3 (italics added).

29   Ibid., p. 6.

30   Ibid., p. 120.

31   Goodman remarks quite mysteriously (that is to say, without sufficient explanation), "if nothing stands apart from all versions [all world-versions], what can be the basis and nature of these constraints [regarding right and wrong versions]? How can a version be wrong about a world it makes? We must obviously look for truth not in the relation of a version to something outside that it refers to but in characteristics of the version itself and its relationships to other versions. . .the answer cannot lie in coherence alone; for a false or otherwise wrong version can hold together as well as a right one. Nor do we have any self-evident truths, absolute axioms, unlimited warranties, to serve as touchstones in distinguishing right *from among other coherent versions* . . . " – *Of Mind and Other Matters* (Cambridge Mass.: Harvard University Press), pp. 36–7 (italics added). The solution seems to be connected with what Goodman calls "right categorization" – in effect, with the solution of "right" projectibles regarding induction. So he adds, "But what makes a category right? Very briefly and oversimply, its adoption in inductive practice, its entrenchment, resulting from inertia modified by invention" (p. 38). The trouble is that the "making" of many divergent worlds (conceded by Goodman to be at least coherent) surely must call into serious question the bare possibility of measuring such entrenchment both pertinently and (*a fortiori*) reliably; *and* the ability *to* gauge reasonable entrenchment points in the direction of a common world (or a common-enough minimal world upon which all the other underdetermined "worlds" Goodman thinks are both actual and "made" depend. On Quine's view, see *Word and Object*, sections 37–9.

32   This bears on but is not quite the point of the dispute between Hilary Putnam and Michael Dummett about so-called "idealist" or "anti-realist"

accounts of truth. See Hilary Putnam, *Meaning and the Moral Sciences* (London: Routledge and Kegan Paul, 1978).

33 See Martin Hollis and Steven Lukes (eds), *Rationality and Relativism* (Cambridge, Mass.: MIT Press, 1982).

34 See particularly Margolis, *Art and Philosophy*, ch. 7, for a sketch of "plausible".

35 This is a charge made by Putnam, for instance, but it is unconvincing. Cf. his "Meaning and Knowledge" (The John Locke Lectures 1976), Lecture II, *Meaning and the Moral Sciences*; and Richard N. Boyd, "Realism, Underdetermination, and a Causal Theory of Evidence," *Nous*, VIII (1973). Kuhn's explicit tolerance of relativism is clear from Thomas S. Kuhn, *The Structure of Scientific Revolutions*, 2nd, enlarged edn (Chicago: University of Chicago Press, 1970), pp. 206–7. Cf. Gerald Doppelt, "Kuhn's Epistemological Relativism: An Interpretation and Defense," *Inquiry*, XXI (1978).

36 Harman, in *The Nature of Morality*, adopts an extreme conventionalist view and construes it as a form of relativism, rather in the manner of the uninteresting variety 3. It is a view more extreme than Hume's, since Hume refuses to construe morality entirely in conventionalist terms.

37 Beardsley, *The Possibility of Criticism*, p. 16.

38 Ibid., p. 36 (italics added).

39 Romantic hermeneutics spans the work of Schleiermacher and, in our own time, E. D. Hirsch, Jr: cf. Hirsch's *Validity in Interpretation* (New Haven, Conn.: Yale University Press, 1967). Cf. also Emilio Betti, "The Epistemological Problem of Understanding as an Aspect of the General Problem of Knowing," tr. Susan Noakes, in Gary Shapiro and Alan Sica (eds), *Hermeneutics* (Amherst: University of Massachusetts Press, 1984). The principal statement of a conservative, anti-relativistic hermeneutics that is still responsive to the radical possibilities of historicity is unquestionably Hans-Georg Gadamer's *Truth and Method*, tr. Garrett Barden and John Cumming from the 2nd German edn (New York: Seabury Press, 1975).

40 See Joseph Margolis, "Nature, Culture, and Persons," *Theory and Decision*, XIII (1981).

41 Cf. Roland Barth, "From Work to Text," in Josué V. Harari (ed.), *Textual Strategies* (Ithaca, NY: Cornell University Press, 1979); also Jacques Derrida, *Of Grammatology*, tr. Gayatri Chakravorty Spivak (Baltimore: John Hopkins University Press, 1974).

42 Cf. Hilary Putnam, "Is Semantics Possible?" and "The Meaning of 'Meaning,'" *Philosophical Papers*, vol. 2 (Cambridge: Cambridge Unversity Press, 1975).

43 For a sample of certain telltale admissions along this line that are unwilling to draw the relativistic conclusion, see Karl R. Popper: *Conjectures and Refutations*, 2nd, rev. edn (New York: Harper Torchbooks, 1968); *Objective Knowledge: An Evolutionary Approach* (Oxford: Clarendon Press, 1972). Also, Karl-Otto Apel, *Towards a Transformation of Philosophy*, tr. Glyn Adey and David Frisby (London: Routledge and Kegan Paul, 1972).

44   See Edmund Gettier, "Is Knowledge True Justified Belief?" *Analysis*, XXIII (1963).
45   See Nicholas Wolterstorff, *Works and Worlds of Art* (Oxford: Clarendon Press, 1980), pt 3.
46   Cf. the brief account in Susan Haack, *Philosophy of Logics* (Cambridge: Cambridge University Press, 1978), ch. 11.
47   See Hilary Putnam, *Philosophical Papers*, vol. 1 (Cambridge: Cambridge University Press, 1975), chs. 7–10; Bas C. van Fraassen, "Semantic Analysis of Quantum Logic," in C. A. Hooker (ed.), *Contemporary Research in the Foundations and Philosophy of Quantum Theory* (Dordrecht: D. Reidel, 1973). For a recent brief overview, cf. M. L. dalla Chiara and P. A. Metelli, "Philosophy of Quantum Mechanics," in Guttorm Fløistad (ed.), *Contemporary Philosophy*, vol. 2: *Philosophy of Science* (The Hague: Martinus Nijhoff, 1982).

2

Historicism and Universalism

For the sake of economy, we shall shift the focus of discussion rather abruptly to certain initial questions of a substantive sort – regarding realism. Our purpose, of course, is to lead to a reconciliation between realism and relativism. We have begun with the formal *minima* of a coherent relativism that promises to escape the native weaknesses of what are generally identified as Protagoreanism and the incommensurability thesis: those doctrines, barely sketched, are very often thought to be the principal forms of relativism; they serve, therefore, to justify an easy dismissal of relativism itself.

Our counterstrategy started with a somewhat formal model of an alternative version of relativism. We had just begun to make its appearance plausible and relevant, and we must now provide at least initial clues regarding its bearing on the general problem of scientific realism. The issues are remarkably complex and difficult to disentangle. By acknowledging conceptual puzzles as they arise in a natural way – without, however, pausing in the middle of preliminaries to attempt to resolve each as it appears – we may perhaps succeed in introducing our third notion of relativism in a sympathetic and uncluttered way without risking too much in the way of promising arguments that, though obviously required, must be postponed for the time being.

In a sense, our policy somewhat mirrors the rather labyrinthine nature of current philosophical dispute, particularly those lines of inquiry that are reaching out, from both directions, to integrate contemporary analytic and Continental European views, to explore the significance of history for the theory of science, and to assess the theoretical import of a very large variety of challenges to what have hitherto been regarded as canonical doctrines. The problem of the reconciliation of realism and relativism proves to be a particularly strategic focus for an extraordinarily large number of current quarrels of importance. Its resolution – at least the viability of its resolution – would go a long way toward forming a comparatively new but responsible setting in which to examine adjusted versions of familiar questions alongside some that are notably often neglected. That at any rate is the intended challenge of the present account and the point of the abrupt shift of scene.

I

It is fashionable to characterize necessity or necessary truth in a Leibnizian manner, as what is true in all possible worlds. But the brilliance of this heuristic device ought not blind us to the fact that, unlike God (in Leibniz's calculation), we cannot suppose ourselves able to individuate all possible worlds. The sense of the notion of necessity is that, whatever we suppose possible worlds to be, nothing we conceive as forming a compossible world could falsify the truth rightly tendered as a necessary truth. Since to conceive or imagine a "particular" compossible world is to conceive or imagine a determinate state of affairs the details of which do not entail incompatible ascriptions among those details, there is reason to think that, whatever may be alleged to be the status of the formal priniple of noncontradiction, conceptual compossibility is parasitic on the semantically rich natural languages with which in various ways we entertain possibilities relative to the actual world. If this much is conceded, then it is a very small step to grasp that, *if* (with due tolerance for counterfactual supposition, correction and change of belief, evolving theories, and the like) what we suppose to be possible relative to the actual world can be specified only within the scope of the particular conceptual schemes and theories that enable us to imagine determinate states of affairs of this sort or that, then

1   different conceptual schemes will permit us to entertain different and different ranges of compossible worlds;
2   confined as we are, within a given historical interval, to a particular conceptual scheme that does not yet feature or even know how to feature distinctions that are to become cognitively accessible at a later time (say, in the sense in which Max Planck first formulated the basic notion of quantum physics at the very beginning of the twentieth century), we cannot make sense of our ever being able to formulate in principle all possibilities with regard to the actual world – nor, therefore, all compossible worlds; and
3   it would not be surprising were human investigators working in real-time terms with competing paradigms (generously construed,

in Thomas Kuhn's sense for instance, as involving a "characteristic set of beliefs and preconceptions,"[1] or, even more globally, "all the shared commitments of a scientific group"[2]) to find their paradigms at least provisionally incommensurable, as relating to differently conceived problems, differently conceived ways of construing events, and the like.

(To suggest a deeper problem: it would not be unreasonable to construe Kant's search for the necessary conditions of human cognition as entirely relativized to his acceptance of Newtonian physics and Euclidean geometry. This points of course to Husserl's criticism. But it also poses the ulterior question – applicable to Husserl as well – of whether there is any sense in which, even if one escapes Kant's parochial vision, one can be said to entertain "all possible worlds" or whether one can be said to entertian necessary truths binding on all possible worlds.)

Kuhn, of course, is understandably uneasy about explicating incommensurability and fixing the concept of a paradigm. He has hardly gone beyond the following formulation:

Proponents of different theories (or different paradigms, in the broader sense of the term) speak different languages – languages expressing different cognitive commitments, *suitable for different worlds*. Their abilities to grasp each other's viewpoints are therefore inevitably limited by the imperfections of the processes of translation and of reference determination.[3]

In his original account, Kuhn had held rather more dubiously that "the proponents of competing paradigms practice their trades *in different worlds*."[4] But, if we do not deny that communities of inquirers may, within their own conceptual horizon, overcome given incommensurabilities, even if they are bound to generate others in the process, if we drop the quarrelsome notion of plural actual worlds, or – better – if we drop the notion of the reality of possible worlds that include the actual world as one only among their number,[5] if we admit that paradigms are not normally assignable clear boundaries, and if we treat "incommensurabilities" in terms of real-time constraints among scientists trying here and now to understand one another's conceptual schemes (and succeeding moderately well) rather than in terms of a principled distinction between globally incommunicable or mutually unintelligible systems, then Kuhn's point is an entirely reasonable one – more reasonable though also much blander and much less difficult to formulate than his seemingly original challenge. (Certainly, we may, by this device, avoid premature assumptions about individuating different conceptual systems.[6])

Let us say,then, by way of a term of art, that human beings cannot in principle *totalize* (all) conceptual compossibilities or (all) possibilities relative to the actual world. So saying, we must construe necessity or necessary truth somewhat in the empirical manner favored by Mill and Quine:[7] that is, in the spirit though not (necessarily) in the letter they favor – viewing what is to be "discovered", rather than defined as a necessary truth, in terms of an appraisal of candidate rules within the whole of actual discourse, drawn from a contingently restricted range of experience. We admit to ourselves, therefore, that we have no straight-forward cognitive access to or assurance regarding such necessary truths, though we do not deny ourselves the advantage of being able to speak of necessary truths, treating them as reasonable posits in accord with empirical inferences of some sort to the best explanation of apparently formal, unchanging conditions of rigor *in* actual discourse, reviewed within a historical or praxical horizon. In fact, Quine himself innocently anticipates a *rapprochement* (that doubtless he would find dismaying), between analytic philosphy and the principal historicized philosophies of Continental Europe, for he applies his argument about the "empirical" nature of necessary truth to the "distinction between necessary and contingent attributes" – that is, to essentialisms and universalisms of every sort, which he rightly says are (within the Millian account) "surely indefensible."[8]

If we reject what in the analytic tradition are characterized as *foundationalism* (the belief that we possess a privileged basis for cognitive certainty) and *essentialism*, or realism construed in the essentialist manner (the belief that, conceding whatever difficulty and self-correction may obtain, the structure of the actual world *is* cognitively transparent to, or representable by, us),[9] then the problem of incommensurability – more pointedly and less misleadingly, the problem of different human communities (differently oriented) understanding one another within the flux of human history – is bound to become much more difficult to resolve than it would otherwise be. As already suggested, recent Continental European philosophies converge on this same pair of doctrines (the denial of totalizing and the denial of foundationalism and essentialism), notably in the attack on the tradition of Western metaphysics that Heidegger pursued and in the attack on so-called logocentrism and the search for "originary" origins pressed by Jacques Derrida.[10] It would not be unfair to say that such doctrines entail the consequence (possibly a radicalized vestige of Kant's achievement) that it makes no sense to ask what the structure of the world is, independent of the conceptual categories in accord with which (however changeably) the question is always set. This is not to deny that there is a physical world that exists independently of inquiry, or that it has a structure in some sense, or even that, *within* the confines of *our* inquiries, *we can* rationally speculate about what the physical world is like independent of those inquiries; it is only to deny that the fruits of human inquiry are, in any principled respect, ever conceptually unaffected by the historically developing forms of inquiry itself, and to insist on the transience of whatever may be elaborated within it. These possibilities help to fix the large sense in which human inquiry is at once realist and idealist. Alternatively, they fix the sense in which the rejection of foundationalism and its allied doctrines entails that a global realist–idealist, or realist–anti-realist, demarcation or disjunction can no longer function – which is hardly to say that, *within* the conceptual space of that new indissolubility, more specialized disputes about the function of science, also said to be about realism, idealism, anti-realism, instrumentalism, and the like, cannot be recovered or appraised without prejudice. Of course, our finding about historicism is itself a would-be universal finding, the work of a certain reflexive assessment of what, on empirical grounds, appears to be only generally true. Historicism is a universalized doctrine found under quite contingent, particular circumstances to be distinctly compelling – but not conceptually inescapable at every possible price.[11] Perhaps it pays to enter a caution here: that historicism signifies (in the present context) only the intrinsically historical career of human inquiry, *not* (at least not necessarily) the mere relativization of all questions of truth, meaning, knowledge, validity, science or the like to the spirit or *Geist* of different cultural eras – in the manner usually associated (in a derogatory sense) with Hegel, nineteenth-century German historians such as Ranke, and Dilthey. Of course, historicism in the latter sense (similar or tantamount to radical relativism or radical incommensurability) is ultimately incoherent if not saved by some absolutist or foundationalist vantage (as Hegel very well understood), since the correct discrimination of different, shifting historical eras *within* which alone epistemic questions are said to have their proper function cannot fail to be self-defeating, completely ahistoricist.[12]

The underlying thread of these reflections appears to be: (1) that empirical inquiry identifies and confirms *general uniformities* within the various contingently limited sectors in which it operates; (2) that it speculates about which of these, under relevant constraints, may justifiably be taken to have uncovered *universal invariances* holding, in some sense, throughout the whole of the actual world or for all possible worlds in which the phenomena examined are supposed to be reidentifiable; and

(3) that it itself posits what it takes to be a *reasonable* basis for justifying inferences in any and all contexts of cognitive interest, from generality to universality. The formula here offered is entirely abstract, but actual efforts to meet the implied demand (valid grounds for universal claims, valid grounds for universal canons of validity) are pursued within the shadow of the same constraints as the actual practices they would review and in accord with the considered achievement and promise of what they take themselves to have inherited and to be engaged in preserving and improving.

Certainly, one large consequence of this way of construing the difference between the general and the universal is that notions such as that of rationality, or rational inquiry or inference to the best explanation, or decidability, cannot fail to be subject to *revision*, in historical terms. If so, then we cannot, on the strength of the record of the "past futures" of the history of science, deny that there are, *now*, truths which we cannot now construe as "effectively decidable."[13] Quite surprisingly, therefore, historicism shows that we cannot convincingly treat the realism of human inquiry in terms of a disjunctive choice between "platonism" or "metaphysical realism," on the one side, and "anti-realism", on the other – in the manner Michael Dummett has proposed.[14] We must rather concede a continuum that avoids the extreme (so-called "anti-realism") of denying that in some "future present" what is now undecidable may yet prove to be decidable – hence, that there remains a fully defensible sense in which "statements of the disputed class [whether about the physical world, mental events, mathematical phenomena, the past] possess [at least sometimes] an objective truth-value, independently of a means of knowing it: they are true or false in virtue of a reality existing independently of us";[15] we must concede a continuum that avoids at the same time the extreme (so-called "realism") of affirming that "the meanings of statements of the disputed class are not directly tied to the kind of evidence for them that we can have, but consist in the manner of their determination as true or false by states of affairs whose existence is not dependent on our possession of evidence for them."[16] Both of the exclusive extremes ("anti-realism" and "realism," in Dummett's usage) are untenable: the question can only be resolved piecemeal within a reasonable review of the actual work of the sciences – which is exactly what, under the banner of historicism, the indissolubility of realism and idealism comes to. Our theory of the real world is and must be "tied" to what we take to be the pertinent evidence available to us; but, in affirming that much, we are not obliged to deny that the evidence itself may justify us in supposing (for reasons of historical and technological limitation) that, at any moment, there may be truths that we do not now and may never (in terms of real-time considerations) actually know.

To remind ourselves of a famous case: Clark Maxwell apparently believed that, if the velocity of light could be measured relative to the velocity of the ether, then the velocity of the ether could be determined; but he also believed that "all methods" that were terrestrially "practicable" for determining the velocity of light would yield "insensible" results, so he thought the project hopeless. But shortly thereafter Michelson actually formulated an experiment for determining the velocity of light and carried it out successfully.[17] Historicism obliges us to acknowledge that during no present interval of time can we reasonably claim that no statement now undecidable will never, in a manageably finite future in which our present cognitive resources will be enlarged, be shown to be decidable (without suffering a palpable change of meaning); *and* that that very tolerance rationally depends on our present ability to construe a vast range of statements as genuinely decidable. Thus interpreted, Dummett's view of realism and anti-realism is itself committed (however surprising it may seem) to an objectionable form of totalizing, or universalism, or essentialism, and must, therefore, be put down. This is the point of the previous suggestion regarding Dummett: it helps to show both that an anti-realist attack on platonism or "metaphysical" or other extreme realisms is not as such an attack on a realism suited to science and that it is (and must be) open in principle to the kind of relativist reading we have already broached; it helps to show in effect the possibility and point of reconciling a disciplined relativism and a disciplined realism, and it confirms in the most powerful way how the entire discussion of realism and its relation to relativism is inexorably affected by construing science as an historicized activity. It is just this conjunction of themes, in fact, that serves as the increasingly common conceptual ground linking Anglo-American and Continental European speculation. Our example also serves as a particularly compelling instance of the kind of evidence that confirms the pertinence of philosophy to science – even its conceptual inseparability from the pursuit of first-order science.

Historicism may be read as the thesis (diachronically applied) that the human condition is such that all claims of universal invariances are problematic in a sense in which general claims are not: in that whatever, within a cognitive practice, could consensually support the general would need to be supplemented in order to support the universal, and in that supporting the universal would depend on assessing in an appropriate way the prior but weaker data favoring the general. Historicism is a thesis in need of a canon that permits us to argue from generality to universality – hence it runs the serious risk of being carelessly formulated as an internally incoherent doctrine. The only way, apparently, in which incoherence can be avoided is to maintain that, whereas general uniformities can be defended on the basis of cognitive powers operative in first-order inquiries (perceptual powers, for instance), universal invariances of any sort can be defended only on the basis of second-order inquiries into the powers acknowledged in first-order inquiries – although, in accord with the caveat just introduced, the distinction between first-order and second-order inquiry is itself a second-order claim or posit subject to whatever degree of strength or weakness may be attributed to inquiries of the relevant second-order sort. In particular, inferences to universal or necessary conditions cannot but be rhetorically supported in terms of the saliences of particular phases of historicized reflection: we deny to ourselves any first-order cogniti*vist* basis on which they may be reliably and actually discriminated. More provocatively put: historicism and universalism themselves depend on transcendental arguments of some sort; or, if such arguments are to be rejected, then first-order arguments themselves cannot fail to be correspondingly enlarged.

Contrariwise, *universalism* may be read as the thesis that the human condition is such that claims of universal invariances are in principle no more problematic than general claims and that, in fact, we do possess first-order cognitive powers capable of directly confirming significant universal claims (the cognitivist thesis). This, too, is a second-order claim of universal force. But universalism, precisely because it posits first-order cognitive powers capable of confirming universal claims of certain privileged sorts at least, claims a variety of conceptual strategies denied to historicism. The historicist is bound to hold that *his* second-order claims of universal scope cannot but be empirically or praxically restricted (restricted by general evidence), cannot therefore support a deductive or otherwise formal canon yielding apodictic or invariant findings (in the manner, say, of a Kantian transcendental argument) or of any comparably strong inductive sort (say, along the lines of Hans Reichenbach's theory that posits a determinable limit for frequencies among natural phenomena – that is, that if their frequencies of occurrence actually have limits, the proper use of inductive procedures must progressively approximate to the actual order of the natural world).[18] This inductivist thesis, it may be noted, is critical for whatever can still be salvaged of the unity-of-science program – in which of course the law-like behavior of quantum physics plays a decisive role;[19] and, yet, the hope of a formulable limit of statistical regularities among the life sciences and the human sciences seems quite incapable of any comparably sanguine satisfaction.[20] (Here, one must observe that first-order induction is not at risk as a working instrument in science. Inductivism, however, is *not* the mere advocacy or commitment to induction: it is the theoretical defense or legitimation of induction as peculiarly suited, perhaps even exclusively suited, to the realist pretensions of science; it is, without question, a second-order thesis. Precisely the same distinction, as we shall see, needs to be made with regard to first-order strategies of falsifying scientific hypotheses – as opposed to second-order falsificationism, Popper's thesis.)

Historicists, we may say, *if* they concede the need to provide grounds for universal claims, cannot but construe the required arguments as transcendental – as second-order arguments formulating the necessary conditions of cognition – but now conceived as restricted by the historical contingencies of actual human inquiry, hence empirically generated from *within* such inquiry. In this sense, historicists cannot but construe transcendental arguments as *sui generis* empirical arguments of an informal and rhetorical (but not for that reason unrigorous) sort formed within and in accord with a critical tradition of such argument. Since historicism does entail a universal claim, it cannot consistently reject transcendental arguments; but, consistently with its own thesis, it cannot concede any first-order cognitive powers of a universalist sort (what may now be called foundationalism or cognitivism or essentialism). This is the sense in which the following serves as a decisive constraint on the internal coherence of all philosophical doctrines (most pertinently, contemporary ones): *historicism and universalism are conceptually incompatible*. Here, then, historicism is not a theory about totalized *Geisten* universally relativizing all cognitive concerns, each within its own "proper" and separate sphere; it is, rather, a theory about the implications of historical (or historicized) existence and inquiry in search of objective and universal structures. In this sense, the contrast between the two sorts of historicism is roughly analogous to the contrast, within disputes triggered by Kuhn's account of scientific paradigms, of opposed conceptions of "incommensurability." (We may take it that, although the need for transcendental arguments has been sympathetically broached here and although a somewhat heterodox characterization of such arguments has been very briefly insinuated, the entire question will have to be much more directly explored.)

II

The fact is that most of the leading philosophical currents of our day *are* historicist in one form or another – be they phenomenological, hermeneutic, Critical, Marxist, Hegelian, structuralist, deconstructivist, pragmatist or analytic in the spirit of contemporary philosophy and history of philosophy of science. Our constraint, therefore, serves as a remarkably economical but powerful criterion of the minimal viability of a large number of well-known theories – which, on inspection, actually seem to be incoherent or at least to have failed to explain the sense in which they mean to reconcile historicism and universalism. Before turning to demonstrate the effectiveness of applying this constraint (as a criterion of philosophical coherence) several distinctions need to be supplied.

The first is the notion of *praxis* – identified only in terms of a least common denominator pertinent to a large variety of contemporary theories. Let us say that a philosophy is praxical if

1   it maintains that the very forms or canons of cognition – particularly of science and rational inquiry – are subject to a process of historical emergence, development, reconstruction, or the like;
2   that such emergence is in some sense influenced or determined by and manifested in the contingent historical development of human labor and the conditions under which labor and production – the socially organized forms of fixing and satisfying human interests and human needs – evolve; and
3   that individual cognitive orientation is, as such, a variant on socially prevalent cognitive practices, which it may contingently modify but which (both individual and social) are subject to human forces not always reflexively detectable even when they are effective – both tacit, then, and not totalizable.

In this sense, praxical philosophy is the dominant form of historicism of our time. Its *locus classicus* is undoubtedly Marx's "Theses on Feuerbach," but it need not take a Marxist form at all. For example, in a fair sense, Heidegger's views about technology and the criticism of Western metaphysics are essentially praxical, however reasonable it may be to judge that Heidegger ultimately departs from that orientation.[21] Equally fairly, John Dewey's conception of "experience" is intended praxically,[22] though hardly in the Marxist manner. More clearly Marxist-oriented, however deviant, are the views of such theorists as Sartre and Adorno and Habermas.[23] To put matters this way is deliberately to leave unresolved the famous question of the distinction between praxical and nonpraxical processes of cognitive change and invention. One can of course regularly find – for instance, in Adorno and Habermas (and, further afield, among the Russian Formalists and reader-reception theorists[24]) – the clear conviction that one must provide for both within the movement of human history. But that question, often notoriously cristic, cannot by itself threaten historicism and normally is intended to max- imize or insure the freedom of cognitive improvisation within the very flux of praxical history. It is not meant to deny, therefore, the con- tingencies under which the search for invariant or universal structures is pursued: this is true even of Jürgen Habermas, who has tried, in our own time (in what may well be the most quixotically sustained attempt), to reconcile a strong conception of *praxis* with the declared discovery of undeniably universal structures.[25]

In the English-speaking world, the praxical orientation, or a kind of historicism very close to it, has recently gathered explicit force in a new series of publications that hopes to picture "the development of ideas in their concrete contexts. By this means [the announcement for the series maintains] artificial distinctions between the history of philosophy, of the various sciences, of society and politics, and of literature, may be seen to dissolve." The general insight shared by those who are praxically oriented – if we stick to common denominators and resist more partisan formulations – is conveniently put by Charles Taylor, who, however, does mean to pursue the theme in a particular way that will prove important to us later. Taylor takes particular note of "the need we often experience to formulate the point of our practices, which need in turn must frequently be met with an historical account." He goes on to say,

> The context in which this need arises is the fact that a basic way
> – I want to argue, *the* basic way – in which we acknowledge and
> mark the things that are important to us in the human context is
> through what we can call social practices. By this I mean roughly:
> ways that we regularly behave to/before each other, which (a)
> embody some understanding between us, and which (b) allow of
> discrimination of right/wrong, appropriate/inappropriate.[26]

This much of Taylor's view is relatively uncontroversial, though par- ticular readings of his (a) and (b) (his own, in fact) will hardly fail to be open to quarrel. The thesis is that theorizing even at the level of science and philosophy is primarily praxical, grounded in and pertinent for the smooth and effective functioning of particular societies. Hence, the praxical thesis conceptually or logically precludes (and denies the need for) *any independent*, ahistorical, cognitively competent, higher-order capacity to review and assess the would-be science and practical knowl- edge of an actual functioning society. In this of course it is distinctly open to challenge; but there can be little doubt that its philosophical bias is congruent with the strongest currents of contemporary Anglo-American and Continental European philosophy. Furthermore, it obliges us to adjust our conception of coming to understand the achievements of the past – out of which our own have presumably sprung: for, where we treat former theorists as pertinent to our own concerns, we do so within a historical tradition that links us to the other's past; and, where we attempt to understand the past in its own terms, we do so within the context of our present understanding of our own linkage to that past. There is, consequently, a very close connection between a praxical and a hermeneutic conception of cognitive issues, that may be more or less integrated or disjoint, depending on one's theory of praxical and non-praxicalized thinking.[27] As we shall soon see, the issue here raised is of considerable importance for the fortunes of relativism.

Another needed notion is that of *transcendental arguments*. These are second-order arguments about the very possibility of a distinct form of cognitive inquiry. In Kant's hands, a transcendental argument marks an invariant species-specific power of human reason that, functioning *a priori* with respect to first-order cognition, can discover the uniquely necessary conditions of such cognition. (Kant, of course, does seem to have had considerable misgivings about the ultimate validity of his exemplary transcendental arguments, those regarding the refutation of idealism. It may be that he was attracted to the view that these are no more than imperfect idealizations of the required ones. Perhaps, then, he himself was attracted to historicized and praxicalized constraints.[28]) In any case, no historicist and no praxically committed philosopher could subscribe to transcendental arguments in the strong Kantian sense (a consideration that has increasingly occupied Habermas). To be redeemed (by way of a heterodox adjustment), transcendental arguments would have to be *empirical* arguments generated from *within* an historically provisional cognitive practice – in search of necessary foundations, unable in principle to insure a unique such account, unable to insure the universal validity of any such account, logically informal but disciplined in accord with a historically developed practice of rationalizing our cognitive powers.

Habermas is uneasy about the implications of a transcendental defense of cognition. Nevertheless, he believes he has managed to formulate the necessary conditions for rational communication free of deception, self-deception, distortion, and domination – conditions capable, therefore, of supporting a universal consensus among all would-be communicants and free of praxical constraint.[29] On the argument, this cannot fail to violate the precept that historicism and universalism are incompatible. In fact, it is a characteristic of numerous historicist theories that they end by embracing some form of universalism. The reason is simply that historicists are often motivated by the wish to avoid relativism – or the appearance of relativism. For instance, this explains at a stroke the subtle way in which Hans-Georg Gadamer's historicism hides an ultimately undefended version of Aristotelian or Aristotelian-like essentialism.[30] Needless to say, a cognitively valid universalism would preclude the need for, as well as the tenability of, a relativisic reading of cognition wherever the first had scope.

Habermas himself candidly admits the irreconcilable attraction of historicism and universalism:

> As long as [the] interests of knowledge are identified and analyzed by way of reflection on the logic of inquiry that structures the natural and the humane sciences, they can claim a "transcendental" status; however, as soon as they are understood in terms of an anthropology of knowledge, as results of natural history, they have an "empirical" status [and thus] cannot . . . be developed within the transcendental framework of objectifying science.[31]

Here he treats the problem in its Kantian form and anticipates a straight-forward resolution. But, in his more recent discussions of the conditions of "communicative competence," Habermas is convinced that the actual conditions of speech favor the "unavoidable fiction" of a universal consensus: that is, that mankind *is* capable of an undistorted, non-deceptive discourse relieved of praxical and historical pressures, by means of which we *can* actually achieve or *can* actually approximate a "rational consensus" among all potential communicants.[32] The thesis of the fiction is a concession to historicism, to the inextricability of praxical and (would-be) ideal communicative concerns. But the very idea that we *can* actually discover and formulate once and for all (and thus subscribe to) the conditions of praxically neutral communication within any and all historicized contexts is both a denial of the putatively fictive nature of the consensus *and* a retreat to a more robust universalism than Habermas is entitled to claim on his own (praxical) grounds.

The search for the universal powers and conditions of human cognition is an obviously persistent concern of reflexive inquiry. For praxically oriented theorists, it is conceptually impossible to concede *first-order* cognitive capacities that can insure universal, essential, foundational, or necessary findings regarding the structure of the actual world or of human inquiry about the world. This is the point of insisting that rational inquiry emerges from, is continuous with, and is affected by, the subcognitive conditions of human survival manifested within the contingent horizon of a particular *praxis* – that itself orients inquiry toward what it provisionally comes to favor as the very forms of disciplined consensus. Inquiry need not abandon the search for universal regularities; indeed, it cannot, if it both recognizes the potentially fatal allure of every uniformity that only appears to have explanatory force as well as the rational need to continue to sort reliable and unreliable structures.

The only solution to this paradox requires second-order reflections on first-order powers, limited and facilitated by the same praxical constraints affecting the very powers we take to facilitate survival. Human inquiry pursues universal conditions without universalism, foundations without foundationalism, essentials without essentialism – by way of transcendental arguments praxically generated and praxically confined: hence, rationally directed at guessing (or, better, directed at proposing or ideally projecting) the necessary within the contingent, the *a priori* within the empirical; hence, also, unavoidably rhetorical at heart, shaping its picture of a rational method for doing so through its own diachronic review of the historically contingent practice it means to review. *There is, therefore, no first-order inquiry without second-order inquiry; are* no cognitive powers acknowledged without the reflexive posit of their competence to sort the actual and the apparent; *are* no contingent cognitive successes without a transcendental attempt to plumb the conditions for their succeeding; and *is* no reasoned confidence in the realism of science and inquiry (however attenuated) without a theory of how *praxis* makes this possible. The radical novelty of this conception is simply that the provisionally posited "necessities" of human cognition are no longer grounded in any *a priori* principled way (as Kant would insist and as, in an even more extreme sense, Husserl proposed).[33] The relatively conservative (slowly changing) nature of transcendental arguments is itself a stunning but *merely empirical contingency*, which permits us (still and effectively) to formulate a fair sense of the characteristic discipline of such arguments. Stated perhaps too succinctly, transcendental reasoning is a rhetorically disciplined adjustment of selected, salient exemplars of second-order reasoning yielding argumentative norms only analogically, not by way of principled argument forms.

There is, however, no reason to think, *if* they are praxically and empirically generated in the manner sketched, that transcendental arguments *could* be counted on to provide "the only possible" theory of the conditions of cognitive success of any sort. That is the Kantian view all right, premised on the species-wide, invariant, praxically and historically unaffected competence of human reason to plumb its own powers. Kant disallows transcendental arguments unconstrained by reflection on first-order achievements, but he seems never to have considered *infra*-species contingencies of the praxical sort – in effect, culturally or historically variable contingencies – as essentially affecting the logical status of (would-be) universally necessary conditions of cognition; hence, he never explicitly perceived *the need to relativize and pluralize transcendental arguments themselves.*[34] He never converted the contextual human limits of transcendental reasoning into praxical, historicized limits – which, it should be said, is precisely the pressure point of Jacques Derrida's extended criticism of Husserl.[35] Husserl seems not to have fully grasped the provisionality of the stage of development of the sciences *with respect to which* he pursued (or of any stage with respect to which he could pursue) the universal, species-wide conditions of human cognition itself. (Nevertheless, true to the Nietzschean origins of his own criticism, Derrida does not "descend" to the question of how to construe truth-value assignments in a positive way.)

Transcendental arguments cannot, on the praxical view, be ascribed any epistemic privilege with respect to science: they cannot "legitimate" science or rational inquiry in this way. But that is hardly to deny the historicized legitimating role of such arguments, once one sees the need to project normative grounds for sorting what is methodologically reliable and unreliable *within* the changing culture of science itself. We alter our conception of the Kantian *quaestio juris* when we historicize inquiry; in fact, we alter the very conception of rationality. But, then, we strengthen rather than weaken the role of transcendental reflection – and in doing that we open the gates to pluralized and relativized speculations of the appropriately disciplined sort. This goes contrary to, for instance, Richard Rorty's recent rejection of transcendental arguments: not in the sense of reinstating the original Kantian project (which Rorty rightly challenges) but in the sense of recognizing the inescapability and importance of second order projections of the presumed realist powers of human cognition.[36] (For the praxical view *is* a profoundly realist view.) It makes little difference whether one incorporates transcendental questions within sciences itself or heuristically distinguishes between first-order and second-order questions; the historicizing of inquiry cannot sweep such questions away in sweeping away essentialism and universalism.[37] When, therefore, proposing a *reductio* of inductivist theories of learning, Karl Popper declares, "I am fortunate in never having been so hard pressed by sceptical attacks or doubts as to have recourse to a transcendental argument," he favors only the "negative use" of such an argument (as against the inductivist) and he believes that the fault of its positive use (as, say, favoring a particular theory of learning) lies in its invariably attempting to defend "the only possible one" for the achievement in question.[38] He rightly condemns the implied universalism, but he fails to consider that his own form of "critical" philosophy (replacing philosophical "justification" with – in W. W. Bartley's terms – "non-justificational" criticism) actually requires a transcendental model of "*rational* criticism" itself (now, no longer uniquely universalized but open to pluralized and relativized formulations).[39] His own replacement of truth by "truthlikeness" (or "verisimilitude") as the "object of our 'rational belief'" can neither be consistently vindicated in the sanguine way he supposes or even attempted without an appeal to transcendental considerations. In Popper, then, we find the attempt to preserve universal regularities by (first-order) *approximation* under (second-order) conditions that make approximation (the assessment of approximation) cognitively inaccessible.[40]

We may, then, claim (and may yet more fully demonstrate) that thinkers as diverse as Popper, Habermas, Gadamer, and Taylor, who are drawn to some version of the historicity of human existence and inquiry but who oppose relativism, and who are uneasily drawn to transcendental considerations that they try to distance themselves from, actually devise alternative forms of the very same underlying theory – which in effect attempts one way or another to reconcile or to approximate a reconciliation of universalism and historicism. The argument has to be rounded out more fully, but the thesis captures the essential thrust of what we have already labeled traditionalism – that is, particularly if a strict universalism or a strict adherence to the transparency thesis or cognitivism is avoided.

The spirit of the thesis is more than adumbrated in Taylor's view. Taylor emphasizes that, in philosophy, in science, in technology, in politics, in economics, we often find that the beliefs and theories we hold – more or less automatically, more or less by way of the "normalization" effected by the historical practices in which we have been groomed – come to be felt to be increasingly responsible for puzzles, paradoxes, dislocations, unsatisfying resolutions of quotidian concerns rather than for the smooth prompting of behavior congruent with a world those beliefs and theories were originally meant to service. Our "society is out of true with the original," he says. And so, "to understand ourselves today, we are pushed into the past for paradigm statements of our formative articulations. We are forced back to the last full disclosure of what we have been about, of what our practice has been woven about."[41] This is "*the* basic way" of understanding our own historical stance if we are "to take a new stance toward our [present] practices." We must "*restore*" a proper picture of the background of our practices, "get clear on the original form" of them, if we are "to *espouse* [now] out of a creative redescription, something one could give reasons for."[42] Presumably we shall find "unsaid," "forgotten," "inarticulated" in our present practices what the "last full-blooded formulation" of the theories original to our own age had already formulated: "We very often cannot raise a *new* issue really effectively until we have re-articulated our *actual* practices."[43]

An essential part of Taylor's purpose is to offset the kind of "relativism" Taylor finds in Richard Rorty's (pragmatic) approximation to the incommensurability thesis – "a kind of philosophical relativism, or at least a view which might be labelled a species of non-realism, according to which reason cannot arbitrate between the alternatives." It is Taylor's purpose to offset the view that, of two competing "pictures of mind-in-world, . . . we cannot argue that one is truer than the other, more faithful to reality or the way things are."[44] The solution lies, Taylor feels, just with placing the competing views within the context of the recovery of what is "original" to our present practices. If we place them so, then "we are not condemned to agnosticism . . . indeed, we cannot be undecided once we understand what is at stake." We are "rescued" from distortion; we repudiate the illusion that our present view alone is intelligible; and we are able to choose the better option in terms of what we have recovered in recovering our own history.[45]

But it is one thing to offset versions or approximations of the incommensurabilist's thesis (what we have called external relativism); it is quite another to suppose that the "original formulation" of our own history will be consensually explicit, or that the projection of how we should construe our present practice in accord with that understanding will once again converge in a strongly consensual way. Taylor seems to have missed the point that the recovery of comparative judgments is *not* tantamount to the defeat of *internal* relativism even if it is decisive against external relativism. Also, he fails to come to terms with hermeneutic and Nietzschean problems regarding the recovery of the past, problems that Gadamer and Foucault (whom he considers) have already shown to require a further argument. In fact, *if* (as seems reasonable) Taylor means to use the expression "paradigm" in a sense sympathetic with Kuhn's usage (though without yielding in the direction of strong incommensurabilism), then there is every reason to think that the kind of relativism Kuhn's view makes possible cannot be precluded by Taylor's own application. At best, then, the thesis – that is, traditionalism – is question-begging.

The fear that spurs such paradoxical reflections is that, within an historicized or praxicalized inquiry, the loss of universalism must doom us also to skepticism or relativism. And the fear is correctly founded –

in the sense that to give up every form of universalism *does* indeed commit us to relativism and pluralism. Historicism entails relativism, not the Hegelianized historicism of the nineteenth century (a form that harbors a secret universalism deployed by historical stages) or the oddly structuralized historicism of Louis Althusser (which reconverts Marxism to such a Hegelianized formula)[46] but the radical historicism of the twentieth century; and, yet, neither relativism nor pluralism entails historicism. Similarly, historicism entails skepticism, not the cartoon pyrrhonism of utter cognitive incapacity but the moderate rejection of all forms of foundationalism;[47] and yet skepticism itself does not entail historicism. Furthermore, once we yield up universalism, then, if relativism and pluralism need neither be incoherently formulated nor threaten whatever general cognitive regularities the practices of science can otherwise legitimately claim, there is no additional need to resist (or fear) the implications of adopting those doctrines. The saving grace of the practices of historicized inquiry is both quite straightforward and simple: in the first place, reasonably confirmed generalizations are empirically possible; second, these appear to be cognitively stabler than theories of cognition and inquiry might lead us to believe if we supposed actual science to be no more than an artifact of such theories; and, third, changes within the entire corpus of generalized scientific findings are remarkably conservative even under the pressure of changing paradigms, research programs, and higher-order theories of science itself.[48]

Contemporary theorists, fearful of the loss of universalism, have tended to favor either of two strategies. Both require what is tantamount to an appeal to transcendental considerations under the condition of an historically restricted cognitive horizon. Broadly speaking, one is Kantian – championing a rational capacity, despite the contingencies of historical and praxical experience, to formulate in a timeless way (for all rationally accessible worlds) the (universal) conditions of universal communication and of the normatively universal assessment of claims and commitments. This is the option favored by Karl-Otto Apel[49] and, equivocally, by Jürgen Habermas.[50] The other is Hegelian – construing historical traditions as themselves preserving at once the partiality and limitation of a transient horizon and, through that, a glimpse of the universal themes and norms of mankind. This is the option favored by Gadamer and Taylor (though without an absolute *telos*). At the moment the second is in the ascendant. Habermas is undoubtedly the touchstone of the intersection between the two.

Perhaps the following remark will serve to fix the curious mix of Kantian and Hegelian elements within what Habermas takes to be the grand solution afforded by speech-act theory – facilitating an escape from the mere contingencies of historical life:

> The validity of a normative background of institutions, roles, socioculturally habitual forms of life – that is, of conventions – is always presupposed. This by no means holds true only for institutionally bound speech actions such as betting, greeting, christening, appointing, and the like, each of which satisfies a *specific* institution (or a narrowly circumscribed class of norms). In promises too, in recommendations, prohibitions, prescriptions, and the like, which are not regulated from the outset by institutions, the speaker implies a validity claim that *must if the speech acts are to succeed*, be covered by existing norms, and that means by (at least) de facto recognition of the claim that these norms rightfully exist . . . . With the illocutionary force of speech actions, the normative validity claims – rightness or appropriateness [*Richtigkeit, Angemessenheit*] – is built just as universally into the structure of speech as the truth claim.[51]

The inherent weakness of Habermas's thesis may be put this way: Habermas concedes that communication may proceed successfully without adherence to such putative norms and without knowing what they are; and yet, as he also claims, its success presupposes the actual regulative force of such norms, the effectiveness of which is open to cognitive testing; but, as he claims further, those norms need not regulate actual discourse – we need only show that they are rationally obligatory even where they are ignored, defied, not fulfilled, or not perceived. There is, in short, a complete failure on Habermas's part to reconcile the modal (particularly the alethic and deontic) aspects of speech acts with their non-modal (empirically contingent but obviously effective) aspects.[52] Alternatively put, Habermas fails to distinguish carefully the constitutive and regulative features of his would-be universal norms; or, what is taken to be regulative of actual discourse and what, in an ideally rational order, would be regulative of human discourse in general. The problem is endemic to all efforts to reconcile historicism and universalism.

III

Perhaps a few essential distinctions may show the grounds for believing that theories, drawn to relativism by the currently perceived force of the historicist and praxical nature of human existence itself, are at least in no greater danger of conceptual incoherence or anarchy than the foundationalist and essentialist theories they would replace.

One must distinguish, first of all, between relativism and pluralism: these are doctrines of entirely different sorts. Relativism is a logical thesis, a thesis about eligible ways of applying truth values or truth-like values to judgments. The interesting question about relativism is *not* about its formal consistency (which is in any case trivially obvious) but about the pertinence of applying it in any particular domain of inquiry – *either* because of some epistemic limitation obtaining in principle or contingently, *or* because of the presumed structure of a certain sector of the world, or both. It is important, therefore, to realize that it is not necessary to construe relativism as a thesis only about the cognitive frailties of man; it is quite possible to hold that men do not or cannot truly know the actual structure of things (in the bipolar sense that relativism opposes) because, on our best theories, there *is* no such unique and independent structure to be known – or, more temperately, there is none answering to particular inquiries (for instance, in interpreting artworks as opposed, say, to approximating causal laws in physics or in formulating evolutionary laws as opposed to the laws of quantum mechanics). Pluralism, on the other hand, is simply a doctrine of social tolerance, of the reasoned willingness of some community to admit – within a certain "space" of inquiry or conduct – a range of alternative practices (including beliefs and behavior) that cannot be reconciled within a coherent theory of the kind that the particular partisans of each such separate practice are capable of generating for themselves. The interesting question about pluralism is *not* a logical question of any sort; in fact, it is well known that the defense of pluralism does not entail advocating relativism or historicism, *or* opposing foundationalism or essentialism. The intriguing question about pluralism concerns rather the possibility of formulating a theory at once determinate and flexible so that it can avoid both a vacuous form of tolerance and the practical difficulty of excluding practices that threaten its own stance of tolerance or its substantive doctrines that tolerance is somehow intended to protect. The dilemma is familiar both in its political form (the democratic tolerance of revolutionary agitation) and in terms of the methodology of science (the admission, despite the "progress" of science, that would-be "canons" cannot justifiably exclude practices deliberately opposed to adhering to any such canons – the informal version of Paul Feyerabend's criticism of Imre Lakatos).[53]

If, then, in a given domain of inquiry, we commit ourselves to a relativistic practice, we cannot avoid adopting as well a congruent form of pluralism. In fact, pluralism can be defended even on absolutist grounds: imagine, for instance, that God has ordained that we should publicly tolerate everything that falls within what is designated as the sphere of private liberty. A ramified relativism precludes, for a given "space" of inquiry, any pertinent form of universalism. Hence, by default at least, it cannot preclude, for that domain, pertinent pluralistic practices – although, contrary to certain popular views, relativism *need not* be committed to the thesis that all alternative claims are equipotent, or that there are equipotent reasons for affirming and denying any and all particular claims, or that there is and can be no viable basis on which to decide questions of the comparative force of competing views.[54] The objection against the "equipotency" thesis (in effect, against skepticism as well) is important all right; but it can only be arbitrarily directed against a moderate relativism, and the equipotency thesis is simply mistakenly thought to be entailed by a moderate relativism. In fact, equipotent values *are* always eligible within a canon or practice of truth-value assignments, and such assignments are incompatible with extreme skeptical claims – for instance, claims about the utter "incommensurability" of different conceptual schemes. All that relativism need concede is that judgments of comparative force are themselves subject to whatever contingencies historicizing and praxicalizing inquiry entail. In particular, relativism is not in the least incompatible with the entirely reasonable thesis that, however untenable in principle all forms of universalism are, the very practice of inquiry tends to confirm the contingently quite conservative history of the process itself – hence the utility of theorizing that particular forms of generality *are* fair candidates for positing particular universal structures; hence, too, that compelling judgements of superior explanatory power and the like *are* entirely accessible and theoretically welcome.[55]

It appears, therefore, that historicism and relativism are quite capable of accommodating coherent theories of the scope that universalist accounts have always presumed to provide – and to do so without disallowing the search for foundations, universals, or necessary connections. What they reserve, however, are their options concerning interpreting the force of any pertinent findings of such sorts – hence, concerning the openness, plurality, and profound sense of contingency with which they ought to be regarded. The historicist's and the relativist's charge is just that the contingency is not at all fatal but that it has been systematically ignored and denied.

It will of course be charged, by some who are opposed, that the notion of relativism here advanced is not, however defensible, the salient or the most interesting version of the doctrine to be considered. Perhaps they are right. There is of course the well-known version of relativism trotted out in order to be exposed as hopelessly incoherent, said nevertheless to be the "central" view – the view, summarized and gleefully dismissed by William Newton-Smith for instance, that "something, s, is true for ψ and s is false for ϕ."[56] That view *is* certainly contradictory – taking s as univocal, taking "true" and "false" *sans phrase* in a bipolar sense, and taking pertinent truth-value assessments as obtaining within the same "world." Also, *any* liberalization along the lines of multiplying "worlds" so that the otherwise offending incompatibles obtain disjunctively (Goodman's apparent escape), or of disallowing a common domain of contest within the one world (Harman's escape),[57] or of displacing "true" and "false" with "relationalized" terms such as "true-in-L" and "false-in-L" (where L designates a particular language, idiom, context, or similar construction), so that the scope of "true-in- . . . " and "false-in- . . . " is disjunctively restricted (where needed) to particular such settings, is utterly uninteresting if viable, bloodless as far as familiar disputes in science, morality, and elsewhere are concerned, and even at times incoherent in ways not unlike that of the "central" doctrine. At the moment, the last of these moves seems to be the favorite form of escape among recent self-styled relativists and their most persistent debunkers – witness the principal complaints of the papers in Hollis and Luke's recent collection, the devices of Kuhn and Feyerabend,[58] and the revival of interest in the view of Protagoras.[59]

There is, however, one absolutely decisive distinction that segregates all such maneuvers (call them relativist, if you wish) from the view (and versions of the view) here defended. We may dub the view here favored "internal" relativism, and all the others, forms of "external" relativism. The external views are committed to the thesis that there is no known (perhaps in principle no possible) procedure or method or practice or policy by means of which justifiably to eliminate, reduce, or disallow contending or divergent or "incommensurable" paradigms, *Gestalten*, "worlds," ontologies, languages, frames of reference, conventions, or the like; and that, since that is so, bipolar truth values are systematically open to gerrymandering in such a way that, within each ("externally") relativized domain, entire sets of "truths" are, where not wanted, not permitted to confront in an evidentially pertinent way otherwise seemingly incompatible sets of "truths" drawn from another cognate or parallel domain. Now, then, external relativism is a form of skepticism or a doctrine of determinate methodological incapacity regarding the resolution of the critical issue (witness Kuhn's uneasiness); whereas internal relativism holds that *we do indeed have a reasonable methodological basis (however logically weak, as far as truth values are concerned) for epistemically supporting or confirming claims that, on a bipolar model, would be or yield incompatibles.* The externalist may account for "conflicting" such systems merely in historical terms, without attention at all to common methodological strategies. One example will suffice. Goodman may be an external relativist when he says, for instance, "I am afraid that my remark . . . about conflicting truths and multiple actual worlds may be passed over as purely rhetorical. They [sic] are not. . . ."[60] He is an external relativist if he means to treat that charge along the same lines that he develops in a related context – where he says,

> I am not so much stating a belief or advancing a thesis or a doctrine as proposing a categorization or scheme or organization, calling attention to a way of setting our nets to capture what may be significant likenesses and differences. Argument for the categorization, the scheme, suggested could not be for its truth, since it has no truth-value, but for its efficacy in worldmaking and understanding. . . . Put crassly, what is called for in such cases is less like arguing than selling.[61]

On the other hand, Quine is an internal relativist when (quite apart from our defending what he says) he holds, advancing his well-known notion of the indeterminacy of translation,

> the infinite totality of sentences of any given speaker's language can be so permuted, or mapped onto itself, that (a) the totality of the speaker's dispositions to verbal behavior remains invariant, and yet (b) the mapping is no mere correlation of sentences with equivalent sentences, in any plausible sense of equivalence however loose. Sentences without number can diverge drastically from their respective correlates, yet the divergences can systematically so offset one another that the overall pattern of associations of sentences with one another and with nonverbal stimulation is preserved.[62]

It is true that Quine also holds, for example, that, regarding analytical hypotheses (by which a given language may be parsed in divergent ways, "The point is not that we cannot be sure whether the analytical hypothesis is right, but that there is not even . . . an objective matter to be right or wrong about."[63] But, here and elsewhere, what he is saying in effect is that we do have a method of pertinently confirming the fit of hypotheses that, on a bipolar model, would yield incompatibles. Perhaps Goodman intends to support a similar view, but his account seems much more obscure.[64] (Certainly, the idea of comparing the "entrenchment" of categories across "world-versions" is, to say the least, difficult to explicate both sympathetically and coherently.)

Now then, if, as has been maintained, relativism is a methodologically positive theory, so-called external relativism is no relativism at all: it is rather a theory (at best) about why certain issues, ordinarily taken *to be* methodologically accessible (*either* nonrelativistically *or* relativistically) are actually *not* open to rational or reasonable resolution at all. Nothing offered here is meant to decide that claim. If it were true, it would of course yield results that might look like the results of a relativistic argument. But, apart from the obvious difference in conception, there remains a most important difference in handling particular claims: the external relativist is bound to hold that, on a pertinently contested point, there simply would be no truth values or truth-like values *to be assigned at all*; whereas the internal relativist is quite capable of maintaining (coherently) that the contending views are *equally* defensible or (even) more or less apt or plausible or the like – though without one's thereby precluding the other. (Of course, it is also possible for the relativist to disconfirm one or both views.) It is worth remarking that internal and external relativism may be compatible if assigned to different ranges of questions; and that, on an *internal* relativistic reading of the question of their tenability, they may even be construed as not incompatible alternative answers to the same question; but it would remain true nevertheless that they could not be construed as the same answer to one and the same question. They are motivated in conceptually diverent ways; for the disproof of external relativism is entirely neutral as between internal relativism and a nonrelativistic view of assigning truth values, and a disproof of internal relativism hardly entails external relativism.

Relativism, then, is a methodologically positive or active theory about the assignment of truth values or truth-like values in some domain of inquiry, in virtue of which some set of claims that, on a bipolar model of truth and falsity, would generate incompatibles does not do so on the model favored. There is no reason to think that, as such, realism precludes relativism; and there is no reason to conflate or identify relativism with pluralism, skepticism, subjectivism, or irrationalism – in particular, irrationalism with respect to assessing incommensurable programs, systems of inquiry or values, paradigms, forms of life, or the like. The only genuinely interesting question about relativism is where and for what reason it should be invoked. But that, of course, is to imply (quite correctly) that it is perfectly capable of being formulated as a coherent thesis.

We are now in a position to draw together a little more closely our investigation of the prospects of relativism and those of an historicized sense of realism. The upshot, which we may here anticipate, is that internal and external relativism are radically distinct and that a historicized or praxicalized account of realism cannot, though it may reasonably defeat external relativism or the incommensurability thesis (which is its most salient version at the present time), preclude the viability of internal relativism. The latter must in fact make conceptual room for it. If we can establish this finding, we shall have justified the economy of pursuing several seemingly somewhat disparate lines of inquiry; for these separate tracks will then be seen to lead independently to the same line of argument.

Notes

1 Thomas S. Kuhn, *The Structure of Scientific Revolutions* (Chicago: University of Chicago Press, 1962), p. 17.

2 Thomas S. Kuhn, *The Essential Tension* (Chicago: University of Chicago Press, 1977), p. 294.

3 Ibid., pp. xxii–xxiii (italics added).

4 Kuhn, *The Structure of Scientific Revolutions*, 2nd, enlarged edn (1970), p. 150 (italics added). For a sense of the standard criticisms of Kuhn's view, see Margaret Masterman, "The Nature of a Paradigm," in Imre Lakatos and Alan Musgrave (eds) *Criticism and the Growth of Knowledge* (Cambridge: Cambridge University Press, 1970); and Carl R. Kordig, *The Justification of Scientific Change* (Dordrecht: D. Reidel, 1971).

5 Cf. Nelson Goodman, *Ways of Worldmaking* (Indianapolis: Hackett, 1978); David Lewis, *Counterfactuals* (Cambridge, Mass.: Harvard University Press, 1973).

6 Cf. Donald Davidson, "On the Very Idea of a Conceptual Scheme," *Proceedings and Addresses of the American Philosophical Association*, XLVI (1973–4).

7 See W. V. Quine, "Two Dogmas of Empiricism", *From a Logical Point of View* (Cambridge, Mass.: Harvard University Press, 1953), and *Word and Object* (Cambridge, Mass.: MIT Press, 1960), ch. 6.

8 Quine, *Word and Object*, pp. 199–200. For a sense of the puzzles of mathematical necessity, in the Quinean context, cf. Charles Parsons, "Quine on the Philosophy of Mathematics," *Mathematics in Philosophy* (Ithaca, NY: Cornell University Press, 1983); Paul Benacerraf, "Mathematical Truth," in Paul Benacerraf and Hilary Putnam (eds), *Philosophy of Mathematics*, 2nd edn (Cambridge: Cambridge University Press, 1983); and Hartry H. Field, *Science without Numbers* (Princeton, NJ: Princeton University Press, 1980), ch. 1.

9 Rejected for instance by Richard Rorty in *Philosophy and the Mirror of Nature* (Princeton, NJ: Princeton University Press, 1979); cf. his *Consequences of Pragmatism* (Minneapolis: University of Minnesota Press, 1982).

10   See for instance Jacques Derrida, *Of Grammatology*, tr. Gayatri Chakravorty Spivak (Baltimore: John Hopkins University Press, 1976).

11   Cf. Michel Foucault, *The Order of Things*, tr. from the French (New York: Random House, 1970).

12   The point is well-perceived by Edmund Husserl – ironically, in pursuing his own completely ahistorical program of apodictic phenomenology. See for insance Edmund Husserl, *Phenomenology and the Crisis of Philosophy*, tr. Quentin Lauer (New York: Harper and Row, 1965). The book includes two complementary essays: "Philosophy as Rigorous Science" and "Philosophy and the Crisis of European Man" – that is, an early and a late specimen of Husserl's attack on naturalism and historicism.

13   Cf. Michael Dummett, "Truth," *Truth and Other Enigmas* (Cambridge, Mass.: Harvard University Press, 1978), p. 17.

14   Cf. ibid., Preface; and Hilary Putnam, *Meaning and the Moral Sciences* (London: Routledge and Kegan Paul, 1978).

15   Dummett, "Realism," *Truth and Other Enigmas*, p. 146.

16   Ibid.

17   Cf. J. Clerk Maxwell, "Ether," *Encyclopaedia Britannica*, 8th edn, vol. 8 (1893), p. 572. The story is given in short form in an extremely clear way in Ian Hacking, *Representing and Intervening* (Cambridge: Cambridge University Press, 1983), pp. 254–61.

18   Hans Reichenbach: *The Theory of Probability*, tr. Ernest H. Hutten and Maria Reichenbach from 2nd German edn (Berkeley, Calif.: University of California Press, 1949); *The Rise of Scientific Philosophy* (Berkeley, Calif.: University of California Press, 1951); *Laws, Modalities, and Counterfactuals* (Berkeley, Calif.: University of California Press, 1976), particularly Appendix, p. 127.

19   See Wesley C. Salmon, *Statistical Explanation and Statistical Revelance*, with Richard C. Jeffrey and James G. Greeno (Pittsburgh: University of Pittsburgh Press, 1971).

20   See for instance Ernest Mayr, *The Growth of Biological Thought* (Cambridge, Mass.: Harvard University Press, 1982).

21   Martin Heidegger, "The Question Concerning Technology," *The Question Concerning Technology and Other Essays*, tr. William Lovitt (New York: Harper and Row, 1977).

22   John Dewey: "The Need for a Recovery of Philosphy," in Dewey et al., *Creative Intelligence: Essays in the Pragmatic Attitude* (New York: Henry Holt, 1917); "Experience, Knowledge and Value: A Rejoinder," in Paul Arthur Schilpp (eds), *The Philosophy of John Dewey*, 2nd edn (New York: Tudor, 1951).

23   Jean-Paul Sartre, *Critique of Dialectical Reason*, tr. Alan Sheridan-Smith, ed. Jonathan Rée (London: New Left Books, 1976); Theodor W. Adorno, *Negative Dialectics*; tr. E. B. Ashton (New York: Seabury Press, 1973); Jürgen Habermas, *Theory and Practice*, tr. John Viertel (Boston, Mass.: Beacon Press, 1973).

24 See for instance, *Russian Formalist Criticism: Four essays*, tr. Lee T. Lemon and Marion J. Reis (Lincoln, Nabr.: University of Nebraska Press, 1965); and Hans Robert Jauss, *Toward an Aesthetic of Reception*, tr. Timothy Bahti (Minneapolis: University of Minnesota Press, 1982).

25 Particularly in *Theory and Practice*, and *Legitimation Crisis*, tr. Thomas McCarthy (Boston, Mass.: Beacon Press, 1975).

26 See Charles Taylor, "Philosophy and its History," in Richard Rorty et al. (eds), *Philosophy in History* (Cambridge: Cambridge University Press, 1984), p. 22. *Philosophy in History* is in fact the pilot volume in the "Ideas in Context" series planned recently for Cambridge University Press.

27 Somewhat different views of this praxical or historicized orientation of philosophy appears in Alasdair MacIntyre, "The Relationship of Philosophy to its Past," and Richard Rorty, "The Historiography of Philosophy: Four Genres," both of which are included in *Philosophy in History*.

28 I have relied here on discussions with Paul Guyer and a paper of his that I have seen in typescript, "Kant's Intentions in the Refutation of Idealism," *Philosophical Review*, XCII (1983). Further suggestions appear in some of his earlier papers: "Kant on Apperception and *A Priori* Synthesis," *American Philosophical Quarterly*, XVII (1980); and "Kant's Tactic in the Transcendental Deduction," *Philosophical Topics*, XII (1981).

29 Jurgen Habermas: *Communications and the Evolution of Society*, tr. Thomas McCarthy (Boston, Mass.: Beacon Press, 1979); *Theory and Practice*.

30 See Hans-Georg Gadamer, *Reason in the Age of Science*, tr. Frederick G. Lawrence (Cambridge, Mass.: MIT Press, 1981); cf. Josef Bleicher, *Contemporary Hermeneutics* (London: Routledge and Kegan Paul, 1980), chs 5–6.

31 Habermas, *Theory and Practice*, p. 21.

32 See Jürgen Habermas: "What is Universal Pragmatics?" *Communication and the Evolution of Society*; "Toward a Theory of Communicative Competence," in H. P. Dreitzel (ed.), *Recent Sociology*, no. 2 (New York: Macmillan, 1970); "A Postscript to *Knowledge and Human Interests*," *Philosophy of the Social Sciences*, III (1973). Raymond Geuss offers the intriguing observation, contrasting Habermas and Adorno, that "In some of this earliest essays Habermas follows Adorno and holds a contexualist view of reflection; then, sometime in the mid 1960s, he seems to have been frightened by the specter of relativism, and retreated into a kind of transcendentalism" – *The Idea of a Critical Theory: Habermas and the Frankfurt School* (Cambridge: Cambridge University Press, 1981), p. 64. Cf. also John B. Thompson, "Universal Pragmatics," in John B. Thompson and David Held (eds), *Habermas: Critical Debates* (Cambridge, Mass.: MIT Press, 1982); and Jürgen Habermas, "A Reply to my Critics," ibid. The reference to the "fiction" appears in Thompson's translation (ibid., pp. 124, 125) of Habermas's "Vorbereitende Bermerkungen zu einer Theorie der kommunikativen Kompetenz," from Jürgen Habermas and Niklas Luhmann, *Theorie der Gesellschaft oder Socialtechnologie – Was liestet*

Systemforschung? (Frankfurt: Suhrkamp, 1971).

33   See for instance Paul Ricoeur, *Husserl: An Analysis of his Phenomenology*, tr. Edward G. Ballard and Lester E. Embree (Evanston, Ill.: Northwestern University Press, 1967).

34   The Kantian position is strongly criticized, on the grounds of the indemonstrability of its exclusive claims, in Stephen Körner, "On Bennett's 'Analytic Transcendental Arguments,'" in Peter Bieri et al. (eds), *Transcendental Arguments and Science* (Dordrecht: D. Reidel, 1979).

35   See Jacques Derrida, *Speech and Phenomena*, tr. David B. Allison (Evanston, Ill.: Northwestern University Press, 1973).

36   Richard Rorty, "Transcendental Arguments, Self-Reference, and Pragmatism," in Bieri et al., *Transcendental Arguments and Science*.

37   This is the crucial weakness of Rorty's *Philosophy and the Mirror of Nature*.

38   Karl R. Popper, *Realism and the Aim of Science* (vol. 1: *From the Postscript to the Logic of Scientific Discovery*), ed. W. W. Bartley III (Totowa, NJ: Rowman and Littlefield, 1983), pp. 316–19.

39   Ibid., p. 27. Cf. W. W. Bartley III, "Rationality versus the Theory of Rationality," in Mario Bunge (ed.), *The Critical Approach to Science and Philosophy* (New York: Free Press, 1964).

40   Popper, *Realism and the Aim of Science*, p. 57. Cf. Popper's *The Logic of Scientific Discovery* (New York: Basic Books, 1959), section 79; and his "Two Faces of Common Sense: An Argument for Commonsense Realism and Against the Commonsense Theory of Knowledge," *Objective Knowledge* (Oxford: Clarendon Press, 1972).

41   Taylor, "Philosophy and its History," in Rorty et al., *Philosophy and History*, pp. 25, 26.

42   Ibid., pp. 19–20, 22.

43   Ibid., pp. 24, 27.

44   Ibid., pp. 28, 29.

45   Ibid., pp. 29–30.

46   Louis Althusser and Etienne Balibar, *Reading Capital*, tr. Ben Brewster (London: New Left Books, 1970), cf. also Jauss, *Toward an Aesthetic of Reception*, chs. 1–2. The trouble with Althusser, very simply, is that, although he means to escape historicism (and the historicized ideologies of engaged agents), his version of a structuralist-like strategy for making Marxism a distinctive science requires that he construe the dynamics of particular societies each entirely within the space of a totalized "problematic" postulated by a putatively autonomous theory. Nevertheless, he seems neither to vindicate its autonomy nor to escape the historicized color of his own convictions regarding each such society. The result is that, in effect (and inadvertently), Althusser recovers, by way of a structuralist-like strategy, what a Hegelian would have posited in historicist and teleological terms. See Mark Poster, *Existential Marxism in Postwar France* (Princeton, NJ: Princeton Universtiy Press, 1975).

47   A particularly straightforward version of a cognate view, without attention

to the historicist issue, appears in Keith Lehrer, "Skepticism and Conceptual Change," in Roderick M. Chisholm and Robert L. Swartz (eds), *Empirical Knowledge* (Englewood Cliffs, NJ: Prentice-Hall, 1973). Cf. Peter D. Klein, *Certainty: A Refutation of Scepticism* (Minneapolis: University of Minnesota Press, 1981).

48 Cf. Dudley Shapere, "The Structure of Scientific Revolutions," *Reason and the Search for Knowledge* (Dordrecht: D. Reidel, 1984).

49 See Karl-Otto Apel, *Towards a Transformation of Philosophy*, tr. Glyn Adey and David Frisby (London: Routledge and Kegan Paul, 1980), ch. 7; cf. also his *Understanding and Explanation*, tr. Georgia Warnke (Cambridge, Mass.: MIT Press, 1984), pt III, ch. 2.

50 See Jürgen Habemas, "What is Universal Pragmatics?" *Communication and the Evolution of Society*.

51. Ibid., p. 54 (I have italicized "must if the speech acts are to succeed").

52 The shift to and from modal formulations and among alternative modals is plain in the entire essay. The Hegelian original from which the developments here traced are at least remotely derived may be drawn fairly clearly from, for instance, the Preface to G. W. F. Hegel, *Phenomenology of Spirit*, tr. A. V. Miller from the 5th German edn (Oxford: Oxford University Press, 1977).

53 See for example Paul Feyerabend, *Against Method* (London: New Left Books, 1975); Imre Lakatos, *Philosophical Papers*, vol 1, ed John Worrall and Gregory Currie (Cambridge: Cambridge University Press, 1978); and Larry Laudan, *Progress and its Problems: Towards a Theory of Scientific Growth* (Berkeley, Calif.: University of California Press, 1977).

54 This seems to be the view taken by Charles Taylor, for instance, in "Rationality," in Martin Hollis and Steven Lukes (eds), *Rationality and Relativism* (Cambridge, Mass.: MIT Press, 1982), particularly at pp. 99–100.

55 Ernest Gellner is correct, in "Relativism and Universals" (repr. in *Rationality and Relativism*) in holding that "the issues of relativism, and that of the existence of human universals, are *not* one and the same issue" (p. 186); although Gellner restricts the question of "human universals" to "whether or not man is one and unique" (ibid.) – which cannot be the whole of the matter and which, in effect, misleads us about the incompatibility of relativism and universalism in the larger sense. In fact, Gellner is an opponent of the thesis here defended; for his main point is that "the Singleness of Man is *not* required for the Uniqueness of the World or of Truth" (p.192), and that the latter claim is the correct or strongest view possible. I should say, *contra* Gellner, that "Relativism is [precisely *not*] about the existence of One World" (p. 200), though I don't deny that some relativists – notably, Goodman – would construe it thus.

56 W. Newton-Smith, "Relativism and the Possibility of Interpretation," ibid., p. 107.

57 Gilbert Harman, *The Nature of Moraliy* (New York: Oxford University Press, 1977).

58 Feyerabend, *Against Method*.
59 See Plato, *Theaetetus*; Jack W. Meiland, "Is Protagorean Relativism Self-defeating?" *Grazer Philosophische Studien*, IX (1979); Chris Swoyer, "True for," in Jack W. Meiland and Michael Krausz (eds), *Relativism: Cognitive and Moral* (Notre Dame, Ind.: University of Notre Dame Press, 1982).
60 Goodman, *Ways of Worldmaking*, p. 110.
61 Ibid, p. 129 (italics added).
62 Quine, *Word and Object*, p. 27.
63 Ibid., p. 73.
64 See also Hilary Putnam, *Reason, Truth and History* (Cambridge: Cambridge University Press, 1981), ch. 2.

3

Objectivism and Relativism

I

Whoever would defend relativism must, on pain of self-confessed stupidity, construe it in a way that is not self-contradictory or self-refuting; and yet it is notorious that its opponents regularly and comfortably identify it in a blatantly stupid form.[1] We cannot help suspecting the objector's practice, because quite obviously the intended lesson needs to be repeated much too frequently to be taken entirely at face value, and because there is no straightforward reason for supposing that the defenders of relativism are that stupid. On the other hand, there is the perfectly reasonable concern – against would-be relativists – that they should not be permitted to tailor the notion of relativism at will solely to escape the damning charge: they must afford an account that suitably bears on a fair portion of those issues that seem to have led to the original complaint. A fair way of passing between these two dangers suggests itself: let us stipulate independent conditions or constraints that a responsive and interesting form of relativism is likely to satisfy, of both the consistency and pertinence sort, without rushing to declare *what* the relativist thesis is or must be. That ought to satisfy all within the field of combat – except, of course, those whose own pleasant game is thereby exposed. The point of the exercise would be to restore a clear sense of the viability of relativism – against the backdrop of its obviously accelerating appeal in the contemporary world but in sympathy with the conviction that, if it is viable, it will surely affect in a profound way our understanding of human rationality and the puzzle of legitimating the alternative forms of inquiry that the human race seems forever bound to encourage. It should be possible in this way to draw out objections or worries about relativism that are not simply occupied with the allegedly inevitable self-refutation.

What shall we need? Well, we shall want to set formal conditions on the truth values (or truth-like values) the relativist's judgments, propositions, claims, or suitable analogues can take, in virtue of which conditions sufficiently close to or like the usually imputed self-refutation obtain but without the obvious penalty; and we shall want to show in some way or other what grounds may be offered for holding that, in *some* sector of inquiry at least (precisely because of the nature of the domain) but not necessarily in all sectors of inquiry, it is at least as reasonable to restrict such judgments in the accommodating way as to refuse to do so; and that doing so really does address a part of deeper concerns about the alleged scope of the relativist thesis. It may prove to be that certain global versions of relativism (for instance, forms of Protagorean relativism[2]) may not be coherent in the sense required. If so, then surely reasonable relativists would abdicate such versions and simply retreat to a more restricted, modular, or modest version, and try to make the case out that even that sort of relativism is stronger than its opponents would be willing to grant. There might have to be a compromise on both sides, and both sides might be sobered by the discovery.

The most minimal formal condition required is straightforward: simply take sets of the offending judgments – supposed to be contradictory or self-refuting – and restrict the truth values or truth-like values they can be assigned, so that, in accord with the new values but not with the old, and without otherwise altering the content of what is claimed, the judgments in question are no longer contradictory or self-refuting. They might be said to be "incongruent," precisely because, on a bipolar model of truth and falsity, they would be incompatible, but now are not. That this is not yet sufficient for any interesting form of relativism is clear enough if we remind ourselves that merely probabilized judgments go some distance to meeting the condition – for example, that it is probable that *Nixon knew about Watergate in advance* and that it is probable that *Nixon did not know about Watergate in advance*. Usually, probabilized judgments are supposed to be assignable the bipolar truth values, "true" and "false," and so would normally be taken to generate (contrary to what we want) contradictions when assigned such values. But the direction in which the formal constraints would need to be spelled out is reasonably clear and reasonably manageable. All we need do is *restrict* the admissible values – values such as "plausible" and "implausible", disallowing "truth" and "falsity" – so that the offending contradictions and self-refutations are precluded (without, of course, needing to disallow contradiction or self-refutation in other ways); then, we should be home free. Of course, the defense may be thought uninteresting. But it certainly clears part of the air. For instance, it disables at a stroke such claims as the following: "implicitly or explicitly, the relativist claims that his or her position is true, yet the relativist also insists that since truth is relative, what is taken as true may also be false. Consequently, relativism itself may be true *and* false. One cannot consistently state the case for relativism without undermining it."[3] It is true that the counter-move is a purely formal one, so it can hardly be thought sufficiently persuasive against more substantive suspicions regarding relativism. By parity of reasoning, however, so too are formal complaints of the sort just cited (the charge of Protagoreanism). One suspects, therefore, that objections of an altogether different sort lurk in the neighborhood, and that, therefore, constraints of another sort will be needed.

Seen this way, relativism is best taken as something more than – but as including at least – a thesis (and the accompanying rationale for it) regarding the assignment of deliberately weakened truth values (or truth-like values) to certain sets of judgments. Narrowly construed, its rationale supplies a theory about the properties or nature of some part of the world, or of some part of the conditions of inquiry with respect to that part of the world, or both, supporting such assignments. Could we, then, in the interest of an honest canvass, add constraints that, joined with suitably amplified versions of the merely formal condition mentioned, would place at greater risk (hence, would mark the greater promise of) the somewhat spare relativism already sketched?

What might be added? The following conditions seem particularly promising.

1   Relativism should not be construed as, or as reducible to, any form of skepticism, cynicism, nihilism, irrationalism, anarchism or the like, although it may be that a well-defended relativism would lend comfort to doctrines of these sorts.
2   Relativism should be construed as precluding, within its scope, any form of foundationalism, essentialism, logocentrism or similar doctrines – without being thought restricted merely to their denial.
3   Relativism should be construed as compatible with, but as not entailing, various forms of historicism, although strong forms of historicism should be construed as entailing relativism.
4   Relativism should be construed as more comprehensive if its rationale is made to depend on properties imputed to a domain of inquiry than if it merely depends on cognitive limitations imposed on whoever makes inquiry in that domain – although the latter strategy need not be refused.
5   Relativism should not be construed in terms of judgments merely relativized (or relationalized) to alternative conceptual schemes, or in terms of the putative incommensurability of such schemes, or in terms of being cognitively confined within the boundaries of

particular such schemes to the exclusion of others; and a theory should not be construed as relativistic merely because it provides for making and appraising judgments that entail an appeal to the categories of particular conceptual schemes, or to schemes subject to the conditions just disfavored.

6   Relativism should not be construed as precluding comparative judgments of the usual sort and range (for instance, of better or worse, or of more or less adequate) conceded within theories that do subscribe to bipolar truth values.

7   Relativism should not, when restricted to particular domains of inquiry, be construed as incompatible in principle with cognitive claims, outside its own scope, that take bipolar truth values.

8   Relativism should not be construed as, or as reducible to, pluralism; and it should be construed as entailing but as not entailed by pluralism.

9   Relativism should be construed as neutral regarding, and as not committed to either affirming or denying (or requiring or precluding), the cognitive adequacy of any single or unified conceptual scheme.

10   Relativism should not be construed as affirming or entailing (or denying, for that matter) the facts of cultural diversity or cultural relativity, whatever they may be, synchronically across cultures or diachronically within particular cultures.

11   Relativism should not be required to resolve claims or disputes by way of supplying evidence or cognitive resources greater or more fruitful than what is normally admitted within any given science or inquiry. In particular, it should not be required to be stated in a global or inclusive rather than a restricted form, or a form more inclusive in scope than any nonrelativistic theory it contends against; and it should be construed as a theory fitted in a conceptually competitive way to the practices of particular forms of inquiry.

These eleven conditions make a very pretty set. Doubtless there are others that would be worth considering in exploring a reasonably ramified version of relativism. But it is hard to suppose that these fail to touch on the points at issue in very nearly all – one is tempted to say, all – of the best-known quarrels about relativism in the recent literature. If so, then any theory that could satisfactorily meet these conditions and the developed formal condition intended would be a fully-fledged form of relativism, quite apart from whether it was specifically linked (as well it might be) to larger issues regarding the practices of science and rational inquiry.

II

Here we may take advantage of a recent account, one of the latest to air the issues raised by our eleven conditions, that offers a decidedly sanguine view about avoiding what it calls the twin disorders of objectivism and relativism. It promises a convenient economy, because it denies to relativism the option of satisfying all or nearly all the conditions mentioned and because it surveys the views of most of the principal opponents of the "disorders" in question. There are actually very few sustained statements of this sort to be had. If we could offset the countermoves it collects from a sprawling literature, then, we might conveniently focus in a brief span the actual prospects of a genuinely disciplined relativism. In fact, if the attack fairly represents a dominant (or the dominant) line of objection to relativism, the best line of defense may well lie (i) in undermining the alleged conceptual dependence of relativism on objectivism; and (ii) in providing a sense in which relativism effectively addresses an ineliminable problem raised *both* by the dependence alleged and by the opposed strategy (i). We may anticipate that the upshot of a successful effort of such a sort would be to bring a merely formally coherent relativism (together with its supporting rationale) into accord with our eleven substantive conditions.

Consider this specimen view. In his recent book *Beyond Objectivism and Relativism*, Richard Bernstein offers the following terminological distinctions:

> By "objectivism," I mean the basic conviction that there is or must be some permanent, ahistorical matrix or framework to which we can ultimately appeal in determining the nature of rationality, knowledge, truth, reality, goodness, or rightness. ... The objectivist maintains that unless we can ground philosophy, knowledge, or language in a suitably rigorous manner we cannot avoid radical skepticism.[4]

> The relativist not only denies the positive claims of the objectivist but goes further. In its strongest form, relativism is the basic conviction that when we turn to the examination of those concepts that philosophers have taken to be the most fundamental – whether it is the concept of rationality, truth, reality, right, the good, or

norms – we are forced to recognize that in the final analysis all such concepts must be understood as relative to a specific conceptual scheme, theoretical framework, paradigm, form of life, society, or culture. ... For the relativist, there is no substantive overarching framework or single metalanguage by which we can rationally adjudicate or univocally evaluate competing claims of alternative paradigms.[5]

Some clarifying observations are in order. First of all, Bernstein means to include as objectivists, for understandable reasons, not only the rationalists and empiricists, and all foundationalists and essentialists, but also Kant and Husserl, although Husserl himself had used the term "objectivist" as inapplicable to the special apodictic certainty appropriate to his own favored form of "transcendental subjectivity."[6] In any case, "objectivism" is a convenient catch-all. Secondly, it is true that relativism is incompatible with an inclusive objectivism (either itself inclusive or restricted) or a restricted objectivism (where itself coordinately restricted). But it hardly follows that "relativism ... is not only the dialectical antithesis of objectivism, it is itself parasitic upon objectivism."[7] That this is neither true nor required nor even particularly central to relativism is worth emphasizing, since relativism is (trivially) incompatible with accounts of knowledge and science opposed to objectivism-*and*-relativism that insist nevertheless that cognitive claims are capable of a measure of "objectivity." (Here, at some risk, we may include as specimen views of the *non*relativist, *non*objectivist sort those of the following at least: Popper, Kuhn, Lakatos, Hesse; Gadamer, Habermas, Ricoeur; Davidson, Putnam; Charles Taylor, MacIntyre, Winch.) Thus, if, as now seems reasonable, objectivist or so-called foundationalist views can be expected to be on the defensive and decline for some time to come, it hardly follows (so far at least) that the status of relativism would be or need be adversely affected by that fact alone, or that the attempt to support relativism would correspondingly decline or have to decline.

The interesting charge advanced (by the would-be opponents of relativism), therefore, is that, although it opposes objectivism, untenable in any case, relativism is committed to the thesis that *only* objectivism could preclude skepticism. Hence, relativism is committed to skepticism, in particular to a version of the (radical) incommensurability thesis (to the effect that claims drawn from different "paradigms" cannot be treated as cognitively competing claims). The counterstrategy is at once clear: construe relativism as (indeed) opposed to objectivism, disallow the skeptical reading (which the sanguine opponent of both objectivism and relativism – so styled – already insists is a viable option), and reinterpret relativism as a thesis about science and rational inquiry viewd in terms of just those conditions. The importance of the relativistic alternative (thus reinterpreted) lies in this: theories of science and rational inquiry may (viably) oppose both objectivism (or foundationalism) and skepticism (or incommensurability or the like); and yet *they may still be usefully sorted as favoring and opposing a refurbished relativism*. Since a great many of the leading discussants of the issue regard themselves as opposed to relativism (if the bare list provided be reasonably accurate), the recovery of relativism promises to be of some significance. The larger strategy, then, is this: (i) show how relativism need not be parasitic on objectivism; and (ii) show how a relativism in accord with (i) can meet the adequacy conditions already enumerated. The fact is that Bernstein never considers the question of defending relativistic theories opposed to objectivism – and very few commentators do. (We shall, in a moment, apply these distinctions to a particular quarrel. Otherwise, the full force and charm of the issue might well be jeopardized. But we need to be careful as well about shaping the conceptual contest that Bernstein's account conveniently invites.)

Admittedly, to say this is not yet to say *what* might be meant by nonobjectivist "objectivity" with respect to science; but the implied burden surely falls on relativists and nonrelativists alike. Here Bernstein is particularly helpful, because his own attempt at specifying the new "objectivity" both brings into focus essential aspects of the history of the issue and unintentionally highlights the decisive lacunae that his effort shares with that of most of those who claim to oppose relativism. A closer look at Bernstein's argument is, therefore, invited.

Bernstein begins in this way. First, he identifies "the central cultural opposition of our time":[8] "many contemporary debates are still structured within traditional extremes. There is still an underlying belief that in the final analysis the only viable alternatives open to us are *either* some form of objectivism, foundationalism, ultimate grounding of knowledge, science, philosophy, and language *or* that we are ineluctably led to relativism, skepticism, historicism, and nihilism."[9] He adds that, "If we see through objectivism, if we expose what is wrong with this way of thinking, then we are at the same time questioning the very intelligibility of relativism."[10] So he rejects the search for "an Archimedean point" (Descartes's obsession); rejects "the Cartesian Anxiety" itself (that is, objectivism); views the "exclusive disjunction of objectivism or relativism" as "misleading and distortive," implausible and unnecessary and tied to the Cartesian Anxiety; and urges us to "exorcise" the Anxiety so that we can pass "beyond" objectivism and relativism to a viable, already somewhat articulated "postempiricist," more "historically oriented understanding of scientific inquiry as a rational activity,"[11]

What is fresh about Bernstein's approach is this: contrary, for instance, to Richard Rorty's dismissal of epistemology (though in complete agreement with Rorty's rejection of objectivism and foundationalism), Bernstein invites us to consider how to characterize objectivity in science and rational inquiry, subject to the rejection of *both* poles of the "central opposition" and subject to the admission (in the Kuhnian spirit) of the indissolubility of science and the history of science. He goes on to salvage in a sympathetic way the essential focus and positive contribution of Kuhn's work on the theory of rational inquiry: "The shift [he says] from a model of rationality that searches for determinate values which can serve as necessary and sufficient conditions, to a model of practical rationality that emphasizes the role of *exemplars* and judgmental interpretation, is not only characteristic of theory-choice but is a leitmotif that pervades all of Kuhn's thinking about science."[12] He adds that, on Kuhn's view (and on his own of course), a paradigm is to be construed as "a concrete exemplar that is open to differing interpretations" but in such a way as *not* to invite the mistaken inference that the contrast between "rules" and "paradigms" is "a contrast between the cognitive and the noncognitive."[13]

Once these remarks are in place, the counterstrategy for defending relativism becomes remarkably simple: merely adopt the reconstructive views advocated and differentiate relativism along the formal lines already mentioned. In short, adopt at least the following.

(a) Reject objectivism.

(b) Deny the exclusive option of objectivism and either skepticism, nihilism, irrationalism, anarchism or the like.

(c) Separate relativism (along the lines already sketched) from all forms of skepticism, nihilism, irrationalism, anarchism and the rest identified in the exclusive option mentioned in (b).

(d) Construe subscribing to the Kuhnian paradigm or exemplar as an instance of subscribing to (a) and (b) – in particular, as subscribing to the view that the norms of rational inquiry are not separable from the actual history of inquiry.

Once matters are put this way, it is clear that the "exclusive option" is not in itself compelling; that the disjoined options may be separately opposed; and that the moderate relativism sketched earlier on is quite different from the so-called relativism of the "exclusive option," unaffected by the defeat or rejection of the latter and certainly compatible with its rejection. The difference intended is simply that between what we have already contrasted as internal and external relativism.

Possibly, Bernstein owes *us* an explanation of why he so arbitrarily supposes that either relativism cannot fail to take the absurdly stupid form it has so often been assigned (Protagoreanism), or why it should be identified with such extreme views as skepticism and nihilism (which, in the sense intended, are utterly opposed to admitting the usual cognitive claims that relativism actually attempts to account for), or why or in what sense it should be linked necessarily, or merely adversely, with historicism and the concession of incommensurable, irreducibly plural conceptual schemes (taken as alternative forms of skepticism and nihilism).[14] On the documentation Bernstein himself offers, the prejudice seems to be very widespread.

III

The prime strategy for redeeming relativism, then, rests with prising it apart from its allegedly symbiotic connection with objectivism. *No one has ever shown that the attempted defense of relativism must fail because objectivism fails (or its more familiar specialized versions fail).* That, after all, would be an extraordinary claim: first, because even the thesis about the stupid form of relativism need take no notice of objectivism; second, because relativism itself has, whenever it has addressed objectivism, opposed it. (To imagine that in doing that it must make itself fatally indefensible for no apparent reason is certainly curious.) Hence, a decisive third option stares us in the face: Bernstein and similar-minded opponents of objectivism deplore and attack the argumentative strategy that would have it that the defeat of objectivism permits only a relativistic defense of science and rational inquiry. So there is an obvious gap in the argument that needs to be filled.

Consider, for example, that, contesting the import of Peter Winch's discussion of the challenge of Zande magic, Charles Taylor (who treats Winch as a relativist of a sort rather close to Bernstein's specifications) admits "incommensurable ways of life" (that is, activities that cannot be carried on at the same time "in principle," and not merely "in practice" – Zande magic and modern science, soccer and rugby football, possibly also pre- and post-Galilean science) but insists nevertheless (against the would-be relativist) that comparative judgments of worth or effectiveness or power (judgments of relative superiority) are not precluded for that reason:

> I entirely agree [Taylor says] that we must speak of a plurality of standards. The discourse in which matters are articulated in different societies can be very different; as we can see in the Azande disinterest in explaining away the paradox Evans-Pritchard put to them in witchcraft diagnosis. The standards are different, because they belong to incommensurable activities. But where I want to disagree with Winch is in claiming that plurality doesn't rule out judgments of superiority. I think the kind of plurality we have here, between the incommensurable, precisely opens the door to such judgments.[15]

The points to be noticed are as follows. First, Taylor's complaint has it that the relativist (*his* relativist) argues unjustifiably from the incommensurability of activities *to* the incommensurability of comparative cross-cultural judgments of such activities, from the impossibility of jointly performing certain activities *to* the impossibility of legitimating certain judgments. Fair enough. But the "relativist's" conclusion trivially follows from the putatively isolating or even imprisoning nature of different conceptual schemes – that he acknowledges. So the force of Taylor's countermove depends on its being the case that the *non sequitur* obtains *because and only because* "different" conceptual schemes are *not* incommensurable – in the sense that we and the Azande *can* understand one another's concepts and standards (which, as it happens, Winch always wished to maintain). Secondly, Taylor's relativistic opponent views matters entirely differently from the relativist (we have) already introduced, who denies *that* opponent's view of incommensurability *and* (also) admits that "judgments of superiority" *are* eligible. To put the matter as forcefully as possible in Taylor's terms, when he insists on "valid transcultural judgments of superiority" but admits that "there is no such thing as a single argument proving global superiority," what does Taylor have in mind (and what could he offer as support) in concluding "wherever the final global verdict falls, it doesn't invalidate but rather depends on such transcultural judgments"?[16] Can he possibly be reinstating here a new form of objectivism?

One should bear in mind that Taylor's theory ultimately must be squared with his own acceptance of the hermeneutic circle. For, as he says,

> we cannot hide from ourselves how greatly this option [for admitting the hermeneutical sciences of man] breaks with certain commonly held notions about our scientific tradition. We cannot measure such sciences against the requirements of a science of

verification: we cannot judge them by their predictive capacity. We have to accept that they are founded on intuitions which all do not share, and what is worse, that these intuitions are closely bound up with our fundamental options. These sciences cannot be "*wertfrei*". ... [17]

But, then, his position *is* a relativism of the sort previously sketched; or is an undefended version of the paradoxical thesis that, in spite of the openness of history, of the hermeneutic circle, of the interpretive fusing of horizons, human standards of rationality and value must in some sense remain essentially fixed, without depending on any form of objectivism;[18] or else is an obscure form of objectivism itself. In the same vein, we may conclude that Kuhnian paradigms cannot insure the defeat of a relativistic theory of science.

Taylor's argument against relativism depends on conflating two quite distinct charges: first, that relativism is committed to the incommensurability thesis; and, second, that relativism is incapable of conceding "judgments of superiority." It is true that any relativism committed to what has been termed the "exclusive option" would be incapable of conceding "judgments of superiority"; but neither Taylor nor anyone else has shown that no pertinent form of relativism can escape the "exclusive option" or that any relativism that escapes or rejects the "option" nevertheless remains incapable of conceding "judgments of superiority." Here is the fatal *non sequitur*. Furthermore, it is difficult to see *how* to exclude a relativistic account of such judgments (once objectivism is repudiated) without at least implicitly subscribing to some even deeper form of objectivism. Such a tension is quite obvious in, for instance, Hans-Georg Gadamer's position, toward which both Taylor's and Bernstein's views noticeably converge. Thus Gadamer characteristically claims,

That which has been sanctioned by tradition and custom has an authority that is nameless, and our finite historical being is marked by the fact that always the authority of what has been transmitted – and not only what is clearly grounded – has power over our attitudes and behavior. ... The validity of morals, for example, is based on tradition. They are freely taken over, but by no means created by a free insight or justified by themselves. That is precisely what we call tradition: the ground of their validity ... tradition has a justification that is outside the arguments of reason and in large measure determines our institutions and our attitudes.[19]

Read correctly, this marks the unmistakable sense in which Gadamer is a closet essentialist – as, indeed, are all traditionalists (in the use assigned that term earlier).

There appears to be absolutely no way, short of falling back to a form of essentialism or universalism or foundationalism (which Gadamer of course opposes), in which the thesis advanced *could* preclude a relativistic reading. Gadamer *does* wish to hold that the "authority" of tradition, changing more or less continuously in its historical process and subject to hermeneutic complexities, effectively fixes its instruction from one distinct phase of that process to another in such a way as to provide an effective, historicized analogue of essentialism. (We have dubbed the thesis "traditionalism.") It is as if the authority of tradition remains recognizable through change *and* as if what it "transmits" (but does not otherwise "legitimate") exhibits a suitably smooth and conservative transition from phase to phase, so that it insures a proper sense of what *is* being thus transmitted. The conceptual lacunae are clear enough. The objectivity of tradition is certainly not demonstrably incompatible with the relativist's thesis. The puzzle is generalizable for all materials subject to hermeneutic review.[20]

A related confusion appears in Richard Rorty's claim that "'Relativism' is the view that every belief on a certain topic, or perhaps about *any* topic, is as good as every other." Rorty adds at once, "No one holds this view." But he goes on to say, "If there *were* any relativists, they would, of course, be easy to refute" (since they would subscribe to the self-refuting Protagorean claim). In any case, he says, "'Relativism' only seems to refer to a disturbing view, worthy of being refuted, if it concerns *real* theories, not just philosophical theories" (that is, "first-level," not merely "second-level," theories). But of course relativism *does* concern real theories of both sorts, once we recognize (*contra* Rorty) that there are no first-level theories without second-level theories or second-level theories without first-level theories. At long last he suggests, "Perhaps 'relativism' is *not* the right name" after all for the doctrine really opposed – that is, "irrationalism," the doctrine (symbiotically but inappropriately) linked, as in Bernstein's account, to the rejection of the privileged grounding of cognitive claims.[21]

If our argument were conceded, we should be catapulted at once "beyond objectivism and relativism" – simply because relativism (the moderate relativism sketched) would then have been recognized as a stronger contender than it appeared to be when viewed as a mere parasite upon the back of objectivism. To that extent, we have justified the implied irony that the usual critics of relativism, who treat that doctrine as flailing away at an already hopeless thesis (objectivism), are themselves the self-appointed victims of that disorder.

But no one will be satisfied. After all, the appeal to Bernstein's original counterstrategy was made in the name of an economy; now, it might be seen as no more than a sly maneuver to gain an unfair advantage by way of a near-irrelevancy. What more should be said? Certainly, the confusion between the two sorts of "relativism" should be accounted for. What may explain the confusion is this: in certain circumstances, the moderate relativist opposes the admissibility of bipolar truth values; somehow, this is converted into his being opposed to the admissibility of *any* truth values (or truth-like values) – hence, converted into his affirming a skeptical or anarchist or nihilist thesis. He thereby becomes the relativist symbiotically dependent on objectivism. But, first of all, even mere indeterminacy of truth value (at a given moment of inquiry or because of real-time constraints) is *not* an expression of skepticism: it is an affirmation of the cognitive standing of a given issue; findings of indeterminacy, after all, *are* assignments of truth value relativized to the available evidence. Secondly, questions once thought to be "intrinsically incapable of determination" – that is, of being determined as true or false – may, *over time*, prove to be actually capable of such determination. Thirdly, it is false to suppose that denying the admissibility of bipolar truth values (for relevant reasons) when weaker values are said to be admissible just *is* an expression of skepticism: on the contrary, it is itself a strong cognitive claim, presumably about the properties of a particular domain of inquiry. Thus, for instance, Quine's doctrine of the indeterminacy of translation is *not* a skeptical thesis; it is (meant to be) a relativist thesis: it holds that alternative (otherwise) incompatible ontologies *can* be empirically supported in given domains and that, *because of the way ontological questions are addressed*, stronger bipolar appraisals of candidate ontologies *cannot* be supported.[22] On the other hand, it may fairly be claimed that Paul Feyerabend (but not Thomas Kuhn) intended to hold a skeptical thesis *in* advancing various versions of the notorious incommensurability claim. For example, Feyerabend *may* have intended such a thesis in holding that "there exist scientific theories which are mutually incommensurable though they apparently deal 'with the same subject matter.'"[23]

The addition of these reflections pretty well settles the plausibility of all of our eleven conditions – at least as far as confirming the strong coherence and relevance of relativism is concerned. But we may round out the argument by collecting whatever substantive considerations may be expected to give relativism a genuine inning. First, then, wherever objectivism is denied or defeated, relativism is facilitated without actually being favored. For its rejection signifies that, in all domains affected, the strongest presumption in favor of bipolar values is disallowed. Nevertheless, the relevance of that rejection is often ignored or denied. For example, when Kuhn's incommensurability thesis is taken as a justified attack on objectivism, or at least on that strong form that holds that there must be a single, omnicompetent, "common, neutral epistemological framework within which we can rationally evaluate competing theories and paradigms or that there is a set of rules ... that will tell us 'how rational agreement can be reached on what would settle the issue on every point where statements seem to conflict,'" it is sometimes insisted that the thesis "has *nothing to do* with relativism, or at least that form of relativism which wants to claim that there can be no rational comparison among the plurality of theories, paradigms, and language games – that we are prisoners locked in our framework and cannot get out of it."[24] Even Popper, who opposes Kuhn's incommensurability thesis, could allow that objection, although he would himself take the incommensurability claim to entail an extreme relativistic thesis.[25]

What is interesting, then, is this: both Kuhn and Popper, opposed on the incommensurability issue, insist on the "objectivity" of comparative judgments within science and on relativism's opposition to that constraint.[26] But, as already explained, their objection is curiously misdirected against (a moderate) relativism and depends on the altogether too easy conceptual slippage that links in one breath "irrationalism, skepticism [and] relativism" (doctrines labeled together thus in order to be discarded together).[27] The opponents of relativism inadvertently impoverish its conceptual resources, and thereby fail to address the challenge that it poses. They claim to support a form of scientific objectivity *opposed to objectivism, always or characteristically or in the most important instances committed to the eligibility of bipolar values.* Nevertheless, they invariably ignore the issue of *legitimating* such values against the relativist's option. *That* issue is almost never frontally addressed; *and* there is no developed argument that actually refutes or seriously weakens the relativistic alternative. In a word: there is no compelling reason why relativism should be restricted to incommensurability contexts.

The following distinctions may perhaps focus our findings in a compendious way: first, adherence or resistance on purely formal grounds to bipolar truth values is a matter utterly distinct from substantive claims about the truth values or truth-like values inquiry into any actual domain can legitimately support; second, the repudiation of objectivism is as such entirely neutral, logically, both to assessing the formal coherence of replacing bipolar values by weaker truth-like values and to assessing the reasonableness of such a replacement in a particular domain; third, the replacement of bipolar values, just as much as their advocacy, is as such opposed to skepticism, incommensurability, anarchism, irrationalism, and the like; and, finally, rejecting the logical eligibility of relativistic truth values solely on the grounds of repudiating objectivism and skepticism or incommensurability itself seriously risks an implicit appeal to an unacknowledged form of objectivism. It is true that objectivism (normally) adheres to bipolar truth values. But that is no reason for supposing that the rejection of objectivism requires our continued subscription to bipolar values in all domains of inquiry. In a fair sense, this is just the issue pressed earlier on in reviewing Dummett's useful version of anti-realism.

IV

Repudiating the more determinate forms of objectivism, then, is bound to encourage even more determinate forms of relativism; for example, repudiating essentialism (say, in accord with Popper's well-known view) or so-called "totalizing" (against the program championed by Lévi-Strauss and other structuralists) or epistemological foundationalism itself.[28] In fact, if Popper's verisimilitude fails, then a scientific realism opposed to essentialism might well be driven to a relativistic position. Similarly, conceptual difficulties affecting univocal applications of the so-called principle of charity (for instance, as in Hilary Putnam's concessions regarding reference to theoretical entities), or difficulties affecting unique extensions of universals (for instance, in accord with Wittgenstein's reflections on the informality of rules governing natural usage, or Goodman's strictures on resemblance), are bound to be favorable to forms of relativism, since they affect truth values so fundamentally.[29]

The strenuousness of resisting relativism will be even more marked as we move on to the special complexities of linguistic and cultural contexts. Here, it is hard to see how the admission of intentional and interpretive considerations, of historicism, and in particular of the profoundly consensual (that is, reflexive) nature of objectivity in the human studies, could possibly fail to strengthen the relativist's hand. Finally, wherever, under the accumulating burden of the themes here broached, questions of rational practice and policy cannot rightly claim to depend on the discovery of independent norms or ontologically "objective values," it is difficult to see how *whatever objectivity* may (reasonably) support moral constraints could preclude a relativistic interpretation of such objectivity.[30] Or, where conceptual issues are thought to require second-order inferences to the best account – noticeably, in speculations about what "there is," under historicized conditions shorn of any sources of apodictic certainty – it is difficult to see how relativistic considerations could be excluded or defeated merely as such.

The entire argument leads to a stunningly obvious question: how, *if* there is no single, timelessly adequate conceptual framework, and *if* there is always an openended plurality of frameworks fitted to parts of the experienced world, and *if* objectivity under these conditions is conceded, can we demonstrate that the very choice of a proper framework *for* resolving particular disputes is invariably, predominantly, characteristically, or generally (for the important cases at least) made in accord with a strong bipolar model of truth values; *or* how, assuming a rational choice fitting framework to question and question to framework, can we demonstrate that, *within* the contexts of inquiry thus provided, the resolution of particular disputes is invariably, predominantly, characteristically, or generally (for the important cases at least) made in accord with a strong bipolar model of truth values? No answer seems to be forthcoming.

A final adjustment suggests itself. It has been argued that conceptual incommensurability, or "conceptual relativism" – the notion that there are *different* conceptual schemes recognizable as such but not translatable or paraphrasable into *our* conceptual scheme (either totally or partially – "cannot be made intelligible and defensible." Donald Davidson, who presses the charge in what is perhaps the most strenuous and compelling way, straightforwardly declares,

> the attempt to give a solid meaning to the idea of conceptual relativism, and hence to the idea of a conceptual scheme, fares no better when based on partial failure of translation than when based on total failure. Given the underlying methodology of interpretation, we could not be in a position to judge that others had concepts or beliefs radically different from our own ... [and] if we cannot intelligibly say that schemes are different, neither can we intelligibly say that they are one.[31]

Here, Davidson is attacking Kuhn's and Feyerabend's use of "incommensurable," which he takes (not at all unfairly) to mean what "not translatable" means.[32] This is *not* to say that "incommensurable" means "not translatable" on the best reading of the phenomena Kuhn and Feyerabend were examining – only that, with considerable uncertainty (and now, perhaps, with much less willingness to risk the issue primarily on the fate of a ramified theory of meaning), they did once favor such an equivalence. Davidson has, then, amplified very usefully

F. P. Ramsey's very pretty point about mentioning to another one's inability to pronounce "marmalade."

Now, Davidson does *not* claim that we *can* actually translate into "our present scheme" whatever any natural-language speaker might say. He does confess, "I think our *present* scheme and language are best understood as extensional and materialist."[33] What, in effect, he shows is that, *if* conceptual schemes are to be individuated as radically different, and *if* "failure of intertranslatability is a necessary condition for difference of conceptual schemes" (as he believes it to be),[34] then Ramsey's paradox obtains and the claim is no longer intelligible. Fair enough. But, *if* actual translation efforts fail, *if* "failure of intertranslat*ability*" is *not* a necessary condition for difference of conceptual schemes, then it may still be entirely reasonable to speak of different (even "radically") different) conceptual schemes, *without* intending either a skeptical or irrationalist reading of Kuhn's rather unfortunate expression "different worlds" *or* a denial of conceptual relativism. One might (with Ian Hacking for instance) speak of a "dissociation" of paradigms or exemplars rather than of a "failure of intertranslatability."[35] The fact is that Davidson has never shown that his own program of intertranslatability is even remotely promising for natural languages or that we have a good enough sense of what could effectively serve as criteria for intertranslat*ability* (or for actual success of translation). Particularly with respect to theoretical terms (without either holding that their meanings are entirely determined by the theories in which they are embedded or that there are no such systematic constraints obtaining),[36] a "dissociation" of investigative practices, habits of thought, historical focus, beliefs and the like might well encourage an inference to conceptual relativism. Under *favorable* circumstances, divergence would yield evidence for at least a robust or moderate relativism; and under no circumstances would it support (or need to support) a thesis of "radically different" conceptual schemes.

We can, therefore, have our cake and eat it too. We can admit "dissociated," plural conceptual schemes in a logical space in which we *lack* a rule of global translatability and in which we *do not claim* the impossibility of translation. That is quite enough for a moderate relativism – and for a recovery of (what is defensible in) Kuhn's account of "incommensurable" paradigms. The question is, granting that much, how *could* the relativistic option be precluded or avoided?

Notes

1   See for example the papers in Martin Hollis and Steven Lukes (eds), *Rationality and Relativism* (Cambridge, Mass.: MIT Press, 1982); and Hans-

Georg Gadamer, *Truth and Method*, tr. Garrett Barden and John Cumming from the 2nd German edn (New York: Seabury Press, 1975), pp. 308–9.

2 Paul Feyerabend holds that "Protagorean relativism is *reasonable* because it pays attention to the pluralism of traditions and values" – *Science in a Free Society* (London: New Left Books, 1978), p. 28; there is some reason to think he believes that Protagoreanism has universal application. Contrast Peter Winch's view in "Understanding a Primitive Society," *American Philosophical Quarterly*, 1 (1964).

3 Richard J. Bernstein, *Beyond Objectivism and Relativism* (Philadelphia: University of Pennsylvania Press, 1983), p. 9; cf. W. Newton-Smith, "Relativism and the Possibility of Interpretation," in Hollis and Lukes, *Rationality and Relativism*.

4 Bernstein, *Beyond Objectivism and Relativism*, p. 8. It is worth remarking that Bernstein observes that "A more appropriate title or subtitle of the book [Gadamer's *Truth and Method*] and indeed of Gadamer's entire philosophic project, might have been 'Beyond Objectivism and Relativism.' Gadamer's primary philosophic aim is to expose what is wrong with the type of thinking that moves between these antithetical poles and to open us to a new way of thinking about understanding that reveals that our being-in-the-world is distorted when we impose the concepts of objectivism and relativism" (p. 115). Gadamer was favorably taken with Bernstein's account of his own work and a letter to that effect is included in Bernstein's book.

5 Ibid., p. 8.

6 Ibid., pp. 10–11; cf. Edmund Husserl, *The Crisis of European Sciences and Transcendental Phenomenology*, tr. David Carr (Evanston, Ill.: Northwestern University Press, 1970), pp. 745–6 (cited by Bernstein).

7 Bernstein, *Beyond Objectivism and Relativism*, p. 37. The charge accords with Gadamer's assessment.

8 Ibid., p. 7.

9 Ibid., pp. 2f.

10 Ibid., pp. 166f.

11 Ibid., pp. 16–23 *passim*.

12 Ibid., p. 57.

13 Ibid.

14 Ibid., pp. 11–12 for instance.

15 Charles Taylor, "Rationality," in Hollis and Lukes, *Rationality and Relativism*, pp. 98, 105. This is not the occasion for attempting to correct standard misinterpretations of Winch's position – including Taylor's. But it should in all fairness be noted that Winch does not seem to have actually opposed cross-cultural comparisons or cross-cultural "judgments of superiority." On Taylor's view, cf. Charles Taylor, "Interpretation and the Sciences of Man," in Paul Rabinow and William M. Sullivan (eds), *Interpretive Social Science*: A Reader (Berkeley, Calif.: University of California Press, 1979).

16 Taylor, "Rationality," in Hollis and Lukes, *Rationality and Relativism*, p. 104.

17 Taylor, "Interpretation and the Sciences of Man," in Rabinow and Sullivan, *Interpretive Social Science*, p. 71. It is interesting to note that Bernstein cites the passage but leaves out the next-to-last line, which reintroduces the threatening relativism: cf. Bernstein, *Beyond Objectivism and Relativism*, p. 135.

18 One should bear in mind Gadamer's endorsement of Bernstein's basic claims – which in a way Taylor also shares; cf. Bernstein, *Beyond Objectivism and Relativism*, Appendix I "A Letter by Professor Hans-Georg Gadamer".

19 Gadamer, *Truth and Method*, p. 249.

20 It applies straightforwardly, for example to the views of Clifford Geertz, "From the Native's Point of View," in Rabinow and Sullivan, *Interpretive Social Science: A Reader*; and Peter Winch, "Understanding a Primitive Society," *American Philosophical Quarterly*, I (1964).

21 Richard Rorty, "Pragmatism, Relativism, and Irrationalism," *Proceedings and Addresses of the American Philosophical Association*, LIII (1980), 727–30.

22 See W. V. Quine, *Word and Object* (Cambridge, Mass.: MIT Press, 1960), ch. 2.

23 Paul Feyerabend, *Against Method* (London: New Left Books, 1975), p. 274. There is an extremely helpful discussion of the difference between Kuhn's and Feyerabend's views in Bernstein, *Beyond Objectivism and Relativism*, pp. 79–93; Bernstein mentions the remark just cited from Feyerabend.

24 Bernstein, *Beyond Objectivism and Relativism*, p. 92. Cf. Donald Davidson, "On the Very Idea of a Conceptual Scheme," *Proceedings and Addresses of the American Philosophical Association*, XLVII (1973–4); Gerald Doppelt, "Kuhn's Epistemological Relativism: An Interpretation and Defense," *Inquiry*, XXI (1978).

25 Cf. Karl R. Popper, *Realism and the Aim of Science* (vol. 1; *From the Postscript to the Logic of Scientific Discovery*), ed. W. W. Bartley III (Totowa, NJ: Rowman and Littlefield, 1983), pp. 156–7; also Thomas S. Kuhn, *The Structure of Scientific Revolutions*, 2nd enlarged edn (Chicago: University of Chicago Press, 1970), p. 150. It is fair to say that Kuhn has muted the strong and distinctive thesis here advanced.

26 Bernstein, for example, reporting quite accurately the debate about incommensurability, explicitly says that "the incommensurability thesis has been rightly taken as an attack on objectivism (not, however, on objectivity)" and that, therefore, it "has nothing to do with relativism" (*Beyond Objectivism and Relativism*, p. 92).

27 Popper, *Realism and the Aim of Science*, p. 18.

28 See Karl R. Popper, "The Aim of Science," *Objective Knowledge: An Evolutionary Approach* (Oxford: Clarendon Press, 1972); Keith Lehrer, *Knowledge* (Oxford: Clarendon Press, 1974); and Rorty, "Pragmatism, Relativism, and Irrationalism," *Proceedings and Addresses of the American Philosophical Association*, LIII. It should be remarked that Popper's opposition to essentialism does not signify that Popper himself has successfully

escaped the charge.

29   See Hilary Putnam, "Meaning and Knowledge" (The John Locke Lectures 1976), *Meaning and the Moral Sciences* Lecture II (London: Routledge and Kegan Paul, 1978); and Nelson Goodman, "Seven Strictures on Similarity," in Lawrence Foster and J. W. Swanson (eds), *Experience and Theory* (Amherst: University of Massachusetts Press, 1970).

30   Bernstein, it appears, agrees with Gadamer's attempt to reinterpret Aristotle's natural law doctrine (so-called) in historicized but objective and (anti-relativistic) terms; cf. Bernstein, *Beyond Objectivism and Relativism*, pp. 156–7; also Gadamer, *Truth and Method*, pp. 278–89, 248–9. It is worth noting how J. L. Mackie, espousing a special doctrine of "moral skepticism," nevertheless attempts to avoid moral relativism: cf. *Ethics: Inventing Right and Wrong* (Harmondsworth, Middx.: Penguin, 1977).

31   Davidson, "On the Very Idea of a Conceptual Scheme," *Proceedings and Addresses of the American Philosophical Association*, XLVII, 11, 20. There is a rather free-wheeling attack on relativism, from the Popperian camp, that rejects the incommensurabilist thesis from the point of view of "the unity of mankind" – construed not as "a literal truth of descent" but as "a program, a proposal for how to act and think": I. C. Jarvie, *Rationality and Relativism* (London: Routledge and Kegan Paul, 1984), p. 14; cf. also, pp. 81, 102. Jarvie's discussion adds little to the argument, except that it regards incommensurabilism as "invalid." But it is useful to take note of it here, if only because it signals the loose convergence among such diverse thinkers as Davidson, Bernstein, Taylor, Gadamer, Apel, Habermas, Popper, Gellner, and Jarvie regarding the "irrationality," "nihilism," "incoherence," or "anarchy" of relativism (reduced to incommensurabilism).

32   Ibid., p. 12. Cf. Thomas Kuhn, "Reflections on my Critics," in Imre Lakatos and Alan Musgrave (eds), *Criticism and the Growth of Knowledge* (Cambridge: Cambridge University Press, 1970), pp. 266, 267; and Paul Feyerabend, "Problems of Empiricism," in R. G. Colodny (ed.), *Beyond the Edge of Certainty* (Englewood Cliffs, NJ: Prentice-Hall, 1965), p. 214. Both are cited by Davidson.

33   Davidson, "On the Very Idea of a Conceptual Scheme," *Proceedings and Addresses of the American Philosophical Association*, XLVII, 10. Cf. also Davidson's "In Defense of Convention T," in Hugues Leblanc (ed.), *Truth, Syntax and Modality* (Amsterdam: North Holland, 1973).

34   Davidson, "On the Very Idea of a Conceptual Scheme," *Proceedings and Addresses of the American Philosophical Association*, XLVII, 12.

35   Ian Hacking, *Representing and Intervening* (Cambridge: Cambridge University Press, 1983), ch. 5: Cf. also Hacking's "Language, Truth and Reason," in Hollis and Lukes, *Rationality and Relativism*.

36   Cf. Putnam, "Meaning and Knowledge," Lecture II, *Meaning and the Moral Sciences*; Dudley Shapere, "The Structure of Scientific Revolutions," in Gary Gutting (ed.), *Paradigms and Paradoxes* (Notre Dame, Ind.: University of Notre Dame Press, 1980).

4

Rationality and Realism

In considering the question of rationality, one could hardly do better than begin with the splendidly helpful paper that Steven Lukes published in 1967 – which assembles many of the most important alternative conceptions in the anthropological and sociological literature but which is nearly entirely wrong about the theoretical constraints on rationality itself;[1] or turn to the quite opposed attempt by Barry Barnes and David Bloor – genuinely searching but nevertheless utterly preposterous – to relativize the question in accord with the influential program of the sociology of knowledge.[2] Lukes's paper errs instructively, because, although it raises the essential issues (which it would be a misfortune to lose a grip on), it draws all the wrong conclusions by a series of *non sequiturs*. The reason, in part at least, undoubtedly lies with Lukes's strong opposition to all forms of cognitive relativism.[3] Barnes and Bloor's account tries to show the way to a balanced relativism, particularly with regard to rationality, but it bungles the effort in a double way: first, because none of the criteria the account offers for sorting relativisms do, singly or collectively, actually demarcate relativistic and nonrelativistic theories (or, more generously, do so for candidates that could really count as interesting versions of relativism); second, because the strategy of the adopted sociology of knowledge does not and cannot distinguish between the merely causal conditions of belief and the normative conditions for the validity of belief claims, or for the truth of beliefs, or for the possession of knowledge by believing agents – where the latter conditions positively entail a conception of rationality and the former merely presuppose such a conception (or, more desperately, suppose that we could work without one). Lukes's position, then, is relevant but quite wrong; and Barnes and Bloor's position, game but wildly irrelevant, even self-defeating. Of course, saying so is meant to signify that drawing the contrast is instructive about the question of rationality. To show this, however, requires a tolerance for what may seem a shift of topic. The sense of shift is only apparent, of course, because one would wish to hold that relativism is rational and not merely coherent, and because the usual theories of rationality strongly incline toward some sort of essentialist or timeless or transhistorical model.

I

Lukes's thesis is quite straightforward. "Some criteria of rationality," he holds, "are universal, i.e., relevantly applicable to all beliefs, in any context, while others are context-dependent, i.e., are to be discovered by investigating the context and are only relevantly applicable to beliefs in that context."[4] Lukes applies the distinction against Peter Winch's now almost too familiar discussion of Zande rationality and understanding.[5] But the way in which Lukes puts his point is obliquely instructive because it is so understandably hasty – without, however, vindicating Winch:

> In so far as Winch seems to be saying that the answer to the ... question [what for society S are the criteria of rationality *in general*?] is culture-dependent, he must be wrong, or at least we could never know if he were right; indeed we cannot even conceive what it would be for him to *be* right. In the first place, the existence of a common *reality* is a necessary precondition of our understanding S's language. ... What must be the case is that S must have our distinction between truth and falsity if we are to understand its language, for, if *per impossibile* it did not, we would be unable even to agree about what counts as the successful identification of public (spatio-temporally located) objects. Moreover, any culture, scientific or not, which engages in successful prediction (and it is difficult to see how any society could survive which did not) must presuppose a given reality. ... In the second place, S's language must have operable logical rules and not all of these can be pure matters of convention. ... It follows that if S has a language, it must, minimally, possess criteria of truth (as correspondence to reality) and logic, which we share with it and which simply *are* criteria of rationality. ... But if the members of S really did not have our criteria of truth and logic, we would have no grounds for attributing to them language, thought or beliefs and would *a fortiori* be unable to make any statements about these.[6]

What Lukes is opposing, here, is the thesis, attributed to Winch, that "rationality itself is context- or culture-dependent." Lukes sides with Alasdair MacIntyre, who holds that "we cannot explain social behavior independently of our own norms of rationality" *and* that "the beginning of an explanation of why certain criteria are taken to be rational in some societies is that they *are* rational"[7] – which in effect signifies that our understanding of the Azande, say, presupposes Lukes's own thesis about universal criteria of rationality.

Now all of this is quite mistaken – but nearly enough right to miss detection. Also, the required correction exposes the extraordinary complexity of the notion of rationality and with it the complexity of the status of the human sciences. These ramifications justify fussing over Lukes's and Barnes and Bloor's alternative accounts.

For example, Lukes claims that "the existence of a common reality is a necessary precondition of our understanding *S*'s language"; *and* that, if that is so, then *S* and we must share the same "distinction between truth and falsity," the same referential practice, the same "operable logical rules" (which could not be "pure matters of convention"), the same "criteria of truth ... and logic" – in effect, the same "criteria of rationality." Lukes never does explain what he means by the expression "our understanding *S*'s language"; or why, if our understanding presupposes a "common reality," it follows that we must also share (among ourselves as well as between ourselves and the members of *S*) the same criteria of truth, reference, logic, rationality. The underlying *non sequitur* depends simply on *the presumed irreconcilability of realism and relativism*: on drawing the conclusion that *sharing the same world entails sharing the same conceptual scheme (of that common world) or the same cognitive criteria, or the same criteria of rationality*. It also supposes, too sanguinely, an easy resolution of questions regarding the status (pertinent to realist–anti-realist disputes) of theories, theoretical entities, the meaning of observationality, phenomenological laws, the entire apparatus of scientific method.[8] Ironically, the play of opposing views on just these questions actually encourages relativistic interpretations of both science and rationality.

Here, reference is often made to Donald Davidson's familiar account, in "On the Very Idea of a Conceptual Scheme,"[9] to the effect that "We cannot make good sense of the idea that there are seriously different total conceptual schemes, or frames of reference, or that there may be radically 'incommensurate' languages (to use Whorf's word)."[10] What is usually not noticed, in Davidson's argument, is that *his* thesis depends (quite tellingly) on a familiar *reductio* of Whorf's hypothesis:[11] if we can translate or interpret the verbal behavior of others, then our conceptual schemes cannot be "radically incommensurate"; and, if we can't, then there's nothing to be said about the properties of the language we fail to understand. The argument counts heavily against certain extravagances of T. S. Kuhn and Nelson Goodman – but it does have its limitation. In particular, when Davidson makes his claim, he intends "conceptual scheme ... to correspond to a whole language; nothing, at any rate [he says], can be left out that is needed to make sense of the rest."[12] Fair enough. But conceding that has nothing to do with (1) sharing all the same particular concepts, or (2) sharing any of the same criteria of truth, reference, logic, or rationality. It is quite possible, *contra* Lukes, to share a common world and, understanding one another, not to have "radically incommensurate" conceptual schemes, while diverging conceptually and while *not* sharing the very same cognitive criteria for getting around in our common world. In fact, Lukes himself gives the game away when – quite correctly – he notices that the view he espouses leads us to suppose that our jointly shared "criteria of truth" would in effect be *criteria* of "correspondence to reality." *If*, however, all forms of foundationalism, essentialism, and the like are eschewed – as hopeless to vindicate[13] – then there *could* be no way to show that we must share the same *criteria* (of correspondence) in merely establishing our sharing a common reality. This is simply the upshot of rejecting what we have been calling objectivism (and what in various other idioms is called logocentrism, onto-theo-logy, the mirror theory, and the like). Alternatively put, there may be some use in a correspondence *theory* of truth, but (short, say, of subscribing to Russell's notion of knowledge by acquaintance) there is no use in correspondence *criteria* of truth – as opposed to criteria (of whatever kind) for *assigning* truth values.

It is true – and important to emphasize – that the conception of rationality *is* a conception that cannot preclude an aptitude for applying cognitive criteria of some sort bearing on truth and reference and predication and the like; for not only must the beliefs, intentions, behavior of a set of creatures cohere in some suitable way, but in addition such creatures must be able to correct or adjust beliefs, intentions, behavior (in a suitably reflexive sense) on the basis of what, from their perspective, functions or counts as counterevidence. Lukes is quite correct to stress this connection.[14] It is just what links rationality and realism.

But it is *not* true that that conceptual linkage entails that we share a "whole language" or "total conceptual schemes" (in Davidson's terms) – or (what is an entirely different issue) the same "criteria" of truth, reference, logic, or rationality (in Lukes's terms). And that means that, contrary to the contemporary fashion, *it is not the case that realism and a moderate (or robust) relativism are incompatible.* (Or, at least, it need not be the case – since "relativism" is defined so arbitrarily or maliciously these days.[15]) In fact, it is important to notice

1   that Davidson's argument against radically incommensurate con-
    ceptual schemes (and analogues of Davidson's argument – Max
    Black's, for instance) has, as such, nothing to do with the issue
    of realism, in any epistemically focused sense;
2   that, when they insist that, "For the relativist there is no sense
    attached to the idea that some standards or beliefs are really
    rational as distinct from merely locally accepted as such," "that
    all beliefs are on a par with one another with respect to the causes
    of their credibility [or rationality] ... [that is,] regardless of truth
    and falsity,"[16] Barnes and Bloor deprive rationality of its necessary
    connection with normative cognitive functions and deprive rela-
    tivism of any possible prospect of functioning as a rationally viable
    option; and
3   that Lukes's realism (minimal in terms of what it asserts, maximal
    in terms of what it infers from what it asserts) does not and
    cannot, contrary to what Lukes suppose, yield any conclusions
    about universal conceptual schemes and universal criteria of truth,
    reference, logic, or rationality.

A short way of putting the point against Lukes is this: it is entirely possible that we share a common world but, for historically pertinent reasons, do not share the same paradigms or criteria for formulating and testing our cognitive claims. What this suggests is that to deny the possibility of that condition is tantamount to rejecting the historicity of human inquiry *and* to subscribing (once again) to foundationalism, essentialism, or some cognitively apt form of the correspondence theory. For, if, as MacIntyre says, we must rely on "our own norms of ration-ality," *how* can we show that those very norms *are not* (in the terms of reproach Lukes favors against Winch) "culture-dependent," "context-dependent," historically local? At the very least, there is a lacuna (the same one that can be traced in Charles Taylor, Hans-Georg Gadamer, and all those who admit the historical nature of human existence but deny even a moderate relativism).

II

In certain recent views of Hilary Putnam's there is a very instructive inadvertence that can be made to lead us out of these difficulties. Once again, it requires a tolerance for a line of inquiry that will, at this point in the discussion, still seem rather tangential to our central concern. In fact, it is not in the least tangential, though it will take some while to show that the considerations that follow bear in an important way on the problems of realism that have yet to be collected.

Putnam accepts an argument of Davidson's to the effect

> that *truth is prior to reference* in the following way: a speaker's understanding of the reference of individual words consists in his grasping the truth conditions for sentences which contain those words. ... Although formally reference appears to be prior to truth, in that logicians define truth in terms of reference, philosophically it is the other way around. What a speaker learns when he learns his native language is the truth conditions for its sentences, or for a subset of its sentences.[17]

At least two points are worth pressing here. First, there *cannot* be any "priority" between words and sentences: words and sentences are linked in a conceptually relational way. It was in fact one of the fundamental mistakes of Quine's theory of language that he believed – and, evidently, Davidson and Putnam, following him – that truth conditions for sentences (Quine's notorious ersatz doctrine of "stimulus meaning") could be provided independently of *all* parsings in terms of constitutive words. But that is impossible: there cannot be any remotely *realist* reading of the truth of sentences without some notion, however inchoate, of reference to the world *via* the terms within such sentences and the terms of other sentences by means of which truth conditions can be confirmed or infirmed.[18] Furthermore, this sense of realism is entirely neutral to the issues at stake in recent disputes about realism and anti-realism.[19]

The issue is vexing when taken in Davidson's sense, which Putnam does not report in the fully relevant respect. For Davidson holds *only* that "an absolute definition of truth fails to yield an analysis of the concept of reference," where by an "absolute" theory is meant a theory of truth

> that satisfies something like Tarski's Convention T: . . . that by recursively characterizing a truth-predicate (say "is true in L") entails, for each sentence s of L, a metalinguistic sentence got from the form "s is true in L if and only if p" when "s" is replaced by a canonical description of a sentence of L and "p" by a sentence

of the metalanguage that gives the truth-conditions of the described sentence.[20]

But an absolute definition is obviously *not* philosophically neutral with respect to truth conditions as, on the contrary, is Tarski's account of the *meaning* of "true." It presupposes – what Davidson never actually shows is reasonable, and what cannot be deduced from the neutral Tarskian conception of "true" – the reducibility of the syntactic–semantic structure of natural languages to the canonical structures Tarski provided for selected formal languages. Here, Davidson specifically intends to contrast the "absolute" use of the primitive, undefined "truth-predicate" with any and all theories that "relativize truth to an interpretation, a model, a possible world, or a domain" – that is, with theories that assign "true" an *epistemic* force. The first achieves the result Davidson wants simply because "the accounts of truth and satisfaction [given in some language] don't suggest *how to go on to the new case* [when a new predicate or a new predicative application is added to the language in hand]."[21] True enough; but then Tarski's truth predicate has *no* epistemic import at all (depends solely on formal equivalences) and his canonical program applies only doubtfully to whole natural languages – and cannot be applied by way of any merely formal or epistemically neutral procedure. It is the conflating of these two features of Tarski's work that gives the false impression of the power of Davidson's thesis. In any case, *reference,* in the epistemically live sense that Putnam favors,[22] *cannot* be posterior to truth along Davidson's lines: Davidson's account is epistemically irrelevant, and Putnam's cannot be construed as a merely formal notion.

The second point to press is simply that Putnam himself insists, in explicating what has been termed "the new theory of reference" (which he takes Kripke and himself to have developed – more or less against Russell's theory), that

> the extension of certain kinds of terms (... "natural kind words," meaning names for such things as natural substances, species, and physical magnitudes) is not fixed by a set of "criteria" laid down in advance, but is, in part, *fixed by the world*. There are objective laws obeyed by multiple sclerosis, by gold, by horses, by electricity; and what it is rational to include in these classes will depend on what those laws turn out to be.[23]

Hence, on Putnam's own theory, meaning and truth conditions entail a rich concept of reference. Furthermore, Putnam indicates his own agreement with Michael Dummett's criticism of Davidson's account, to the effect that *two* distinct notions of truth are required: one, an "internal," purely formal *"equivalence principle"* (capturing Tarski's neutral truth predicate), which has no explanatory power; the other, an "external," interpreted, justificatory notion that does have an *"explanatory role* in an account of understanding" – and which, in having that, indissolubly links truth and reference within a theory of meaning.[24]

Putnam disagrees with Dummett's apparent collapsing of truth into justification, of course – essentially on the grounds that truth but not justification "cannot be lost," is not tensed or relativized or a matter of degree. Hence, Putnam holds, "truth [is] an *idealization* of justification" – which marks his well-known contrast between "internal realism" and "metaphysical realism."[25] But the fact remains that, on Putnam's view, the meaning (hence, the truth conditions for the use) of natural-kind terms (which, presumably, organize our sciences) is not conventional or subjective, and positively requires determinate *reference* to the real world (at least reference as determinate as predication itself). Furthermore, on Putnam's view, the rationality of human behavior can apparently be gauged by behavior and dispositions favorable or unfavorable to bringing our terms into line with these realist considerations. So truth (*a fortiori*, meaning) and reference are conceptually symbiotic.

Once we accept this much, it is but a step to see as well that – on any "interpreted" theory of truth that resists doctrines functionally similar (in any of a very large number of ways) to (say) Russell's theory of knowledge by acquaintance (to what in a larger sense is "foundationalism" or, in the Continental European idiom, the "philosophy of presence" or "logocentrism") – *there is and can be no principled basis for insuring uniquely determinate truths about the world.* Perhaps the point should be put in a somewhat different way. By *realism* – in an epistemically fundamental sense – we may mean either of two doctrines:

1 there is an actual world, structured in some way independent of human inquiry, that human inquirers have (some) knowledge of;
2 there are denumerably many facts about the actual world as it is structured independent of human inquiry, that human inquirers have (some) knowledge of.

Doctrine 1 is compatible with supporting a realism (*sans phrase*) in which the ingredients of our science, sorted in terms of the structures of the world independent of inquiry and the structures of inquiry that affect our access to the independent world, *cannot* be disjoined from one another (roughly, the upshot of Kant's view of the relationship between transcendental idealism and empirical realism, without any concession to Kant's own theory of transcendental reasoning or of constraints on empirical knowledge); doctrine 2 entails a disjunction between such "realist" and "idealist" ingredients (roughly, the upshot of admitting that Putnam's contrast between "internal" and "metaphysical" realism does specify – against Putnam's own intention – viable alternatives,[26] without any further consideration of Putnam's own theories of language or of constraints on empirical knowledge).

Broadly speaking, doctrine 1 requires that realism be an *en bloc* doctrine – what may fairly be termed a pragmatist doctrine, in the sense that, though there may be a (second-order) ecological or evolutionary or survivalist justification for realism, there cannot be a (first-order) cognitivist justification, a particular cognitive discrimination that confirms the fact of the matter. This is also why there *cannot* be a first-order testable *bloc* science, in Quine's sense, though there can be a first-order *bloc*-testing of "a whole group of hypotheses" within the larger whole of science, in Duhem's sense.[27] To see matters this way is, in effect, to hold that, if we subscribe to a realism in accord with doctrine 1, we cannot, merely on those grounds, draw Lukes's conclusions about sharing common concepts or common criteria of truth, reference, logic, or rationality. Lukes, in effect, has suppressed his conviction that the only viable realism – hence, the only convincing ground for a viable form of rationality, taken as having an epistemic function – *must* be a form of doctrine 2: metaphysical realism, or a realism that makes no concessions to idealism (that is, a kind of foundationalism or essentialism). But that, of course, is both indefensible in itself and (*a fortiori*) significantly harder to defend than any version of doctrine 1.

It is a further – stronger – thesis, going very far beyond merely demonstrating the *non sequitur* of Lukes's argument, that, given a realism in accord with 1, *and* the denial of 2, there are indefinitely many (shall we say) "cognitively defensible" accounts of the constitutive phenomena of the world, if there is any such account. Putnam hesitates here between characterizing this position – in effect, his own – as internal realism or internal non-realism, because of his wish to reconcile the executive metaphysical theories of Quine, Goodman, and Dummett at least. He offers the following useful distinction:

> On [the] perspective [of metaphysical realism], the world consists of some fixed totality of mind-independent objects. There is exactly one true and complete description of "the way the world is." Truth involves some sort of correspondence relation between words and

thought-signs and external things and sets of things. ... [On] the *internalist* perspective, ... *what objects does the world consist of?* is a question that it only makes sense to ask *within* a theory or description. Many "internalist" philosophers, though not all, hold further that there is more than one "true" theory or description of the world. "Truth," in an internalist view, is some sort of (idealized) rational acceptability – some sort of ideal coherence of our beliefs with each other and with our experiences *as those experiences are themselves represented in our belief system* – and not cor-respondence with mind-independent or discourse-independent "states of affairs."[28]

Putnam also wishes to contrast the internalist view with the relativist's, but that is because (prejudicially) he simply defines these alternatives in such a way that "the non-realist position [the internalist's] ... assumes an *objective* notion of rational acceptability"; whereas, although it also rejects metaphysical realism, the relativist's regards "truth or rational acceptability as *subjective*": "The whole *purpose* of relativism, its very defining characteristic [he says], is ... to *deny* the existence of any intel-ligible notion of *objective* 'fit'. Thus the relativist cannot understand talk about truth in terms of *objective* justification-conditions."[29]

Two distinctions should put everything into manageable order. First of all, Putnam contrasts internalism and relativism in the way he does (understandably but arbitrarily), because he takes Kuhn and Fey-erabend – as champions of the incommensurability thesis – to be para-digmatic relativists (hence, also, subjectivists);[30] but it is entirely possible (and entirely reasonable) to formulate relativism as not Protagorean or skeptical or subjectivist or anarchist, but committed instead (without contradiction) *to* cognitively viable notions of "objective fit," *within the constraints of an internalist metaphysics.* So seen, Putnam may be said not to have shown that (or even how) the internal realist (or non-realist) can fail to be a relativist or at least to accommodate the relativist (who could easily be one of Putnam's own favored sort of theorist – that is, one committed to the notion of objective fit, consistently with affirming "more than one 'true' theory or description of the world" where the alternatives are not mutually compatible or reconcilable with one another). Secondly, if "objective fit" is relativized to conceptual scheme (though not in the radical sense Davidson opposes), and if no meta-physical realism can force or lead us to the "one true and complete description of 'the way the world is'" – which is certainly not tantamount to incommensurability – then, just as *truth claims* or *truth values* (as opposed to truth *tout court*) are relativized to conceptual schemes, *so too is reference.* "'Objects' do not exist independently of conceptual schemes," says Putnam. "Since the objects *and* the signs are alike *internal* to the scheme of description, it is possible even trivial to say what matches what."[31] "Trivial" is actually not a helpful charge here (though the point is clear enough), once we treat linguistic usage in a richly historicized way, pluralized for different societies, and specialized in terms of a division of labor. The deeper insight remains that truth, meaning, and reference are conceptually inseparable distinctions for any realist conception of science compatible with doctrine 1 above, whether or not one approaches matters from the view of metaphysical or internal realism and whether or not one is a relativist. Furthermore, *if* (and *because*) rationality is a notion that has an epistemic function – linking human behavior to our very mode of understanding reality – *the theory of what it is to be rational cannot be prised apart from the theory of science.*

A final word of warning is in order. In effect, Putnam *is* a kind of moderate conceptual relativist, provided only that (on his view) alternative "internalist" characterizations of the world preserve a measure of "objective fit" *and* that alternative conceptual schemes are not attenuated so far that they exhibit the extreme incommensurability he opposes in Kuhn and Feyerabend. Nevertheless, quite ironically, he is himself tempted by a more extreme form of relativism than the moderate relativist is likely to favor. This is undoubtedly due to his attraction to Quine's thesis about the "inscrutability of reference" and Davidson's thesis that "truth is prior to reference."[32] But it also explicitly involves his appeal to the Skolem–Löwenheim theorem.[33] From purely formal considerations of that theorem – which of course have no direct connection with the actual conditions of cognitive inquiry of an empirical sort – Putnam is led to affirm that "the truth conditions for 'A cat is on a mat' don't even exclude the possibility that 'cat' refers to *cherries*."[34] But, from the modestly relativistic concession that reference cannot be uniquely fixed under the conceptual conditions acknowledged, it hardly follows that there is any radical indeterminacy or inscrutability of reference that *would "fit" the actual conditions of human existence and human inquiry.* Furthermore, *if* predication would not support a comparably radical finding, and *if* predication and reference *are* conceptually linked in epistemic contexts, then the radical view Putnam espouses is both untenable and tantamount to utter conceptual chaos. The elementary point is that the Skolem–Löwenheim theorem is entirely formal and *lacks altogether any linkage with human cognitive constraints pertinent to a realist science* – realist in at least the minimal sense of doctrine 1 above. Roughly, the Skolem–Löwenheim theorem, like Tarski's account of the meaning of "true," is entirely formal and thus ontologically neutral; but neither Davidson's use of Tarski's account of truth predicates nor Putnam's use of the Skolem–Löwenheim theorem is neutral in the same sense. By pressing this distinction, one is led to see that the strong extensionalism Davidson favors, the would-be priority of truth over reference, and the recovery of reference relativized to conceptual schemes regimented in accord with Davidson's view of truth obscure the fact that no merely formal programs of these sorts bear *as yet* on the substantive question of what our cognitive practices reveal about the logical behavior of actual realist claims, and obscure the fact that a moderate relativism may indeed accord best with those same practices. To put the point in a nutshell, the attempt to solve the question of what a reasonable form of scientific realism would be like – by purely formal means *or* by means that can be applied in purely formal terms *first* (which is Davidson's preference[35] and one Putnam is equivocally attracted to) – is both undefended in terms of any second-order legitimation and utterly contrary to the praxical or historicist orientation introduced earlier. In fact, such a formalism stands fairly accused of failing to come to terms with just the sort of anti-realist constraint that Dummett has usefully favored – of which, it may be said, both Davidson and Putnam appear to have conceded the generally salutary purpose, even where they have not entirely agreed with Dummett's own local formulation. Put another way, the tolerance for radical epistemological possibilities that one finds in Quine, Goodman, Davidson, Putnam and others strongly attracted to their views is simply the obverse side of their distinct penchant for a purely formal treatment of human cognition itself – that is, for their *not* locating actual cognitive practices within the historical life of psychologically and linguistically apt human societies. In rejecting all forms of cognitive transparency, they *lean* in the direction of what we are here calling pragmatism; but they fail to draw their epistemological speculations out of a reasonably rich and plausible account of actual human survival. This is why, adhering to holism, they have no epistemic grounds for favoring the distributed claims of any actual science.

III

This leads us back to Lukes's sanguine *non sequitur* and the heroically self-defeating irrelevance of Barnes and Bloor's reductive (putatively relativistic) sociology of knowledge. For, if only a form of internal realism is viable (or internal non-realism, or anti-realism or even irrealism – to accommodate, without prejudice, here, all candidate theories that are strongly pragmatist, opposed to metaphysical realism, and committed to the symbiosis of realism and idealism), then the shift to internal realism is bound to affect substantively, decisively, possibly even radically, what we may defend as an adequate theory of rationality.[36] For example, if we adopt a strongly historicized and praxicalized account of concepts and human understanding – which Lukes appears to favor[37] – then it is quite impossible to reach any of the universalized conclusions regarding rationality Lukes himself draws *from* a minimally realist thesis. This is not to say that cultural or rational universals are impossible to confirm empirically. It is to say rather that *universalism* is incompatible with historicism, with praxical accounts of understanding, with pragmatism, with internal realism deprived of foundationalist pretensions (in effect, with Kantianism); and that would-be *universals* are themselves only *general* uniformities offered as candidates for universality *via* critical inferences to the best explanation of human life.

Alternatively put, social understanding, socially shared identification of objects, and the like, do *not* presuppose species-wide universals or species-wide criteria of truth and rationality: an empirically accessible conservatism of a conceptual and cognitive sort (undoubtedly linked to biological uniformities and to the relatively slow pace with which biologically constrained conceptual variability occurs within different societies and within the same societies diachronically considered) is quite sufficient to account for the *contingent* stability of such understanding. There is no other recourse. *The fact is that, under the constraints conceded, no one can successfully demonstrate what timeless conceptual uniformities obtain that account for obviously effective social understanding.*

Historicism and universalism are simply incompatible; but universals themselves are empirically contingent general regularities sorted under historical or praxical constraints – as the likeliest universalizable candidates we have. This is what, ultimately, is missed in those last, desperate versions of would-be timeless (totalized and transhistorical) theories of rationality advanced by Jürgen Habermas and Karl-Otto Apel.[38] Lukes cannot draw the conclusion he wants – from his own assumptions; and Habermas and Apel actually violate the conceptual constraints under which they attempt to theorize about rationality.

Carl Hempel provides the counterpart universalist conception of rationality favored by the partisans of the unity-of-science program – that is, by those largely indifferent to historical and praxical contingencies.[39] But that alternative is unsatisfactory for counterpart reasons. First of all, it is doubtful whether, if human psychology and the disciplines that depend upon the phenomena it examines cannot be reduced physicalistically – which seems most plausible[40] – it is possible in principle to match nomic universals with all *bona fide* instances of causal interaction. Secondly, if we have no clear strategy for insuring the universalism of the hypothetico-deductive model of explanation, once empirical generalizations of the causal sort are denied approximative status with respect to universal covering laws – for instance, by attacks on essentialism, by attention to ineliminable referential contingencies, by attention to the absence of empirical evidence exhibiting probabilized regularities as (invariably) tending asymptotically toward fixed limits of variation – then, if interaction be conceded, even the domain of physical forces (certainly that portion intimately involved in human action) cannot form a closed domain. Here we may recall Davidson's rather gentle criticism of Hempel's account of explaining rational action under covering laws: "in the sense in which rationality is a trait that comes and goes, it can't be an assumption needed for every reason explanation. People who don't have the trait are still agents, have reasons and motives, and act on them."[41] But, further, Davidson's attenuated acceptance of Hempel's nomological approach cannot but be similarly undermined by the requirement (his own) of "strict laws [for the domain in question: psychology] belonging to a *closed* system of laws and ways of describing events [where] there are no such laws governing the occurrence of events described in psychological terms."[42]

We are being forced inexorably, by these and similar considerations, to concede that the viability of candidate theories of rationality and the very structure of such theories cannot be less fundamentally affected by historicized and praxical constraints than the theory of science itself. Once we give up metaphysical realism (in all its protean forms), reductive physicalism (in all its forms), the "closed system" status of the domains of the human sciences, the question of rationality will be seen to be more of a puzzle – of a piece with the theory of science itself – than an independent source of assured universal constraints (of the sort Lukes obviously favors) by means of which to temper our account of social understanding and the methodology of science. The intelligibility of human behavior, intra- and inter-culturally or intra- and inter-linguistically, will, then, be seen to be the result (in some sense) of the joint functioning of general biological uniformities (most plausibly linked to cognitive aptitude) *and* the radically historicized, contingent hermeneutic aptitudes of particular human beings.

Quite sensibly, Hempel (and, with him, Davidson) took the hypothetico-deductive model of explanation in science to provide the most promising model – or, a salient part of that model – of rationality: a rational agent, on that view, is one who behaves (implicitly or explicitly) in accord with the most powerful cognitive model we possess. The generally admitted fact of scientific progress draws us in this direction. The trouble is that that model is in the deepest trouble itself, because the logical status of scientific laws is in doubt, because the deductive model of explanation is in doubt, and because the conceptual connection between explanatory models and the living, historical practice of scientific inquiry is unclear. This, of course, is precisely what is associated with the difficulties unearthed by such investigators as Kuhn, Lakatos, and Feyerabend.[43] We simply do not have a suitable model of the rationality of science, though we have some clues.[44] Consequently, when theorists – Mario Bunge, perhaps most notably[45] – construct a rational model of technology and purposive behavior as guided by the universal laws of nature, they cannot fail to be open to the same difficulties as inhere in our attempts to model the rationality of science.

IV

Amid all these difficulties, however, one conceptual clue stands out above all others: we must concede that man is rational even if we are unable to model his rationality convincingly. We cannot merely *assume* human rationality – because of the reflexive nature of the would-be hypothesis. At present, man is the sole paradigm of the scientist, the cognitive agent, the psychologically endowed creature, the language-user, the purposive and rational being. The study of all else (the *human* study of all else) is conceptually dependent on this condition[46] – which is at once the joint theme of analytic forms of realism and anti-realism and of the hermeneutic dependence of the physical on the human sciences. But the structure of all the roles mentioned is hardly self-evident: rationality itself is a second-order, contingently persuasive ascription – within historicized reflection – of the stablest general features of our own *cognitively* focused existence, those that seem to stand the best chance of universally fitting the achievements of science and intelligent behavior. There is, inevitably, a normative function to be assigned science and intelligence and, correspondingly, an equilibrating congruity between these and rationality itself. This is the sense in which rationality is ultimately construed in pragmatist terms: it marks the effective survival of the human species *via* whatever its investigative and testing practices may be; it marks it, that is, *en bloc*, *not* in particular privileged propositions.

Hence Barnes and Bloor are quite right to discredit Lukes's and Martin Hollis's thesis "that all cultures share a common core of beliefs and rationally-justified patterns of inference," "cultural universals" that (against what, in an impoverished sense, they themselves take to be relativism) insure the sharing of truth and the mutual understanding of men of different cultures.[47] They rightly remark, "reality is, after all, a common factor in all the vastly different cognitive responses that men produce to it. Being a common factor it is not a promising candidate to field as an explanation of that variation."[48]

Nevertheless, they fail to grasp the puzzle of rationality, because they impoverish both relativism *and* the conditions of cognition. Regarding the first, they offer three would-be features:

1   "that beliefs on a certain topic vary" – which cannot differentiate between relativistic and nonrelativistic theories;
2   "that which of these beliefs is found in a given context depends on, or is relative to, the circumstances of the users" – which again is entirely neutral; and
3   their so-called "equivalence postulate" – "that all beliefs are on a par with one another with respect to the causes of their credibility. It is not that all beliefs are equally true or equally false, but that regardless of truth and falsity the fact of their credibility is to be seen as equally problematic."[49]

Now, part of the point of 1–3 is to disallow all versions of metaphysical realism, of foundationalism, of objectivism, of what Hollis terms an epistemically neutral "bridgehead" linking all culturally variable forms of life.[50] But part of the point Barnes and Bloor wish to support is that relativism (on their reading) is tantamount to an utter skepticism with respect to a rationally justified confidence in *any* form of reasoning; so they claim, explicating the "equivalence postulate," that "Our two basic modes of reasoning (deduction and induction] are in an equally *hopeless* state with regard to their rational justification."[51] Rationality, then, cannot be linked (as with Lukes) to any cognitively assured set of beliefs or any timelessly secure form of reasoning. Fair enough. But that hardly shows that relativism is equivalent to Barnes and Bloor's own extreme form of skepticism; or that the rejection of theories of rationality in accord with metaphysical realism leads directly to skepticism; or that the retreat to the sociology of knowledge must eschew evaluating beliefs as true or false and as rational or irrational because of links to truth and falsity, and "must search [instead] for the causes of [their] credibility";[52] *or* (most damagingly) that it is even possible to explore the causes of beliefs *without a positive commitment to cognitive appraisal and to some positive view of rationality*. In this sense, Barnes and Bloor's program is utterly self-defeating.[53]

The required conception of rationality, then, must situate us between the extremes of metaphysical realism and mere skepticism; it must be cognitively sanguine, hence realist; it must, in escaping universalism, essentialism, and the like, accommodate the profoundly historicized and praxical nature of human existence; *and*, as a second-order thesis, it cannot, on pain of contradiction, be formulated in cognitiv*ist* terms. If these constraints be conceded, then there is only one – extremely persuasive – option before us: some version of Charles Sanders Peirce's biologically motivated view of human rationality (suitably spare, suitably adjusted, suitably relieved of Peirce's own fandango, neutral to other controversies) must be at least as close to the *beginning* of a satisfactory orientation as we could possibly get. A few tantalizing lines will confirm this: "every simple truth of science is due to the affinity of the human soul to the soul of the universe, imperfect as that affinity no doubt is";[54] "Certain general ideas of action [that is, the regularities of natural forces], prevail throughout the universe, and the reasoning mind is itself a product of the universe. These same laws are thus, by logical necessity, incorporated in his own being."[55] The point of Peirce's floridly expressed conception is that rationality cannot be an explicitly formulizable procedure; that the "abductive" or hypothesis-forming ability that we have cannot be justified on the grounds of rational strategies that are more than heuristic devices or recipes (against, say, Mill's Canons); that, without the "natural prompting" that belongs to our having successfully evolved *within* nature itself, if we had "to search blindfold for a law which would suit the phenomena, our chance of finding it would be as one to infinity."[56] This means that we *are* justified in formulating would-be canons of reasoning, that there must be promisingly stable but changing methodological regularities (not assured a timeless validity) that our evolutionary and ecological achievement insures in an empirically contingent way. In short, realism, whether of the externalist or internalist sort, is unintelligible without a counterpart theory of human rationality. (Peirce, of course, links his sanguine myth about rationality to his equally sanguine myth about the long run of science. He does not attempt to specify determinate truths about either.)

Rationality, then, is a theory of an explanatory sort that we know no way of avoiding – in attempting to understand, reflexively, our own cognitive aptitude. That we have a cognitive aptitude is, broadly speaking, a biological fact, in the sense that the survival of our species depends on the intervention of sustained inquiry. It is a theory of a cognitivist sort *if* we subscribe (in subscribing to that) to some form of metaphysical realism (or a cognate doctrine); and it cannot be cognitivist *if* we subscribe to a realism of the non-"metaphysical" sort here supported, which, otherwise (paired in Putnam's way, in terms of internal and external realisms), would remain seriously ambiguous. So rationality is, minimally, a species-specific model of the cognitively informed capacity of creatures – human and nonhuman – to survive, in the biological sense of reproducing populations. Cognition is justified on noncognitivist grounds, then, which is why rationality must in large part be accounted for in terms of "tacit" congruities between the uniformities of nature and the uniformities of mind. The theme of the biologically tacit, which is Peirce's notion (and which, as such, invites a useful comparison with Michael Polanyi's notion), captures three of the strongest themes of an adequate realism that is not epistemically tendentious:

1   that the realist import of human cognitive powers is itself entailed in the subcognitive conditions of species survival;
2   that distributed realist claims of every sort are conceptually parasitic on the holism of 1; and
3   that the realism of cognitive claims can escape at one and the same time all forms of objectivism (in the sense in which we have used that term) *and* all forms of a representational theory of knowledge or mind (which we merely take note of here, in the manner of a promissory note).

It would not be unreasonable to characterize 1–3 as the heart of what at the present time is usually meant by *pragmatism*.

Of course, there is also the familiar temptation to construe the rational as the moral or in some such way – that is, as providing normative direction for human conduct and behavior. In the same sense in which there must be general uniformities that yield recipes for scientific inquiry, so must there also be general prudential concerns that any rationally "responsible" (*species-wide*) policy must accommodate.[57] But, once we view matters thus, we must see that any *infra*-species-wide model of rationality (in particular, normative action-guiding models for particular societies or individuals) cannot fail to be ideologically partisan or tolerant of a plurality of nonconverging partisan models – historically situated, context-bound, to use Lukes's own terms (applied, ironically, almost as terms of opprobrium). At any rate, such models cannot be expected to draw support from those models that (in the internal realist sense) minimally fit the admitted achievement of human science, even though that achievement must, rationally, also inform and constrain intelligent behavior. The attempt to draw universal ethical norms from inquiry itself was of course dear to Peirce (his "logical socialism") and has been to such philosophers as Habermas and Apel, who have tried to improve on Peirce in this respect.[58] (We shall return to Habermas and Apel for the required details in chapter 7.) But, apart from the inevitable failure of their efforts, which follows from the incompatibility of historicism and universalism, any attempt to merge rationality and morality (or any doctrine of normative policy) must enrich our realism well beyond anything that the *explanatory* function of rationality would require or could support.

Rationality in the latter sense, precisely because it trades on biologically subcognitive uniformities in the species, in virtue of which we suppose man to have an aptitude for discerning selected uniformities in nature *and* for cognitively accommodating the conceptual orientation of diverse societies, *does not entail* (*contra* Lukes) universal criteria of rationality, universal criteria of truth, universally shared concepts. All that is required is that given criteria, given concepts, given beliefs, given theories are and can be shared by *particular* aggregates of cognitively apt agents actually in communication with one another; moving from one such group to another, there is no reason to suppose that universal and invariant concepts and criteria are employed in each. The success of *particular* communications does not require it – which of course goes against Apel and Habermas. Endorsing the search for normative universals that would fit actual communicative success concedes the explanatory irrelevance of such a search, as well as the futility of supposing that there could be only one such thesis suited to, or ideally convergent or congruent with, all candidate generalities of the pertinent sort. If, in spite of being realists in the minimal sense provided, we cannot insure a uniquely correct scientific account of the world – in a sense, the point of convergence between Kuhn and Putnam – then we cannot insure a uniquely correct account of rationality either.[59] Realism and rationality are conceptually linked concepts; but their connection is fully compatible with, and, given current views of realism itself, rather economically and favorably served by, a modest or robust relativism. In particular (to fix our ideas by a single application), *if*, on some realist view – Einstein's, for instance[60] – the predictive and practical success of a science not only does not as such entail the truths of the effective theories invoked, or the reality of the entities they posit, but also does not enable us to decide uniquely what *the* methodology of science is (legitimating the actual success in question or confirming the truth of theories and the reality of theoretical entities), then, correspondingly, we cannot expect to draw on the theory of scientific method for a unique model of rationality. Divergent and incompatible theories of science (fitted to the success posited) are bound to be matched by divergent and incompatible models of rationality. Also, the *social* tolerance of individually divergent and incompatible convictions about rational method (roughly, Feyerabend's thesis) may even be favored on pragmatist or survivalist grounds.[61]

Notes

1   Steven Lukes, "Some Problems about Rationality," *Archives européennes de sociologie*, VIII (1967).

2   Barry Barnes and David Bloor, "Relativism, Rationalism and the Sociology of Knowledge," in Martin Hollis and Steven Lukes (eds), *Rationality and Relativism* (Cambridge, Mass.: MIT Press, 1982).

3   Cf. Introduction to Hollis and Lukes, *Rationality and Relativism*; and Steven Lukes, "Relativism: Cognitive and Moral," *Proceedings of the Aristotelian Society*, XLVII (1974). Lukes is somewhat drawn – ultimately opposed – to moral relativism: cf. pp. 171–2 and section iv.

4   Lukes, "Some Problems about Rationality," *Archives européennes de sociologie*, VIII, 260. This pretty much recapitulates "Relativism: Cognitive and Moral."

5   Peter Winch, "Understanding a Primitive Society," *American Philosophical Quarterly*, I (1964).

6   Ibid., pp. 260–2.

7   Alasdair MacIntyre, "A Mistake about Causality in Social Science," in P. Laslett and W. G. Runciman (eds), *Philosophy, Politics and Society*, 2nd ser. (Oxford: Basil Blackwell, 1962), p. 61. The reference is cited by Lukes and the thesis is opposed by Winch.

8   See for example Hilary Putnam, *Meaning and the Moral Sciences* (London: Routledge and Kegan Paul, 1978). Bas C. van Fraassen, *The Scientific Image* (Oxford: Clarendon Press, 1980); Nancy Cartwright, *How the Laws of Physics Lie* (Oxford: Clarendon Press, 1983); and Ian Hacking, *Representing and Intervening* (Cambridge: Cambridge University Press, 1982).

9   Donald Davidson, "On the Very Idea of a Conceptual Scheme," *Proceedings and Addresses of the American Philosophical Association*, XLVII (1973–4).

10   Donald Davidson, "Psychology as Philosophy" (Comments and Replies), *Essays on Actions and Events* (Oxford: Clarendon Press, 1980), p. 243.

11   See Max Black, "Linguistic Relativity: The Views of Benjamin Lee Whorf," *Models and Metaphors* (Ithaca, NY: Cornell University Press, 1962).

12   Davidson, "Psychology as Philosophy," *Essays on Actions and Events*, p. 243. Cf. Charles Taylor, "Rationality," in Hollis and Lukes, *Rationality and Relativism*.

13   For purposes of economy, we may take it that the principal analytic arguments against versions of foundationalism are summarized in Richard Rorty, *Philosophy and the Mirror of Nature* (Princeton, NJ: Princeton University Press, 1979). See also Nicholas Rescher, *The Coherence Theory of Truth*

(Oxford: Clarendon Press, 1973).

14 The point is not really featured by Davidson, who speaks rather more of testing rationality than of its conceptual connection with being a cognitively apt and critical agent: it is not enough to have beliefs, or beliefs that guide action, or beliefs that guide action successfully. See Donald Davidson, "Hempel on Explaining Action" and "Mental Events," in *Essays on Actions and Events*. The point is central, however, in Jaakko Hintikka, *Knowledge and Belief* (Ithaca, NY: Cornell University Press, 1962).

15 See Hilary Putnam, "Beyond Historicism," *Philosophical Papers*, vol. 3 (Cambridge: Cambridge University Press, 1983).

16 Barnes and Bloor, "Relativism, Rationalism and the Sociology of Knowledge," in Hollis and Lukes, *Rationality and Relativism*, pp. 27, 28.

17 Putnam, "Beyond Historicism," *Philosophical Papers*, vol. 3, pp. 291–2.

18 See W. V. Quine, *Word and Object* (Cambridge, Mass.: MIT Press, 1960), ch. 2. Certainly, one of the most celebrated remarks of the book is the following: "Occasion sentences and stimulus meaning are general coin; terms and reference are local to our conceptual scheme" (p. 53). See also Joseph Margolis, "Behaviorism and Alien Languages," *Philosophia*, III (1973).

19 See Putnam, *Philosophical Papers*, vol. 3.

20 Donald Davidson, "Reality without Reference," in Mark Platts (ed.), *Reference, Truth and Reality* (London: Routledge and Kegan Paul, 1980) pp. 133, 131.

21 Ibid., pp. 131, 133.

22 Putnam, "Beyond Historicism," *Philosophical Papers*, vol. 3, pp. 295–6.

23 Putnam, "Reference and Truth," ibid., p. 71.

24 Ibid., pp. 82–3. Michael Dummett's William James Lectures, which apparently develop these issues, have yet to be published. See also Dummett's "What is a Theory of Meaning? (II)," in Gareth Evans and John McDowell (eds), *Truth and Meaning* (Oxford: Clarendon Press, 1976), p. 74.

25 Putnam, "Reference and Truth," *Philosophical Papers*, vol. 3, pp. 84–6. See also Putnam's *Reason, Truth and History* (Cambridge: Cambridge University Press, 1981), ch. 3.

26 Putnam: "Realism and Reason," *Meaning and the Moral Sciences*; "Two Philosophical Perspectives," *Reason, Truth and History*; "Why there isn't a Ready-made World," *Philosophical Papers*, vol. 3.

27 See Pierre Duhem, *The Aims and Structure of Physical Theory*, tr. Philip Wiener (Princeton, NJ: Princeton University Press, 1954), ch. 6; W. V. Quine, "Two Dogmas of Empiricism," *From a Logical Point of View* (Cambridge, Mass.: Harvard University Press, 1953). There is a useful compendium of the principal views about the so-called Duhem–Quine thesis in Sandra G. Harding (ed.), *Can Theories be Refuted?* (Dordrecht: D. Reidel, 1976).

28 Putnam, "Two Philosophical Perspectives," *Reason, Truth and History*, pp. 49–50.

29 Putnam, "Two Conceptions of Rationality," ibid., p. 123.

30   Ibid., pp. 113–19.
31   Putnam, "Two Philosophical Perspectives," ibid., p. 52. Cf. also Putnam's "Models and Reality," *Philosophical Papers*, vol. 3.
32   Cf. W. V. Quine, "Ontological Relativity," *Ontological Relativity and Other Essays* (New York: Columbia University Press, 1969).
33   See Putnam, *Reason, Truth and History*, ch. 2 and Appendix.
34   Ibid., p. 35.
35   See Donald Davidson, "Reality without Reference," *Inquiries into Truth and Interpretation* (Oxford: Clarendon Press, 1984).
36   The question about metaphysical realism is complicated in a further regard by certain pertinent remarks of Michael Dummett's. See his "What is a Theory of Meaning?" in Samuel Guttenplan (ed.), *Mind and Language* (Oxford: Clarendon Press, 1975); and "What is a Theory of Meaning? (II)," in Evans and McDowell, *Truth and Meaning*.
37   Cf. Steven Lukes, *Power: A Radical View* (London: Macmillan, 1974), ch. 4.
38   Jürgen Habermas, *Communication and the Evolution of Society*, tr. Thomas McCarthy (Boston, Mass.: Beacon Press, 1979); Karl-Otto Apel, *Toward a Transformation of Philosophy*, tr. Glyn Adey and David Frisby (London: Routledge and Kegan Paul, 1980). Thus seen, John Searle's insistence on the necessary and sufficient conditions of speech acts is, apart from its departure from John Austin's original orientation, a pale version of Habermas's argument, in spite of the fact that Habermas obviously relies on the prior validity of Searle's and similar accounts. Cf. John R. Searle, *Speech Acts* (Cambridge: Cambridge University Press, 1969).
39   Carl G. Hempel, "Rational Action," *Proceedings and Addresses of the American Philosophical Association*, XXXV (1962).
40   See Joseph Margolis: *Philosophy of Psychology* (Englewood Cliffs, NJ: Prentice-Hall, 1984); *Culture and Cultural Entities* (Dordrecht: D. Reidel, 1983); *Persons and Minds* (Dordrecht: D. Reidel, 1978).
41   Donald Davidson, "Hempel on Explaining Action," *Essays on Actions and Events*, p. 266.
42   Ibid., p. 262 (italics added). Cf. Davidson's "Mental Events," also in *Essays on Actions and Events*; and Joseph Margolis, "Prospects for an Extensionalist Psychology of Action," *Journal for the Theory of Social Behavior*, II (1981).
43   The full adequacy of their particular views is not at stake.
44   See for instance Thomas S. Kuhn, "Second Thoughts on Paradigms," *The Essential Tension* (Chicago: University of Chicago Press, 1977); Ernan McMullin, "Values in Science," *Proceedings of the Philosophy of Science Association*, vol. 2, ed. P. D. Asquith and T. Nickles (1983) – I have seen this essay only in manuscript; W. H. Newton-Smith, *The Rationality of Science* (London: Routledge and Kegan Paul, 1981); Kurt Hübner, *Critique of Scientific Reason*, tr. Paul R. Dixon Jr and Hollis M. Dixon (Chicago: University of Chicago Press, 1983). How remarkably scanty our clues here

are may be judged from these discussions.

45 Mario Bunge, "Toward a Philosophy of Technology," in Carl Mitcham and Robert Mackey (eds), *Philosophy and Technology* (New York: Free Press, 1983). Cf. Joseph Margolis, "Three Conceptions of Technology: Satanic, Titanic, Human," in Carl Mitcham (ed.), *Philosophy and Technology*, vol. 7 (Greenwich, Conn.: JAI Press, 1984). Of course, it is Imre Lakatos who is the principal (failed) advocate of a discovery of a model of rationality drawn from the historically shifting forms of scientific inquiry but not prejudicially linked to merely favoring any particular contingency of such inquiry. Cf. Paul Feyerabend, *Against Method* (London: New Left Books, 1975), ch. 17.

46 See Margolis, "Animal and Human Minds," *Culture and Cultural Entities*.

47 Barnes and Bloor, "Relativism, Rationalism and the Sociology of Knowledge," in Hollis and Lukes, *Rationality and Relativism*, p. 35. Cf. also Martin Hollis, "The Social Destruction of Reality," in the same collection.

48 Barnes and Bloor, "Relativism, Rationalism and the Sociology of Knowledge," ibid., p. 34.

49 Ibid., pp. 22–3.

50 Cf. Hollis, "The Social Destruction of Reality," in Hollis and Lukes, *Rationality and Relativism*.

51 Barnes and Bloor, "Relativism, Rationalism and the Sociology of Knowledge," ibid., p. 41.

52 Ibid., p. 23.

53 A discussion quite sympathetic with the view here pressed may be found in Russell Keat and John Urry, *Social Theory as Science* (London: Routledge and Kegan Paul, 1975), pp. 204–12.

54 *Collected Papers of Charles Sanders Peirce*, 8 vols, ed. Charles Hartshorne, Paul Weiss, and Arthur W. Burks (Cambridge, Mass.: Harvard University Press, 1931–58), vol. 5, p. 47.

55 Ibid., p. 603.

56 Ibid., vol. 6, p. 10. Cf. Michael Polanyi, *Personal Knowledge*, corrected edn (Chicago: University of Chicago Press, 1962).

57 I have tried to explore such minima in *Negativities: The Limits of Life* (Columbus: Charles Merrill, 1975). For a recent sample of action-guiding conceptions of rationality, largely focused in individualistic terms, see Richard B. Brandt (ed.), "Rational Actions," special double issue of *Social Theory and Practice*, IX (1983).

58 Karl-Otto Apel, *Charles S. Peirce: From Pragmatism to Pragmaticism*, tr. John Michael Krois (Amherst: University of Massachusetts Press, 1981). (The expression "logical socialism," John Krois tells me, Apel believes he coined. But Max Fisch confirms that the thesis is clearly Peirce's.)

59 For a compendious account of the current state of rationality theory, see Jon Elster, "Rationality," in Guttorm Fløistad (ed.), *Contemporary Philosophy* vol. 2: *Philosophy of Science* (The Hague: Martinus Nijhoff, 1982). Elster may well equivocate on "rationality" – as a theory of action within which "rational" and "irrational" behavior may be sorted, or as a

theory of the normatively preferable alternative itself (cf. p. 120). For he appears to favor the thesis "that intentionality does not presuppose rationality," which suits neither option. Cf. also Charles Taylor, "Interpretation and the Sciences of Man," in Paul Rabinow and William M. Sullivan (eds), *Interpretive Social Science: A Reader* (Berkeley, Calif.: University of California Press, 1979).

60 See for example Arthur Fine, "Einstein's Motivational Realism," in James T. Cushing et al. (eds), *Science and Reality: Recent Work in the Philosophy of Science* (Notre Dame, Ind.: University of Notre Dame Press, 1964).

61 See for instance Husain Sarkar, *A Theory of Method* (Berkeley, Calif.: University of California Press, 1983); and Howard Margolis, *Selfishness, Altruism, and Rationality* (Chicago: University of Chicago Press, 1982). Cf. also, McMullin, "Values in Science," in *Proceedings of the Philosophy of Science Association*, vol. 2.

5

Realism and Relativism

I

There is an elementary objection to the so-called redundancy theory of truth (associated with the name of F. P. Ramsey[1]) that is very nearly completely neglected and that has really nothing to do with deeper worries (so-called realist worries) about insuring a sufficiently robust relationship between competent human inquiry and a cognitively accessible world – for instance, along the lines pressed so famously by J. L. Austin.[2] It is, however, an objection that directly bears on the viability of relativism. The reason the expression "is true" is not, contrary to what Ramsey claimed, "an obviously superfluous addition" to a particular proposition asserted[3] is simply that *it need not be the case* that, *if* they take truth values or truth-like values at all, all propositions asserted take the bipolar values "true" and "false." After all, it is not incoherent to maintain that propositions in a given sector of inquiry may be ascribed only relativistic values. Hence, *if*, say, we conceded that, for reasons bearing on the properties of a given sector, particular claims could only be plausible and never simply true (so that claims that on a model of bipolar truth values would be incompatible would now be jointly plausible), it would clearly be false to hold that "*p* is true" is, as such, a redundant form of "*p*". A similar but more heterodox consideration – debatable along entirely different lines and motivated for altogether different reasons – affects the question of reference to fictional entities: if it were thought that one could refer to Sherlock Holmes, that Holmes could never have existed, and that in referring to Holmes a speaker could still coherently acknowledge Holmes's nonexistence, then, correspondingly, it would not, in purporting to make reference in one's assertion, be redundantly entailed that one intended to refer to what exists.[4]

There can be no doubt that a certain "standard" view of discourse holds to something very much like the redundancy theory of truth (with whatever further caveats might be thought advisable: for instance, regarding proposition-like formulations that take no truth values at all, though they appear to, and are normally taken to, as Ramsey himself tried to show in analyzing general propositions); and there can be no doubt that the "standard" view insists on something very much like the so-called Axiom of Existence.[5] But, if it is an open question *what are* our cognitive powers with respect to the actual world and *what are* our communicative interests, then it may be premature to disallow an objection to the redundancy theory – or, for that matter, to the Axiom of Existence – if there are no insurmountable difficulties of a purely formal sort regarding internal consistency and coherence. It would be premature or biased if its only vice were that, though coherent, it went counter to the larger intent of the redundancy thesis itself. (A similar defense could of course be mounted for the bare eligibility of resisting an exclusively extensional treatment of reference.)

The fact is that, once we deny all forms of the cognitive transparency of the world, once we concede that we cannot legitimately require more rigor of our inquiries than what we suppose particular domains inquired into can support, once we are alerted to currently unresolved puzzles pertinent to the very issue at stake (for instance, regarding the truth of theories in science, the existence of theoretical entities, the status of scientific laws; or regarding the ineliminability of relatively equipotent but opposed ontological parsings of given bodies of putatively factual data; or regarding the ineliminability of relatively equipotent but opposed interpretations of human history, art, linguistic communication, or behavior), then we cannot rightly disallow the objection to the redundancy theory. Our assessment of the point of such resistance goes hand in hand with whatever progress we can claim regarding such questions.

The conceptual connection between such seemingly formal matters as those of the redundancy theory of truth and the Axiom of Existence and such substantive matters as that of the validity of competing forms of realism is so natural that heterodox views about the former are bound to color otherwise seemingly standard disputes about the latter. For example, a retreat from the redundancy theory along the lines suggested may (wrongly) be taken to entail an endorsement of skepticism – hence, a rejection of realism; or, a retreat from the Axiom of Existence may (correctly) be seen to neutralize (as far as reference alone is concerned) the realist import of postulating unobservable theoretical entities. A so-called anti-realist, then, with respect to such unobservables could be said, on the weakened view of reference, to have drawn a premature conclusion about the ontological status of such entities – a matter entirely distinct from that of the force of realist presumptions regarding the causal, explanatory, or perceptual role of real entities.[6] The point is that the very perception of what counts as a realist or anti-realist thesis may be decidedly colored by formal considerations not usually drawn into standard disputes; *and* that some such considerations are actually favored by systematic forms of relativism – which nevertheless mean to support a robust form of realism.

Relativism is an empirically motivated thesis to the effect that, in particular sectors of inquiry, it is methodologically advisable to retreat from insisting on a strong bipolar model of truth and falsity, while not denying that the affected propositions or claims *are* genuinely such and, as such, are to be ascribed suitable truth-like values – just such, in fact, that on the bipolar model (but no longer) would yield and confirm incompatibles. In the spirit of the foregoing remarks, relativism is not only not opposed to realism, but its advocates are positively committed to realism every bit as pertinaciously as are the partisans of what – in a deliberately shadowy manner – I have called the "standard" view. The trouble of course rests with what may be meant by speaking of *realism*.

About realism, it needs to be said at once that there are extraordinarily few theorists who deny that, *in some sense*, they are realists about science and rational inquiry. Naturally, they will dispute what that entails; and the nature and direction of contemporary disputes about realism in science suggest that there may even be some contingent benefit to be had from retiring the term from active debate; it may have become by now hardly more than an advertising slogan. (Of course, to suggest the benefit is not to retire the term at all.) In any case, realism is, minimally, the generic thesis that the world is so ordered that human inquiry is effectively "linked" to its structures, so that human behavior is cognitively informed by that "linkage"; and that human inquiry is so ordered that some suitable portion of its normal processes and products (generating states of belief and generating propositions or claims) are so "linked" to the world's structures as to yield cognitively informed behavior. *What* the linkage is and *what* its scope is are of course the principal foci of contention *among realists*. Realism, then, is a theory that (at least initially) refuses to disjoin so-called ontological and epistemological questions. The denial of realism entails disjoining the two to the extent at least that either the world is rendered cognitively inaccessible or inquiry is cognitively stalemated or defeated.

The principal opponents of realism are the skeptics. Peter Klein has identified three principal (not necessarily separate) forms of skepticism (which he then undertakes to refute):

1   Direct Skepticism, which holds that "It is not the case that S can know that p"
2   Iterative Skepticism, which holds that "It is not the case that S can know that S can know that p"; and
3   Pyrrhonian Direct Skepticism, which holds that "There are no better reasons for believing that S can know that p than there are for not believing that it is not the case that S can know that p."[7]

With these distinctions in mind, it becomes problematic, frankly, whether or why what are often termed relativistic theories (the reason for the caution will be clear in a moment) should be said to be either anti-realist or skeptical. For example, Richard Bernstein offers the following clarificatory remark:

> As I have characterized the relativist, his or her essential claim is that there can be no higher appeal than to a given conceptual scheme, language game, set of social practices, or historical epoch. There is a nonreducible plurality of such schemes, paradigms, and practices; there is no substantive overarching framework in which radically different and alternative schemes are commensurable – no universal standards that somehow stand outside of and above these competing alternatives.[8]

In context, it is clear that Bernstein believes that *any* sustained opposition to the incommensurability thesis (as presented), whether apodictic (as with Husserl) or nonabsolutist (as in his own view), is at once a repudiation of skepticism – a fortiori, a repudiation of relativism and (one supposes) a defense of a sanguine form of realism. We can only conjecture here regarding Bernstein's views, since, on close inspection, it turns out that he does not actually speak of realism. But the fact that he links "relativism, skepticism, historicism, and nihilism" together, essentially without distinction, and (apparently) without needing such distinctions at this point,[9] without any caveats about mutual entailments, strongly suggests that skepticism and relativism are (for Bernstein) pretty well the same doctrine[10] – hence suggests that relativism is opposed to even the most minimal realism. A very characteristic and telltale mark of the "realist" is his insistence on "objectivity" in human inquiry – although (very plainly) what is substantively meant by the term cannot fail to be affected by puzzling over the redundancy theory in the way already suggested. It is certainly very difficult to disengage altogether the notion of the "objective" from the presumption (however attenuated) of the old correspondence theory of truth.[11] But, if correspondence fails in any epistemic sense, and if "objectivity" in inquiry is to be affirmed, then we do need a fuller account of realism and of relativism to redeem the notion. We have of course already taken note of the inconclusiveness of Bernstein's attack on relativism. But now we need to consider the issue from the side of realism as well – for instance, with regard to the relationship between skepticism or the incommensurability theory and realism. And here it will pay to bear in mind the often unobserved bias (and the import of the bias) of what we have termed the redundancy theory of truth. We have, it should be remembered, emphasized that the formal advocacy of a bipolar model of truth values and the advocacy of objectivism (in the sense already given) are quite independent matters.

To be sure, the firmest specimens of the incommensurability thesis are to be found in well-known statements made by Paul Feyerabend and Thomas Kuhn.[12] Nevertheless, it would be very difficult to deny that Feyerabend and Kuhn *are* realists (of some sort) in accord with the minimal notion here developed. Thus, for instance, precisely where he advocates favoring "hypotheses inconsistent with *observations, facts, and experimental results*," Feyerabend supports the proposal by remarking that "there is not a single interesting theory that agrees with all the known facts in its domain."[13] Neither Feyerabend nor Kuhn directly addresses the issue of (minimal) realism, and there is nothing in what they say that would incline any reader to suppose that they were skeptics in any of the senses mentioned. Feyerabend actually opposes "epistemological anarchism" to skepticism.[14] In his more strident moments, it is true that he can be found to say,

> Briefly, but not incorrectly: *today science prevails not because of its comparative merits, but because the show has been rigged in its favor.* ... The lesson to be learned [he insists] is that *non-scientific ideologies, practices, theories, traditions can become powerful rivals and can reveal major shortcomings of science if only they are given a fair chance to compete.* It is the task of the institutions of a free society to give them such a fair chance. The excellence of science, however, can be asserted only *after* numerous comparisons with alternative points of view.[15]

But that is not to oppose realism, in the skeptic's sense: it is to endorse realism.

Let us construe realism, then, as, minimally, the rejection of skepticism. No interesting version of realism in science could possibly be confined to that least denominator: certainly, nothing regarding the reality of unobservable entities or the truth of theories. Also, incommensurability itself may (but need not) be construed skeptically. There is a perfectly eligible sense in which Kuhn, for instance, does *not* intend the incommensurability of evolving scientific problems and standards to constitute a defense of skepticism in science – even in the absence of a neutral language, a *tertium quid*, in terms of which to overcome such incommensurability without remainder. The overlapping of problems, standards, procedures, observations, practices, and the like insures, Kuhn believes, a basis for making the work of one group of incommensurabilists intelligible to the members of another, without the support (impossible anyway) of an omnicompetent third language.[16] Furthermore, this thesis of incommensurability Kuhn takes to be compatible with progress in science – which insures Kuhn's minimal realism; and it constitutes a form of relativism without skepticism – which insures the nonequivalence of the incommensurability thesis and skepticism and the nonequivalence of relativism and skepticism. As Gerald Doppelt very neatly maintains, "Kuhnian incommensurability [is] compatible with a considerable overlap between the language, problems, data and standards of rival paradigms; certainly sufficient overlap to account for the shared context of rational debate which Kuhn as well as his critics find to be a pervasive feature of scientific development"; and "the balance of reasons or the demands of scientific rationality never unequivocally favor one paradigm (either the old or the new) over its rival."[17]

It is of course true that, in the Postscript to the second edition of *The Structure of Scientific Revolutions*, Kuhn himself both denies that he is a relativist with regard to scientific progress (since he affirms, "I am a convinced believer in scientific progress" – "later scientific theories are better than earlier ones for solving puzzles in the often quite different environments to which they are applied") *and* declares that there *are* criteria of "accuracy of prediction, particularly of quantitative prediction; the balance between esoteric and everyday subject matter; and the number of different problems solved. ... [Also, there are criteria of] simplicity, scope, and compatibility with other specialities [and others, so that] scientific development is, like biological, a unidirectional and irreversible process."[18] But Kuhn clearly does not show *how his* version of incommensurability and the absence of a neutral third language *can* legitimate both the "unidirectionality" of progress and the fixity or verisimilitudinal aspects of scientific rationality, once we deny (with him) "that successive theories grow ever closer to, or approximate more and more closely to, the truth."[19]

The fact is that Kuhn toys with the relativist ascription;[20] but he is unable to legitimate, at every stage of the confrontation of competing paradigms, the possibility of a minimal realism, of a measure of "objectivity" and rationality, *in which* claims logically more powerful than what we have been calling relativistic claims (claims that on a bipolar model would be incompatible but, retreating from that model, now are not) obtain. Once the incommensurability thesis is reconciled (as it obviously can be) with realism, once we deny that "there is (or must be) a single universal framework of commensuration,"[21] it becomes quite impossible to refuse to countenance a robust relativism of the sort here briefly sketched. Kuhn himself may have been troubled by the firm relativism of his own commitment – and he seems, as by the projection of somewhat transparadigmatic criteria of progress, to have tried to escape its clutches; but, at the very least, there is a yawning conceptual chasm between the admission of (nonskeptical) incommensurability and the affirmation of an objectivity that precludes relativism within the central tradition of the philosophy of science. Nevertheless, to admit the eligibility of relativism is a far cry from concluding, with the Edinburgh and Bath sociologists, that the failure of Kuhn's more conservative efforts and the failure of the rejection of the incommensurability thesis leave intact the position of the sociology of scientific knowledge, that – since "paradigms 'transform the world' so that scientists belonging to different paradigm communities can be seen as 'responding to different worlds' and will inevitably talk through each another" – "there is nothing within [the anti-relativist movement] to stop the sociologist assuming, say, all scientific knowledge to be relative [relativistic] and proceeding accordingly."[22] If the sociology intended is simply a skepticism, as may well be the case,[23] then it hardly fits the central tradition of science; and, if it is meant to accommodate the central tradition itself, then it will have to exceed the recent reading of the sociology of knowledge (in the direction of epistemology, which cannot fail to be normative) and it will have to turn to an assessment of the relationship between bipolar truth values and relativistic values *within the epistemic space of minimal realism.*

Minimal realism, then, is a theory about the human condition, formulated in the sparest way so as to offset skepticism but not so as to insure any of the determinate would-be truths of any favored first-order science or inquiry. In contemporary philosophy of science, it is the fortune or fate of Kuhn's incommensurability thesis to have been marked as the emblem of a gathering consensus about the negative constraints on any hereafter promising realism; for the acceptance of Kuhn's general thesis (despite its fuzziness and the fuzziness of its trailing literature) *does* contribute much to our picture of a viable realism. In particular, the defeasibility of any candidate theory is now expected to be tested in terms of at least the following considerations;

1   denial of the cognitive transparency of nature – hence of universalism, essentialism, and related doctrines;
2   construal of science as the work and achievement of historical communities;
3   acknowledgement of incommensurability within the diachronic movement of science;
4   rejection of skepticism;
5   rejection of objectivism – that is, of any formulable universal framework of commensuration;
6   disqualification of any fallibilist or linear theory of scientific progress or linear theory of verisimilitude;
7   adherence to holism – that is, legitimation without reference to general cognitive privilege or to privileged first-order truths.

These form a somewhat overlapping set of constraints, and they apply directly only to what we are here calling minimal realism. Our claim is that, given the current state of philosophical reflection, any comprehensive realism would accommodate minimal realism, and no comprehensive realism would remain content with minimal realism itself. Furthermore, the conditions enumerated are distinctly due to second-order reflections and are, accordingly, open, on changing second-order grounds, to challenge, alteration, refinement, addition, *and* relativistic elaboration. Put another way, whatever universal scope these constraints may be supposed to enjoy must be compatible with the inherent limitations of minimal realism itself – that is, without pretending to be confirmed by any first-order evidence: they are in this sense strongly rhetorical and noncognitivist in nature, but not for that reason without rigor. We may say, tendentiously once again, that these gathering themes (1–7) begin to collect what we shall mean by advocating pragmatism.

II

By and large, in the sense in which minimal realism is a theory of the human condition *vis-à-vis* cognition in general, something like Peircean pragmatism (shorn of Peirce's doctrine of the long run) and something like a Heideggerean phenomenology of *Dasein* (shorn of Heidegger's developing views of the privilege of poetry – apotheosized in Hölderlin) are reasonably fair alternative (and converging) accounts of what the rejection of skepticism minimally requires.[24] (This may strike one as a wild leap, but it is not.) The potential compatibility and comparability of pragmatic and phenomenological formulas at this strategic juncture suggests in an important way fuller prospects for reconciling Anglo-

American and Continental European versions of realism. Certainly, without deliberate intention, Kuhn's incommensurability thesis is congruent with both lines of speculation.

But, beyond this initial step, what we must appreciate is that there are an enormous number of developed objections to realism *that are not really opposed to minimal realism at all*. The absence of a rough typology of realism has misled a great many. What we may anticipate is that, assuming minimal realism to be consensually favored at the present time, more complex and more pointed forms of realism are bound to be more controversial. Hence, not only are second-order speculations about realist *minima* inescapably relativistic (on pain of contradiction) but the assessment of detailed claims of a more specialized and more advanced sort – for instance, regarding the existence of theoretical entities, the relationship between theory and observation, the status of scientific laws, the nature of causality, the conditions of scientific rationality, the import of predictive and technological success, the function of explanation, the unity of the natural and human sciences, the persistence of intentional and intensional complexities, the confirmation of truth, the tolerance of incompatible accounts of the actual world or of plural actual worlds, and the like – are bound to diverge, even more strikingly, along relativistic lines.

The lesson is easily illustrated; for, by way of the most superficial paradox, there are no avowed anti-realists that are not also realists. Consider Michael Dummett's views, for instance, which afford some of the most sustained "anti-realist" criticisms that have so far been developed – of what may be called the formal epistemology of realism. That Dummett is a realist is explicit in the following important statement:

> Baffled by the attempt to describe in general the relation between language and reality, we have nowadays abandoned the correspondence theory of truth, and justify our doing so on the score that it was an attempt to state a *criterion* of truth in the sense in which this cannot be done. Nevertheless, the correspondence theory expresses one important feature of the concept of truth which is not expressed by the law 'It is true that *p* if and only if *p*' and which we have so far left quite out of account: that a statement is true only if there is something in the world *in virtue of which* it is true. Although we no longer accept correspondence theory, we remain realists *au fond*; we retain in our thinking a fundamentally realist conception of truth. Realism consists in the belief that for any statement there must be something in virtue of which either it or its negation is true: it is only on the basis of this belief that we

can justify the idea that truth and falsity play an essential role in the notion of the meaning of a statement, that the general form of an explanation of meaning is a statement of the truth-conditions.[25]

Dummett explains the sense in which he is an anti-realist opponent of realism (while remaining a realist) in the following way: "the anti-realist interprets 'capable of being known' to mean 'capable of being known *by us*,' whereas the realist interprets it to mean 'capable of being known by some hypothetical being whose intellectual capacities and powers of observation may exceed our own.'" The anti-realist claims, for realist reasons, that the "realist's" conception (in question) "is quite spurious." So the *anti-realist* position holds "that a *realist* interpretation is possible only for those statements which are in principle effectively decidable (i.e. those for which there is no serious issue between the realist and anti-realist)."[26] The sense in which Dummett is a realist is the sense in which he is at least a minimal realist – that is, opposes skepticism. But Dummett does not discuss skepticism *and* he does not discuss (Kuhnian) incommensurability. The sense in which he is an anti-realist is the sense in which he is (to a considerable extent, though not utterly) an opponent of the "realist" he himself identifies – of what, more recently, has come to be called (in Hilary Putnam's idiom) a "metaphysical realist."[27] But both Dummett and Putnam have in effect conceded that they cannot satisfactorily formulate the full conditions for "effective decidability"; and the diachronic nature of scientific practices and the implications of incommensurability raise serious questions about the reasonableness of an extreme and uncompromising anti-realism (of Dummett's sort).

There is, however, a further concession that may be drawn or wrung from Dummett, one that returns us to the issue posed by Ramsey. It is linked to an adjustment in the view Dummett first favored in his influential paper "Realism" and which he believes he has now corrected: "to give up the principle of bivalence," he says, "does not mean going back on the principle of *tertium non datur*, the principle that, for no statement, can we ever rule out both the possibility of its being true and that of its being false, in other words, the principle that there can be no circumstances in which a statement can be recognized as being, irrevocably, neither true nor false."[28] The term "irrevocably" signifies, for Dummett, an adherence to a strong form of realism in which the *semantic* principle of *tertium non datur* is supported at the same time that "effective decidability" (with all its inherent difficulties) is also supported. It is in fact in terms of the decidability issue that Dummett himself argues that "the redundancy theory [associated with Ramsey and Wittgenstein] must be false"; for,

If we do not yet understand the object-language, we shall have no idea of the point of introducing the predicate "true," as applied to its sentences, in accordance with the truth-definition [the Tarskian truth-definition]; the truth-definition, which lays down the conditions under which an arbitrary sentence of the object-language is true, cannot simultaneously provide us with a grasp of the meaning of each such sentence, unless, indeed, we already know in advance what the point of the predicate so defined is supposed to be.[29]

But, either because at least Kuhnian incommensurability obtains in the history of science, or because, if the decidability issue is as substantive as Dummett (rightly) insists it is, the issue of what *epistemic* and *ontological* constraints operate in different sectors of inquiry to affect the logical force of what can be decided must be equally substantive, the principle of *tertium non datur* must itself, in given sectors of inquiry, be open to challenge along relativistic lines. There is no reason why the question should be closed; and, in admitting it, we should concede as well that an answer either way – for or against the principle, in cognitive contexts taken distributively – is rightly interpreted as articulating a form of realism. So seen, the term "irrevocably" could be resisted, on historicist and relativistic grounds, while at the same time challenging *tertium non datur*.

The point can also be made by considering the different and distinct ways in which Dummett uses the term "realist": first (pejoratively), to signify those who subscribe to a correspondence *criterion* of truth or, alternatively, those who interpret "capable of being known" to mean "capable of being known by some hypothetical being whose intellectual capacities and powers of observation may exceed our own"; second (favorably), to signify those who construe realist claims in terms of human decidability (so-called anti-realists); and, third (also favorably), to signify those who maintain that "for any statement there must be something in virtue of which either it or its negation is true" (*tertium non datur*). Now, the third sense is neither tantamount to, nor entailed by, the second; furthermore, to insist on the necessity of adhering to the third is, in context, either arbitrary or undefended – in either case, vulnerable to an "anti-realist" objection of Dummett's own sort. Why should we not, therefore, charge Dummett with a knowledge that titans more knowledgeable than himself have: to the effect that *tertium non datur* always obtains? There seems to be no satisfactory rejoinder.

It is argued in addition by another (quite different sort of) anti-realist, Bas van Fraassen, that Dummett's view of realism "is quite idiosyncratic," since it treats realism as "relating, not to a class of entities or a class of terms, but to a class of *statements*." Van Fraassen says, in opposition, "I do not conceive the dispute [as, say, regarding scientific realism] as being about language at all."[30] Furthermore, Dummett's thesis (on his own reading) leads him, troublesomely, to construe nominalists – those anti-realists "who denied the existence of universals and the referential character of general terms"[31] – as realists (of the sort he was opposing): in effect, therefore, Dummett concedes restrictions on his own usage.

Now, these issues are remarkably complex and far-reaching, and deserve a moment of additional reflection. Realism, in the minimal sense, *is* a doctrine nearly no one opposes – certainly not Dummett any more than van Fraassen. *That* form of realism has nothing whatsoever to do with "statements" (in van Fraassen's derogatory sense, in the sense pressed, perhaps most doggedly, by Michael Devitt[32]); hence, also, it has nothing whatsoever to do with the theory of truth. Nevertheless, as soon as one goes beyond minimal realism (which, as remarked, is too slim a thesis to be of any interest on its own) – as soon, for instance, as one abandons foundationalism and all forms of cognitive transparency – one must reconcile realism with idealism (roughly, in the Kantian spirit, though without necessarily adhering to anything like Kant's sanguine analysis of what the structure of the mind is alleged to contribute to the objectivity of the sciences). And, as soon as that is conceded, then, contrary to van Fraassen and Devitt (and all those critics of Dummett who have failed to distinguish Dummett's anti-realism from positivism), the question of realism – in particular, the question of scientific realism – cannot fail to acknowledge that the theory of truth is *constitutive* of any viable realism.

This is certainly part of Dummett's reason for opposing the redundancy theory of truth (sometimes also called the "eliminative" or "disquotational" theory of truth). *In* the sense in which "*Realism says nothing semantic at all*," "does not strictly entail any doctrine of truth at all,"[33] it is quite true that the minimal realist acknowledges that there must be a great many facts about the world he believes without confirmation and even without a clear sense of the conditions of "warranted assertibility" or the like – also, that the world must be determinately structured in ways he may never fathom or even suspect; but that is a concession Dummett himself makes, and presses as serving the correspondence theory against the redundancy theory of truth.

What this shows (against his critics) is the genuine *relevance* of Dummett's form of anti-realism in examining or disputing the viability of any full-blooded realism. It does *not* show that Dummett's thesis is actually the right one (which, granting the force of the episode involving Michelson's measurement of light, it cannot possibly be). If, however, epistemic considerations are constitutive of a ramified realism (as opposed to minimal realism) – that is, a realism fitted to our science and, therefore, to whatever constitutive constraints bear on the objectivity of our science   then one cannot plausibly disjoin theorizing about the nature of truth, reference, meaning, or method from what is essential to theorizing about realism itself; and one cannot eliminate truth, reference, meaning, or method (along the lines suggested[34]), regardless of how we finally manage to equilibrate the requirements of realism and theories of these more semantic and anthropocentric sorts. Furthermore, in pursuing these issues, we are hardly obliged to hold that "meanings" must be formulable in terms of truth conditions or the like.

Dummett's anti-realism, then, raises a pertinent question about a constitutive linkage between truth and realism. This is why it is perfectly reasonable for Dummett to sort (with regard to realism) the bearing of different "*semantic*" principles, bivalence and *tertium non datur* (that is, respectively, "every statement is either true or false" and "no statement is neither true nor false").[35] Here, Dummett wishes to press several distinct claims: first, that the redundancy thesis (to which in a sense Tarski subscribes) must be false, if in order to introduce the predicate "true" for the distributed sentences of an object language we must already understand the meaning of those sentences – otherwise we could not understand the point of applying the "Tarskian truth-definition framed in a metalanguage" to any of those sentences[36] second, that "if the principle of *tertium non datur* is violated, more specifically, if we allow that there are sentences that are neither true nor false, then the equivalence thesis could not hold [namely, the thesis that, for any sentence A, A is equivalent to 'It is true that A', or to ⌜S is true⌝, where S is a ('structural–descriptive') name of A]."[37]

Tarski of course is the author of what may well be the most memorable version of the equivalence thesis. Dummett obviously means to reconcile his own anti-realism with (at least) Tarski's conception, provided that (1) we reject the redundancy reading of "true," and (2) we distinguish carefully between Tarski's abstract "truth-definition" fitted to any "arbitrary sentence" and his "structural–descriptive" account of any such sentence relative to which "true" is actually applicable to it.

It is, then, in accommodating (1) and (2) that one may well hold, with Dummett, that *tertium non datur* cannot be modified or replaced; or, with others, that the law of excluded middle cannot be given up. In fact, it has been argued that "If LEM [the law of excluded middle, '$p \vee \neg p$'] is a theorem of a system, and if Tarski's (T) schema holds for that system

['(A)' is true iff A: the equivalence thesis], PB [the principle of bivalence, 'every wff of the system is either true or false'] must also hold."[38] But two countermeasures suggest themselves: either there is no pertinent sense in which Tarski's formal truth definition *can* be admitted independently of his theory about structural–descriptive conditions for applying it to the particular sentences of an object language – except at the price of utter vacuity; or else, granting the division, if the alleged "neutrality" of the truth definition is said to insure that *tertium non datur* holds and must hold for all particular sentences, it must do so only in so far as the neutrality of the truth definition is preserved – which is to say, *not* invoking, without further supporting evidence regarding the propriety of doing so, the "structural-descriptive" conditions for applying the truth definition *distributively*.

Tarski himself was not sanguine about satisfactorily construing natural languages thus; alternatively, if the "equivalence thesis" (or Tarski's so-called "adequacy condition") requires the indissolubility of these two ingredients (the truth definition and the structural–descriptive conditions), then "violating" *tertium non datur is not at all tantamount to violating a philosophically neutral thesis*. Relativism, as in effect has been argued, requires (in a sense that distinguishes relativistic values from mere indeterminacy) the violation of *tertium non datur*. But the essential issue is that one cannot convincingly maintain that those structural constraints *we* rightly impose on semantically or epistemically interpreted formulas (actual sentences) *are*, at that very level of actually interpreting or representing the real world, bound to be straightforwardly derivable from whatever is alleged to be metaphysically neutral. Dummett cannot, then, consistently identify the difference between Tarski's truth definition and Tarski's structural-descriptive conditions and still hold *tertium non datur* to be metaphysically neutral; or, subscribing to his own strong version of anti-realism, he cannot consistently deny that insisting on *tertium non datur* is itself, in some pertinent sense, subject to anti-realist challenges of its own. In a word, the defense of relativism with regard to realist issues is *not* the advocacy of indeterminacy of truth-value gaps (Frege's concern): it is intended as an accommodation of what we may (on broadly empirical grounds) take to be the truth-like values that are epistemically supportable in particular sectors of inquiry.

This marks the sense in which Dummett flirts with a (metaphysical) realism he is at pains to oppose. This is also the sense – the very interesting sense – in which Davidson's extensionalism cannot fail to be vulnerable to anti-realist challenges based on a close reading of Tarski's own adequacy condition. The irony remains that, *in* accord with Tarski's structural-descriptive program, and independently of Tarski's or David-son's convictions about the properties of natural languages or of the normal inquiries of science (in particular, the human sciences), *whether* this domain or that lends itself to the full application of Tarski's adequacy condition cannot fail to be, in however generous a sense, a contingent, empirical matter – a matter that cannot be resolved on formal grounds alone. *This* is the neutral and deeper function of a Dummett-like anti-realism (meant to serve a reasonable realism): one that neither caters for Dummett's own unreasonably restrictive view of decidability, nor for Dummett's (and others') narrow adherence to *tertium non datur*.

Tarski's adequacy condition, it must be remembered, stipulates a material equivalence between sentences in an object language and sen-tences in a metalanguage. It is in this sense not addressed to the realist issue at all – though it may be brought to bear on it, as Davidson has done and as Tarski himself briefly considers. It would be a mistake, however, to hold that *Tarski's* adherence to the redundancy or dis-quotational notion of truth – contrary, possibly, to Ramsey's concern or that of others[39] – was "simply a device for talking about non-linguistic reality while appearing to talk about sentences."[40] For, as soon as the matter is viewed thus, conceding the indissolubility of the truth definition and the structural-descriptive conditions, Tarski's account cannot fail to be seen as a very strong, partisan theory of the nature of reality – for which, let it be said, Tarski (thus interpreted) offers not the least shred of evidence. We might, much more reasonably, insist that the (nearly vacuous) point of the ("amazingly neutral") truth definition is merely that *some* subset of sentences of natural languages may be viewed as sufficiently well-formed to be, for the mere reason of being thus formed, assignable values designated as truth values: all the virtues of Tarski's formal canon then accrue to them, although they cannot for that reason alone be *distributively* identified.

The *epistemically* relevant sense of "true," the sense that is inescapably linked to the realist issue (once one proceeds beyond the minimal sense, already remarked), cannot construe the correspondence theory as limited to object language and metalanguage viewed in formal terms alone. That sense imposes an additional, higher-order constraint on whatever may (for the sake of the argument) be conceded at the "lower," merely formal level at which Tarski's account functions. This is the point of Dummett's scruple; this is what Putnam has learned from Dummett; and this pro-vides a fair sense in which a relativistic criticism of *tertium non datur* need not compromise (if we read the issue thus) any of the purely formal features of whatever sentences meet Tarski's constraints drawn from purely formalized languages. This shows at once not merely the pecu-

liarly easy error of conflating Tarski's correspondence theory with epistemically realist correspondence theories but also the peculiarly double
confusion that flows from that error regarding the analysis of knowledge.
For it is one thing to suppose that, in accord with the Tarskian account,
truth may be "eliminated" while *at the same time* the sentences of natural
languages may be ("neutrally") taken to conform with Tarski's structural-
descriptive conditions; it is quite another to suppose that, in the epistemic
context, truth may again be "eliminated" as far as the *formal* analysis of
knowledge is concerned, while *at the same time* the formal properties
of the sentences of any disciplined science will, in general, conform with
the thus-extended application of Tarski's (or a Tarskian-like) account.
The first move – and even much of the second – forms the heart of
Davidson's program;[41] the second appears most prominently in Keith
Lehrer's detailed analysis of knowledge and marks the fatal formalism
of so much of Anglo-American epistemology.[42]

To return now to van Fraassen, in opposing realism in the sense of
opposing scientific realism he advances a thesis he calls "constructive
empiricism," which (though explicitly dubbed anti-realist) is also
opposed to Dummett's anti-realism: "Certainly," he says,

> I wish to define scientific realism so that it need not imply that all
> statements in the theoretical language are true or false (only that
> they are all capable of being true or false, that is, there are con-
> ditions for each under which it has a truth-value); to imply also
> that the aim at least is that the theories should be true. And the
> contrary position of constructive empiricism is not anti-realist in
> Dummett's sense, since it also assumes scientific statements to
> have truth-conditions entirely independent of human activity or
> knowledge.[43]

In effect, van Fraassen's grasp of the contingencies of the history of
science leads him to favor the realist against Dummett's anti-realist, while
at the same time he opposes that version of realism (so far saved) that,
in addition, fails to meet the strictures of "constructive empiricism";
"*Science aims to give us,*" he says, "*theories which are empirically
adequate; and acceptance of a theory involves as belief only that it is
empirically adequate.*" This is anti-realism and constructive empiricism.[44]
Part of the point is that "belief" is construed as "believing-true" *and*
that "acceptance" of a theory is *not* necessarily tantamount to believing
it true: that belief that is part of "accepting a scientific theory is only
[the belief] that it 'saves the phenomena', that is, correctly describes
what is observable." But we accept theories for other reasons; we even

prefer one theory over another that is "empirically equivalent." The reason is said to be "pragmatic," to involve "pragmatic virtues" that "do not give us any reason over and above the evidence of the empirical data, for thinking that a theory is true." In effect, "to accept one theory rather than another one involves also a commitment to a research programme, to continuing the dialogue with nature in the framework of one conceptual scheme rather than another."[45] By contrast, scientific realism commits us to the following: *Science aims to give us, in its theories, a literally true story of what the world is like; and acceptance of a scientific theory involves the belief that it is true.*[46]

Van Fraassen's account, then, is a subtle and deliberately lean version of empiricism – stricter about observationality than logical positivism and ontologically more economical than the usual scientific realism. Whether it can be effectively defended remains to be seen. Our concern, here, is not primarily with defending or attacking it. Nevertheless, several important qualifications link van Fraassen's thesis in a fruitful wasy with our own project. First of all, in terms of van Fraassen's program, there are well-known difficulties distinguishing between observable and unobservable entities, distinguishing between observing entities and observing that something is the case, distinguishing between putatively theoretical and non-theoretical parts of our language, distinguishing between observation *tout court* and experimentally guided and informed observation, and distinguishing between phenomenological and theoretical laws.[17] It is certainly not clear that there is, or could be, a uniquely satisfactory resolution of these complexities or a resolution, fitted to the central practices of science, that would favor van Fraassen's program in that spirit. Secondly, the very conditions for debating what form of realism best suits the history of science is by no means clearcut or likely to yield similarly unique or congruent solutions. Hence, quite apart from the fortunes of van Fraassen's particular doctrine, there is good reason to suppose that the nature of debates about realism in science is bound to accommodate some relativistic tolerance of competing onto-logical persuasions.

Consider, for example, that both van Fraassen and Nancy Cartwright oppose relying on inference to the best explanation, where such infer-ence, as involving accepting explanatory theories, is thought to commit us at once to the existence of the entities postulated by the theory.[48] (The scientific realism here opposed is most explicitly formulated by Wilfrid Sellars.[49]) Cartwright, like van Fraassen, characterizes her pos-ition as anti-realist; but it does not accord entirely with van Fraassen's and indeed is opposed to his thesis. Cartwright begins with a strikingly bold position that goes much further in the anti-realist direction than van Fraassen's "agnostic" view of "the existence of the unobservable aspects of the world described by science."[50] She declares straight out that "the falsehood of fundamental laws is a consequence of their great explanatory power" – which is not meant (as is van Fraassen's thesis) as a favorable gloss on Duhem's empiricism, since Cartwright wishes to reconcile her anti-realism with a part of the claims of scientific realism that van Fraassen wishes to oppose. The pivot of her position rests entirely with the contrast between "phenomenological" and "theoretical" (or "fundamental") laws, as she finds those terms used in the practice of physics – not of philosophy. "Phenomenological laws," she holds,

> describe what happens. They describe what happens in superfluids or meson-nucleon scattering as well as the more readily observed changes in Faraday's dense borosilicate glass, where magnetic fields rotate the plane of polarization of light. For the physicist, unlike the philosopher, the distinction between theoretical and phenomenological *has nothing to do with what is observable and what is unobservable*. Instead the terms separate laws which are fundamental and explanatory from those that merely describe.[51]

It is certainly true that realists, such as Sellars, have argued that, if "theoretical laws are false and inaccurate, then phenomenological laws are more so." But Cartwright "urge[s] just the reverse."[52] The heart of her thesis, then, is this:

> The appearance of truth [in explanatory theories] comes from a bad model of explanation, a model that ties laws directly to reality. As an alternative to the conventional picture I propose a *simulacrum* account of explanation. The route from theory to reality is from theory to model, and then from model to phenomenological law. The phenomenological laws are indeed true of the objects of reality – or might be; but the fundamental laws are true only of objects in the model.[53]

In this general approach, Cartwright and van Fraassen converge – except for the fact that van Fraassen is more radically opposed to scientific realism (however agnostically) in adhering to the reality only of the *observable*, whereas Cartwright is not opposed to scientific realism wherever it construes the real in terms of the *phenomenological* (even if, inevitably, that includes the unobservable). Furthermore and quite independently of the quarrel between Cartwright and van Fraassen, van Fraassen nowhere satisfactorily contrasts the observable and the unobservable – in such a way as to disallow the admission of (putatively unobservable) theoretical entities. For, although, he maintains that "what is observable [is] a theory-independent question" – in fact, he maintains that that distinction "is an empirical distinction" – the notion of "empirical adequacy" he favors merely requires "saving the [observable] phenomena," *which are not and do not need to be independently defined or specified.*[54] On van Fraassen's view, it is entirely possible that theories that do not demarcate the observable and unobservable "save the phenomena" nevertheless; saving the phenomena seems nowhere to require a distributive demarcation between the observable and unobservable. Cartwright's explicit principle for rejecting van Fraassen's empiricism is just that "Casual reasoning provides good grounds for our beliefs in theoretical entities": "no inference to the best explanation; only inference to most likely cause."[55] She offers an instructive example, notable because it is not entirely settled even today. It concerns an experiment in the mid-nineteenth century, by William Crookes, involving the rotation of the vanes of the radiometer (which Crookes invented) closed in a glass bowl in which an imperfect vacuum obtains. An early explanation of the radiometer's motion appealed to light pressure. This proved an insufficient explanation and attention turned to the implications of the action of gas molecules within the glass (conceding the imperfect vacuum). James Clerk Maxwell accounted for the motion not in terms of the pressures the postulated molecules exerted bouncing with differential rates between the two sides of the vanes (painted black and white) but rather in terms of the slippage of the gas over the surface of the vanes producing tangential stresses because of differential heating in the gas itself. Of this explanation Cartwright says,

> The molecules in Crookes's radiometer are invisible, and the tangential stresses are not the kinds of things one would have expected to see in the first place. Yet ... I believe in both. I believe in them because I accept Maxwell's causal account of why the vanes move around. In producing this account, Maxwell deploys certain fundamental laws, such as Boltzmann's equation and the equation of continuity, which I do not believe in. But one can reject theoretical laws without rejecting theoretical entities. In the case of Maxwell's molecules and the tangential stresses in the radiometer, there is an answer to van Fraassen's question: we have a satisfactory causal account, and so we have good reason to believe in the entities, processes, and properties in question.[56]

What is at stake here is not the solution to Crookes's puzzle but the nature of reasonable normative constraints on arguments favoring scientific realism in the context of such puzzles. Van Fraassen agrees with Cartwright on the intermediary status of theoretical models. As he puts it, "the notions of *truth* and *model* belong to semantics [not syntactics]"; "[the] acceptance of theories ... does not require belief that all significant aspects of the models have corresponding counterparts in reality. ... The locus of possibility is the model, not a reality beyond the phenomena."[57] Now, van Fraassen does address the issue of postulating unobservable entities on the basis of Hans Reichenbach's Principle of the Common Cause, which in effect maintains that "every statistical correlation (at least, every positive dependence) must be explained through common causes" – which, van Fraassen rightly observes, "means then that the very project of science will necessarily lead to the introduction of unobservable structure behind the phenomena."[58]

Van Fraassen clearly resists the principle, holding to his empiricism. But it is not entirely clear whether he thereby meets the strong claim that Cartwright advances, which rests not so much on correlation as on causal agency within the pointedly artifactual context of experiment;[59] contrariwise, it is not clear whether Cartwright makes good her own case, either in the sense in which the use of fundamental laws may be taken to have a stronger realist import than she concedes or in the sense that phenomenological regularities may be able to be brought into more economical accord with something like van Fraassen's empiricism. What we see is that it is not at all evident that all considerations admitted to be relevant to formulating norms governing how arguments about scientific realism are to be assessed are themselves uniformly weighted or ranked by all informed discussants – or able to be; and it is not evident that a uniformly "objective" policy is possible, that would preclude relativistic claims about different sorts of puzzles. Furthermore, *it is not at all clear that the absence of such objectivity precludes a favorable measure of rigor or disallows our construing relativistic claims as enjoying as much objectivity as the field permits.* Also, if the redundancy theory of truth is dampened in the direction suggested, then the differences among strong realists such as Sellars and rather differently oriented anti-realists such as van Fraassen and Cartwright will correspondingly be dampened as well – though not eliminated. In particular, if van Fraassen is prepared to characterize himself as "agnostic" with respect to unobservable entities, and if the gap between "acceptance" of a theory and "belief" in entities is reduced by the dampening intended – so that "believing" may signify "believing-plausible" as well as "believing-true" – then the disagreements in question will be considerably attenuated. But it must be remembered that such attenuation is itself gained at the cost of accommodating relativism.

If we partition anti-realism between Dummett's kind of undertaking and that of Cartwright and van Fraassen, we cannot ignore the fact that they are really opposed to one another; for Dummett's version supports, *distributively,* a decidability constraint, and Cartwright's and van Fraassen's (diverging between themselves) rejects such a constraint in favoring alternative forms of scientific holism. Dummett's project is essentially advanced in a formalistic way relatively unaffected by the history of science; Cartwright's and van Fraassen's is essentially attentive (in different ways) to the complexities of that history and, hence, implies that the other misses the peculiar, holistic, integrity of theorizing in science in close accord with observation and/or experiment. In a word, Cartwright and van Fraassen distinguish carefully between the *truth* and the *success* of a theory; Dummett appears to ignore that distinction and to insist very strenuously on truth. It is not unimportant, as we shall see later, to distinguish carefully between these two forms of anti-realism. For Hilary Putnam's and Richard Boyd's sanguine view of scientific realism fails to come to terms convincingly with the complexities of the second version of anti-realism (Cartwright's and van Fraassen's – not to mention Kuhn's and Feyerabend's closely related "idealism") and fails to bridge convincingly the complexities of reconciling the first version (Dummett's) with (a Quinean-like) holism.⁶⁰ Clearly, the second version favors relativism; and the first, though it does not favor relativism, is (with an adjustment that may be turned against Dummett himself) capable of being reconciled with relativism.

III

There appears to be a natural setting for relativism with regard to speculations about realism that the practice of the physical sciences invites. In fact, we may approach the prospects of relativism in a fresh way because of the foregoing review. For the standard opponents of relativism bring two extreme charges against the doctrine, charges that are peculiarly extravagant if not maliciously favored, notably unresponsive to the actual disputes about scientific realism. There are those who hold that relativism is or entails skepticism – that is, a global skepticism about the very cognitive competence of man; and there are those who hold that relativism is not or does not entail skepticism, that it is committed to cognitive competence but that, in advancing its claim, it necessarily contradicts itself. There are also those who add that relativism is committed to or entails the incommensurability thesis, either as a form of skepticism or as a distinct form of cognitive competence; and that in the latter case there is, where relativism is pertinent, no common sector of shared practice in which rules, principles, norms operative within given subsectors of life could possibly resolve issues ranging *across* such (exclusive) subsectors, even though such larger considerations are normally thought to arise and to require resolution.[61] (In effect, the thesis is a version of the skepticism it pretends to avoid.)

These are all desperate measures effectively derailed by actually demonstrating how a cognitively focused relativism committed to the pertinent dampening of the redundancy theory can be fitted in a robust way to standard disputes about scientific realism. The strategy advises us, in effect, that, once we persuade ourselves of the formal coherence of relativism, to go on to demonstrate its substantive relevance in this domain or that depends on a thorough and sustained examination of the particular disputes of a particular domain. There can be no straightforward declension of the argument from one domain to another; but it is, nevertheless, not unreasonable to argue that, if relativism can claim an application central to the interpretation of the work of the physical sciences, it is very unlikely that it will fail to have at least as central a role in disputes regarding the human sciences.

What is essential is that we resist selling relativism short by invoking pertinent truth values only in contexts of ambiguity or contingent ignorance or lack of information. When, for instance, it is argued, as in disputes about Henry James's *The Turn of the Screw*, that the story is inherently ambiguous (if indeed it actually is), so that incompatible interpretations may be textually defended by collecting in a coherent way all (presumably all) determinate features of the undisputed story, it would not be to the point to claim that the opposed parties were engaged in a debate ordered along relativistic lines. The confirmation of incompatible readings supported by an ambiguous text is *not* equivalent to *retreating from bipolar truth values* to a model in which incongruent claims obtain (that is, pertinent claims that, on a bipolar model – but no longer – would be incompatible). Similarly, probabilized judgments that, if not probabilized (that is, if detached from their admittedly indecisive probabilizing evidence), would be incompatible are not to be viewed in the same way as insisting on relativistic values – because, say, of real-time limitations of an apparently structural sort bearing on the nature of human cognition in this domain or that. For example, in the case of questions about scientific realism, *there is no clearly unique, convergent, or principled ordering* of pertinent considerations linking observationality, causality, controlled experiment, technological and artifactual innovation, scientific progress, models, and fundamental laws –

whether or not construed in terms of incommensurability (of the restricted nonskeptical and nonexclusionasry sort) – that would convincingly
insure the adequacy of a bipolar model with regard to claims of scientific
realism. Attention to the import of denying the cognitive transparency
of the world, of affirming the historicized nature of human existence
and human cognition, of conceding even relatively benign forms of
incommensurability, attests to the likelihood that, even in epistemic
terms (*not* restricted to the contingencies of particular evidence), we can
hardly expect to preclude relativism or to disallow its occupying a
distinctly central place in our conceptual system.

Nevertheless, the most powerful version of the defense of relativism
cannot but be based on the claim that the nature of the questions raised,
the properties of the entities or phenomena under examination, the very
structure of the disciplines in question disallow resorting to a bipolar
model of truth values. Here, of course, the argument can hardly be more
than an invitation to make a fresh start, although the input of our survey
of the issues of realism within the physical sciences cannot be restricted
merely to limitations on human cognition. We may at least anticipate
what would lend support to a more ontological reading of our thesis.
Certainly, as in the interpretation of literary texts, the meaning of
historical events, linguistic communication itself, the impossibility
(admittedly only alleged at this point) of demarcating or individuating
words and sentences, artworks, human actions in purely extensional
ways, the entire problem of reidentifying cultural phenomena that are
intensionally discriminated, cannot fail to raise profound difficulties for
any simple bipolar model.[62] The complexities of intentionality go very
deep, clearly threatening the unity of the sciences as well as what we
can justifiably claim to mean in speaking jointly of "objectivity" in the
natural and human sciences. Furthermore, ontological disputes, disputes
about what "there is" in the world, disputes about real entities and real
properties, appear to be quite intractable to exclusive resolution in terms
of a bipolar model – which, at least for the sake of the argument, the
recent work of Quine and Goodman amply confirms. And, finally,
transcendental arguments regarding the legitimation of any first-order
cognitive discipline appear (despite premature death notices) to be both
ineliminable – if first-order disciplines are themselves ineliminable –
and, granting historicism, incommensurability, and the non-transparency
thesis, utterly unlikely to yield to a bipolar model. But these are very
large issues that deserve a fresh inning.

There is a final consideration that bridges to some extent the difference
between epistemological and ontological uses of the relativistic thesis –
that neither denies the difference nor the complexities in terms of which

particular claims may, from time to time, seem to favor the one focus or the other. Einstein's speculations about realism are instructive here. They have to do, primarily, with Einstein's understanding of what realism in theoretical physics comes to, and with his long-standing conviction that quantum physics yields an inherently incomplete description of the physical phenomena it addresses.[63]

Einstein appears to have subscribed to a paradoxical combination of views: on the one hand, he rejects the possibility that physics could conform with the pretensions of the correspondence theory of truth; on the other, he construes physics as committed to the description of physical reality as it is independent of human observation. But he sketches an ingenious and coherent solution. In the first place, he adheres to a form of scientific holism and denies the testability of individual concepts and assumptions; secondly, he denies that even causality is "empirically determinable" – that is, directly testable in an empirical sense;[64] and, thirdly, as Arthur Fine neatly remarks, he "entheorizes" both his holism and his concept of causality – which is to say, he holds that, in physics, we can test only the viability on empirical adequacy of our theories, even our theories of what we mean and what we are testing.[65]

In abandoning correspondence, we must of course abandon verisimilitude, at least that form of verisimilitude that Karl Popper had advocated (call it verisimilitude$_1$), since, on Popper's view, verisimilitude signifies approximation to the truth and, hence, is parasitic on a cognitively accessible use of the very notion Popper claims we cannot use.[66] Einstein recovers a sense of realism, then, by way of coherence considerations, under conditions that include the salience of holistic testing (such as it is) *and* his own convictions (or biases or prejudices) about *what* reality independent of human observation must be like.

As is well known, the cornerstone of his conviction was that the fundamental laws of physics – what of causality must be preserved at all costs – must make no essential use of probabilistic concepts: "I don't believe," Einstein writes, "that the fundamental physical laws may consist in relations between *probabilities* for the real things, but for relations concerning the things themselves."[67] Now, of course, this conviction runs diametrically counter to the conviction of quantum physicists, who operate with an entirely different *sense* of what independent physical reality must be like or of what our cognitive relation to the actual world must be like. We may at any rate say, of Einstein, that he abandoned truth and adhered to some form of "truthlikeness" (verisimilitude$_2$, let us say), by which we are to understand that the *representations* offered by our science (both models, rather in the sense in which van Fraassen speaks of them, *and individual claims, which are holistically collected and governed as to truth value by our theories* – in a sense that yet does not deny or disqualify the saliences of our testing efforts) provide us with the only picture of physical reality that we can ever obtain.

Once we see matters in this way, rejecting transparency and correspondence, adhering strictly to holism, construing realism by way of entheorizing, *there remains no possibility of precluding a robust relativism at the center of our philosophy of science.* But what Einstein's remarks oblige us to grasp as well is that the sense of realism itself cannot fail, on those conditions, to conform to or be governed by certain personal values, or insistent convictions, about the nature of reality. These, too, are inevitably subject to dialectical challenge – which the contest between relativity and quantum physics confirms; but, even with (or perhaps because of) this further complication, there is no way in which, within the boundaries of scientific holism, coherence or pragmatist concerns could mitigate the full pertinence of relativism.

There seem to be no other avenues of escape.

Notes

1 See F. P. Ramsey, "Facts and Propositions," *Foundations of Mathematics*, ed. Richard B. Braithewaite (London: Routledge and Kegan Paul, 1931; Paterson, NJ: Littlefield, Adams, 1960).
2 See J. L. Austin and P. F. Strawson, ("Truth" symposium), *Proceedings of the Aristotelian Society*, suppl. vol. XXIV (1950); and J. L. Austin, "Unfair to Facts," *Philosophical Papers* (Oxford: Clarendon Press, 1961).
3 Ramsey, "Facts and Propositions," *Foundations of Mathematics*, p. 143 (1960 edn).
4 See Joseph Margolis, "Fiction and Existence", in Joseph Margolis (ed.) *The Worlds of Art and the World* (Amsterdam: Rodopi, 1983).
5 See John R. Searle, *Speech Acts* (Cambridge: Cambridge University Press, 1969), ch. 4; and Joseph Margolis, "The Axiom of Existence: *Reductio ad Absurdum*," *Southern Journal of Philosophy*, XV (1977).
6 This bears, for instance, on differences regarding the viability of scientific realism among Ian Hacking, *Representing and Intervening* (Cambridge: Cambridge University Press, 1983); Hilary Putnam, *Meaning and the Moral Sciences* (London: Routledge and Kegan Paul, 1978); and Bas C. van-Fraassen, *The Scientific Image* (Oxford: Clarendon Press, 1980).
7 Peter D. Klein, *Certainty: A Refutation of Scepticism* (Minneapolis: University of Minnesota Press, 1981), p. 11.
8 Richard J. Bernstein, *Beyond Objectivism and Relativism* (Philadelphia: University of Pennsylvania Press, 1983), pp. 11–12.

9   Ibid., p. 3f.

10 Cf. ibid., p. 8.

11 One sees this, for instance, in Tarski's semantic conception of truth and in Popper's appeal to Tarski's notion, even in the context of favoring his well-known doctrine of verisimilitude. See Karl R. Popper, "Two Faces of Common Sense" and "Philosophical Comments on Tarski's Theory of Truth," *Objective Knowledge: An Evolutionary Approach* (Oxford: Clarendon Press, 1972).

12 For example, Thomas S. Kuhn, *The Structure of Scientific Revolutions*, 2nd enlarged edn (Chicago: University of Chicago Press, 1970), p. 150; and Paul Feyerabend, *Against Method* (London: New Left Books, 1975), pp. 30–1 (ch. 17).

13 Feyerabend, *Against Method*, pp. 30–1.

14 Ibid., p. 189; cf. pp. 297–8.

15 Paul Feyerabend, *Science in a Free Society* (London: New Left Books, 1978), pp. 102–3.

16 See Gerald Doppelt, "Kuhn's Epistemological Relativism: An Interpretation and Defense," *Inquiry*, XXI (1978); repr. (with omissions) in Jack W. Meiland and Michael Krausz (eds), *Relativism: Cognitive and Moral* (Notre Dame, Ind.: University of Notre Dame Press, 1982). Bernstein's summary of the issue, at least partly dependent on Doppelt's account, is thorough and helpful (*Beyond Objectivism and Relativism*, pp. 79–93).

17 Doppelt, "Kuhn's Epistemological Relativism," in Meiland and Krausz, *Relativism: Cognitive and Moral*, pp. 118, 119.

18 Kuhn, *The Structure of Scientific Revolutions*, p. 206.

19 Ibid. Cf. the criticism of Israel Scheffler, *Science and Subjectivity* (Indianapolis: Bobbs-Merrill, 1967); Roger Trigg, *Reason and Commitment* (Cambridge: Cambridge University Press, 1973).

20 Kuhn, *The Structure of Scientific Revolutions*, pp. 206–7.

21 Bernstein, *Beyond Objectivism and Relativism*, p. 85.

22 H. M. Collins and T. J. Pinch, *Frames of Meaning: The Social Construction of Extraordinary Science* (London: Routledge and Kegan Paul, 1982), pp. 14–15. Cf. also H. M. Collins and G. Cox, "Recovering Relativity: Did Prophecy Fail?" *Social Studies of Science*, VI (1976); and, for a sample of standard contemporary objections, Larry Laudan, "Explaining the Success of Science: Beyond Epistemic Realism and Relativism," in James T. Cushing et al. (eds), *Science and Reality: Recent Work in the Philosophy of Science* (Notre Dame, Ind.: University of Notre Dame Press, 1984).

23 See Barry Barnes and David Bloor, "Relativism, Rationalism and the Sociology of Knowledge," in Martin Hollis and Steven Lukes (eds), *Rationality and Relativism* (Cambridge, Mass.: MIT Press, 1982).

24 See *Collected Papers of Charles Sanders Peirce*, 8 vols. ed. Charles Hartshorne, Paul Weiss, and Arthur W. Burks (Cambridge, Mass.: Harvard University Press, 1931–58), vol. 5, pp. 47, 603; and W. V. Quine, *Word and Object* (Cambridge: MIT Press, 1960), p. 23. Also, Martin Heidegger,

Introduction to *Being and Time*, tr. John Macquarrie and Edward Robinson from the German edn (New York: Harper and Row, 1962); "Hölderlin and the Essence of Poetry," tr. Douglas Scott, in Martin Heidegger, *Existence and Being*, ed. Werner Brock (South Bend, Ind.: Gateway, 1949); and Paul de Man, "Heidegger's Exegesis of Hölderlin," *Blindness and Insight*, 2nd rev. edn (Minneapolis: University of Minnesota Press, 1983).

25 Michael Dummett, "Truth," *Truth and Other Enigmas* (Cambridge, Mass.: Harvard University Press, 1978), p. 14. This very strong *realist* commitment is, unaccountably, completely overlooked, even denied, in Michael Devitt's sustained criticism of Dummett's anti-realism. See *Realism and Truth* (Princeton, NJ: Princeton University Press, 1984), ch. 12. Contrary to Devitt's claim, Dummett does *not* reduce the metaphysics of realism to a question "only" of "verificationist truth conditions" (p. 7): it apparently has (in Devitt's idiom), an "evidence-transcendent" feature *for Dummett*. But the matter requires further sorting. See also, Crispin Wright, "Critical Study: Dummett and Revisionism," *Philosophical Quarterly*, LI (1981).

26 Dummett, "Truth," *Truth and Other Enigmas*, p. 24 (I have italicized "realist"). These remarks appear in a Postscript (1972) to the original paper. In fact, in the Postscript Dummett adds, "I am no longer so unsympathetic to realism: the realist has a lot more to say for himself than is acknowledged in the article. The dispute is still a long way from resolution" (p. 24).

27 Cf. Putnam, "Realism and Reason,", *Meaning and the Moral Sciences*

28 Dummett, Preface to *Truth and Other Enigmas*, p.xxx; cf. also "Realism," repr. in the same collection.

29 Ibid., p. xxi.

30 Van Fraassen, *The Scientific Image* pp. 37, 38; Dummett, "Realism," *Truth and Other Enigmas*, p. 146 (cited by van Fraassen).

31 Dummett, "Realism," *Truth and Other Enigmas*, p. 147.

32 Devitt, *Realism and Truth*.

33 Ibid., pp. 34, 35.

34 This goes against Donald Davidson's view favoring the eliminability of reference: "Reality without Reference," *Inquiries into Truth and Interpretation* (Oxford: Clarendon Press, 1984).

35 Dummett, *Truth and Other Enigmas*, p. xix (Preface).

36 Ibid., pp. xx (Preface), 4–5 ("Truth").

37 Ibid., p. xx (Preface).

38 Susan Haack, *Deviant Logic* (Cambridge: Cambridge University Press, 1974), p. 67. See also P. T. Geach, *Logic Matters* (Oxford: Basil Blackwell, 1972), section 2.5.

39 See Stephen Leeds, "Theories of Reference and Truth," *Erkenntnis*, XIII (1978).

40 Devitt, *Realism and Truth*, p. 29.

41 Perhaps the single most strategic comment of Davidson's bearing on this vexed issue is the following, from "The Inscrutability of Reference": "Truth is relative to an object language, but not to a metalanguage" (*Inquiries into*

Truth and Interpretation, p. 223). The remark must be read in the light of another, in "Reality without Reference," where Davidson is clearly concerned with the analysis of natural languages suited to a realist science: "By a theory of truth, I mean a theory that satisfies something like Tarski's Convention T: it is a theory that by recursively characterizing a truth predicate (say 'is true in L') entails, for each sentence s of L, a metalinguistic sentence got from the form 's is true in L if and only if p' when 's' is replaced by a canonical description of a sentence of L and 'p' by a sentence of the metalanguage that gives the truth conditions of the described sentence" (ibid., p. 215).

42 See Keith Lehrer, *Knowledge* (Oxford: Clarendon Press, 1974). Lehrer's account is examined more closely in chapter 10 below.

43 Van Fraassen, *The Scientific Image*, p. 38.

44 Ibid., p. 12.

45 Ibid., p. 4.

46 Ibid., p. 8.

47 See ibid., ch. 2; also, Grover Maxwell, "The Ontological Status of Theoretical Entities," *Minnesota Studies in the Philosophy of Science*, ed. Herbert Feigl et al., vol. III (Minneapolis: University of Minnesota Press, 1962); Isaac Levi, "Confirmational Conditionalization," *Journal of Philosophy*, LXXV (1978); Nancy Cartwright, Introduction to *How the Laws of Physics Lie* (Oxford: Clarendon Press, 1983).

48 Van Fraassen, *The Scientific Image*, pp. 19–23; Cartwright, Introduction to *How the Laws of Physics Lie*. See also Pierre Duhem, *The Aim and Structure of Physical Theory*, tr. Philip P. Wiener from 2nd French edn (Princeton, NJ: Princeton University Press, 1954), ch. 1.

49 Wilfrid Sellars, "Phenomenalism," *Science, Perception and Reality* (London: Routledge and Kegan Paul, 1963), p. 97n: "to have good reason for espousing a theory is *ipso facto* to have good reason for saying that the entities postulated by the theory really exist"; the remark is cited by van Fraassen.

50 Van Fraassen, *The Scientific Image*, p. 72.

51 Cartwright, *How the Laws of Physics Lie* p. 2 (italics added).

52 Ibid., p. 3.

53 Ibid., p. 4.

54 Van Fraassen, *The Scientific Image*, pp. 57–8, 12.

55 Cartwright, *How the Laws of Physics Lie*, p. 6.

56 Ibid., pp. 6–7.

57 Van Fraassen, *The Scientific Image*, pp. 43, 201–2.

58 Ibid., pp. 25–31; cf. Hans Reichenbach, *The Direction of Time* (Berkeley, Calif.: University of California Press, 1963); and Wesley C. Salmon, "Theoretical Explanation," in Stephen Körner (ed.), *Explanation* (Oxford: Basil Blackwell, 1975).

59 See Hacking, *Representing and Intervening*.

60 There is a very helpful summary of recent debates on these matters in Jarrett Leplin, Introduction to Jarrett Leplin (ed.), *Scientific Realism* (Berkeley,

Calif.: University of California Press, 1984). Leplin's entire anthology collects the most salient views. See particularly Ernan McMullin, "A Case for Scientific Realism"; Richard N. Boyd, "The Current Status of Scientific Realism"; Arthur Fine, "The Natural Ontological Attitude"; and Larry Laudan, "A Confutation of Convergent Realism."

61   Cf. Gilbert Harman, "Moral Relativism Defended," *Philosophical Review*, LXXIV (1975); and *The Nature of Morality* (New York: Oxford University Press, 1977).

62   I have pursued these issues in some depth in *Persons and Minds* (Dordrecht: D. Reidel, 1978); *Art and Philosophy* (Atlantic Highlands, NJ: Humanities Press, 1980); *Philosophy of Psychology* (Englewood Cliffs, NJ: Prentice-Hall, 1984); and *Culture and Cultural Entities* (Dordrecht: D. Reidel, 1984).

63   I rely very heavily here on the extremely instructive paper by Arthur Fine, "Einstein's Realism," in Cushing et al., *Science and Reality*. This is not, however, to agree entirely with Fine's characterization or assessment of various forms of realism mentioned in the course of his explication.

64   The phrase appears, in a clear version of Einstein's view, in a letter to J. J. Fehr, 25 March, 1952 (cited by Fine, ibid., p. 107).

65   Cf. ibid., pp. 107–10. The term "entheorizes" is Fine's.

66   See Karl R. Popper, *Realism and the Aim of Science* (vol. 1: *From the Postscript to the Logic of Scientific Discovery*) ed. W. W. Bartley III (Totowa, NJ: Rowman and Littlefield, 1983), pp. xxxv–xxxvii, 57–8.

67   From a letter to M. C. Coodal, 10 September 1945 (cited in Fine, "Einstein's Realism," in Cushing et al., *Science and Reality*).

Part Two

Foundations and the Recovery of Pragmatism

6

The Legitimation of Realism

I

Construed in any sense minimally pertinent to the accomplishments of science, realism is a thesis about a certain favorable linkage between the cognizable features of the world *vis-à-vis* the cognizing powers of human inquirers. So stated, the thesis is of course vacuous, although it helps us to see at once why a correspondence reading of realism is so attractive, and to begin to tally the very large variety of doctrines that, in more interesting respects, may be said to be versions of realism. To support realism, then, cannot fail to collect what, in the jargon, is the work of epistemology and ontology: to theorize about the structure of the actual world is to theorize about our competence to grasp that structure, and to claim any cognitive competence is to claim that its exercise entails some grasp of the actual world's structure. Again, this is logically trivial – but, again, not for that reason unimportant. For one thing, science cannot be supposed to be effectively self-corrective without explicit, ongoing appraisals of the relationship between its putative powers and its putative achievements; and, for another, the history of science is at least the history of what, in retrospect, have come to be viewed as errors in cognitive and methodological presumption. There is no disjunctive contrast to be fixed once and for all between the first-order inquiries of science and the second-order inquiries of philosophy: the distinction is no more than a distinction of convenience regarding practices that need not pause to classify their various concerns in just that way; but the classification does serve to draw attention to what can hardly fail to be included in a reasonable overview of the responsible work of science, as well as in the ongoing efforts of a responsible science itself. Also, of course, the minimal sense of realism must be essentially opposed to and essentially opposed by (Pyrrhonian) skepticism, for realism presupposes and addresses a science minimally competent in the respect noted. Skepticism either challenges, by assertion, any such presumptive confidence, or worries that presumption by nonassertive or ironically assertive strategies that cannot or will not be reconciled with the realist project itself.[1] In this sense, realism need not be opposed to idealism, unless, by "idealism," one means those forms of epistemic subjectivism in which (as with classical British empiricism) it becomes problematic whether and in what way what we are directly acquainted with experientially, ideas or sensa, are cognitively linked with the structures of the actual world. This is just the point of the familiar charge of the implicit skepticism of subjective idealism. Certainly, a Kantian-like or Husserlian-like idealism is not meant to oppose realisms suitable to the work of the sciences. A convenient way of putting the point is simply to affirm that to reconcile realism and idealism does not entail construing cognitive competence in any way initially or essentially restricted to representations (of would-be reality) – hence, does not as such render the realist vulnerable to skeptical doubts about the adequacy of representations of any sort (whether, say, Cartesian or Lockean). Thus interpreted, we may understand, by *idealism*, whatever is at least minimally entailed regarding the mind's contribution to the formation of our science, in denying to (scientific) realism any and all forms of cognitive transparency, objectivism, correspondence, and the like. To say this much of course signifies that the cognitive indissolubility of realist and idealist elements extends to the intransparency of the mind as well – hence, affects in an essential way the viability of whatever may be characterized as a transcendental argument: for example, it precludes the synthetic *a priori*.

Broadly speaking, there are only two lines of strategy favoring the legitimation of realism: one directly concerns claims about our cognizing powers; the other concerns such claims only indirectly, by inferring in some way that what we initially concede to be the human condition – notably, the actual survival and viability of the human species, or, more narrowly, the living practices of actual societies – signifies that we must possess suitable cognizing powers (whatever they may be) sufficient for such survival and viability. We may say that the first line of strategy is circular, in that it speculates about what we suppose to be our cognizing powers, once we concede a certain characteristic set of determinate truths having realist import; and the second line of strategy is circular, in that it speculates that we must suppose we do have cognizing powers, since, on the strength of what appears to be cognitively salient in the whole of human existence, we allege that we are unable to resist the conviction that the survival and viability of the stock depends on the complex, collectively successful interventions of human inquiry. This sort of cautious formulation, of course, actually encourages the marginal puzzles of the skeptic. The skeptic is in a sense artifactually incubated by any and every retreat from a flat insistence on the utter certainty and reliability of human inquiry: he is marginal, however, in the sense that the doubts he generates he generates *in the minds* of those already disposed to entertain the concession just mentioned, and in the sense that, in the limit, the realist and the skeptic cannot consistently be supposed to engage in an exchange intelligible within the terms of reference of the *realist*.

In any case, varieties of the first line of strategy may be termed *epistemic*; those of the second, *pragmatist* (or, *non-epistemic*). Broadly speaking, *no* adequate form of legitimation of the realism of science could be formulated – if the undertaking were countenanced at all – without providing some epistemic argument. This of course risks, though it need not actually embrace, a privileged claim that, beginning with a genuinely open question about, say, how a (realist) science is conceptually possible (informally reminiscent, at least at this point, of the Kantian transcendental question), we somehow manage to exercise a "higher" cognitive resource straightforwardly competent to meet the question. The important theoretical manoeuvre here is, of course, whether and how we may address the epistemic issue squarely and adequately even if we abandon appealing to any such privileged cognitive resource.

On the other hand, the entire movement of contemporary philosophy, to the extent that it honors the question, has moved increasingly in the direction of the pragmatist strategy. This offers the obvious advantage of precluding at once any pretense of privilege, both because its would-be rationalization of science legitimates realism on *non*-epistemic grounds and because in doing even that it addresses science *en bloc*, only holistically. Still, precisely in doing that, it betrays a possible inadequacy: for the whole point of legitimating *science is* to provide a reasoned basis for favoring one or another competing conception of the findings and practices of actual inquiry *within* the history, *and* within the horizon of the possible reform, of the work of human investigators. That means, in effect, that we must attend to epistemic issues focused on the *distributed* achievements of science – for example, regarding the realist status of theoretical entities posited in attempting to explain the observational data collected in Crookes's radiometer experiments.[2] Failure to address such questions is simply a failure to come to terms with the full realist issue, in the very context in which it is first pertinently broached.

There can be no doubt that the resolution of such questions is *not* merely airy, higher-order speculation about the organized practices of first-order science – itself *autonomous, intact, sufficiently guided by*

*rational considerations without attending at all to such speculations, closed
in a principled way against them, unaffected by them except by way of
entirely contingent or systematically irrelevant intrusions.* No. If, for
example, the illicit privilege suggested a moment before (the essential
cognitive transparency of nature) directly distorts, weakens, misleads,
or impoverishes the actual progress of science, then the conceptual
symbiosis of first- and second-order considerations can hardly be denied.
It would then be an odd economy to suggest that, once such threats
were "therapeutically" exposed, science could continue very nicely by
itself, without any further intrusion of "transcendental" philosophy.
This, as will be recognized, is very close to the strategy advocated by
Richard Rorty. We shall turn to it again shortly. But for the moment
we must concede that the double risk of circularity hovers over every
speculation about the realist import of science.

That circularity is benign enough, if we do not pretend to establish
our cognizing powers *ab initio* by such strategies – although, under
certain circumstances (whether defensibly or not), even the effort to
legitimate such powers *ab initio* need not be viciously circular; it would
be eligible, for instance, *if*, on some argument, it were thought possible
to possess cognitive powers that were self-certifying, self-insuring, "self-
presenting," self-confirming, self-evidently or indubitably apt for securing truths about the actual world. Clearly, the latter strategy is a sub-
strategy of the first of the two main lines of argument already acknowledged. Call it *cognitivism*, in the sense that it postulates a determinate
cognizing competence to grasp and articulate, *distributively*, *certain*
truths having realist import; and that that competence is reflexively
sufficient to insure itself as well: schematically, cognitivism holds that,
for some apparently autonomous set of (realist) propositions or truths,
Kp entails KKp. (This helps to explain, incidentally, why the advocacy
of synthetic *a priori* truths is a form of cognitivism – hence, why Kant's
version of transcendental idealism is not a version of the cognitive
indissolubility of realism and idealism of the sort here favored. This is,
also, the heart of Husserl's objection to Kant – though it must also be
applied to Husserl – and it serves as a clue to the heterodox possibilities
involved in recovering transcendental reasoning in praxical or historicized
terms.) Normally, of course, such an entailment would be disallowed;
the rule, then, is at least one way of conceding the cognitive *privilege*
of some set of distributed claims or judgments (or, conceivably, of some
particular source or competence or power, such as sensory awareness,
from which or in accord with which such privileged judgments issue;
or, perhaps, of some set of thus-disclosed facts or states of affairs that
we may affirm in such claims or judgments).

Here we must be careful not to construe epistemic epithets as merely psychological, even though, since knowledge entails or involves psychological states and abilities (like belief, inference, and the like), the ascribability of epistemic attributes entails the ascribability of psychological attributes. If, in particular, a cognitivist attribute is ascribed, then that ascription will entail the ascribability of a pertinent psychological attribute, simply because it will "involve" such an attribute.

A reasonable – perhaps even the most ramified – contemporary account of such attributes is provided by Roderick Chisholm. Chisholm first introduces the notion of "self-presenting" properties (or states), and then says of self-presenting properties that they "involve" psychological properties – in the following sense: "Whatever is self-presenting is *implied by* what is psychological. That is to say, for every self-presenting property, there is a psychological property which is necessarily such that, if one has the psychological property then one has the self-presenting property"; alternatively, "every self-presenting property is necessarily such that, if one conceives the property, then one conceives some psychological property."[3] For Chisholm, "The mark of a self-presenting property is this: every property it entails is necessarily such that, if a person has it and also considers whether he has it, then *ipso facto* he will attribute it to himself."[4] For Chisholm, then, "a person's self-presenting properties *are* objects of certainty for that person," possessing "the highest degree of epistemic justification" – hence, "foundational" for human knowledge; also, such properties are (epistemically) "supervenient" (from "merely" psychological properties), in the sense of the schematism already adduced: cognitivist properties may be expected to function foundationally, in that (for instance, as with self-presenting properties) they conform to the rule "Kp entails KKp" and provide epistemic grounds for whatever is evident about other properties.[5]

It is in the spirit of such considerations that Chisholm introduces the crucial foundational formula for "the directly evident": "What justifies me in thinking I know that a is F is simply the fact that a is F."[6] This apparently meets Sextus Empiricus's constraint that (in effect) things are evident in themselves or through other things. Someone's illness may be evident through his symptoms; but self-presenting states are "directly evident." Chisholm does not, of course, attempt to offer supporting evidence for his claim, for that would (appear to) entail treating the "directly evident" as merely evident through something other than itself – which, even if reasonable, would be insufficient for its purpose. But it is relatively uncontroversial to remark that, whatever may be supposed to be directly evident (for example, one's moods or beliefs or sensations, or even macroscopic physical objects perceived under certain circumstances[7]), there is no compelling sense in which rejecting the thesis – without yet embracing skepticism – is simply inadmissible or obviously mistaken or the advocacy of an uncertainty that significantly strains the conceptual tolerance of those already distinctly favorably disposed to the minimal realism of science. Furthermore, the effort to legitimate the cognitivist thesis, precisely because it is a second-order undertaking, need not (and on certain interpretations cannot) be construed as undermining the first-order cognitive competences alleged.

Whether the thesis can be suitably defended is not our immediate concern. We are here merely trying to understand the nature of the available strategies for legitimating alternative forms of realism. Cognitivism offers a foundational legitimation of realist claims – although whether, for instance, a ramified form of scientific realism could be adequately legitimated on such grounds (as Chisholm posits) seems dubious; or whether, with respect to the realist status of science, we should constrain any would-be legitimation severely within the competence of such foundational claims (possibly in a sense analogous to Bas van Fraassen's "constructive empiricism"[8]) is not straightforwardly obvious. No salient lines of relevant elaboration are suggested in Chisholm's account.

The critical point at stake is this: on a cognitivist thesis, although we may distinguish the foundational assurance of a proposition (answering to a self-presenting state) from the theoretical account of the epistemic status of that proposition, the two are peculiarly closely linked. For, pursuing our specimen, in merely reflecting on whether one has a certain self-presenting property, one is said to be completely justified in attributing it to himself; hence, the exercise of the pertinent first-order cognitive power and the exercise of the first-order power to reflect on the exercise of the other are sufficient to justify formulating the *second-order* rule in accord with which the *foundational* reliability of that first-order power may be affirmed.[9] On this theory, we do not need to legitimate – to justify in the pertinent second-order sense – our competence to have and recognize self-presenting states *in order to have and recognize such states; and* the mere exercise of such a competence entitles us to move to formulate the (legitimating) "rule of evidence" that is always and only instantiated in that very exercise. Cognitivism, then, or the foundational elaboration of cognitivism, exhibits the peculiarly strong philosophical feature that a putative first-order cognizing power in effect provides a sufficient conceptual basis in itself for positing its own (second-order) legitimation. This is certainly extraordinary, in the straightforward sense that *such* second-order *legitimation* – that is, efforts to provide the conceptual grounds sufficient for demonstrating, displaying, vindicating, in some strong sense, the respect (possibly open to alternative interpretations) in which our cognitive powers *are* rightly construed as competent in the way they *are* (as, say, in having realist import) – is, now, quite effortlessly (in effect, self-evidently) supplied. For such efforts are precisely what are usually taken to be the concern of transcendental inquiry (perhaps not canonically, in Kant's sense): here, in cognitivist theories and in the foundational extension of such theories, the would-be transcendental question is answered merely by articulating what a *first-order* reflection on a certain *first-order* cognitive capacity ("transcendentally") implies.

Needless to say, if we give up cognitivist strategies, or if we give them up as far as the realist import of a ramified science is concerned, the usual complexity of the second-order issue (legitimation) will be entirely restored, *even if* we hold to the first (the epistemic) line of strategy – that is, to one directly concerned with distributed cognitive claims or the putative competence through the exercise of which such claims are said to function as they do. In fact, it is an irony that the rejection of the cognitivist or foundationalist thesis quite often leads either to ignoring or to positively rejecting the conceptual need for any legitimation. Thus, for instance, Richard Rorty straightforwardly affirms,

> I construe [Donald] Davidson's argument against the notion of "conceptual scheme" and against the "scheme–content distinction" as an argument for pragmatism, and thus against the possibility of epistemology. Davidson, in other words, seems to me to have found a transcendental argument to end all transcendental arguments – one which tears down the scaffolding upon which the standard paradigms of "realistic" transcendental arguments were mounted. ... I suggest that abandoning the scheme–content distinction and accepting pragmatism does, in a sense, mean abandoning philosophy. Philosophy *does* depend upon transcendental arguments for its existence, *if* philosophy is conceived of as a non-empirical criticism of culture [or] the legitimation of knowledge-claims.[10]

The irony may be put this way: on the one hand, the cognitivist or foundationalist legitimation of realism is hardly more than one quite specialized version of an *epistemically* focused strategy – one in fact that, at times, tends to obscure even the need for legitimating questions, in view of the very power of its first-order claims; and, on the other, there are enormously many questions regarding the realist status of the first-order work of science that invite inquiry and *rationally affect the fortunes and direction of science itself* – questions that cannot be dismissed merely in dismissing cognitivism and foundationalism.[11] On the contrary, *if* Rorty is right in rejecting all versions of cognitive privilege – of *those* forms of realism that treat the cognizable world as transparent to human cognition or that treat human cognition as capable of undistortedly representing the structures of the actual world (or of grasping such structures in some other, similarly potent way – Aristotle's, for instance)[12] – and *if* there is a formulable sense (seemingly impossible to deny) in which we are thereupon rationally enjoined to direct the inquiry and theorizing of science in accord with the intended corrective, then it seems quite impossible to deny a viable and pertinent role to transcendental or legitimating concerns. Rorty simply takes it – without any argument at all – that every effort at legitimating realism cannot but be a version of the "mirror" thesis he opposes. But that is an odd fancy.

There is, then, no way of sustaining a first-order cognitive discipline – a science – without reflectively assessing, correcting, adjusting, exploring what we should reasonably construe as its very competence. But that just is to raise second-order questions. Furthermore, the history of every first-order discipline will, on that concession, be a function in part at least of such reflections: first-order and second-order work are really no more than heuristically distinguished aspects of a rationally continuous discipline – not discrete, or hierarchically ordered, or formally distinct undertakings. It is therefore a complete *non sequitur* to suppose either that pursuing second-order or transcendental concerns is to be committed to any form of cognitivism or that to reject cognitivism is to give up transcendental concerns. The most that can be said is that, once we give up Cartesian and Kantian versions of the "mirror" thesis (which versions Rorty so vigorously opposes), our conception of transcendental reasoning is bound to take a heterodox turn. It will have to give up the synthetic *a priori*, and it will have to concede that it cannot achieve any uniquely correct solutions. (Here, then, a relativistic reading of transcendental arguments begins to dawn.)

A larger adjustment suggests itself. What we are calling the epistemic strategy probably takes at least three distinct forms: either (1) it is fully cognitivist, in the sense already provided; or (2) it is subordinated within a pragmatist (or non-epistemic) strategy; *or* (3) it is committed to a privileged metaphysics or methodology *affecting cognitive claims distributively but without genuinely cognitivist or foundationalist grounds*. In the analytic tradition, there can be little doubt that the systematic advocacy of physicalism and extensionalism (associated, for instance, with the work of Quine and Davidson) is characteristically pursued in this third way – *blindly*, in epistemic terms, one may say, precisely because of an overly strict adherence to what is (wrongly) taken to be the import of rejecting the analytic–synthetic demarcation. For the rejection of that distinction rightly obtains only at the level of second-order inquiry – consistently with pragmatism; but it may (and must) be reclaimed in acceptably provisional ways *within* a holistic realism, in order to accommodate the achievements of science itself. It is against the inclusive form of epistemic privilege (ranging over both cognitivist *and* the "blind" but not thereby *non*-epistemic strategies) that Rorty rightly inveighs. (In the Continental European tradition, following the example of Heidegger and Jacques Derrida, such presumptively transcendental claims are dubbed "philosophy of presence" or "logocentrism" or the like.[13]) But Rorty fails to segregate the second of these strategies from the other two; it is precisely there that his would-be final subversion of philosophy collapses. (We may, then, adopt the term "logocentric" for theories falling within the union of the first and third strategies, or for the third strategy alone: foundationalism, then, may be logocentric without actually being cognitivistic. We shall return to the issue.)

The *non sequitur* of Rorty's rejection of philosophy suggests the importance of even a modest catalogue of the relevant strategies for legitimating realism in science. Merely to acknowledge, for instance, the observational underdetermination of explanatory theories within the very practice of science – as well as the substantive bearing on the problems and direction of actual research, of disputes about the conceptual relations linking observational data, phenomenological laws, causal inference, and explanatory theory (for example, as in disagreements of the sort abstracted by van Fraassen and Nancy Cartwright) – amply confirms how premature Rorty's conclusion is. *If* in exploring the legitimation of our cognitive competence (those very first-order competences Rorty fully acknowledges, in supporting science) we need not construe our power cognitivistically or logocentrically – either in first-order or in second-order terms – then a Rortian view of transcendental arguments cannot fail to impoverish the conceptual resources with which we ought to pursue a rational review *of* the very undertakings of science. The conclusion falls out quite naturally merely by considering that there are (epistemically pertinent) ways of exploring the realism of science other than by insisting on that (the cognitivist's) strategy.

Certainly, one sees that, even if Chisholm's version of a narrowly cognitivist strategy is allowed, there is no obviously salient or compelling application of it that could be expected to decide the right version of realism *in science*. Also, against even this concession, it is by no means clear that, as in invoking Wittgenstein as Chisholm does, in explaining the directly evident, there is any assured sense in which the pertinent support of cognitive claims may actually be shown to rest – or need to rest – on formulable *grounds* or, consequently, on "valid general principles of evidence."[14]

Chisholm cites approvingly a passage in Wittgenstein's *On Certainty* regarding the use of (the apparent avowal) "I know," as if Wittgenstein were there supporting something like Chisholm's own theory of the evident and the directly evident.[15] But the truth is that Wittgenstein was actually drawing us away from any cognitivist or foundationalist views – toward an altogether different strategy. For he plainly maintains, in what appears to be the same general context as that of Chisholm's citation, that "Giving grounds, ... justifying the evidence, comes to an end; but the end is not certain propositions' striking us immediately as true, i.e. it is not a kind of *seeing* on our part; it is our *acting*, which lies at the bottom of the language-game."[16] Once we grasp his point, it is neither clear, nor straightforwardly convincing to maintain, that Chisholm has actually addressed the most economical objection to his thesis: namely, that it is unnecessary (as well as threateningly extravagant). For, what Wittgenstein very simply shows is that we *can* come to a "stopping place," an end to "Socratic questions" – as Chisholm insists we must[17] – without appeal to grounds or evidential rules of the foundational kind Chisholm favors. Wittgenstein's answer, then, lies in (implicitly) adopting a version of the *second* principal strategy (the non-epistemic strategy) for legitimating realism. Of course, whether we should say that Wittgenstein was a realist in some strong and interesting sense needs to be considered in a fresh way. But at the very least, with regard to just the kind of properties and states Chisholm wishes to treat as self-presenting, Wittgenstein shows us how to *ground* the seeming compellingness of pertinent propositions in the viable *practices* and *activities* of a society rather than in *epistemically* specified cognitive (that is, cognitivist) powers. In effect, Wittgenstein moves to a non-epistemic, pragmatist legitimation of our cognitive capacities – for which reason, of course, he must give up, in so doing, the direct legitimation of distributed claims. For the argument holds only *en bloc*.[18] Alternatively put, Wittgensteinian "forms of life" signify an extremely abstract acknowledgement of the praxical nature of human cognition – without, that is, any account of the historically determinate conditions under which human life is actually produced and reproduced (as on the Marxist view).

We may take a moment to reflect, here, on the fact that we have ineluctably moved from a focus on relativism to a focus on realism. The issues have their own life, of course. But perhaps it may be fairly said that, when we directly entertained the question of the viability of relativism, we had our eye always cocked for the possibility of reconciling a viable relativism with a realism suited to science. Correspondingly, in now sorting the complexities of realism – in cognitively pertinent terms – we mean to attend constantly to the potential bearing of our realist options upon the fortunes of the relativism we have provisionally fashioned.

II

We can hardly fail to be reminded, here, of Quine's holism – as well as of its connection with the fate of the analytic–synthetic distinction.[19] Certainly, the legitimation of cognitive powers on *non*-epistemic grounds, precisely because it gives up altogether the pretense of being able to confirm, in a strongly realist sense, cognitive claims taken singly (a retreat required, in any case, in having rejected the analytic–synthetic distinction – Quine's crucial challenge to Carnap), *cannot* be taken to exhibit the error that, say, Rorty claims to have exposed in rejecting transcendental arguments. On the contrary, it is deliberately concerned with avoiding that putative error. The trouble with the *non*-epistemic legitimation of science is simply that it can provide absolutely no grounds for assessing – *internally* with respect to the pragmatist orientation itself (that is, internally with respect to the biological viability of a race dependent on cognitive intercession) – *any* differential grounds for appraising distributively the various parts *of our first-order science.* Here is the crucial difference between Duhem and Quine, and here is the puzzle Rorty fails to address. For Quine never explains how to decide rationally *which* option we should favor among alternative sets of distributed claims within our first-order science; and Rorty expressly favors the competence of our actual science *to* decide such questions, but fails to see the need (given the conceptual dangers he himself warns us about) to explain the connection between the holistic pragmatism he favors and science's self-corrective powers. In short, both Quine and Rorty favor holistic defenses of realism; but *both* neglect to discuss the contingencies of realism itself *within the scope of a pragmatically competent science* – say, in accord with their own general realist convictions about the direction science is bound to take. Thus, Quine clearly commits himself to a very strong form of extensionalism; and Rorty, to an equally strong (though unspecified) form of physicalism.[20] But there *is* no way to make sense of such commitments, except in terms of some thesis about the legitimation of *distributed* claims. Quine, therefore, is obliged to reconsider the viability of *some* operable distinction between analytic and synthetic criteria; and Rorty is obliged to explain why we should have confidence in the progressive or eventual achievement of an *adequate* physicalist science. Neither, however, rises to the occasion. In that sense, both have inadvertently subscribed to (the "blind" version of) logocentrism. Furthermore, *under holistic constraints*, only a transcendental argument could recover – dialectically – the realist status of distributed scientific claims and strategies of inquiry.

The move to pragmatism precludes the logocentric privilege of extensionalism and physicalism and the unity-of-science program, though it does not preclude their (piecemeal) eligibility. This is why prioritizing formal, uninterpreted schemata for whatever is to count as correctly disciplined empirical inquiry – for example, Davidson's application of a Tarskian-like program to psychology[21] – cannot fail to be "blind" in the logocentric sense, cannot fail to signify an unearned cognitive privilege. Pragmatism does avoid the indefensible claims of a strong cognitivism. But it must incorporate, or be supplemented by, some substantive guidelines (epistemically focused guidelines) bearing on the realist import of science. (This is what one senses in the permanent appeal of correspondence over coherence theories of truth.)

There is otherwise no way to articulate the merely minimal, *en bloc* realism of *science*, in terms of comparing the developing phases of its history, say, as opposed to the strangely coherent structure of certain systematic delusions. Speculations about scientific rationality, for instance, are intended as just such a supplement. The point is a most important one, clarifying for example why it is that Quine's holism may be either ultimately incoherent (since it risks *some* operative segregation of the analytic and synthetic at least for the sake of supporting a strong physicalism and extensionalism) or ultimately irrelevant to Quine's own realist objectives (since it cannot draw, from holism itself, *any* basis for favoring or for confirming the *distributed* power of physicalism or extensionalism – for affirming, say, that "Intensional objects can indeed be banished, and good riddance; but the extensional abstract objects, numbers notably, remain to be reckoned with (and that not in one sense alone)."[22]

Similarly, the point at stake helps to explain the natural tendency, among those drawn to a coherence theory of truth or science, to supplement coherence considerations by *pragmatist* ones, where the holism of the latter is internally differentiated so as to support a more distributive sense of realism.[23] Otherwise, certainly as far as realism is concerned, coherentist accounts tend to become fatally formalistic (for example, like Keith Lehrer's well-known anti-foundationalist analysis of knowledge[24]). This is why analytic epistemology so often risks being empty and uncompelling (even at times irrelevant) in contrast to the more historical and problem-oriented methodology of current theories of science. Without taking sides on the issues raised respectively in the two domains, one sees at once the distinct difference in relevance, for realist questions, of the epistemological reflections, say, of such authors as Quine, Lehrer, and Fred Dretske,[25] on the one hand, and Kuhn, van Fraassen, Cartwright, and Ian Hacking,[26] on the other.

It is really only when one adopts a strong cognitivism or foundationalism that the otherwise formalist nature of most analytic epistemology seems to escape its own limitations. This, of course, is precisely the appeal of such an undertaking as Chisholm's.[27] However, even in Chisholm there seems to be an important lacuna that affects the assessment of his intended foundationalism. The natural (but hardly easy) way of identifying what is missing is to draw on Edmund Husserl's criticism of "objectivism" – without, it must be said, subscribing to Husserl's own conception of the apodictic science of phenomenology. Husserl's point may be gathered from the following remark: "There are all sorts of problems that stem from naïveté, according to which objectivistic science holds what it calls the objective world to be the totality of what is, without paying any attention to the fact that no objective science can do justice to the subjectivity that achieves science."[28] What Husserl is pressing here, admittedly in the form of an *obiter dictum*, is simply that there is no way to consider legitimating cognitive claims without addressing the issue of how such claims are related to the very life of the agent ("subjectivity"), said to have achieved a reliable science.

An essential part of Husserl's complaint, of course, is addressed to Brentano's "not yet [having] overcome objectivism and psychological naturalism," in spite of the fact that Brentano had correctly "promoted psychology [as] a science of vital intentional experience" against "sensualism" (or British-style empiricism) and in spite of the fact that he, Husserl, had of course been correctly oriented by Brentano (though with a radical shift from objectivism to *a priori* idealism – to which Brentano objected) to the primacy of intentional phenomena.[29] But it is also essential to Husserl's complaint that the advocates of *both* an empiricist objectivism *and* a Brentano-like psychological naturalism (even with its recovery of intentionality) fail to "see that from the very beginning they necessarily presuppose themselves as a group of men belonging to their own environing world and historical period. By the same token, they do not see that in pursuing their aims they are seeking a truth in itself, universally valid for everyone."[30] In short, claims of universal validity cannot be legitimated without, at the very least, explaining how to overcome the contingencies of historical existence – which cannot (as such) insure such universality. (This, of course, is an essential part of Husserl's objection to Kant's transcendental arguments, addressed too innocently to a specifically Newtonian physics and a Euclidean geometry.) Husserl leaps to the phenomenologically ("transcendentally") apodictic – which many would regard as quite impossible to vouchsafe; and Brentano holds to the "descriptively" apodictic (to what is "naturalistic" or "objectivist" on Husserl's view, even though reflexive, intentionally qualified, and ampliative in terms of experience).[31]

The point is that Chisholm does not address in a sustained way the double question of how his own conception of self-presenting properties (certainly treated more in the spirit of Brentano than of Husserl) and of how historicizing the entire question of epistemic certainty can be satisfactorily construed so as to legitimate his own claims about the directly evident. Husserl had grasped the need for transcendental or legitimating grounds for first-order claims; but he insisted on the apodictic nature of those higher reflections. Brentano, perhaps in a way not very distant from Husserl's own early version of apodictic science regarding psychological phenomena, had attempted to assign necessity directly to what is disclosed within a reflexive first-order attention (that is, relative to "noticing" as opposed to mere "sensing" or the like); but Brentano had not effectively met the threatening contingencies Husserl posed. Also, if we recall that Wittgenstein effectively provides an alternative that is reasonably congruent with Chisholm's own emphasis (in spite of the not altogether decisive difference Chisholm himself draws attention to regarding the priority of the intentional over the linguistic or of the linguistic over the intentional – the focus of his differences with Wittgenstein[32]), we may see that enlarging the psychological and epistemic to include the intentional does not in itself legitimate a cognitivist account and does not rightly yet address the prospects of foundationalism vis-à-vis realism in science.

It is also not obvious, of course, that Husserl's version of transcendental apriorism could – any more than Kant's, which Husserl believed failed to overcome the objectivist and historicist limitations it would have had to – be said to have succeeded in realizing its own apodictic objective or to have escaped the contingencies of history.[33] In fact, Chisholm effectively rejects Husserl's "transcendental–phenomenological idealism." He does so by the following interesting maneuver: Husserl, Chisholm claims, inferred from "(i) The world cannot be experienced, or even thought, except as being relative to transcendental subjectivity, to the 'I think' that must accompany all presentations" to "(ii) everything that exists and everything that could possibly exist is necessarily relative to the 'I think'." But, argues, Chisholm, (ii) does

not follow from (i), even if (i) is "unassailable." In effect, siding with
the British and American realists of the first part of the twentieth
century – notably, with the central charge of G. E. Moore's "Refutation
of Idealism"[34] – Chisholm sees the weakness of Husserl's claim as
analogous to that of all those idealisms that hold that we are confined
to "the circle of our own ideas" (representationalism). Hence, on Chisholm's view, even if Husserl is right in advancing "(iii) transcendental
subjectivity itself is *not* thus relative to anything else," accepting (i) does
not commit us to Husserl's further apodictic claim," (iv) transcendental
subjectivity is the Absolute to which all else in the world is relative."[35]
This is indeed a stunningly simple demonstration of the inherent *non
ysequitur* of *all* Husserl's struggles to achieve a transcendental cognitivism.
In particular, it suggests the serious doubts that need to be raised
about what Jacques Derrida has summarized as "the self-presence of
transcendental life" in Husserl's work: the self-disclosing nature of the
transcendental mind, in monological contexts, utterly unmediated by
language.[36]

It is of course entirely possible that Husserl's notion of the apodictic
is *not* the notion of an actually accessible conceptual necessity or universal
constraint that *we* can with certainty discern. It may, in this sense, be
meant heuristically or directively, although the concept of a phenomenological science can hardly have been intended in a merely heuristic
way. Every determinate claim of the relevant kind may be potentially
defective, in terms of the conditions and constraints of historical (or
historicized) reflection within the limited horizon of any *Lebenswelt*: so
Husserl may have intended to draw attention primarily to the peculiar
stability, generality, difficulty of denying or satisfactorily replacing
(within our *Lebenswelt*) apparent conceptual necessities of the phenomenological sort. Husserl may, then, have pursued foundational questions
(of a sort radically different from Kant's) without presuming to possess
effectively foundationalist resources (and perhaps something similar is
true of Kant, given his dissatisfaction with his own transcendental
proofs). This would certainly be a reasonable reading of the thrust of
Merleau-Ponty's phenomenology, which, after all, pursues an authentic
strand of Husserl's own speculation.[37] But, in any case, Husserl clearly
opposed the possibility of apodictic or *a priori* certainty with respect to
the natural or objective world (of every familiar science); and, in pursuing
this theme – against Kant and Brentano in particular – he meant to
confirm that *cognition*, as the activity and achievement of an agent that
is alone capable of pursuing science, is never as such, in part or whole,
the matter of any natural or objective science. This is the minimal thesis
of "subjectivity" to which Chisholm alludes in his analysis of Husserl.

But what it means is that, *if* any genuinely apodictic findings are accessible, they are accessible only at the level of phenomenological reflection and never at the level of "naturalistic," "objectivist," "historicist" or similar inquiries. The question remains, therefore, *how* to salvage the apodictic in terms congenial to Brentano and/or Kant, once it is admitted that empirical science is subject to the historicized contingencies of a *Lebenswelt* – even if it is true that such contingencies must also (reflexively) affect the prospects of phenomenological science itself. Chisholm cannot then have failed to lay himself under an obligation, in accommodating the minimal thesis regarding subjectivity.

Nevertheless, Chisholm does find foundationalist sources within the intentional, along "objectivist" lines, more or less in accord with Brentano's emphasis. He appears to miss the fundamental objection posed by Husserl, however, because *he* notes the doubtfulness of Husserl's preference for the apodictic disclosures of subjectivity rather than Husserl's more pertinent insistence on the historicized contingencies of intentional awareness itself. In effect, Chisholm accepts Husserl's (i) but "naturalizes" it: "I believe," he says,

> that "transcendental subjectivity" is something that must be taken into account by any serious philosophy of mind and certainly by any adequate "phenomenology." One cannot describe it, so far as I can see, in terms of bodily states or even of thoughts or feelings. But when Husserl describes the place of transcendental subjectivity in the world – or, rather, the place of the world in relation to transcendental subjectivity – he proposes a philosophical description of evident psychological phenomena (and one which many of his followers could not accept).[38]

Chisholm does not, however, attempt a full legitimation of his naturalized account of intentional self-evidence. It is true that he shows how to preserve the realism of intentionally qualified experience – against mere subjectivism; but he develops an account that is still more like an intentionalized empiricism, with a realist upshot of course, than one that weighs the actual bearing of distributed phenomenological reports on a realism suited to science. (One suspects, therefore, a more logocentric strategy in Chisholm's program.) There is no attempt to provide a full-scale examination of the characteristic problems of legitimating realism in science *from* the vantage of the foundational sources Chisholm subscribes to.

The foundationalism seems to be conflated with the realism; but, then, it leaves oddly undefended (however strongly favored) a realism

(Chisholm's) that falls more or less within Wilfrid Sellars's "manifest image."[39] On the other hand, the phenomenological theme does manage to point unmistakably to the "naïveté" (Husserl's term) of Sellars's own rejection of the *epistemic* role of "subjectivity" – which cannot fail to bear on Sellars's extreme scientific realism as much as on the ordinary sensory reports Sellars would discount.[40] If we combine, then, Husserl's worries about the historical and cultural contingencies of human inquiry together with Wittgenstein's ("pragmatist") alternative to foundationalism of the sort Chisholm favors, we cannot fail to see the indecisiveness of Chisholm's program thus far developed. For example, suppose that, in a Humean-like sense, we cannot either reflexively detect a persisting cognizing self or be certain of its identity through an apparent or "quasi"-identity;[41] or, therefore, be certain that what is predicated in reflexive first-person discourse of the "self" is true of it as thus persisting.[42] In fact, what emerges is a clear sense of the inadequacy of any mere empiricism (or intentionalized "empiricism"), whether idealist in the sense of subjectivism or realist in the sense Chisholm is prepared to share with Husserl, to provide foundationalist or logocentric directives sufficiently pertinent to the needs of a realism suited to science. We are bound, therefore, to look elsewhere.

III

We have been arguing, in effect, that (second-order) questions of legitimation, particularly with respect to realism in science, are coherent, viable, substantively pertinent with regard to the rational direction of the very (first-order) work of science, hence both symbiotically linked to first-order inquiry and ineliminable on rational grounds. We have not directly specified the logical character of legitimation itself; and, to be candid, references to "legitimating" inquiries rather than "transcendental" deductions or arguments reflect a deliberate avoidance of the more canonical term in favor of a much less controversial one – both because it seemed more natural to try to show the plausibility of holding on to the second-order inquiries here broached without yet invoking technical objections, and because it seemed desirable to leave altogether open the question of what logical form (if any) pertinent arguments should be said to take. The latter question remains entirely open still: particularly, in opposition to the (cognitivist or logocentric) versions advocated by Kant and Husserl and to those counterarguments (Rorty's, for instance) that refuse to consider other or more heterodox versions of legitimation (or transcendental arguments).

But we have also begun to shape something of a reasonable strategy of legitimation: it should begin along pragmatist lines, so as to obviate cognitivisms and foundationalisms of every sort (essentialisms, universalisms, logocentrisms, and the rest). It should establish a minimal realism, by non-epistemic considerations of an *en bloc* sort. And then, on *epistemic* considerations internal to (that is, benignly circular regarding) the putative achievements of science and inquiry – and on the strength of (internally) distributed weightings of reliability, importance, and the like – *we should continue as before*.

We ground our realism, minimally, as pragmatists: in effect, we reject cognitivism (and logocentrism) and treat realism holistically. Then, within the space of *that* advantage, we return to *epistemic* considerations – now, distributively – by testing the realist possibilities and the import of legitimating efforts grounded in certain favored features of the ongoing first-order practice of our science, *about which we have, diachronically, always raised the same realist concerns and which have, therefore, always been affected by the symbiotic linkage between such first- and second-order work.*

Pragmatist without epistemic legitimation, we may say, is blind; and epistemic without prior pragmatist legitimation is indefensible because it is cognitivistic or logocentric. The first maxim explains why Quine's and Donald Davidson's physicalism and extensionalism are (as forms of realism suited to science) entirely blind: there is, for instance, no epistemically pertinent sense in which to treat linguistic behavior as elicited "responses" to "stimulations" – either with respect to the observed behavior of a native speaker *or* with respect to a field linguist's observation of such behavior – *if*, for example, "A visual stimulation is perhaps best identified, for present purposes [or in whatever way the account may be refined along the same lines], with the pattern of chromatic irradiation of the eye" (even if we restrict ourselves to "the microscopically same irradiations");[43] correspondingly, there is no empirically pertinent "translation manual" in which "we can infer from it nothing about the relations between words and objects."[44] Both doctrines try to provide a promising realism suited to the first-order practices of science solely in terms of a noncognitivist or pragmatist holism (however much the distinction between first- and second-order issues may be collapsed); and both, it may be added, fail to address what is salvageable in Husserl's challenge to naturalism and objectivism (which betrays their sense of a distributed realism). Finally, both suppose (*without argument*) that empirically pertinent semantic and referential distinctions can always be suitably reconciled – *in pertinently realist terms* – in accord with a merely programmatic physicalism or a merely extensional syntax legitimately already in place on holistic grounds alone. (We have already touched on the problem in exploring Davidson's use of Tarski's Convention T and Putnam's use of the Skolem–Löwenheim theorem.) But these are entirely undefended and indefensible maneuvers – *logocentric*, precisely in attempting to rescue an epistemic privilege from a non-epistemic holism.

The second maxim signifies what the defeat of cognitivism and logocentrism entails as well as the promising conceptual option of integrating pragmatist and internal epistemic strategies of legitimation. It teaches us, in effect, that, contrary to Quine's and Rorty's resistance, there can be no form of realism pertinent to the actual work of science *that does not address itself to the (realist) import of distributed claims*. What both seem to have feared, unnecessarily, is that advocating an *epistemic* strategy could not but undo the repudiation of a principled demarcation between the analytic and the synthetic. But that is simply a mistake. All that is needed is the concession that distributed realist claims are appraised only *within* the boundaries of a pragmatist strategy blind to cognitivist privilege or logocentric pretension. We cannot ignore the rational function of such internal speculation, simply because the *en bloc* success of our very science makes no sense except in terms of ongoing, differentially weighted commitments regarding all the alternative possibilities of choice – reflexively collected and diachronically assessed within the scope of our first-order science. Curiously, to say this is to say no more than is already entailed in Quine's insistence (which Rorty opposes), that science and philosophy are seamlessly one.

But, if we concede the distributed (epistemic) blindness of pragmatism and the indefensibility of logocentrism, and if we concede the consequent contingencies – particularly, the historicized contingencies of horizon and bias – there can be little doubt that the very enterprise of legitimating realism cannot be construed in a way that precludes relativistic procedures, either diachronically or synchronically. There simply is no sense in which the pertinent questions of realism in science can be timelessly or uniquely resolved. This is the reason why a reflexively therapeutic conception of philosophy cannot possibly exhaust the pertinence of second-order questions with regard to any well-established first-order empirical inquiry. There will always be choices to be made regarding the realist import of observation, experiment, invention, procedure, problem, puzzle, explanatory theory, postulation of entities, causal inference, comparative assessments and prejudices of what is central to an ongoing science – choices *needed* in order to act rationally *as* scientists. Such choices will always be hostage to the perceived contingencies of the successes and failures of our historicized science; and there is no *a priori* reason why all pertinent speculation about such choices should converge ideally toward some single solution.

We may gather the essential threads of the argument in the following way. There is no point to fitting holism to science without fitting it to the whole of science; and there is no way of doing that without fitting it to the ordered claims of a distributive science. But there is no way of addressing the latter without a ramified theory of truth applied to both a second-order (holistic) reading of science *and* a first-order reading of the distributed claims of science. Both are required by any viable theory of scientific realism; and no appreciation of the special power of the (first-order achievement of the) developed sciences can fail to come to terms with the symbiosis of first- and second-order questions. Here, then, is the common failing of Rorty's rejection of philosophy and of the pertinence of truth and theories of truth,[45] of Quine's insistence on disjoining the empirical testing of science *en bloc* and the would-be first-order testing of distributed claims that cannot in any way overcome the inherent opacities of single propositions (with regard to reference and truth), *and* also (drawing on an earlier discussion) of Gadamer's and Taylor's reliance on the crypto-universalism and crypto-cognitivism of appealing to the "tradition" of human inquiry within the boundaries of historicized horizons. Rorty's thesis fails because it denies what is entailed by its own commitment to science; Quine's, because it tries to insure a reasonably realist reading of science without accepting its full price; Gadamer's and Taylor's, because it smuggles into its own account sources of cognitive assurance that it cannot and would be unwilling to legitimate. Hence, Rorty urges us to abandon philosophy but preserve science; Quine insists on the inscrutability of reference and the indeterminacy of translation within a science scrutable enough to "make our theories true"; and Gadamer and Taylor reassure us that the relativistic threat to our apparently stable sciences posed by historicized existence is safely offset by a universal-like tradition forever lurking in that same history. To grasp the *aporia* of each is to grasp as well the sense in which science and philosophy are continuous with one another, the sense in which philosophy must be strongly pragmatist to be viable and in which a viable pragmatism cannot fail to accommodate the moderate relativism here espoused.

The truth is that an epistemic strategy for legitimating realism, if not committed to any form of cognitivism or logocentrism, cannot but be relativistic.

Notes

1 Cf Peter Klein, *Certainty* (Minneapolis: University of Minnesota Press, 1960); and Arne Naess, *Scepticism* (London: Routledge and Kegan Paul,

1968), especially ch. 1.

2   See Nancy Cartwright, *How the Laws of Physics Lie* (Oxford: Clarendon Press, 1983).

3   Roderick M. Chisholm, *The Foundations of Knowing* (Minneapolis: University of Minnesota Press, 1982), p. 10.

4   Ibid.

5   Ibid., pp. 11–13.

6   Roderick M. Chisholm, *Theory of Knowledge*, 2nd edn (Englewood Cliffs, N.J.: Prentice-Hall, 1977), p. 21.

7   See Norman Malcolm, *Knowledge and Certainty* (Englewood Cliffs, N.J.: Prentice-Hall, 1963).

8   See Bas C. van Fraassen, *The Scientific Image* (Oxford: Clarendon Press, 1980), ch. 2.

9   Cf. Chisholm, *Theory of Knowledge*, p. 19.

10 Richard Rorty, "Transcendental Arguments, Self-Reference, and Pragmatism," in Peter Bieri et al. (eds), *Transcendental Arguments and Science* (Dordrecht: R. Reidel, 1979), p. 78; see also Rorty's *Philosophy and the Mirror of Nature* (Princeton, N.J.: Princeton University Press, 1979). The reference to Davidson is to "On the Very Idea of a Conceptual Scheme," *Inquiries into Truth and Interpretation* (Oxford: Clarendon Press, 1984).

11 For a brief formulation of Chisholm's view of foundationalism, see *Theory of Knowledge*, p. 63. Cf. also Keith Lehrer, *Knowledge* (Oxford: Clarendon Press, 1974).

12 In effect, this suggests the limited scope of Rorty's own "mirror" metaphor in characterizing the philosophical tradition he rejects: cf. *Philosophy and the Mirror of Nature*, ch. 1.

13 See Jacques Derrida, *Of Grammatology*, trs. Gayatri Chakravorty Spivak (Baltimore: Johns Hopkins University Press, 1976).

14 Chisholm, *Theory of Knowledge*, p. 17.

15 The passage is from Ludwig Wittgenstein, *On Certainty*, ed. G. E. M. Anscombe and G. H. von Wright, tr. Denis Paul and G. E. M. Anscombe (Oxford: Basil Blackwell, 1969), section 243.

16 Ibid., section 200.

17 Chisholm, *Theory of Knowledge*, ch. 2.

18 This is surely the proper and valuable point of Norman Malcolm's reading of Wittgenstein. See his "Wittgenstein's *Philosophical Investigations*," *Knowledge and Certainty* (Englewood Cliffs, N.J.: Prentice-Hall, 1963); cf. also Sidney Shoemaker, *Self-Knowledge and Self-Identity* (Ithaca, NY: Cornell University Press, 1963).

19 See W. V. Quine, "Two Dogmas of Empiricism," *From a Logical Point of View* (Cambridge, Mass.: Harvard University Press, 1953).

20 Cf. Rorty, *Philosophy and the Mirror of Nature*, for instance at p. 354.

21 See Davidson: "Reality without Reference," *Inquiries into Truth and Interpretation*; "Mental Events," *Essays on Actions and Events* (Oxford: Clarendon Press, 1980).

22 The difficulty has always dogged Quine's projects. Yet in a recent review he confirms his adherence to these programs without any acknowledgement of their seeming arbitrariness. See W. V. Quine, "Four Hot Questions in

Philosophy" (review of P. F. Strawson, *Skepticism and Naturalism: Some Varieties*), *New York Review of Books*, 14 February 1985, p. 32.

23 This is the key to, for instance, Nicholas Rescher's *The Coherence Theory of Truth* (Oxford: Clarendon Press, 1973).

24 Lehrer, *Knowledge*.

25 See Fred I. Dretske, *Knowledge and the Flow of Information* (Cambridge, Mass.: MIT Press, 1981).

26 See Ian Hacking, *Representing and Intervening* (Cambridge: Cambridge University Press, 1983).

27 The characteristic failure, however, of analytic foundationalism to come to grips with the realist issue in spite of its seemingly larger resources may be gauged rather quickly from, to cite a pertinent specimen, John L. Pollock, *Knowledge and Justification* (Princeton, NJ: Princeton University Press, 1974), pp. 54–6, where Pollock briefly considers the issue of "scientific realism" – actually restricted, instructively, to Bertrand Russell's quite general thesis that "we infer the existence of physical objects as the simplest explanation of why things appear to us in the way they do" (p. 54). Cf. also ch. 8; and Bertrand Russell, *The Problems of Philosophy* (New York: Holt, Rinehart and Winston, 1912).

28 Edmund Husserl, "Philosophy and the Crisis of European Man," *Phenomenology and the Crisis of Philosophy*, tr. Quentin Lauer (New York: Harper and Row, 1965), p. 185.

29 Ibid., pp. 189–90.

30 Ibid., pp. 186–7. Cf. also Husserl: "Philosophy as Rigorous Science," in the same collection; and *The Crisis of European Sciences and Transcendental Phenomenology*, tr. David Carr (Evanston, Ill.: Northwestern University Press, 1970), pp. 68–70, 298. (Brentano, by the way, was not opposed to characterizing himself as an empiricist.)

31 For a convenient overview of Brentano's descriptive psychology, see Roderick M. Chisholm, "Brentano's Descriptive Psychology," in Linda L. McAlister (ed.), *The Philosophy of Brentano* (Atlantic Highlands, NJ: Humanities Press, 1976).

32 See for instance Roderick M. Chisholm: *The First Person* (Minneapolis: University of Minnesota Press, 1981), ch. 1; *Perceiving: A Philosophical Study* (Ithaca, NY: Cornell University Press, 1957), ch. 11.

33 See also Husserl, *The Crisis of European Sciences and Transcendental Phenomenology*. Broadly speaking, this is the focus of Derrida's criticism of Husserl: see Jacques Derrida, *Speech and Phenomena*, tr. David B. Allison (Evanston, Ill.: Northwestern University Press, 1973), pp. 24–32. Cf. Chisholm: *The Foundations of Knowledge*, ch. 8; and *The First Person*, ch. 3.

34 G. E. Moore, "Refutation of Idealism," *Mind* XII (1903).

35 Roderick M. Chisholm (ed.), Editor's Introduction to *Realism and the Background of Phenomenology* (Glencoe, Ill.: Free Press, 1960), especially pp. 21–2, 25.

36 See Edmund Husserl, *Logical Investigations*, 2 vols, tr. J. N. Findlay (New York: Humanities Press, 1970), First Investigation; also Derrida, *Speech and Phenomena* (the phrase quoted appears on p. 6).

37 See Maurice Merleau-Ponty, *The Visible and the Invisible*, tr. Alphonso Lingis (Evanston, Ill.: Northwestern University Press, 1968).

38 Chisholm, Editor's Introduction to *Realism and the Background of Phenomenology*, p. 20.

39 Cf. Wilfrid Sellars, "Philosophy and the Scientific Image of Man," *Science, Perception and Reality* (London: Routledge and Kegan Paul, 1963).

40 Cf. Sellars, "The Language of Theories," ibid., for instance at p. 126.

41 Cf. Derek Parfit, *Reasons and Persons* (Oxford: Clarendon Press, 1984), section 80.

42 Cf. Chisholm, *The First Person*, particularly the bearing of ch. 5 on ch. 7.

43 W. V. Quine, *Word and Object* (Cambridge, Mass.: MIT Press, 1960), p. 31.

44 Davidson, "Reality with Reference," *Inquiries into Truth and Interpretation*, p. 221.

45 See Richard Rorty, Introduction to *Consequences of Pragmatism* (Minneapolis: University of Minnesota Press, 1982).

7

Pragmatism without Foundations

I

Possibly some among us would concede that the history of science reliably testifies to the realist achievement of science. Beyond this grudging acknowledgement, there is often said to be rather little consensus about the nature and analysis of human knowledge and little prospect of wider consensus.

Perhaps the defensiveness of this small piece of tact is already plain: it is the mark of the street-wise theorist who anticipates that there are more detailed difficulties involved in speculating about the conditions of knowledge than ever he can anticipate. One impulse bids us abandon altogether the theory of knowledge – and canonical philosophy in general – but hold on sensibly to the fruitful work of science. This, of course, is the fashionable advice tendered by Richard Rorty. Rorty applauds Thomas Kuhn's argument, for instance, demonstrating the inadequacy of "the traditional epistemological paradigm" when applied in the context of revolutionary science.[1] But Rorty concludes that, instead of trying to find an alternative paradigm, "Kuhn should have simply discarded the epistemological project altogether."[2] He urges that we do so.

His advice seems absurdly simple and profoundly decent until we naggingly observe that science itself – certainly the powerful tradition of inquiry that so commands the Western mind – quite naturally generates its own second-order questions. To admit that is simply to admit, in a fairly noncontroversial sense, that science is seamlessly continuous with philosophical reflection on the nature of reality, of knowledge, of method, of meaning, of truth. We cannot have our science and eat our epistemology. This is what baffles Rorty in reviewing the destructive power of the so-called "holism" and anti-foundationalism of Wilfrid Sellars and W. V. Quine.[3] How they could have supposed they were *continuing* the enterprise of epistemology, once they had demonstrated the inherent error of its ways, simply escapes Rorty. The answer, of course, is the straightforward one that, at least implicitly, *they* did not characterize its essential problem as Rorty does.

Rorty maintains that

> the desire for a theory of knowledge is a desire for constraint – a desire to find "foundations" to which one might cling, frameworks beyond which one must not stray, objects which impose themselves, representations which cannot be gainsaid. ... Epistemology proceeds on the assumption that all contributions to a given discourse are commensurable. ... By "commensurable" I mean able to be brought under a set of rules which will tell us how rational agreement can be reached on what would settle on every point where statements seem to conflict.[4]

This is admirably clear, and helps to explain why, in Rorty's opinion, "the holistic, antifoundationalist, pragmatist treatments of knowledge and meaning which we find in Dewey, Wittgenstein, Quine, Sellars, and Davidson are almost equally offensive to many philosophers, precisely because they abandon the quest for commensuration and thus are 'relativist.'"[5] Of course, with the uncertain exception of Wittgenstein, those mentioned explicitly – one might almost say, enthusiastically – pursue epistemology and ontology, apparently mindless of the fact that they have done their own work too well. Less fancifully stated, they must suppose that the theory of knowledge examines the question of the foundations of knowledge without being committed *a priori* to there being any fixed foundations to be discovered. Rorty correctly observes that the strongest contemporary currents of epistemology have undermined foundationalism; he wrongly concludes that the question of epistemic foundations has therefore lost its conceptual relevance. For that reason, he prematurely disposes of philosophy. But, once we grant that human beings have knowledge, it is hopeless to deny the relevance and admissibility of the Kantian-like questions, "How is such knowledge possible?" "What are its necessary and sufficient conditions?"

How these are to be construed and answered may be counted on to sort the genuine foundationalist and whoever, like those Rorty himself names and favors, honors the questions and rejects the foundationalist answer. Quine himself, it should be remembered, denies the discontinuity of philosophy and science, in rejecting Carnap's distinction between internal and external questions.[6] The distinction of second-order questions is itself a distinction of provisional relations *within* a complex practice that cannot possibly proceed level by separate logical level. "True, no experiment may be expected to settle an ontological issue"; but this is designed more to explain the multiplicity of defensible ontologies than the pointlessness of the issue, for Quine takes the claim to apply to scientific theory just as well. Also, as he rather neatly observes, the philosopher "can scrutinize and improve the system from within, appealing to coherence and simplicity; but this is the theoretician's method generally. He has recourse to semantic ascent, but so has the scientist."[7] Semantic ascent merely captures the advantage of whatever agreement shifting from the "material mode" to the "formal mode" makes possible, without pretending to anything like the tenability of Carnap's distinction between internal and external questions.

Now, we can view what Quine says here – somewhat against his own inclination (in one regard), certainly against Rorty's (in another) – as redeeming, under significantly altered conditions, the entire traditional range of fundamental philosophical questions. The tradition holds that these are *foundational* or *transcendental* questions, second-order questions about what makes human knowledge conceptually possible. Two qualifications suggest themselves, both of which are already implicit in what has been drawn from Quine, neither of which, doubtless, he would care to put in just this way. First of all, foundational or transcendental questions are questions internal to the very practice of science – second-order, *sui generis* empirical questions: they are reflexively projected by attending to what we take our cognitive achievement to be and by querying what could conceivably and plausibly serve as the preconditions (the "external" or *a priori* conditions, in that sense) of the practice at stake. Secondly, the question arises relative to the historical contingency of our own particular phase of science; that is, it is a foundational question, but it does not (or at least it need not) arise in a *foundationalist* way. This, then, provides, at one and the same time, for the *reductio* of Rorty's position and for the radical transformation of Kant's doctrine of transcendental questions. One way or another, foundationalist theories hold to a fixed, certain, or strongly privileged cognitive access to the real world, on which all other cognitively relevant claims depend, however weakly.[8]

So seen, foundationalist views are rather more protean and persistent than the standard examples suggest. It is one thing to discharge the indubitability of sense data and Cartesian self-evidence. It is quite another to question, with the foundationalist's motive in mind, the suppler, slier, rather decentered doctrines of the analytic–synthetic demarcation, essentialism, the totalized structure of thought and language (Wittgenstein's *Tractatus*, for instance), progressivism in science, and the synthetic *a priori*. Perhaps a brief illustration will help to show the natural dangers of the undertaking. Karl Popper, for example, strongly opposes essentialism in scientific explanation. He offers three views of science, the second of which he takes to be seriously mistaken but correctible and the third, essentialist and utterly wrong:

(1) *The scientist aims at finding a true theory or description of the world* (and especially of its regularities or "laws"), *which shall also be an explanation of the observable facts.*

(2) *The scientist can succeed in finally establishing the truth of such theories beyond all reasonable doubt.*

(3) *The best, the truly scientific theories, describe the "essences" or the "essential natures" of things – the realities which lie behind the appearances.* Such theories are neither in need nor susceptible of further explanation: they *are ultimate explanations*, and to find them is the ultimate aim of the scientist.[9]

Popper wishes to steer a third course between the essentialist view (which he finds embodied in Galilean science) and the instrumentalist view of science (to the effect that universal laws or theories are not proper statements about reality but only rules or instructions for deriving singular observational statements from other singular observational statements).[10] Popper accepts (1) and attenuates (2) along the lines of his falsifiability thesis – in a way that yields what he himself dubs a "modified essentialism." As he says, "although I do not think that we can ever describe, by our universal laws, an *ultimate* essence of the world, I do not doubt that we may seek to probe deeper and deeper into the structure of our world or, as we might say, into properties of the world that are more and more essential, or of greater and greater depth."[11] In effect, this is the nerve of Popper's well-known doctrine of verisimilitude – on which progress in science depends. Granting the strict impossibility of (2) and (3) – and what amounts to the fallibilism of the falsifiability thesis – theories exhibit more or less "truthlikeness or *verisimilitude*" but not truth,

if and only if (a) their truth contents and falsity contents (or their measures) are comparable, and either (b) the truth content, but not the falsity content, T_1 is smaller than that of T_2, or else (c) the truth content of T_1 is not greater than that of T_2, but its falsity content is greater. In brief, we say that T_1 is nearer to the truth, or more similar to the truth, than T_2, if and only if more true statements follow from it, but not more false statements, or at least equally many true statements but fewer false statements.[12]

This seems quite straightforward, but it has the extraordinary disadvantage of presupposing *some* pertinent measure of approximation to the ultimate truth about, or essential natures of, things that Popper insists are never accessible. Otherwise, he would never be able to distinguish his position from either the true essentialist's or the true instrumentalist's, both of whom he cordially abhors. Popper wants to hold at one and the same time that nature is inexhaustibly and immeasurably deep – so that we can never really tell how our contingent science is related moment by moment to what may be discovered – and that, nevertheless, our science can genuinely claim progress and a distinct measure of verisimilitude. The project is quite impossible; but, more than that, it turns out to be a cryptic form of foundationalism itself, just at the point at which it would free us forever from its clutches. Popper's error lies, precisely, in maintaining both the immeasurable inexhaustibility of nature *and* the epistemic standing of verisimilitude; for to take the first seriously is to preclude the second. This is not to preclude the reasonableness of a conviction regarding scientific progress or of the relative fruitfulness of one program of research over another. It is only to treat it as a regulative notion governing compared bets *within* a practice blind to its own convergence (however slight) toward the ultimate revelation of nature.

It is interesting to speculate that, in a much more attenuated form, a cognate difficulty besets Quine's fundamental contribution to the puzzle of analyticity. For, though he says in no uncertain way that "For all its a priori reasonableness, a boundary between analytic and synthetic statements simply has not been drawn,"[13] he also says, linking the dogma of reductionism and that of analyticity ("at root identical"),

> The dogma of reductionism survives in the supposition that each statement, taken in isolation from its fellows, can admit of confirmation or infirmation at all. My countersuggestion, issuing essentially from Carnap's doctrine of the physical world in the *Aufbau*, is that our statements about the external world face the tribunal of sense experience not individually but only as a corporate body. ... The unit of empirical significance is the whole of science.[14]

This, which incorporates Quine's stronger version of the so-called Duhem thesis – since, on Quine's view but not on Duhem's, "any statement can be held true come what may, if we make drastic enough adjustments elsewhere in the system"[15] – does appear to commit Quine to the thesis that science as a whole *is* somehow cognitively testable.[16] It is in this spirit that Quine speaks metaphorically of (apparently) testing individual statements "in terms of varying distances from a sensory periphery": "the edge of the system must be kept squared with experience."[17] The image is absolutely fundamental to the argument of the first two books of *Word and Object*: socialized, "stimulus synonymy" and "stimulus analyticity" may, as Quine concedes, still not be "behavioristic reconstructions of intuitive semantics, but only a behavioristic ersatz";[18] but there can be little question that, for Quine, "analytical hypotheses" are *not* required for determining the stimulus meaning of the "observation sentences" of native speakers or of fixing "stimulus synonymy" and "stimulus analyticity" themselves. Quine characteristically asks, "how does the linguist *pass* these bounds?" The answer is that he *then* invokes his own "analytical hypothesis," his own culturally favored categoreal networks.[19] So the relative neutrality of Quine's executive approximation to understanding an alien speaker *via* stimulus meaning entails *some* demarcation (in terms of first-order cognitive competence) between the analytic and the synthetic. And to that extent, though the major thrust of his entire philosophical effort is to undermine foundationalism, Quine remains something of a crypto-foundationalist. Alternatively, *if* he merely retreats to a pragmatist defense of the holistic validity of science, then, *in* eschewing epistemic grounds for distributed claims, Quine ineluctably renders defenseless or undefended his own extensionalist and physicalist programs (which would otherwise have point *only* for systems of distributed claims). This, of course, is just the sense in which Quine's account is "logocentric" (in the narrow sense given).

It is no accident that both Quine and Popper consider the bearing, on their own doctrines, of those most original speculations of Charles Sanders Peirce's that seem particularly opposed to foundationalism. Here is what Quine says:

> Peirce was tempted to define truth outright in terms of scientific method as the ideal theory which is approached as a limit when the (supposed) canons of scientific method are used unceasingly on continuing experience. But there is a lot wrong with Peirce's notion, besides its assumption of a final organon of scientific method and its appeal to an infinite process. There is a faulty use of numerical analogy in speaking of a limit of theories, since the notion of limit depends on that of "nearer than" which is defined for numbers and not for theories. And even if we by-pass such troubles ..., still there is trouble in the imputation of uniqueness

("*the* ideal result"). For ... we have no reason to suppose that man's surface irritations even unto eternity admit of any one systematization that is scientifically better or simpler than all possible others. It seems likelier, if only on account of asymmetries or dualities, that countless alternative theories would be tied for first place. Scientific method is the way to truth, but it affords even in principle no unique definition of truth. Any so-called pragmatic definition of truth is doomed to failure equally.[20]

In effect, Quine politely accuses Peirce of an illicit foundationalist impulse – a peculiarly pervasive one, in fact, drawn not to positing particular truths (in the manner of the Cartesians or the sense-datum theorists or the Kantians or the Carnapians) but rather to positing the necessary *method* for arriving (in the long run) at the truth. His own objection concerns more the tolerance of alternative ontologies (or grammars) compatibly fitted in divergent ways "with the totality of speech dispositions, yet incompatible with one another"[21] than it concerns the denial that science is the way of truth.

Quine is the advocate of an interesting realism, in which convergence, even compatibility, of provisional theories and ontologies is not required of reasonable claims about the way the world is: "The last arbiter [of truth about the world] is so-called scientific method, however amorphous,"[22] he says. But, curiously, as we have seen, Quine himself falls back implicitly to some sort of cognitive testing of science *en bloc*; and this, even assuming his tolerance for relativism (in effect, in the extended short run) is actually a sort of foundationalist mate of Peirce's own fallibilism. Most succinctly put, *if* the demarcation between the analytic and the synthetic is seriously denied, then the pragmatic testing of science taken as a whole *cannot* be cognitively managed *in principle* – though it can tolerate, *within* its practice, any number of competing confirmatory strategies; it must, ultimately, be construed in terms of something like the continued viability of the race, in terms of mere biological survival. But that is perfectly plausible and sufficient. Any departure would require that science *could* be tested by partitioning its more reliable and less reliable portions – but that, precisely, would be foundationalism once again.

Popper's use of Peirce is both more indirect and more wholehearted in its approval. What Popper wishes to show (alluding favorably to Peirce) is that natural phenomena are neither entirely physically determined ("clocks," in Popper's idiom) nor entirely due to chance ("clouds"); that indeterminism is correct (which is not to deny causal connections); that "rational human behavior ... is something *inter-*

mediate in character between perfect chance and perfect determinism –
something intermediate between perfect clouds and perfect clocks"; and
that "such non-physical things as *purposes, deliberations, plans, decision,
theories, intentions*, and *values*, can play a part in bringing about physical
changes in the physical world."[23] Popper seems not to have quite appreciated the complexity of Peirce's views of the relationship of chance, the
evolving law-like habits of nature, and the role of human intelligence as
the organ of nature's own self-discovery. For instance, Peirce's doctrine
of evolutionary love provides a richer biologically but *not* epistemically
centered account of human success in hitting on explanatory hypotheses
(abduction) more favorably than mere chance, blind circumstance, or
any self-corrective method could possibly insure – once foundationalism
is rejected.[24] Popper inevitably falls back, therefore, to a cognitive and
methodological principle, which we have already criticized in the context
of reviewing the doctrine of verisimilitude. Falsification applies distributively; but evolution can only contribute a noncognitive and holistic
defense of realism. Since Popper addresses the rationality of the actual
practices of science, the deliberate use of falsificationist strategies should
rationally support our confidence in verisimilitudinal progress. But that
is now impossible – for reasons internal to Popper's own account.
Without some plausible rationale for *relying* on falsificationist procedures
(for instance, the calculus Popper himself proposes), either the potential
infinitude of possible hypotheses (Peirce's emphasis – not, let it be said,
Popper's) or the possibility of short-term or accumulating biases and the
potentially misleading successes of our hypothesizing art would seriously
call into question both the doctrine of verisimilitude (which Popper is
at times prepared to scuttle) *and* the conceptual linkage between relying
on falsificationism and adhering to verisimilitude.

Apart from this intriguing matter, what Popper seeks to do is to
construe human inquiry, rather along Peircean lines, as both the result
of a long process of Darwinian evolution and itself best characterized
by analogy with that process. Human inquiry has evolved, he says, in
order, precisely, to maximize verisimilitude, proceeding fallibly *along
falsificationist lines*:

> the growth of our knowledge is the result of a process closely
> resembling what Darwin called "natural selection"; that is, the
> *natural selection of hypotheses*: our knowledge consists, at every
> moment, of those hypotheses which have shown their (com-
> parative) fitness by surviving so far in their struggle for existence;
> a competitive struggle which eliminates those hypotheses which are
> unfit. ... all problems of pure knowledge are *problems of explan-*

ation ... solved by proposing explanatory theories; and an explanatory theory can be criticized by showing that it is either inconsistent in itself or incompatible with the fact or incompatible with some other knowledge. Yet this criticism assumes that what we wish to find are *true* theories – theories which agree with the facts. It is, I believe, this idea of *truth as correspondence with the facts* which makes rational criticism possible ... our aim is to find true theories or at least theories which are nearer to the truth than the theories which are known to us at present.[25]

Here, in a very real sense, the fundamental weakness of Popper's account can be seen to be a minor version of Peirce's own – though it must be specified somewhat differently. Peirce's is far the more important error, because it actually eludes Popper's comparatively simple blunder and both brings us to what is probably the most liberalized version of foundationalism possible and discloses (thereby) an extremely powerful consideration in evaluating the better prospects of epistemology at the present moment. Frankly, Popper fails to see that the denial of essentialism, the insistence on the unfathomable depth of nature, the reliance on falsifiability without foundationalism, and the admission of the historical nature of science itself all conspire to make verisimilitude *cognitively inaccessible*; or, alternatively, Popper fails to see that he cannot reconcile the *distributed* (but potentially limitless) use of falsifiability, in the service of scientific realism or realist progress, without some epistemic connection between falsifiability and verisimilitude or some other doctrine similarly associated with an evolutionary picture of human cognition.

Rightly seen, this also explains the special courage and pathos of Imre Lakatos's methodology of scientific research programs. Popper's confidence in the demarcation between science and metaphysics (that is, "pseudoscience") betrays a reliance on episodic falsification once and for all that cannot be squared with rejecting foundationalism. Lakatos admits, by way of contrast, that, "whereas Popper acknowledged the *influence of metaphysics* upon science, I see metaphysics as an integral part of science."[26] Falsifiability is proposed as a reliable demarcation criterion in the *Logic of Scientific Discovery*;[27] there, it directly entails the rejection of induction and inductivism, and confirms Popper's charge that the positivists simply endorsed "the invasion of metaphysics into the scientific realm."[28] Nevertheless, Popper never satisfactorily addresses the problem of plausibly postponing refutations in particular cases or the problem of reconciling his well-known principle of scientific honesty – that "*criteria of refutation* have to be laid down beforehand:

it must be agreed which observable situations, if actually observed, mean that the theory [at stake] is refuted" – with the actual facts of the history of science: as much, say, with the practice of Newtonian science as with the practice of Freudian pseudoscience.[29] (To press the point against Popper, however, is *not* to concede that Lakatos has made a satisfactory case out for the indefinite postponement of refutations.[30])

Lakatos is much exercised, therefore, to decide whether Popper is merely a naïve "falsificationist" (who holds that "any theory which can be interpreted as experimentally falsifiable, is 'acceptable' or 'scientific'") or a "sophisticated falsificationist" (who holds that "a theory is 'acceptable' or 'scientific' only if it has corroborated excess empirical content over its predecessor or rival, that is, only if it leads to the discovery of novel facts."[31] But there is good reason to believe that Lakatos's own emendation (favoring sophisticated falsification) is still too strong and does not accord with the history of science either – for instance, as in holding that an improved theory T', must be able to explain "the previous success of [a competing] T, that is, [that] *all the unrefuted content of T is included* (within the limits of observational error) in the content of T'."[32] There seems to be no way of forming a comprehensive rational method for insuring that, in any episode in the history of science, T' reliably contributes thus to real scientific progress. This is simply another way of making verisimilitude cognitively inaccessible; or (alternatively) of admitting that there can be no privileged internal–external demarcation regarding the practice of science itself. (But, again, to admit this is *not* to concede that there is no viable distinction to be made between theory and observation.[33])

Accordingly, Lakatos, unlike Popper, begins not with falsifiable hypotheses but with research programs – which are not falsifiable in the naive falsificationist's manner; nevertheless, he believes they can be shown to be *better* along the lines suggested, so that "progress is marked by instances verifying excess content rather than by falsifying instances, and 'falsification' and 'rejection' become logically independent."[34] The truth is that Lakatos, too, is drawn in two rather different ways; and his own best view is that his "meta-criterion" of the better theory permits indefinite postponement of final assessments, "rearguard skirmishes for defeated programs [that is, defeated by inductivist and naive falsificationist criteria]," and (most important) can only serve "more of a guide to the historian of science than to the scientist."[35]

Popper is more sanguine but equivocal about verisimilitude. In addition to the fact that his own proposals for a sophisticated falsificationism provide an explicit basis for Lakatos's own adjustment, Popper actually states that through the "*temporary* successes of our theories

... we can be reasonably successful in attributing our refutations to *definite portions* of the theoretical maze" – which he candidly notes is inexplicable on Duhem's and Quine's views.[36] But, *if* our successes are genuinely "temporary," contingent, fragmented though collected in relatively inclusive theories, subject to chance runs of apparent progress, then, once again, verisimilitude can never be cognitively accessible in the realist sense – though Popper's meta-criterion can serve effectively as a heuristic and regulative rational principle within the practice of science. It cannot claim to satisfy the requirements of the correspondence theory of truth, which (in spite of the perceptible difficulties of Wittgenstein's and Schlick's versions), Popper eventually defended most enthusiastically – once Tarski's theory came to his attention.[37] In any case, it is conceptually impossible, without adhering to some cognitivist or foundationalist thesis (to some assured demarcation of decisive synthetic evidence), to maintain that, under historicized conditions of inquiry, realist progress, verisimilitude, can be reasonably attributed "to *definite portions* of the theoretical maze." Alternatively put, Popper is unclear about whether he wishes to treat verisimilitude as a second-order, holistic, regulative constraint that has no cognitive standing, or whether he wishes to link it more directly to first-order, distributive, and cognitive constraints on sorting the realist import of various clusters of particular falsifications. He appears to favor the first explicitly, but he requires the second implicitly.

Lakatos correctly notes that Popper's insistence on empirical corroboration in support of verisimilitude suggests the need to recover an attenuated inductivism at least. Understandably, Popper resists this line of development. Hence, verisimilitude becomes more a matter of pious optimism than of actual approximation to the Truth: "I am a metaphysical realist, and an epistemological optimist in the sense that I hold that the truthlikeness ('verisimilitude') of our scientific theories can increase: this is how our knowledge grows."[38] But, then, Popper cannot manage to distinguish satisfactorily his own position from that of the skeptic, and cannot really distance himself sufficiently from Quine and Duhem. He cannot escape merely ordering his *beliefs*. And Lakatos, precisely because *he* favors the most sanguine Popperian view, explicitly holds "that the 'logic of the growth of knowledge' *must* include – in addition to Popper's *logico-metaphysical* theory of verisimilitude – *some* speculative *genuinely epistemological* theory concerning scientific standards with verisimiltude" – effectively, some attenuated form of inductivism.[39] But, then, *he* cannot escape the merely heuristic status of his own practice. In short, Popper holds that, "from a rational point of view, we should not 'rely' on any theory, for no theory has been shown to be true, or can be shown to be true.... But we should *prefer* as basis for action the best-tested theory."[40] But this, precisely, is to give up the realist interpretation of verisimilitude in the strong epistemic sense and to retreat to a pragmatic form of assessing realist beliefs that remains blind to correspondence.

II

Now, the importance of this longish detour lies in our having thereby gained a reasonably full appreciation of the sense in which realism cannot – once freed from foundationalist assumptions – remain directly accessible epistemically.[41] We can remain realists, but the only defense possible pretty well requires that we turn to pragmatist or biological grounds *and* obliges us to refuse to draw a sharp demarcation between realist and idealist theories. This may not be quite what Popper has in mind when he speaks of his "world 3 [as] autonomous," of the fact that "almost all our subjective knowledge (world 2 knowledge) depends upon world 3, that is to say on (at least virtually) *linguistically formulated theories*"; but what he says seems remarkably close to that admission.[42] In any case, once we gain this perspective, we must see that there is no possibility of escaping a moderate relativism with regard to the fruits of science and no possibility of sustaining a universal regulative principle of any methodological sort with respect to the enterprise of science itself. As it turns out, this dual limitation can be traced directly to an essential inadvertence in Peirce's own theory; and its exposure helps to reveal what may well be the very last vestige of foundationalism within the current range of philosophical endeavors that seek to reconcile the strongest movements of analytic and Continental European philosophy. Short of a return to foundationalism, then, our account may be fairly taken to isolate the most plausible constraints on the future prospects of philosophical speculation oriented to saving the major tradition. At the very least, we have canvassed the most influential and most likely argumentative strategies that could possibly disallow or strongly disfavor a relativist reading of realism.

Consider Peirce. He seems never to have wavered from the dictum that "logic is the doctrine of truth, its nature and the manner in which it is to be discovered."[43] But he developed the notion in two rather different ways – at least roughly collected by the eventually opposed terms "pragmatism" and "pragmaticism." In a sense, the two are already adumbrated in the following well-known remark of the early paper "How to Make our Ideas Clear": "The opinion which is fated to be ultimately agreed to by all who investigate, is what we mean by the truth, and the object represented in this opinion is real. That is the way I would explain reality."[44] In effect, in both directions, Peirce never wavered in identifying the real and the knowable. However, more characteristically in the pragmatic period, he treats inquiry as serving to bring specific doubt to an end, settling beliefs, moving episodically and finitely to an actual consensus among poised agents; more characteristically in the pragmaticist period, or in his pragmaticist worries about the inadequacy of construing the function of inquiry as leading to action (and habits of action) suited to determinate circumstances of doubt, he treats science as inseparable from the *infinite* effort of a universal inquiring community. On the one hand, he says,

> The whole function of thought is to produce some habits of action ... every purpose of action is to produce some sensible result. Thus, we come down to what is tangible and conceivably practical, as the root of every real distinction of thought, no matter how subtle it may be; and there is no distinction of meaning so fine as to consist in anything but a possible difference of practice.[45]

On the other, Peirce had already stressed, in an earlier remark, that

> The real ... is that (more exactly: the object of the opinion) which, sooner or later, information and reasoning would finally result in, *and which is therefore independent of the vagaries of me and you.* Thus, the very origin of the conception of reality shows that this conception essentially involves the notion of a *Community*, without definite limits, and capable of definite increase of knowledge.[46]

The parallel of Popper's distinction between inductivism and falsificationism is reasonably clear – as well as Peirce's pragmaticist analogue of the doctrine of verisimilitude and the inextricable mingling of realist and idealist claims. The upshot is that Peirce ultimately treats reality as *never known* – ultimately, as unknowable – by any finite inquiring mind, in order to insure that it is "known" only in the long run. The following brief remarks capture this theme perhaps as well as any: "The final Interpretant does not consist in the way in which any mind does act but in the way in which every mind would act ...";[47] "the catholic consent which constitutes the truth is by no means to be limited to men in this earthly life or to the human race, but extends to the whole communion of minds to which we belong, including some probably whose senses are very different from ours."[48] Peirce, then, actually tries, as does Popper – in an effort that, as we have seen, Quine positively refuses to countenance – to integrate a methodological commitment to scientific progress at the same time as he retires the possibility of measuring such progress within the boundaries of any historical inquiry. It is only his unusual metaphysics of evolution – which Popper does not share – that permits Peirce to defend a *non-epistemic* (biological) basis for his confidence. This confirms the sense in which Popper's error is merely a special instance of Peirce's, since Popper has no conceptual basis for the *methodology* of verisimilitude. Neither has Peirce, of course, but he simply refuses to construe the approximation to Truth methodologically. Perhaps the contrast may be captured by the following interpretation: Popper, in effect, is a metaphysical realist, though only to the extent that verisimilitude is progressive; and Peirce avoids the choice between metaphysical realism and anti-realism (or internal realism – in Putnam's idiom) because on neither pragmatist nor pragmaticist grounds can reality or truth be assigned any conceptual role apart from whatever is internal to the mere contingencies of human inquiry. That is why Popper's thesis is incoherent; and Peirce's, simply inadequately self-critical. Popper's confidence depends on cognitive powers he effectively denies; Peirce's, on cognitive powers that, for ultimately noncognitive reasons, cannot support the sanguinely linear fallibilism he actually favors.

So seen, though it may strike us at first as unlikely, the most telling objection to foundationalism, or to the attempt to support scientific realism on methodological grounds, may be drawn quite simply from the fact that Peirce was an optimist about fallibilism and that, although his was a coherent-enough view, it hardly provides a *necessary* – or even a likely presupposition for the enterprise of science itself. There is no cognitive advantage in adhering to a methodology that yields no measurable gains in the extended short run: biological optimism reasonably justifies the generic (or minimal) realism of science, but not any of its detailed accomplishments or determinate claims. If we grant this conclusion, we are led at once to a decisive turning-point in contemporary philosophy. To abandon foundationalism while holding on to science is to embrace some form of fallibilist self-correction. But, when fallibilism is itself applied *self-referentially*, so that the very procedures of correction are denied any cognitive fixity, it becomes equally clear that we cannot even begin to identify any methodologically necessary conditions of Peirce's "whole communion of minds" or "catholic consent." Whatever biological confidence justifies our continued realism remains in force in the absence of consensus (where consensus is either an artifact of contingent and fragmented inquiries or else ultimately unknowable) or in the actual presence of nonconverging and incompatible theories and practices (à la Quine, or, for that matter, à la Feyerabend). The result is that a tolerance for competing, historically relativized traditions of inquiry can never be conceptually weaker than, or conceptually forced to be replaced or supplemented by, the regulative presupposition of a universalized community of inquiring minds committed – if not (by necessity) to certain truths fated to be discovered – at least to the essential rules by which such truths are in principle asymptotically approximated or capable of approximation by serial extensions of the short run. That there are no such measurable extensions is equivalent to admitting that, however it arises out of social *praxis*, science is incurably ideological and contingent. Confidence about infinite inquiry has no bearing on the comparative appraisal, here and now, of competing rules of inquiry. Certainly, convergence is not obviously fated to obtain. (*A fortiori*, no essentialist or universalist theory of rationality can be drawn from the effective practices of science.)

Fallibilism, reflexively conceived, is simply the transcendental discovery that verisimilitude and its pragmatic counterparts are methodologically inaccessible. Nevertheless, it is quite clear that Peirce construes logic as the normative (ultimately, ethical) provision of the rules of inquiry by which the universal community of science pursues its infinite purpose: "Thinking is a kind of action, and reasoning is a kind of deliberate action; and to call an argument illogical, or a proposition false, is a special kind of moral judgment."[49] The rules of logic appear, therefore, to be not merely conventionally or "internally" regulative of aggregated and episodic beliefs but actually (ethically) constitutive of the very activity of the rational inquiry of science itself: "Logic is the means of attaining the end of thought."[50]

Here, then, is the touchstone of the fatal flaw of that most interesting recent attempt to reconcile analytic and Continental European philosophy – particularly, Peircean pragmatism and hermeneutic and Frankfurt Critical philosophy – found in the work of Karl-Otto Apel and Jürgen Habermas. Their efforts represent the most attenuated version of foundationalism that can be found at present. They are particularly important because they devote themselves at one and the same time to bridging the gap between *Naturwissenschaften* and *Geisteswissenschaften*, to linking all forms of rational inquiry and principled conduct by means of universal norms, and to avoiding all forms of relativism within the constraints of historicized practice. There could hardly be a more comprehensive undertaking. The fact that they fail – and must fail – therefore, leads us to the brink of confronting once and for all the stubborn empirical contingency with which transcendental reflection (or what

Habermas now calls the "rational reconstruction of universal competences") must be undertaken.[51] The search for universal or necessary
conditions goes on as before; but now, once the methodological lacuna
of Peirce's own venture is made clear and is clearly seen to be both
tolerable and ineliminable, the prospect of, and the need for, actually
discovering such constraints become either lame, otiose, or quite impossible – though not actually incoherent.

Apel is particularly open about the dangers of ethical relativism and
ideologically skewed science and the explicit need to go beyond Peirce's
own "transcendental semiotic" in providing a foundation for the human
and natural sciences and the practical commitments of men.[52] He
emphasizes, along with Gadamer, that "the human scientist [or the
interpreter of texts and behavior, or the committed agent, for that
matter] should not deceive himself into thinking he can take up a neutral
standpoint outside history ... the power of history as the mediation of
tradition still also exists in the age of historicism."[53] So he wishes to
concede the initial contingency, ideological shaping, and relativity of all
human engagements; but he hopes, by an enlargement of Peirce's own
insight, to escape mere submission to all such constraints: "A man who
wishes to proceed logically in the sense of Peirce's synthetic logic of
inquiry has to surrender all the private interests of his finite life, also
the private interest in *his* personal salvation ... to the interest of the
indefinite community since only the community has a chance to reach
the ultimate truth" – Peirce's so-called principle of "logical socialism."[54]

Apel, it must be noted, freely acknowledges (with Peirce) "the uncertainty concerning the actual attainment of the goal [of objective knowledge, secured at best by a postulated, transcendental consensus]," which
(he claims) must therefore "be replaced by an ethical principle of engage-
ment and hope."[55] This is why, in Apel's opinion, the logical rules of
inquiry cannot be reduced, in the manner of early pragmatism (or in
that of Hume or the positivists – that is, by "scientism," in Apel's sense,
by the reduction of human subjects to mere observable objects, to be
studied in accord with some explicit canon), but can only be managed
by a so-called "transcendental hermeneutics" already adumbrated in
Peirce's later pragmaticism: the required method of understanding
"works towards agreement about the meaning of concepts which *must
be presupposed by every formulizable type of theory-formation*."[56] "The
ethics *presupposed* by logic as the precondition of its possibility," Apel
says, "*implies*, therefore, the obligation to apply logic and science"; "the
entire complex of science, logic and the ethics of argumentation must
apparently either be accepted as a whole or – if this is meaningful and
possible – negated as a whole."[57] The universal condition is thus an

ethical injunction *to* subscribe to whatever logical and methodological conditions are judged necessary to the realization of the universal community. Apel speaks of "realizing the *ideal* communication community in the real one," and his *a priori* (ultimately, his ethical) principle regarding argument and inquiry "presupposes two things: first, a *real communication community* whose member he has himself become through a process of socialization, and second, an *ideal communication* community that would basically be capable of adequately understanding the meaning of his arguments and judging their truth in a definitive manner."[58]

But the *reductio* of Apel's position remains quite elementary and unaffected by these subtleties. First of all, Apel acknowledges that, by cultural grooming, one actually becomes a member of some viable but limited communication community – without knowledge of the supposed requirements of any ideal communication community and without any need to avail oneself of them. Secondly, even the intention to accept the would-be rules of an ideal community need never actually entail prescribing (or even discovering) any substantive constraints *as* universally necessary. Thirdly, Apel never shows how any would-be universal rules could be realized in historical time, or how we could ever know that they were. Fourthly, by the very force of Peirce's account, we can (and perhaps always must) proceed with some set of provisional, quite tentative rules (conceivably, different ones for different societies) without any cognitive basis for supposing that these will or must converge in the long run. And, finally, whatever they may be, the necessary conditions of the universal community cannot be invoked except conditionally – that is, *on* actually subscribing ethically to its realization; but there is no independent ethical, logical, methodological, or cognitive need to subscribe *to* its realization, and it is not even clear that it is a possible undertaking.

This is just what the full rejection of foundationalism entails. Under the conditions of historicized existence, we remain forever burdened with reflections about the contingency, relativity, nonconvergence, and ideological bias of our own practices. That disclosure, however, cannot be taken to signify a progressive realization of an ideal community's behavior or an incrase in verisimilitude; at best it signifies only the stablest projection, *within* some current interval of inquiry, of what reflexively appear to be the least and most reliable features contributing to the supposed realist achievement of that community's practice. Empirically but not in principle, noticeably stable general regularities do obtain. Even Apel's program depends upon them, but it does not quite recognize that they are sufficient for our needs. Apel insists on more; but his would-be universals are peculiarly pale and in any case indemonstrable, and they undoubtedly reflect the embarrassment of an incipient relativism and the threatening abandonment of a Kantian-like (or, even more accurately, with Peirce, an Hegelian-like) confidence.

Habermas's program is rather similar to Apel's, except that it construes the Peircean objective in terms of what Habermas calls "the construction of the ideal speech community." "No matter how the intersubjectivity of mutual understanding may be deformed," he says, "the *design* of an ideal speech situation is *necessarily implied* in the structure of potential speech, since all speech, even intentional deception, is oriented toward the idea of truth." Still, "On the strength of communicative competence alone ... and independent of the empirical structures of the social system to which we belong, we are quite unable to realize the ideal speech situation, we can only anticipate it."[59] The defect is obvious once again. Pursuing his "universal pragmatics," Habermas rightly says that "we can proceed from the fact that functioning language games, in which speech acts are exchanged, are based on an underlying consensus."[60] But from this it hardly follows either that the consensus of any historical community entails ideally necessary rules within its own internal practice, or that consensus (say, in Wittgenstein's sense) entails any rules at all, or that the conditions of unrestricted intercommunity exchange entail universal rules. One might even see in Habermas's maneuver an analogue of that peculiarly detached arbitrariness (hardly intended) that haunts the work of the Frankfurt school – for instance, in Marcuse's invention of the proper interests of the working class, now that it no longer is capable of finding them for itself.[61] But in Habermas and Apel the presumption is more ambitious, since it posits an idealized but putatively necessary (imperative) rule of intelligence itself. It is, however, a rule that claims our allegiance through all the changes of historical time and yet fails to demonstrate that it is ever actually needed for the provisional achievements of any.

In fact, in Habermas, one may take note of certain telltale tendencies that undermine his own position. For one thing, Habermas wrongly accuses Wittgenstein (of the *Investigations*) of construing "forms of life" in the manner of closed systems (in the technical sense of that term);[62] secondly, in historicizing the discovery of the universal rules of the ideal speech community, Habermas repeats Peirce's error regarding the linear nature of progress; and, thirdly, in attempting to overcome the "dialogic" contingencies of the hermeneutic dimension of human life, Habermas pretends (merely pretends) to be able to discover an adequate emancipatory and "universalistic" science.[63] Wittgenstein, as we have already seen, really refuses to treat "forms of life" in cognitive terms, though they serve as the precondition for cognitive inquiry itself. Peirce, of course, cannot legitimate his own brand of verisimilitude. And Habermas simply fails to explain what the conceptual connection could possibly be between a praxically centered human existence and the *discovery*, under *or* beyond praxical conditions, of transhistorical universals.

This brings us to the finding that pragmatism neither does, nor can, nor need, sustain any cognitively motivated commitment to foundationalism; and that the claims of foundationalism itself predictably appear to take increasingly attenuated and unlikely forms in the effort to avoid the full implications of relativism and historicity. Once the coherence of a foundationless pragmatism is made clear, however, we have before us the prospect of an entirely new vista of philosophical options. What we need to explore are the alternative possibilities that transcendental reflection can generate about plausibly stipulated (but hardly necessary) conditions for a viable realism and communicative practice. There can and need be no unique solution here.

The search for foundations (without embracing foundationalism) is, therefore, the clue to the viability of a philosophical inquiry that pursues Kantian-like questions about the legitimation of science without pretending that its historically best candidates are either timelessly confirmed, convergent toward some uniquely adequate thesis, powerful enough to disqualify relativistic contenders at every point of contest – or, of course, secretly assured of some decisive cognitive privilege. The search for the universal foundations of knowledge goes on as before: but that search is now seen to take the form of inspecting alternative, diachronically conservative, general regularities or conditions that, by arguments to the best explanation (themselves alternatively persuasive in accord with different weightings of pertinent considerations), are historically judged to be among the best candidates that have as yet been found for such status. So seen, our clue is the key to what, in our own time, we are obliged to treat as the evolving form of transcendental arguments, once foundationalism is rejected and once historicism is embraced – *should* we be prepared, for example against the contemporary critics of epistemology, to acknowledge both the legitimacy of second-order philosophical questions and the impossibility of retreating to crypto-foundationalist or crypto-essentialist resources. But this is precisely what "pragmatism" has come, or is best taken, to mean. Alternatively put, what our inquiries have led us to is the reaffirmation of the incompatibility of historicism and universalism – this time, not so much from the side of relativism as from the side of realism. And so we have confirmed in effect the conceptual lacuna previously noted – among the arguments of a surprisingly varied and yet similar-minded group of opponents of relativism: including (to draw together the various figures addressed in a somewhat sprawling argument) Taylor, Gadamer, Bernstein, Popper, Putnam, Lakatos, Kuhn, Habermas, and Apel.

Notes

1   T. S. Kuhn, *The Structure of Scientific Revolutions*, 2nd, enlarged edn (Chicago: University of Chicago Press, 1970), pp. 120–1; cited in Richard Rorty, *Philosophy and the Mirror of Nature* (Princeton, NJ: Princeton University Press, 1979), pp. 324–5.
2   Rorty, *Philosophy and the Mirror of Nature*, pp. 324–5.
3   Cf. ibid., ch. 4.
4   Ibid., p. 316.
5   Ibid., p. 317.
6   W. V. Quine, *Word and Object* (Cambridge, Mass.: MIT Press, 1960), pp. 270–6; cf. Rudolf Carnap, "Empiricism, Semantics, and Ontology," *Meaning and Necessity*, 2nd, enlarged edn (Chicago: University of Chicago Press, 1956).
7   Ibid., p. 276.
8   See Keith Lehrer, *Knowledge* (Oxford: Clarendon Press, 1974), Rorty, *Philosophy and the Mirror of Nature*, ch. 3.
9   Karl R. Popper, "Three Views concerning Human Knowledge," *Conjectures and Refutations: The Growth of Scientific Knowledge*, 2nd, rev. edn (New York: Harper Torchbooks, 1968), pp. 103–4.
10 Cf. Nancy Cartwright, *How the Laws of Physics Lie* (Oxford: Clarendon Press, 1983).
11 Karl R. Popper, "The Aim of Science," *Objective Knowledge: An Evolutionary Approach* (Oxford: Clarendon Press, 1972), pp. 196, 197.
12 Popper, "Two Faces of Common Sense," ibid., p. 52.
13 W.V. Quine, "Two Dogmas of Empiricism," *From a Logical Point of View* (Cambridge, Mass.: Harvard University Press, 1953), p. 37.
14 Ibid., pp. 41, 42.
15 Ibid., p. 43.
16 Cf. Sandra G. Harding (ed.), *Can Theories be Refuted? Essays on the Duhem–Quine Thesis* (Dordrecht: D. Reidel, 1976).
17 Quine, "Two Dogmas of Empiricism," *From a Logical Point of View*, pp. 43, 45.
18 Quine, *Word and Object*, p. 66.
19 Ibid., p. 68 (italics added). Cf. p. 42; also Joseph Margolis: "Quine on Observationality and Translation," *Foundations of Language*, IV (1968); and "Behaviorism and Alien Languages," *Philosophia*, III (1973).
20 Quine, *Word and Object*, p. 23. Cf. *Collected Papers of Charles Sanders Peirce*, 8 vols ed. Charles Hartshorne, Paul Weiss, and Arthur W. Burks (Cambridge, Mass.: Harvard University Press, 1931–58), vol. 5, p. 407 (cited by Quine).

21 Quine, *Word and Object*, p. 27.

22 Ibid., p. 23.

23 Popper, "Of Clouds and Clocks," *Objective Knowledge*, pp. 226, 228, 229.

24 Cf. *The Collected Papers of Charles Sanders Peirce*, vol. 6, p. 307.

25 Popper, "Evolution and the Tree of Knowledge," *Objective Knowledge*, pp. 263, 264.

26 Imre Lakatos, "Popper on Demarcation and Induction," *Philosophical Papers*, vol. 1, ed. John Worrall and Gregory Currie (Cambridge: Cambridge University Press, 1978), p. 148, n. 2.

27 Karl R. Popper, *The Logic of Scientific Discovery*, 2nd, rev. edn, with additional revisions (New York: Harper Torchbooks, 1965), ch. 1.

28 Ibid., pp. 37, 40.

29 Cf. Imre Lakatos: *Proofs and Refutations: The Logic of Mathematical Discovery*, ed. John Worrall and E. G. Zahar (Cambridge: Cambridge University Press, 1976); and "Popper on Demarcation and Induction," *Philosophical Papers*, vol. 1, pp. 146–8. Popper's statement appears in his *Conjectures and Refutations*, p. 38, n. 3 (cited by Lakatos).

30 Cf. Ian Hacking, *Representing and Intervening* (Cambridge: Cambridge University Press, 1983), chs. 8, 15.

31 Lakatos, "Falsification and the Methodology of Scientific Research Programmes," *Philosophical Papers*, vol. 1, pp. 31–2, Cf. "Popper on Demarcation and Induction," in the same collection.

32 Lakatos, "Falsification and the Methodology of Scientific Research Programs, "ibid., p. 32 (italics added). Cf. also Larry Laudan, *Progress and its Problems: Towards a Theory of Scientific Growth* (Berkeley, Calif.: University of California Press, 1977); and Paul Feyerabend, *Against Method* (London: New Left Books, 1975).

33 Cf. Hacking, *Representing and Intervening*, ch. 10.

34 Ibid., p. 150.

35 Ibid., pp. 152, 154.

36 Popper, "Truth, Rationality, and the Growth of Scientific Knowledge," *Conjectures and Refutations*, pp. 240–3 (italics added).

37 Ibid., ch. 10.

38 Karl R. Popper, "Remarks on the Problem of Demarcation and Rationality," in Imre Lakatos and Alan Musgrave (eds), *Problems in the Philosophy of Science* (Amsterdam: North Holland, 1968); cf. also J. W. N. Watkins, "Hume, Carnap and Popper," in Imre Lakatos (ed.), *The Problem of Inductive Logic* (Amsterdam: North Holland, 1968).

39 Lakatos, "Popper on Demarcation and Inductivism," *Philosophical Papers*, vol. 1, pp. 159–67, particularly p. 165.

40 Popper, "Conjectural Knowledge: My Solution of the Problem of Induction," *Objective Knowledge*, pp. 21–2.

41 Cf. Hilary Putnam, *Meaning and the Moral Sciences* (London: Routledge and Kegan Paul, 1978).

42 Popper, "Two Faces of Common Sense: An Argument for Commonsense Realism and against the Commonsense Theory of Knowledge," *Objective Knowledge*, p. 74.
43 *Collected Works of Charles Sanders Peirce*, vol. 7, p. 321.
44 Ibid., vol. 5, p. 407.
45 Ibid., p. 400.
46 Ibid., p. 311 (first italics added).
47 Ibid., vol. 8, p. 315.
48 Ibid., vol. 5, p. 311.
49 Ibid., vol. 8, p. 191.
50 Ibid., vol. 2, p. 198.
51 Jürgen Habermas, "Was heisst Universalpragmatik?" *Sprachpragmatik und Philosophie*, ed. Karl-Otto Apel (Frankfurt: Suhrkamp, 1976); cf. Thomas McCarthy, *The Critical Theory of Jürgen Habermas* (Cambridge, Mass.: MIT Press, 1978), ch. 4.
52 Cf. Karl-Otto Apel: *Charles S. Peirce: From Pragmatism to Pragmaticism*, tr. John Michael Krois (Amherst: University of Massachusetts Press, 1981), particularly ch. 9; "The A Priori of the Communication Community and the Foundations of Ethics: The Problem of a Rational Foundation of Ethics in the Scientific Age," *Towards a Transformation of Philosophy*, tr. Glyn Adey and David Frisby (London: Routledge and Kegan Paul, 1980); and "The A Priori of Communication and the Foundation of the Humanities," *Man and World*, V (1972).
53 Apel, "Scientistics, Hermeneutics and the Critique of Ideology: Outline of a Theory of Science from a Cognitive–Anthropological Standpoint," *Toward a Transformation of Philosophy*, p. 64. Cf. Jürgen Habermas, "A Review of Gadamer's *Truth and Method*," *Understanding and Social Inquiry*, ed. Fred R. Dallmayr and Thomas McCarthy (Notre Dame, Ind.: University of Notre Dame Press, 1977).
54 Apel, "From Kant to Peirce: The Semiotical Transformation of Transcendental Logic," *Toward a Transformation of Philosophy*, p. 90.
55 Apel, "Scientism or Transcendental Hermeneutics? On the Question of the Subject of the Interpretation of Signs in the Semiotics of Pragmatism," ibid., p. 105.
56 Ibid., pp. 107–9.
57 Apel, "The A Priori of the Communication Community and the Foundations of Ethics: The Problem of a Rational Foundation of Ethics in the Scientific Age," ibid., p. 261.
58 Ibid., pp. 282, 280.
59 Jürgen Habermas, "Towards a Theory of Communicative Competence," *Inquiry*, XIII (1970) 372 (second italics added). Cf. also Richard J. Bernstein, *The Restructuring of Social and Political Theory* (New York: Harcourt Brace Jovanovich, 1976), pt IV, particularly pp. 219–25.
60 Jürgen Habermas, "Introduction: Some Difficulties in the Attempt to Link

Theory and Praxis," *Theory and Practice*, John Viertel (Boston, Mass.: Beacon Press, 1973), p. 17f. Cf. also, McCarthy, *The Critical Theory of Jürgen Habermas*, ch. 4.

61 Cf. Herbert Marcuse, *One-Dimensional Man* (Boston, Mass.: Beacon Press, 1964).

62 Habermas, "A Review of Gadamer's *Truth and Method*," *Understanding and Social Inquiry*.

63 See Thomas McCarthy, "Rationality and Relativism: Habermas's 'Overcoming' of Hermeneutics," in John B. Thompson and David Held (eds), *Habermas: Critical Debates* (Cambridge, Mass.: MIT Press, 1982).

8

A Sense of *Rapprochement* between Analytic and Continental European Philosophy

I

We are at a very curious moment in intellectual history. On the one hand, we are witnessing, in all explanatory disciplines, a profound retreat from the principal sources of conceptual assurance and stability regarding the fixed canons of science; and, on the other, we are witnessing an equally profound disbelief in the capacity of theoretical and meta-theoretical anarchy to account for the palpable successes of orderly inquiry or to justify the charge of the futility of examining the grounds for the putative rigor of such inquiry. In short, methodological speculation has produced a vacuum, and efforts to fill it have conceived a chaos.

The pressure points through which we have been led to this disorder are reasonably easy to map, at least by way of prominent specimen views that have shaped the recent history of theorizing about the conditions of rational inquiry. For example, in the view of Rudolf Carnap, who, in an important sense, gave a more characteristic stamp to the Vienna Circle than even Moritz Schlick, and whose extravagant notions of philosophical rigor have haunted Western theorizing down to our own day in a more than vestigial sense – despite their nearly utter collapse – one can mark certain decisive conceptual commitments that have simply led us astray.

Much of this is a matter of common record. In fact, two of Carnap's master themes were masterfully undermined, more than thirty years ago, in W. V. Quine's "Two Dogmas of Empiricism," perhaps one of the two or three most famous brief papers of modern analytic philosophy.

Quine shows the sense in which, first, the disjunctive, so-called analytic–synthetic distinction (alternatively, the disjunctive distinction between differences of meaning and differences of belief) cannot be conceptually managed by means of applying suitably formulable rules and criteria; and the sense in which, secondly, the attempt to reduce the statements of science to the utterances of immediate experience fails to specify a way in which such statements, taken singly, can be said to be rigorously confirmed or infirmed.[1] Broadly put, what Quine did and what he knew he was doing was to demonstrate that we lacked – and, on the evidence, probably could not supply – a principled distinction between fact and meaning or a principled procedure either for translating any of the claims of a disciplined science into the idiom of sensory or immediate experience or for decisively testing the validity of any particular such claims in an empirically acceptable way. In effect, he showed that neither could the certitude or self-evidence or evidential relevance and reliability of the truths of reason and the truths of experience be counted on to afford cognitive foundations for the canonical reformulation of science, nor could the disjunctive distinction between what the real world contributes and what the mind separately contributes to the organization of knowledge (the famous realist–idealist problem) ever be legitimately redeemed. He himself saw the exposure of the two dogmas involved as effecting "a blurring of the supposed boundary between speculative metaphysics and natural science [and] a shift toward pragmatism."[2]

This was a remarkably powerful and early prophecy of the demise of the strongest model of analytic philosophy. And yet, ironically, Quine himself became, in the interval from the early fifties to perhaps the very late seventies (and even, trailing off somewhat, into the eighties), the undoubted (even self-conscious) master of the deeper programmatic assumptions of that tradition of philosophy that flowered for a short interval within the very range of Carnap's marvellously sanguine expectations. In particular, for all the subversive force of the argument of the "Two Dogmas" paper, Quine somehow managed to believe in – and, in this spirit, to lead and collect and give heart to a large army of intellectual workers, ranging beyond philosophy (in the narrow professional sense) to all the sciences and all forms of rational inquiry – and to insist on the pervasive program of extensionalism, which Carnap *really* wished to press and of which the dogmas Quine exposed were primarily the most strategic, most familiar, and apparently most manageable manifestations. In short, it is not in the least clear – it is not even reasonably coherent to hold – that extensionalism (very roughly speaking, the double claim that the description of human behavior could be managed by a language confined to what was [supposed] adequate for purely physical phenomena and that the language of immediate experience could satisfy the same constraint) is conceptually the best, or empirically the best confirmed or most promising, theory of the fundamental structure of all the sciences and studies, once the force of the "Two Dogmas" argument is acknowledged. How could we suppose – how could Quine suppose – that, once we grasped the blurring of science and metaphysics, once we denied the demarcation between the mind and the world, once we recognized the fatuousness of self-disclosing truths unaffected by local conceptual schemes, once we admitted the limitation of all inquiry within the boundaries of alternative systems of thought (systems, that is, the boundaries of which we can never fix for certain), *there was any principled basis left on which to prefer any single alternative conceptual strategy for science, or, in particular, that most strenuous one (extensionalism) that, when applied, presupposed the adequacy of a thoroughgoing physicalism and the eliminability of intentional contexts*? Carnap, of course, was very clear about what he was seeking to do.[3] (And, of course, he anticipated to a significant degree Quine's queries and challenges.) Quine, we are obliged to suppose, must have realized how effectively his own argument subverted the extensionalism *he* clearly shared with Carnap. Nevertheless, Quine has remained remarkably devoted to the rejection of intentionality, the possibility of "regimenting" natural languages along strongly extensionalist lines, and the presumptive adequacy of physicalism.[4] These cannot possibly be more than dogmas of Quine's own choosing – now rendered all the more curious when we pay due respect to Quine's demolition of the cornerstones of those very doctrines, achieved in the defeat of the doctrines Carnap first favored. But the enormously widespread persistence (even refinement and strengthening) of the extensionalist model – despite the general acceptance of Quine's account of the two central dogmas, as well as Alfred Tarski's compelling conviction that natural languages could not be expected to be formally regimented in a suitably extensionalist way – is a historical paradox that bears close examination.[5] The fact is that the recent pursuit of the old model, with whatever adjustment, has simply never felt obliged to retrace its own conceptual foundations. It has, therefore, shown, by turns, a distinct insensitivity to diachronic contingencies and an openness to historical changes in theoretical orientation without bothering to explore the import of our capacity to be drawn to just such changes.

The odd thing is that the same impulse which motivated such subversive reflections within the analytic tradition of Anglo-American philosophy (itself, of course, shaped by highly selective European currents) was at work, in an entirely different spirit, within the mainstream of Continental European philosophy. Strange as it may seem, Quine and

Heidegger converge in this respect, though both would probably have shuddered to have anyone think so. Now, of course, it is even fashionable not to blink at the linkage.[6]

II

We can perhaps fix Heidegger's conception – at least the main thrust of *Being and Time* – risking an excessive economy, in two sentences: "Entities are grasped in their Being as 'presence' [*Anwesenheit*]; this means that they are understood with regard to a definite mode of time – the '*Present*' [*die Gegenwart*]";[7] and "historicity [*Historizität*] is possible as a kind of Being which the inquiring Dasein may possess, only becaue historicality is a determining characteristic for Dasein in the very basis of its Being."[8] Heidegger's complex point is that human existence (Dasein) is, in each of us, characterized by a distinctive disposition and capacity (because of language) to inquire into the entities and schemes of entities that compose our sciences *and* into the precondition of Being, which these multiply ordered entities or beings reveal (and which provide the only way in which Being can be revealed in historical time). Dasein is distinctive, therefore, because it is uniquely suited by its very nature to understanding Being (the *a priori* condition of every science and intelligible inquiry – which, however, is not itself the object of any particular science). Hence, Being is not an entity; it is never exhausted by the systematic disclosure of any (manifest) entities; it can only be grasped through the ordered manifestation of such entities; there is and can be no Kantian or transcendental assurance of the universal validity of any such schemata; what authenticity they have depends on a condition that is not itself open to use as a criterion of validity; what is compelling about such schemata, taken serially, depends on the conditions of historical existence within the horizon of which they thus appear (*erscheinen*); at best, they themselves have an historical appropriateness (and nature) and are replaced by others for a similar reason; we can discover *how* such prevailing schemata arise (by an inquiry prior to, and deeper and more certain than, science and metaphysics: that is, by what Heidegger means by phenomenology), though we cannot discover in that (or any) way *which* historicized schemes are ultimately more accurate or valid; and, consequently, these reflections undermine the timeless pretensions of traditional science and philosophy (they achieve, that is, what Heidegger calls *Destruktion*).[9]

Put perhaps more straightforwardly, Heidegger construes human existence as inherently historical, committed to making conceptual order of the world it appears to confront, succeeding to a degree in so doing within the limits of its own temporary framework, incapable of escaping that historicized limitation, incapable for that reason of discovering any certain or permanent basis for the schemes it does favor, disposed in spite of that to treat its own schemata as universally or transhistorically adequate, and incapable of exhausting all eligible such schemes. In a fair sense, Heidegger tried to redeem a radical sense of human history in opposition to the misleadingly ahistorical notion of history that, in the spirit of the metaphysical tradition Heidegger contests (or "de-strukts"), Hegel is said to champion.[10] For, on Heidegger's view, Hegel is committed to the thesis that "the true Present is eternity," that past and future – what was but is no longer and what is now not yet but will be – oblige us to construe the show of history, of apparent change and development, as nothing more than the temporal presentation of what is eternally present. Heidegger holds instead (presumably on the basis of a phenomenological disclosure) that the very condition of Dasein (the existential nature of man, if you please) is "primordially" temporal; hence, the "time" the world manifests – being disclosed to Dasein – answers to this radical historicity. This, perhaps, is the meaning of that most extraordinary statement of Heidegger's: "Temporality temporalizes world-time, within the horizon of which 'history' can 'appear' as historizing within-time. 'Spirit' does not fall *into* time; but factical existence 'falls' as falling *from* primordial, authentic temporality."[11] Hegel's "time" is the temporal or dialectical disclosure of the eternal Present; Heidegger's, the inherent condition of human existence, for which and in the process of which alone alternative "worlds" of entities reveal how reality authentically but transiently appears. Furthermore, there *is* no eternal "point of view."

   Now, the irony of Heidegger's very persuasive insistence on the radical historicity of human existence is this. *In* calling into question the valid fixity or cognitive transparency or eternalizing interpretation of any human representation of the world (metaphysics and science, in short), Heidegger *should have grasped* the reflexive import of this very insight on his own phenomenological claims; that is, the so-called "deeper" insight of his own method surely cannot escape the threat of limitation, distortion, illusion, prejudice, error, inattention, indifference, habit, and the like, of contingent time (or existence), any more than the false confidence of traditional metaphysics – from which, perhaps, Heidegger's own way of working ought rightly to be conceptually distinguished. He rejected all traditional claims to certitude and the discovery of the fixed structures of the world; but he somehow reserved to himself the capacity, not (to be sure) to discover those structures by a higher "method," but to discover (nevertheless) *how* it is, given the nature of human existence, we are tempted by that ancient confidence and *how* we *must* (essentially or timelessly) orient ourselves to an authentic relationship to Being – admittedly disclosed only through the shifting and partial schemata of the entities of particular cognitive disciplines.[12] In doing that, Heidegger could not have failed to make some essentialist claim about the nature of Dasein – and, therefore, about responsible forms of inquiry as such.

This, perhaps, is a fair extension of Jacques Derrida's critique of Edmund Husserl (the founder of phenomenology) to Heidegger himself, whom Derrida there professes to follow.[13] Derrida's very telling objection against Husserl (and, by extension, against Heidegger) is simply that so-called phenomenological disclosures presuppose that "temporality has a nondisplaceable center, an eye or living core, the punctuality of the real now"; as Husserl has it, "The actual *now* is necessarily something punctual (*ein Punktuelles*) and remains so, *a form that persists through continuous change of matter.*"[14] Here, following Heidegger's lead, Derrida is surely recalling and extending Heidegger's own criticism of Hegel's apparent falsification of the very condition of human existence. For, as Derrida says, "what is at stake is indeed the [cognitive] privilege of the actual present, the now. This conflict, necessarily unlike any other, is between philosophy, which is always a philosophy of presence, and a meditation on nonpresence – which is not perforce its contrary. . . ."[15]

In short, on the argument linking Derrida and Heidegger (regardless of any wavering or inconsistency on the part of either), any presumed cognitive privilege, certitude, disclosure of "presence" or "self-presence," the eternal or actual *now*, or the like, must be an artifact in some ineliminable way of the radical historicity, temporality, Dasein (shall we say?) of human existence. But, if so, phenomenology, like metaphysics and science, is rendered radically contingent, structured by a dependence on conditions of historical existence that cannot ever be recovered as the "originary" or first or ultimately reliable source (*das Anfangende*).[16] This, if affirmed (as by Husserl and, in effect, by Heidegger too), would be self-defeating, perhaps incoherent, and it is precisely what Derrida means to reject in affirming his own famously opaque doctrine of *différance*.

By a kind of cunning of history, the division of labor between the analytic tradition centered in Quine's criticism of Carnap (and his assuming the peculiarly difficult post of defending extensionalism without foundations against his own insights) and the Continental European tradition centered in Heidegger's and Derrida's progressively cannibalizing criticism of Hegel and Husserl and Heidegger himself (along the lines of an increasingly radical sense of the meaning of human historicity) symbiotically require one another, converge, and enrich each other's doctrine in ways unlikely to have been achieved in isolation. Certainly, this is close to the realization that we find ourselves in at present.

III

What is symptomatically curious about both movements is their respective blindness to their own faults and deficiencies. Many have noticed, for example, that the tradition that moves through Heidegger and Derrida (and, thinking of Nietzsche, who precedes and influences both, through such other figures as Foucault and Deleuze) has spawned a tribe of thinkers that have a remarkably impoverished sense of the specifically historicized and historicizing nature of human existence – in spite of their own emphasis on historicity. One may quarrel with this finding, of course; but it is hard to deny it, particularly in reviewing the work of Heidegger and Derrida. Heidegger and Derrida are concerned with the radical threat and radical openness of historical existence, but not particularly with the fine processes of historicized thinking. That really comes clear in Hans-Georg Gadamer's departure from the views of his own mentor, Heidegger. For Gadamer understands his project as one of explaining the interpretive dialogue between past and present within genuinely historical processes (*Horizontverschmelzung*), in such a way as to reject anything like the methodological canon and cognate notion of truth favored in the natural sciences or, by a touchingly hopeless gesture (as in the work of Wilhelm Dilthey), any analogue of these allegedly adjusted to the study of human history; and in such a way as to save an essential and timelessly human tradition from the disorders of a mere relativism that Gadamer thought implicit in Heidegger's inchoate sense of history.[17] The irony, then, is that Heidegger (and, in a sense, Derrida as well) poses (but never addresses) the puzzle of how to understand the nature and rigor of a thoroughly historicized examination of human culture and human existence once we give up the pretense of traditional metaphysics and science (which, in their search for essences, foundations, cognitively transparent structures, timeless universals, and the rest, have profoundly ignored or falsified historicized existence and inquiry – once, that is, we commit ourselves to what Heidegger meant by the inexhaustibility and yet "disclosedness" or historical revelation of Being). Despite its rather florid tone, the thesis manages to remind one of Popper's opposition to essentialism and (oddly) to appear sparer, because it is never tempted by the prospect of verisimilitude.

In his later work, Heidegger turns increasingly to some strange redemptive attitude toward Being that loses completely the force of the courageous stance regarding Dasein already sketched. And Gadamer ingeniously – but utterly without defense – tries to retrieve a conservative (or timeless) truth about human nature *within* the very processes of history (thus overturning Heidegger and retreating to a tamer version of Hegel's grand scheme, which he believed himself to have opposed). Gadamer is rightly seen, therefore, as the pivotal figure here, because he grasps and thoroughly focuses how utterly untenable are the older ahistorical canons and norms of truth within the reflexive study of human history itself – once we are committed to a Heideggerian conception of time – and because, in spite of that, he himself (perhaps through a fear of relativism and the threatening barbarity he links with it) falsifies the historicist theme by pretending to recoup somehow, through historical contingency, the unchanging values and concerns of an underlying human nature. Human nature, we may happily anticipate as well as reconfirm, remains transhistorically the same through historical variation and change. In this sense, the division of labor between Heidegger and Gadamer, within the Continental European tradition they share, parallels the much more economical (but also more puzzling) double function that Quine performs within the analytic tradition. (In a word, Gadamer is a "traditionalist" – in the technical sense supplied earlier on; by a pretty irony, so is Quine.)

There is, in fact, a similar betrayal of the historicist thesis in Jürgen Habermas, who attempts to integrate hermeneutic, Frankfurt Critical, and Marxist views of history. For Habermas, after deriving a thoroughgoing historicism from his own fundamental praxical concerns, manages somehow to reserve (through his reading of speech-act theory, evidently) the universally valid forms of communication – and hence, apparently, of science.[18] It is a persuasive doctrine, however – that is, a generalization aspiring to universal validity but confined to being forever tested by the shifting visions of historical change, an axiom necessarily *manqué* but all the more vigorous and appealing for that reason – that *historicism and universalism are incompatible*. This, in a real sense, *is* the underlying theme of convergence between the analytic and Continental European traditions: the attenuation, on internal grounds, of the extensionalist canon, which still requires a sense of human history in order to see itself as the most forceful contemporary bid to preserve the "philosophy of presence" and to see that, thus construed, it cannot legitimate its own persistence; also, the exposure as vacant and ahistorical of a conception of human history that has lost full contact with, or hope in, the rigors of methodological discipline centered in the actual practices of sustained inquiry – and, thus alienated, is content either to rehearse the errors of "logocentric" thinking or to claim a higher calling for man or to fall back merely to subtler versions of the old mistakes because there is (it is said) no viable alternative to defend. The challenge, precisely, is to find the fluid forms of just such an alternative.

In the Continental European tradition, it is perhaps chiefly in such figures as Habermas and Paul Ricoeur that one finds a sustained effort to provide a tenable sense of the methodology of inquiry (and of the world it addresses) within an historicized conception of human existence. Habermas fails, for the reason given; and Ricoeur pursues the matter with great caution but not with much specificity or actual methodological focus.[19] The charm of both, however, lies in their deliberate effort to marry the "rigor" of the analytic tradition and the "wisdom" of the Continental European. Correspondingly, on the analytic side (the contrasts, of course, are intentionally oversimple), the historicist theme has been increasingly internalized within an attenuated notion of the sanguine expectations of the unity-of-science program – without much serious effort to incorporate explicitly the work of Heidegger, the hermeneutic figures, the Frankfurt Critical movement, the phenomenologists, or the Marxists. The obvious specimen, here, is provided by Thomas Kuhn. For Kuhn's notions of discontinuous paradigm shifts, of the contrast between normal and revolutionary science, of incommensurabilities at the level of theoretical discourse within the actual working practices of (principally) the physical sciences effectively attempt to provide a genuine sense of historicized thinking struggling to preserve, with as few concessions as possible, whatever may be thought to be left of the extensionalist program Carnap originally spawned.[20] Kuhn thought to radicalize (and thereby to redeem) the unity-of-science program by historicizing it. But the result was that he could not legitimate his own professed confidence in scientific progress; and, under the quite reasonable pressure of his own critics regarding the potential incoherence of the incommensurability thesis, he increasingly muted the difference between normal and revolutionary science, turned more and more concessively to the canon he had originally challenged, and gradually lost the force of the historicist theme that the Continentals had already prepared.

The point is that the sense of history within the analytic tradition is remarkably thin – if not almost altogether lacking – even among those (such as Quine or, most strikingly, the Wittgenstein of the *Investigations* turned against the Wittgenstein of the *Tractatus*) who have undermined traditional metaphysical and extensionalist canons for reasons congruent with historicism but cast in terms as ahistorical as what they wished to challenge, or those (such as Kuhn or, even more explicitly, Imre Lakatos) who have directly attempted to fuse a historical sensibility with the search for universal canons in science.[21] Wittgenstein is the only one of these who eschews the vision of the canon altogether; but, confining himself within the "forms of life" historical contingencies allotted him, he never explained the systematic import of his own powerful reflections. There is, therefore, a touch of conceptual anarchy there. Lakatos is the most touchingly candid of these, because he alone was wrong in a heroic way in believing that a really close attention to the actual practices of historical science would still vindicate a transhistorically stable model of rational method flexible enough to accommodate all the vagaries of human inquiry.[22] Paul Feyerabend is obviously the most historically suspicious of the analytically oriented philosophers of science – and, in this respect, also the one most clearly infected by Continental European views of historical existence; but, since he has chosen a completely anarchical view of science, he cannot even pretend to explain the significance of the great turning-points in science he himself insists upon.[23]

In a sense, it is just this weakness in the analytic tradition that attracts the Continental – appearing in, for instance, the tentative (and perhaps simplistic) overtures of such thinkers as Habermas and Ricoeur. The only other alternatives promising a suitable methodological rigor – at least for the human sciences – would have to favor structuralism or Marxism. But structuralism is explicitly opposed to historicism; and Marxism itself oscillates between a structuralist-like temptation (as in Althusser or, in a more generalized form, in Foucault) and, perhaps through a fear (once again) of being dubbed Hegelian, a marked inclination to insist that a genuinely praxicalized sensibility must avoid altogether the pretense of transhistorical canons.[24] The Continental European tradition is seeking to find a way either of recapturing the rigor of the analytic tradition – excessively favored at home even after its implied defeat or after attention to its serious limitations – by attenuating its claims in the historicist spirit, or by matching that rigor by another drawn from more native Continental sources. The odd blindness of Quine, on this side of the fence, and of Habermas, on that side; the hankering for universal structures on the part of Lakatos, on this side, and the cognate but gratuitous confidence of Gadamer, on that side; the easy anarchism of Feyerabend, on this side, and the almost priestly refusal by Heidegger and Derrida to address the problem of methodological reconstruction, on that side; all these items confirm the one-sidedness and symbiotic linkage of the two major streams of thought in the Western world. *And* they confirm the conceptual vacuum (and promise) of the present moment in intellectual history.

IV

In tracing the unexpected confluence of these two lines of thought, we are also entitled to sketch the future history of their mutual recognition. Historicism is undoubtedly the major theme that will be pursued. Conceptually, this cannot but enhance certain increasingly standardized forms of philosophical objection – of the sorts already sampled. For instance, it entails the eclipse of all forms of totalizing: either of the classical structuralist sort (as in Lévi-Strauss, preeminently) or of that historically layered sort that Althusser and Foucault (for rather different reasons) have favored; or of the quite different sort that mingles universalizing with essentialist tendencies, as, in the rejection of a strongly realist interpretation of nomological universals or natural laws, in the critical work of Karl Popper against inductivism and the like.[25] It also means, of course, the eclipse of all forms of essentialism, whether or not fused with foundationalist claims – fashionably captured quite recently (perhaps through the converging influence of John Dewey and Heidegger and Derrida) by Richard Rorty, but also, more bafflingly, in the recent work of Nelson Goodman.[26] It also signifies the retreat of foundationalism, whether directly fused with strongly realist commitments or not; and it challenges, even along nonfoundationalist lines, a forced choice between sharply demarcated realist and idealist elements in science – notably, for example, in the exploratory work of Hilary Putnam and Michael Dummett.[27]

Finally, it signifies the considerable retreat of extensionalism. Here one must remember that, already in Quine's account (though without sustained analysis there), it had been acknowledged that alternative *blocs* of statements could be reconciled with admitted data critical to the confirmation or disconfirmation of scientific claims – could in fact preserve the same truth values for such *blocs*, despite widespread divergencies, within each, of assignable truth values to seemingly cognate statements.[28] What this means is that Quine's own subversion of Carnap's program ineliminably built into the adjusted canonical view a profound intensionality (that is, complications unmanageable by either Carnap's or Quine's devices) that could not fail to surface and to suggest (or require) a sympathetic historicist reading. Once we see that, within the extensionalist canon, room must be provided for intensional variation (*not* even traceable or explicable in extensionalist terms), we are bound to ask for the legitimating grounds for favoring particular conceptual schemes *and* for the reliability for supposing that there *are some* relatively neutral, ground-level "data" (for instance, Carnap's protocol sentences) that, once admitted, would enable us to discard with a clear conscience "mere" intensional curiosities.[29] The brute fact is – it is remarkable how regularly it has been ignored – that, once the analytic–synthetic distinction has been put in jeopardy, once foundationalism has been repudiated, once the realist–idealist demarcation has been denied, once historicist constraints have been embraced, once nature is admitted to be inexhaustible, the extensionalist project is either rendered completely unreasonable, arbitrary, magical, stubborn, blind, untutored, grandiose, or else completely domesticated for finite, very small, provisional, and entirely derivative applications within the competence of a larger understanding (that it can have no basis for supposing could be progressively analyzed in its own favored way).

Read rather against Quine's own systematic intentions, the Quinean criticism unexpectedly demonstrates the conceptual linkage between the attack on a thoroughgoing extensionalism *and* the need for a fundamental modification of the Kantian reading of the realist–idealist problem (since Kant, but not his historicizing successors, believed he could disengage to some extent at least the organizing contribution of the knowing mind and of the world known, within the body of science: in effect, it is this sanguine confidence on Kant's part that, despite his apparently late interest in the significance of history, marks the profoundly anti-historicist nature of his entire enterprise). Put more pointedly, Quine's radical version of the holistic theory of testing science (Duhem's thesis) risks the very possibility of such testing. To reserve a privileged set of "data" smacks of foundationalism, essentialism, naive realism, the rejection of his own rejection of the dogmas of empiricism and, ultimately, the rejection of holism – but it *is* the extreme move plausibly (perhaps even necessarily) required to save an extensionalism fitted to a working science. Alternatively, to specify the testing "data" in a way that is *not* privileged – for instance, along the pragmatist lines Quine professes to favor – *is*, in effect, to historicize science and the theory of science, to focus scientific realism as a deep conceptual puzzle, to concede an inability to justify the demarcation of realist and idealist components within science, and (most important) to acknowledge that the variable, open ended, nontotalized conceptual schemes in use in the developing practice of actual cognitive disciplines cannot be antecedently supposed (and are not even reasonably likely) to be reducible to, or intertranslatable in terms of, any extensionalist idiom – without serious (and unassessable) loss or distortion. To admit the force of these findings, however, *is* to concede – very much against the philosophical grain – that Quine and Heidegger actually converge in an important way, despite the picturesque differences in their local argots. It is as if Quine wished (though to propose it is a pure fantasy) to press Heideggerian *Destruktion* or Derridean deconstruction in exposing the dogmas of empiricism and empiricist science.

We are led to a most intriguing consideration. To adopt a thorough-going historicism, along the somewhat radicalized lines sketched, is to acknowledge that, in every cognitive undertaking, we are in the grip of conceptual schemes whose systematic boundaries, essential rules of inter-nal orderliness, relationship to the world independent of our linguistic access, relationship to other similar such conceptual schemes, propensity and capacity for change and evolution, we cannot ever finally fix or fully fathom. When, therefore, Quine appears to accommodate these difficulties, we cannot help noticing in his account a distinctly limiting naïveté, which undoubtedly explains his own sanguine philosophical hopes. For, when he considers the field linguist's attempt to understand some native speaker in the bush, Quine says, "It is only by ... outright projection of prior linguistic habits that the linguist can find general terms in the native language at all, or, having found them, match them with his own. ... The method of analytical hypotheses [that is, the method of segmenting the heard utterances of the native into con-veniently short recurrent parts, permitting one to compile a list of would-be native words, in certain favored contexts of apparent use, unverifiably, and without supposing word for word equivalences] is a way of cata-pulting oneself into the jungle language by the momentum of the home language."[30] Here we must realize that Quine restricts himself to explicitly constructed procedures *for* establishing whatever would-be translations may interest us. But in doing that he has somehow neglected to consider that the intralinguistic puzzles of our communication are exactly the same as the interlinguistic puzzles he is attempting to manage; *and* that the extensional equivalences he himself tries to invoke, both inter- and intralinguistically (what he sketches in terms of his well-known ersatz procedure of "stimulus meaning"), function as such only on the sufferance of our facility in a natural language whose own extensionally reductive properties we simply don't know and don't know how to establish. In a word, Quine's procedure is explicitly extensionalist but depends on a *tacit*, ultimately unrecoverable linguistic and conceptual commitment (unrecoverable, that is, in any realist, essentialist, foun-dationalist, or similar sense – *not* inaccessible to second-order speculation *within* historicized constraints).

In this respect, strange as it may seem, something like Heidegger's strong emphasis on historicity is really required in order to discipline the unwarranted optimism of Quine's own program *and* to complete an account of whatever complex form of legitimation it may support. Put as succinctly as possible, on Heidegger's view, every human encounter with what thereby presents itself as something "within-the-world" (what is inexorably linked to our total praxical involvement with the world) constitutes an *interpretation* that depends on our already having been oriented in one way rather than another *by* our prior involvements, but not in a way we can straightforwardly or explicitly detail: "The ready-to-hand [*Zuhandenheit*: things first encountered and construed in terms of our work and effective survival] is," he says,

> always understood in terms of a totality of involvements. This totality need not be grasped explicitly by a thematic interpretation. Even if it has undergone such an interpretation, it recedes into an understanding which does not stand out from the background [the effective criticism of Quine's view]. And this is the very mode in which it is the essential foundation for everyday circumspective interpretation. In every case this interpretation is grounded in *something we have in advance* – in a *fore-having* [*Vorhabe*].[31]

We do not merely have a conception of things, then, we have a "fore-conception" of them (*Vorgriff*): "we set our sights 'foresightedly'" – which is to say, (1) the function of our concepts depends on a prior conceptual orientation, which is in effect our history; (2) it is for that reason only that things are interpretable at all; and (3) the attempted recovery of such fore-conception cannot itself fail to be similarly encumbered. "An interpretation," says Heidegger, "is never a presuppositionless apprehending of something presented to us (*eines Vorgegebenen*]."[32]

The full and marvellous irony of this confrontation between Quine and Heidegger – and, through them, of the analytic and Continental European traditions – now begins to emerge. The analytic tradition cannot be salvaged any longer, except through the thoroughly alien historicist theme linking Nietzsche, Heidegger, and Derrida[33] – or, in addition, by way of what Ricoeur has aptly termed the "hermeneutics of suspicion," the associated interpretive traditions of Marx and Freud, in which familiarly specialized (even more pertinent) forms of "fore-conception" are explored.[34] On the other hand, there can be no reconstruction of the putatively tacit conceptual framework (within which our explicit, working conceptual framework operates) without *some* regularization along extensionalist lines. So the deconstructive enterprise running from Nietzsche to Heidegger and Derrida remains altogether vacant without the risked discipline of the analytic sort, *and* even self-defeating to the extent that it itself pretends to disclose (as it inevitably must) the inherent limitations of disregarding its own corrective. This, then, pre-records the future history of Western philosophy that our past and present history cannot and would not wish to escape. It will have to be a form of reflexive, second-order speculation, within historicist constraints, regarding the best recommendations of what (both diachronically and pluralistically) may be taken to be the universal structures of our science. To give up the project is to fall back to intellectual anarchy. To believe that such structures can be fixed once and for all is to falsify the new direction and to fall back to traditional forms of confidence. And to believe that, even in the flux of things, certain doctrines can be assured a privileged stability nevertheless is to betray a deep penchant for incoherence and the ubiquity of the variable forms of dogma and philosophical bad faith.

V

Seen through American eyes, the converging themes of the entire movement of contemporary Western philosophy are decidedly pragmatist in cast. This is not to say that the specific doctrines favored by Peirce or Dewey or James are correct or vindicated, or that current theories are returning to their specific views. It is not even to lay much importance on the term "pragmatist." The fact remains, however, that in nearly all contemporary speculations about reality, cognition, methods of inquiry, certain large conceptual tendencies that had not been expected to converge in this way and that now promise a distinctly novel, even radical, orientation capable of being shared throughout the Western tradition are struggling to find a coherent expression. Of course, these converging tendencies are as much phenomenological, Marxist, hermeneutic, deconstructive as they are pragmatist. It was in fact to dramatize just this convergence that we explored the unlikely similarities between Heidegger's emphasis on the historicity of human existence and Quine's on the import of holism and the fate of the analytic–synthetic distinction.

To avoid parochial misunderstanding, then, but to continue to press a partisan taste in terms, let us construe "pragmatism" as a term of art. We shall take any philosophy to be *pragmatist* to the extent that it distinctly favors three doctrines, regardless of its conceptual sources or variant details. It must, first, oppose foundationalism with respect to whatever cognitive powers it presupposes. Hence, the epistemological

claims of platonism, Cartesian and Kantian certainty, sense-datum theories, Husserlian reduction, totalized systems of the structuralist possibilities of any cultural or cognitive domain, the discovery of the "true"
or "single" language of nature, even the discovery of the fixed laws of
nature, are all precluded. Secondly, it must compensate for this first
constraint by presupposing that, in a sense not epistemically privileged
or even fundamentally epistemic in nature, a certain tacit condition
regarding the survival of the human species obtains: namely, that our
cognitive powers and our theories of those powers must be judged
sufficiently grounded in reality for our sustained adherence to them not
as such to entail the extinction, near-extinction, or related jeopardy of
the human species or of strategically engaged parts of the human species.
Thirdly, relative to these two constraints, it must provide for the cognitive success of valid forms of inquiry in terms continuous with, and
dependent upon, the conditions of social *praxis* – that is, the historically
variable activities by which apparently viable societies intervene in nature
and reproduce their kind. Ultimately, the unified import of the second
and third constraints fixes the minimal, seemingly ineliminable sense of
realist claims – whether for the interventions of science or of human
activity at large. The import of what is denied by the first constraint
fixes the sense of all those privileged forms of realism that, one way or
another, treat human cognition as essentially transparent and non-
distorting in facilitating pertinent access to the actual world. The concepts
of *praxis* and technology, then, confirm at one and the same time the
"opacity" of man's cognitive relationship to the world and, *via* the
survivor's intervention, the assurance of his realist inquiries.

Preeminently, both Heidegger and Marx exhibit, in this sense, a
pragmatist orientation: Heidegger, more in *Being and Time* than in "The
Question concerning Technology" or "The Turning";[35] Marx, notably
in the *Theses on Feuerbach* and the *Grundrisse*.[36] But the pragmatist
strains in Heidegger are perhaps more clearly developed among those he
has influenced – for instance, within the hermeneutic tradition, Gadamer
(*Truth and Method*) as opposed, say, to Dilthey; and, among the exis-
tentialists, Sartre, particularly in his effort to reconcile existentialism and
Marxism.[37] Among relatively recent Continental European thinkers of
importance, one may note that the Wittgenstein of the *Investigations*
but not of the *Tractatus* may reasonably be said to be a pragmatist in his
treatment of philosophical issues.[38] Husserl's search for the indubitable
foundations of knowledge and the characterization of the transcendental
ego mark him as a clear target of pragmatism. But descriptive phenomenology, notably in the work of Merleau-Ponty, is obviously capable of
functioning in the pragmatist manner.[39] Among the more eclectic think-

ers influenced in varying degrees and ways by Marxism, phenomenology, Heidegger, hermeneutics, existentialism, and structuralism, the pragmatist bent is particularly noticeable in Habermas, Marcuse, Bourdieu, and Apel.[40] So-called analytic structuralism, as instanced, for example, in Lévi-Strauss, is a ready target of pragmatism, for much the same reasons that the totalizing tendencies (altogether abstracted from *praxis* and historicity) that appear in the *Tractatus* and the work of such early linguistic structuralists as Saussure are criticized. Genetic structuralism, on the other hand, particularly associated with Piaget and those he has influenced, attempts to restore the primacy at least of the tacit conditions of the developing powers of human cognition, conceding, in particular, the primacy of human action within real-life contexts. Unfortunately, Piaget himself has rather little to say about the social import of *praxis* and treats cognitive (and linguistic) development more in terms of structurally fixed transformations than in terms of actual *praxis*.[41] This helps to explain, for instance, the sense in which Lucien Goldmann, combining Marx (via Lukács) and Piaget, is more clearly oriented in the pragmatist manner than either Piaget or Lukács.[42] The possibility, within this eclectic network, of leaning toward radical relativism and conceptual anarchy – though still distinctly pragmatist in orientation – is perhaps best illustrated in the work of Jacques Derrida.[43]

In fact, the principal thrust of current pragmatist developments distinctly favors the following doctrines: first, that, in rejecting foundationalism and conceding the historicity of human inquiry, we can no longer meaningfully oppose realism and idealism as independent alternatives regarding the cognitive status of science; and, second, that, in linking the ultimate realist import of competing theories to the tacit conditions of species survival, we can no longer insure an exclusively adequate or correct account of "what there is." Realism now signifies that the explicit dialectical opposition and replacement of ontologies manage to be suitably continuous with the ecological, essentially precognitive, conditions under which the race persists; and idealism now signifies that candidate theories can be tested only relative to our remembered record of the fortunes of earlier theories and our current conception of how to continue to test theories informed by that record. Constrained by these adjustments, relativism now signifies the tolerance of alternative ontologies that – consistently with what, on the best transcendental evidence, we take to be the requirements of system, meaning, simplicity, coherence, validity – may be fitted to the corpus of the developing data of our contingent and essentially incomplete inquiries. The idea that formulated ontologies incompatible with one another could not possibly be jointly validated (in whatever way ontologies can be validated) presupposes correspondence criteria of truth, a strong commitment to the ubiquity of bipolar truth values, and a correlated commitment to some cognitively pertinent strict demarcation of realist and idealist alternatives. Yet even our conception of the requirements of system, simplicity, and the rest cannot possibly escape a measure of relativization. To avoid those presuppositions, therefore, is to apply the force of skepticism against claims of exclusive truth and to reinterpret the new realist import of well-defended theories as falling within the competence of what we may now more profoundly characterize as the instrumental nature of human inquiry. Instrumentalism need no longer be opposed to realism and need no longer be construed as a form of subjectivism or subjective idealism.[44] In fact, there is no way to avoid reconciling realism and instrumentalism, once holism is conceded. Realism is itself the transcendentally imputed import of the results of diachronic inquiry interpreted as improved approximations to the way the world is (verisimilitude$_2$). Hence, it cannot be freed from its conceptual dependence on idealist and instrumentalist constraints; and it cannot be freed from its effective dependence on our contingently dominant technology and social *praxis*.

There are, one may say, two decisive conceptual foci for contemporary philosophy, and these, as it happens, are decidedly congenial to the pragmatist orientation:

1   human engagements involving the real world are inescapably and ineliminably technological;
2   transcendental discoveries are a species of empirical discovery.

These two theses prove to be nicely complementary, in that they entail or presuppose the historical and social nature of human existence and cognition, the equivocally liberating and confining orientation of changing and partial horizons, the reflexive discovery of our cognitive capacities with respect to alternative horizons, the continuity of precognitively ordered and cognitively informed survival and work, the socialized sense of active and effective human intervention, the reasonableness of assessing the reality of theoretically postulaed entities in terms of causally relevant experiment and invention, and the viability of nonconverging and even incompatible theories of the nature of reality and of man's cognitive relation to reality. Without any doubt, these are among the most salient and insistent philosophical claims of our day and appear, with equal regularity, in both the Anglo-American and the Continental European literature.

Thesis 2 draws attention to the unique role of man as the sole agent of ontological and epistemological discovery – hence, to the sense in which (opposing Heidegger's characteristic worry) man cannot be reduced to a merely technologically accessible object, *even* if there is a defensible sense in which he remains an object of inquiry: very simply put, thesis 1 itself has transcendental import. The relevant lesson is a dual one. In the first place, it is precisely man's transcendental grasp of the technological grounding of his own sustained survival and cognitive achievements – his active intervention in nature – that most plausibly insures his sense of the structure of the real world and of his capacity to discern it. And, in the second, it remains an empirical question as to what is actually disclosed about technologically accessible reality – both nonhuman and human. There is no possibility – and no need – to escape a technological orientation; there is no need for a flight to Being writ large; there is only a need to realize that theoretical overviews of reality and human cognition, disclosed reflexively within a particular historical horizon of successful *praxis* and its attendant ideologies, are bound to be continually replaced. But such replacements are rationally constrained

  (i)   by the need to make coherent sense of the relationship of antecedent overviews relative to their own horizons and the present vantage;
  (ii) by the interpreted record of the continuity of human inquiry itself;
  (iii) by the technological clues transcendentally favored as affording the most convincing overview within any present horizon; and
  (iv) by the inevitable concession that, both diachronically and synchronically, no exclusively valid overview could possibly be constructed.

In a reasonable sense, this is to combine Heidegger's emphasis on historicity and *alētheia* and Marx's emphasis on the priority of the social conditions of production over individual consciousness.

This is why such recently fashionable views as Richard Rorty's repudiation of philosophy (particularly, of ontology and epistemology), Paul Feyerabend's radical anarchism regarding science, and Thomas Kuhn's stock insistence on the mere discontinuity of paradigms are decidedly premature and arbitrary. Rorty ignores or rejects the possibility of transcendental arguments; Feyerabend ignores the methodological import of whatever, even on his own view, proves to be scientifically pertinent; and Kuhn fails to locate relevant discontinuities within a larger conception of continuous human inquiry. There is, frankly, something wrong-headed about historicized reflections on the powers of human cognition that seriously conclude that philosophy is altogether misguided (Rorty) or that science is altogether incapable of rational direction (Feyerabend) or that different paradigms of inquiry commit their adherents to living in altogether different worlds (Kuhn). All three writers exhibit that distinctly contemporary emphasis of pragmatism that relies primarily on the thesis of historicity. But each is nonplussed by the challenge of relativism and the puzzle of recovering a measure of objectivity and methodological discipline in the absence of foundationalist guarantees. Failing to resolve the matter, each announces the impossibility of a solution from a pretended vantage that would itself have required a transcendent privilege obviating his own skepticism. It is perhaps because the Kantian conception of transcendental arguments has led us to suppose that such arguments must enjoy foundationalist grounds of certainty, are impossible under the condition of historicity,[45] and are fundamentally opposed to empirical reasoning that Rorty, Feyerabend, and Kuhn may have been drawn too early to their own discouraged conclusions. But they are extravagances in any case.

The pivotal issue remains how to recover transcendental reflection under the constraints of a radically historicized pragmatism. The answer, quite simply, lies with grasping the primacy of social *praxis* and, through that, the inescapably technological orientation of our reflection on the nature of reality. Transcendental questions may be conceded to take their familiar Kantian form: "How is (this or that kind of) human cognition possible?" where the querying doubt (unlike that of Rorty, Feyerabend, or Kuhn) is heuristic or methodological – not skeptical or, beyond skepticism, already (transcendently) supplied with the secret knowledge (somewhat in the spirit of the later Heidegger – perhaps also of Derrida) of the impossibility or necessary failure of cognition. But now transcendental questions can no longer be interpreted in terms of the cognitive competence of any singular, privately informed, or solipsistic agent;[46] they must construe cognition as the achievement of an inquiring society – as conformable with the practices and routines of a socially shaped inquiry. Inevitably, therefore, they must be brought to bear on the evolving conditions of social *praxis* under which an effective science itself evolves. Thus seen, the technological represents pragmatism's best clue linking the tacit and cognitively explicit features of whatever realism we can justifiably ascribe to our science and effective routines of life. Transcendental questions concern what – reflecting on what, within the margin of survival of the species, best appears to constitute our knowledge of the world – appear to be the necessary and enabling conditions of such knowledge. The answers are not entailed or deducible from such knowledge; they are concerned, rather, with proposed conditions that may be taken as the wider *presuppositions* on which such knowledge itself depends. So transcendental arguments are "inferences" – if one wishes so to speak – even, "inferences to the best explanation," regarding the presuppositions of human cognition. Hence, they are peculiarly occupied with the conditions of knowledge, meaning, truth, reference, validity, coherence, consistency, and the like – with just those and only those conditions that oblige us to theorize that there can, in principle, be no more than one global system within which all pertinent conceptual distinctions can be intelligibly made, that force us to concede that postulating *any* plurality of such systems is either incoherent or else self-deceptive.

For example, reference to what is true-in-L and true-in-L' presupposes a language capable of distinguishing L and L' and of specifying what meets those conditions in a way not restricted by the qualifications of L and L'. Put in the simplest terms: the presumption of one actual world is the obverse side of presuming that *all* intelligible speculations about reality must, as such, be addressed to the same community of investigators. To say this is *not* to disallow incommensurable, incompatible, divergent theories: it is only to disallow the coherence of "our" acknowledging a determinate "world" unintelligible to us, or to insist that determinately plural "worlds" cannot but be discriminated as such within the same ken of intelligibility. What Feyerabend and Kuhn neglect, therefore, is just the transcendental condition under which the radical difference between two theories (any two theories) informing observation and experiment are actually recognizable as such – hence, recognizably not so radically opposed as to preclude *our* entertaining and comparing them. And what Rorty neglects is just the elementary fact that the very admission of science presupposes the possibility of grasping the transcendental conditions under which science functions as such.

Furthermore, to say that transcendental arguments are "inferences" is to say only that they are open to rational appraisal, not that there is a fixed or formulable canon by which their appraisal may be said to be governed. Transcendental arguments are *not* like formal metalogical arguments: there *can* be no relevant restriction in the scope of their premises or accessible evidence (as formally axiomatized systems presuppose), simply because they are the fruit of the continuous and undivided reflexive effort of the entire species functioning ultimately as a single cognitive community to discover what (and whatever) it can make out to be the limits and powers of its entire cognitive capacity – the same limits and powers, one must suppose, as inform inquiry at any and every object-language and metalanguage level. Again, to say that they are inferences "to the best explanation" is to say only that the power of a transcendental argument rests with the ongoing consensus of the cognitive community that weighs the dialectical advantages to itself of competing theories, not that transcendental arguments answer to a canon in any way like whatever provisional canons may obtain for inferences to the best explanation *within* the practice of an established science.

The inferences of transcendental arguments are, in this sense, *always external to a cognitive practice* as far as its purpose is concerned (that is, they are directed to its presuppositions). But they are always, and cannot but be, generated under the contingent conditions of some such particular practice; they are, therefore, speculations about conditions external to a practice made exclusively *within the historical and empirical conditions of such a practice.* This explains the temptation, the impossibility, and the unimportance of every effort to conflate the transcendental and the transcendent. That transcendental arguments, therefore, are a species of empirical argument (thesis 2) is, broadly speaking, the consequence of Heidegger's thesis of historicity; and that our best clue about the validity of such arguments lies with the stablest technological features of social *praxis* (thesis 1) is, broadly speaking, the consequence of Marx's thesis about the relation of production and consciousness. The technological, therefore, performs a double role. On the one hand, in accord with Heidegger's and Marx's view, it signifies how reality is "disclosed" to humans – primarily because it is through social production, invention, experiment, intentional action, and attention to the conditions of survival (both precognitively and through explicit inquiry) that our sense of being in touch with reality is vindicated at all; but, contrary to the thrust of Heidegger's late qualification, the correction of all theories of cognition and reality thus informed is itself inevitably historicized and subject to the ideological limits of any successor stage of *praxis*. There is no escape from the historical condition, but the recognition of that fact itself is the profoundly simple result of transcendental reflection *within* the very condition of history – which obviates, therefore, the inescapability of Heidegger's various pessimisms. On the other hand, the technological signifies how the study of the whole of reality – of physical nature, of life, of the social and cultural activities and relations of human existence – is unified in terms of our own investigative interests. Hence, at the very least, not only can the theory of the physical sciences not afford to ignore the systematic role of the actual historical work of particular human investigators (for instance, against the model of the unity-of-science program); but, also, we can neither preclude the scientific study of man nor insure that the human sciences must conform to any canon judged adequate for either the physical or life sciences. The primacy of the technological, therefore, facilitates a fresh grasp of the methodological and explanatory peculiarities that the human studies may require – for example, regarding the analysis of causality in the human sphere, the relation of causality and nomologicality, and the bearing of considerations of rationality, understanding, interpretation on the explanation of human behavior. Located against this backdrop, the Quinean program is as much an extravagance as the Heideggerian – and for the same reason: it betrays its own most forceful insight.

Seen in its transcendental role (as insuring inquiry a measure of objectivity relativized to the conditions of *praxis* and dialectical review) and applied to the human sciences (as modelling the methodological distinction of such sciences), the technological may fairly be interpreted as helping to preserve whatever distinction bears on human freedom and dignity, the thrust and direction of human inquiry, the balance between realist and idealist components of cognition, the tolerance of plural, even incompatible, theories compatible with a common *praxis*, the provision of grounds for disclosing ideological distortion without appeal to foundationalism, the admissibility of a moderate relativism consistent with objectivity, and such similar doctrines as the recent currents of pragmatism have been advancing. In this sense, the praxical does *not* signify a subterranean structure fixed either for a totalized world history or for allegedly distinct but bounded phases of an open-ended human history: it signifies only the refusal to disengage science and philosophy from the tacit, biologically grounded impulses of human societies to survive and reproduce themselves. But that is probably as much as one can ask of any relevant theory – and more than most can afford.

Notes

1 W. V. Quine, "Two Dogmas of Empiricism," *From a Logical Point of View* (Cambridge, Mass.: Harvard University Press, 1953).

2 Ibid., p. 20.

3 See Rudolf Carnap, "Psychology in Physical Language," tr. George Schick, in A. J. Ayer (ed.), *Logical Positivism* (Glencoe, Ill.: Free Press, 1959).

4 See for instance W. V. Quine, *Word and Object* (Cambridge, Mass.: MIT Press, 1960), for instance sections 1, 45, 47.

5 See Alfred Tarski, "The Concept of Truth in Formalized Languages," *Logic, Semantics, Metamathematics*, tr. J. H. Woodger, 2nd edn, John Corcoran (Indianapolis: Hackett, 1983). Perhaps the most sanguine but entirely programmatic (or promissory) pursuit of the extensionalist program is to be found in the work of Donald Davidson, particularly "In Defence of Con-

vention T," in Hugues Leblanc (ed.), *Truth, Syntax and Modality* (Amsterdam: North Holland, 1973); and "Mental Events," *Essays on Actions and Events* (Oxford: Clarendon Press, 1980).

6 In a sense, this may be taken to be the principal charm of Richard Rorty's *Philosophy and the Mirror of Nature* (Princeton, NJ: Princeton University Press, 1979).

7 Martin Heidegger, *Being and Time*, tr. John Macquarrie and Edward Robinson (New York: Harper and Row, 1962), p. 25 (pagination to German edn).

8 Ibid., p. 20.

9 Cf. for example ibid., pp. 4, 7, 9, 11, 12, 13, 17, 20, 22, 24, 25, 27, 28.

10 Cf. ibid., pp. 3, 428–36.

11 Ibid., pp. 431, 436: "Der 'Geist' fällt nicht in die Zeit, sondern: die faktische Existenz 'fällt' als verfallende aus der ursprünglichen, eigentlichen Zeitlichkeit."

12 The full reversal of Heidegger's "de-struktive" theme, already implicit in *Being and Time*, is perhaps nowhere more explicit than in the lecture "The Onto-theo-logical Constitution of Metaphysics," collected in Martin Heidegger, *Identity and Difference*, tr. Joan Stambaugh (New York: Harper and Row, 1969).

13 See Jacques Derrida, *Speech and Phenomena and Other Essays on Husserl's Theory of Signs*, tr. David B. Allison (Evanston, Ill.: Northwestern University Press, 1973), particularly "The Voice that Keeps Silence," n. 4 (p. 74), and of course the entire essay "Différance," which depends on and ultimately opposes Heidegger's notion of *Differenz*.

14 Derrida, "Signs and the Blink of an Idea," ibid., p. 62. The quotation from Husserl's *Ideas: General Introduction to Pure Phenomenology* is cited by Derrida — the translation is modified by Derrida's translator, from W. R. Boyce Gibson's translation of *Ideas* (New York: Humanities Press, 1931), p. 237. Cf. also Paul Ricoeur, *Husserl: An Analysis of his Phenomenology*, tr. Edward G. Ballard and Lester E. Embree (Evanston, Ill.: Northwestern University Press, 1967).

15 Derrida, "Signs and the Blink of an Idea," *Speech and Phenomena*, p. 62.

16 In Heidegger's idiom, against Hegel: "The Onto-theo-logical Constitution of Metaphysics," *Identity and Difference*, pp. 48–9.

17 Hans-Georg Gadamer: *Truth and Method*, tr. Garrett Barden and John Cumming from the 2nd German edn (New York: Seabury Press, 1975); *Philosophical Hermeneutics*, ed. and tr. David E. Linge (Berkeley, Calif.: University of California Press, 1976); *Reason in the Age of Science*, tr. Frederick G. Lawrence (Cambridge, Mass.: MIT Press, 1981).

18 Jürgen Habermas: *Communication and the Evolution of Society*, tr. Thomas McCarthy (Boston, Mass.: Beacon Press, 1979); *Knowledge and Human Interests*, tr. Jeremy J. Shapiro (Boston, Mass.: Beacon Press, 1968).

19 Paul Ricoeur, *Hermeneutics and the Human Sciences*, ed. and tr. John B. Thompson (Cambridge: Cambridge University Press, 1981).

20 Thomas S. Kuhn: *The Structure of Scientific Revolutions*, 2nd, enlarged edn (Chicago: University of Chicago Press, 1970); *The Essential Tension* (Chicago: University of Chicago Press, 1977). See Imre Lakatos and Alan Musgrave (eds), *Criticism and the Growth of Knowledge* (Cambridge: Cambridge University Press, 1970); and Gary Gutting (ed.), *Paradigms and Revolutions* (Notre Dame, Ind.: University of Notre Dame Press, 1980).

21 Imre Lakatos, *Philosophical Papers*, vol. 1, ed. John Worrall and Gregory Currie (Cambridge: Cambridge University Press, 1978).

22 For a sense of the historical problem, see Larry Laudan, *Progress and its Problems: Towards a Theory of Scientific Growth* (Berkeley, Calif.: University of California Press, 1977).

23 Paul Feyerabend, *Against Method* (London: New Left Books, 1975).

24 Cf. Louis Althusser and Etienne Balibar, *Reading Capital*, tr. Ben Brewster (London: New Left Books, 1970); Michel Foucault, *The Order of Things*, tr. from the French (New York: Random House, 1970). An extremely succinct sense of the ambiguity of Marx's relationship to Hegel – and, therefore, of Marxism to Hegelianism – may be drawn from two brief remarks, cited in G. A. Cohen, *Karl Marx's Theory of History: A Defense* (Princeton, NJ: Princeton University Press, 1978), p. 27: "new, higher relations of production never appear before the material conditions of their existence have matured in the womb of the old society itself" (from Marx's *Critique of Political Economy*) and "truth appears only when its time has come – and therefore never appears too early, nor ever finds that the public is not ready for it" (from the Preface to Hegel's *Phenomenology of Mind*). Both Hegel and Marx have a teleological sense of history. But, if, as Cohen urges, "The world spirit is a person, but it is not a human being" (p. 1), then history's *telos* is essential to the life of *that* being; on the other hand, Marx's famous materialist reversal of Hegel need not be, and on most views is not meant to be, symmetrical in this respect – for there *is*, for Marx, no entity (no "species-man") to be comparably identified whose essential *telos* is realized in time, although *men* universally do strive for freedom. The open-ended nature of Hegelian history is still *internal to the essential development of the world spirit itself*. The open-ended nature of Marxist history, on the other hand, does not constitute the internal and essential development *of any thing or entity*; on the contrary, man transforms himself by his labor. Put in Marx's own terms, man is uniquely a "species-being" (*Gattungswesen*), not because there is an abstract entity, man, that individual men somehow labor to realize the *telos* of, but rather because men alone are capable of intentionally addressing in their labor objectives that are species-wide: "It is just in his work upon the objective world that man really proves himself as a species-being. ... The object of labor is, therefore, *the objectification of man's species-life*" – from *Karl Marx: Early Writings*, tr. and ed. T. B. Bottomore (New York: McGraw-Hill, 1963), p. 128. In Hegel, the Idea (of Freedom) originally internal to the world spirit realizes itself in the material world; in Marx, men are capable of addressing the

objective of universal freedom: they *transform* themselves (even when not thus enlightened) by their labor. But man is characterized as a species-being only in virtue of the universality of his objective, not in virtue of an essential relationship between material history and the internal *telos* of *Geist*. This accounts for the characteristic (particularly, the recent) disinclination of Marxists (both Eastern and Western European) to subscribe to structuralist or transhistorical canons.

25 Karl R. Popper: *Objective Knowledge: An Evolutionary Approach* (Oxford: Clarendon Press, 1972), particularly "Conjectural Knowledge: My Solution of the Problem of Induction" and "The Aim of Science"; and *Realism and the Aim of Science*, vol. 1: *From the Postscript to the Logic of Scientific Discovery*, ed. W. W. Bartley III (Totowa, NJ: Rowman and Littlefield, 1983), ch. 1. Cf. also Nancy Cartwright, *How the Laws of Physics Lie* (Oxford: Clarendon Press, 1983), Essay 3.

26 Rorty: *Philosophy and the Mirror of Nature*; and *Consequences of Pragmatism* (Minneapolis: University of Minnesota Press, 1980). Also, Nelson Goodman, *Ways of Worldmaking* (Indianapolis: Hackett, 1978).

27 Michael Dummett: *Truth and Other Enigmas* (Cambridge, Mass.: Harvard University Press, 1978), particularly, "Truth," "Realism," and "The Significance of Quine's Indeterminacy Thesis"; "What is a Theory of Meaning?" in Samuel Guttenplan (ed.), *Mind and Language* (Oxford: Clarendon Press, 1975); "What is a Theory of Meaning? (II)," in Gareth Evans and John McDowell (eds), *Truth and Meaning* (Oxford: Clarendon Press, 1976). Also, Hilary Putnam: *Meaning and the Moral Sciences* (London: Routledge and Kegan Paul, 1978); "Two Conceptions of Rationality," *Reason, Truth and History* (Cambridge: Cambridge University Press, 1981); *Philosophical Papers*, vol. 3 (Cambridge: Cambridge University Press, 1983).

28 Quine, *Word and Object*, section 7.

29 Cf. Joseph Margolis, "Behaviorism and Alien Languages," *Philosophia*, III (1973).

30 Quine, *Word and Object*, section 15.

31 Heidegger, *Being and Time*, p. 150.

32 Ibid.

33 Cf. Friedrich Nietzsche, "On Truth and Lie in an Extra-moral Sense," in *The Portable Nietzsche*, ed. and tr. Walter Kaufmann (New York: Viking, 1954).

34 See Paul Ricoeur, *Freud and Philosophy*, tr. Denis Savage (New Haven, Conn.: Yale University Press, 1970), ch. 2.

35 Martin Heidegger, "Die Frage nach der Technik," *Die Technik und die Kehre* (Pfullingen, Gunther Neske, 1954); tr. William Lovitt, in *The Question Concerning Technology and Other Essays* (New York: Harper and Row, 1977).

36 Karl Marx: *Theses on Feuerbach*, in *Karl Marx: Selected Writings*, ed. David McLellan (Oxford: Oxford University Press, 1977); *Grundrisse*,

Foundations of the Critique of Political Economy, tr. Martin Nicolaus (New York: Vintage Books, 1973).

37 Jean-Paul Sartre, *Critique of Dialectical Reason*, ed. Jonathan Rée, Alan Sheridan-Smith (London: New Left Books, 1976).

38 Cf. Ludwig Wittgenstein, *On Certainty*, ed. G. E. M. Anscombe and G. H. von Wright, tr. Denis Paul and G. E. M. Anscombe (Oxford: Basil Blackwell, 1969).

39 Maurice Merleau-Ponty, *Phenomenology of Perception*, tr. Colin Smith (London: Routledge and Kegan Paul, 1962); *The Visible and the Invisible*, ed. Claude Lefort, tr. Alphonso Lingis (Evanston, Ill.: Northwestern University Press, 1968).

40 Representative texts include Habermas, *Knowledge and Human Interests*; Herbert Marcuse, *Reason and Revolution* (New York: Oxford University Press, 1941) and *One-Dimensional Man* (Boston, Mass.: Beacon Press, 1964); Pierre Bourdieu, *Outline of a Theory of Practice*, tr. Richard Nice (Cambridge: Cambridge University Press, 1977); Karl-Otto Apel, *Towards a Transformation of Philosophy*, tr. Glyn Adey and David Frisby (Boston, Mass.: Beacon Press, 1980).

41 Cf. L. S. Vygotsky, *Thought and Language*, tr. Eugenia Hanfmann and Gertrude Vakar (Cambridge, Mass.: MIT Press, 1962), for an early criticism of Piaget; Roland Barthes, *Elements of Semiology*, tr. Annette Lavers and Colin Smith (London: Jonathan Cape, 1967); Paul Ricoeur, *Interpretation Theory: Discourse and the Surplus of Meaning* (Fort Worth: Texas Christian University Press, 1976). For Piaget's most recent views, see Massimo Piattelli-Palmarini (ed.), *Language and Learning: The Debate between Jean Piaget and Noam Chomsky* (Cambridge, Mass.: Harvard University Press, 1980). Piaget's view of *praxis* is essentially biological but hardly social or cultural.

42 Cf. Lucien Goldmann: *Essays on Method in the Sociology of Literature*, ed. and tr. William Q. Boelhower (St Louis, Mo.: Telos Press, 1980); *Lukács and Heidegger: Towards a New Philosophy*, tr. William Q. Boelhower (London: Routledge and Kegan Paul, 1977).

43 Cf. Derrida: *Speech and Phenomena*; and *Of Grammatology*, tr. Gayatri Chakravorty Spivak (Baltimore, Johns Hopkins University Press, 1976).

44 Cf. Popper: *Objective Knowledge*, pp. 194–7, 261–5; *Conjectures and Refutations* (London: Routledge and Kegan Paul, 1962), ch. 3. Also, Ernest Nagel, *The Structure of Science* (New York: Harcourt Brace, 1961), ch. 6.

45 Cf. P. F. Strawson, *The Bounds of Sense* (London: Methuen, 1966).

46 Cf. Apel, *Towards a Transformation of Philosophy*.

9

Cognitive Issues in the
Realist–Idealist Dispute

On the textbook view, realism is the historical opponent of nominalism as well as of idealism, two seemingly unrelated antagonists. But, under the pressure of Kantian and Kantian-like thinking, the oppositions themselves significantly change and elements of both quarrels begin to converge and even to adhere rather naturally to one another. The idea that material objects exist independently of, without any dependence on, mind – in effect, independently of any conditions of cognition – is an intuitively very compelling conviction, which of course the details of astronomy and the early history of our planet are thought (in a non-question-begging way) to support. But that conviction is hard to separate from the corollary that a world independent of mind – in particular, a material world – must have a determinate structure of its own. There is, therefore, a very natural connection between the seemingly metaphysical claim originally termed *realist* (the thesis of a structured world independent of cognition) and the epistemological concerns of realist-minded investigators – that is, between the view that there are truths about the actual structures of the real world that do not depend on the cognitive capacities of human investigators ("metaphysical realism") and the view that, with whatever qualifications may be imposed, those structures are cognitively accessible to such investigators ("epistemological realism"). Hence it is hard to separate the original realist thesis from a further consideration: whether

1 the "real world" is ultimately unknowable; or
2 being knowable, its actual, determinate structure is open to discovery; or
3 though unknowable "in itself" – that is, on the essential condition of mind-independence – we are nevertheless able to formulate a valid description of the world-as-it-impinges-on-us.

One may not unfairly claim that contemporary analytic maneuvers with the dialectical possibilities of these three alternatives mark the Kantian-like character of current versions of *realism* – in fact, also, of certain forms of what is now often called anti-realism.[1]

If so, then, since theories closer to alternative 3 tend now to pre-dominate in the analytic tradition, it becomes problematic both to dis-tinguish the realist and idealist (or anti-realist) views from one another and to confirm in a new way that the realist thesis (*so* distinguished) is correct or perspicuous. Furthermore, if 3 is favored, then the potential inadequacy of nominalist views of concepts (or universals) extended spontaneously in the contexts of disciplined inquiry – that is, in epis-temically serious regards, not merely formally – cannot fail to surface and to link up with the other opposition. Alternatively put, since in a variety of ways most analytic commentators (as we have earlier remarked) insist that the description of the world is radically dependent on the theories or categories of description favored by human percipients, it is difficult to see how, assuming nominalism, the original realist com-mitment regarding the world's independence of mind can be reconciled with *any* putatively valid account of the detailed and determinate nature of the world or its parts – that is, of the world cognized. For, on any view of natural languages and of inquiry conducted in a natural language, it seems impossible to deny that even the effective extension of so-called linguistic "conventions" (about the use of general terms) would require some very complex dependency on spontaneously discriminated simi-larities or resemblances in the world (beyond whatever exemplars were first posited) in virtue of which such putative conventions could be workable at all; and that, without prejudice to viable solutions, is never conceded or accounted for by a strict nominalism. The irony is that a realist reading of universals need not be cognitivist (along the lines of alternative 3 as opposed to 2, although the usual defense of nominalism incorporates a strong objection to every form of cognitivism. Hence, nominalism threatens to disable its own capacity to accommodate a realism suited to science – by adhering to constraints both unnecessary in themselves and excessive for the task. In a word, every seemingly promising nominalism is a purely formal exercise, obliged to mute or ignore actual problems of human inquiry (even when addressed to what is taken to be a real domain of numbers). But there is no point to a nominalism disengaged from epistemic concerns: it intends a peculiar economy of referents and attributes without attention to the humanly active science by which its would-be domain is first posited and mapped.[2]

Realism, in the sense minimally suited to science, requires both a mind-independent world (certainly, a mind-independent physical world) *and* (in some suitably robust sense) the cognitive accessibility of that world. In the current idiom, alternative 2 (usually) links "metaphysical" realism[3] to some form of cognitivism. That is, it both affirms a structured world independent of cognition and, *if* it concedes a human ability to know *that* mind-independent world (as opposed to conceding a possible race of titans or gods capable of knowing what we cannot know), then it must also affirm some form of cognitivism or transparency. Still, since alternative 3 opposes cognitivism but is committed to some form of realism in the epistemological sense, 2 may well devolve into 3. Anti-realism, then, at least one prominent version of it (Michael Dummett's), opposes metaphysical realism (or "realism," for short), in the sense in which that doctrine takes truth and falsity to apply to realist statements quite independently of our capacity to decide the matter; in this sense, anti-realism remains *entirely* neutral to the foundationalist issue. (It remains quite possible, nevertheless, that an anti-realist may actually be a cognitivist. Perhaps Chisholm is one such theorist; and perhaps Dummett's advocacy of *tertium non datur* signifies something threatening cognitivism – or at least a restricted form of logocentrism.)

Alternative 3 marks the setting in which realism (in the initial generic sense given) and anti-realism (as just construed) need not be incompatible; although *diachronically* tolerant concessions regarding our ability to decide truth claims – within the terms of alternative 3 – cannot quite keep realism from appearing to favor (a measure of) metaphysical realism (despite the intended difference in their respective rationales). Recall Clerk Maxwell's view of the measurement of light. *Within* (the minimal commitments of) realism, the theory of science is sometimes said, also, to favor *scientific realism*,[4] which (usually) maintains – with respect to *either* 2 or 3 – that unobservable entities introduced by "successful" explanatory theories are real (for that reason) and are not merely instrumentally or heuristically employed devices; or that their causal efficacy (*not* equivalent to their explanatory success) constitutes the grounds for affirming their reality. It is, however, also possible to speak of scientific realism in the sense that countenances only observables or only what phenomenological laws are said to be true of; such restricted versions are usually also said to be forms of anti-realism. There is, then, another, actually more pertinent, version of *anti-realism* (than Dummett's) that disputes the reality of unobservable or theoretical entities, or at any rate disputes the thesis that the "success" of their "explanatory" role is what confers the status of being "real" on such entities, or that disputes the thesis that unobservable entities can be shown to have causal efficacy.[5] Just as "realism," "metaphysical realism," and "scientific realism" are quite distinct theses, so too are the alternative forms of "anti-realism." Also, alternative 3 may or may not concede some form of logocentrism (not, however, extended from strictly cognitivist claims) – for instance, by prioritizing extensionalist or physicalist constraints for the very idiom of a "legitimate" science, in the manner of Quine and Davidson – and may or may not be constrained by holist or pragmatist limitations on distributed cognitive claims. So, all in all, we must admit that there is no reliably central or stable use of the terms "realist," "idealist," and "anti-realist" that we can take for granted in sorting through a rather puzzling literature.

These complications suggest the need for a certain caution regarding the appraisal of versions of realism adjusted to accommodate or resist the formidable pressures of post-Kantian idealism – especially because the first version of anti-realism (sketched above) is also taken to be a form of idealism.[6]

I

Let us first consider the record – that is, several of the more salient views of our day exhibiting the tendencies in question – without, however, defending or attacking particular doctrines or even adequately classifying positions known to be related or opposed to one another. In the Postscript to his influential and much-discussed theory of scientific paradigms, Thomas Kuhn offers the following explicit finding:

There is, I think, no theory-independent way to reconstruct phrases like "really there"; the notion of a match between the ontology of a theory and its "real" counterpart in nature now seems to me illusive in principle. Besides, as a historian, I am impressed with the implausibility of the view. I do not doubt, for example, that Newton's mechanics improves on Aristotle's and that Einstein's improves on Newton's as instruments for puzzle-solving. But I can see in their succession no coherent direction of ontological development. On the contrary, in some important respects, though by no means in all, Einstein's general theory of relativity is closer to Aristotle's than either of them is to Newton's. Though the temptation to describe that position as relativistic is understandable, the description seems to me wrong. Conversely, if the position be relativism, I cannot see that the relativist loses anything needed to account for the nature and development of the sciences.[7]

It is difficult to make sense of Kuhn's thesis unless we suppose that, for him, ontological relativity does not constitute sufficient grounds for construing a theory of scientific knowledge as relativistic. The reason is caught up in Kuhn's conception of "puzzle-solving." Roughly, his view is that, in spite of the fact that, for reasons of a historical nature, different scientists belong to different educational and puzzle-oriented communities and make different "group commitments" in terms of the "paradigms" they favor in coming to grips with the world, still "the stimuli that impinge upon them are the same. So is their general neural apparatus, however differently programmed. Furthermore, except in a small, if all-important area of experience even their neural programming must be very nearly the same, for they share a history, except the immediate past."[8] The relativism of ontology, perception, and paradigms and the selection of putatively solvable problems are seen by Kuhn, therefore, to rest on an underlying biological uniformity in the human species in virtue of which divergent paradigms of the *success* of scientific work *themselves confirm their nonrelativistic import.*

This may seem a far-fetched interpretation of Kuhn's thesis,[9] but it proves both plausible and instructive about other influential views that diverge from his own. He says very plainly, "An appropriately programmed perceptual mechanism has survival value. To say that the members of different groups may have different perceptions when confronted with the same stimuli is not to imply that they may have just any perceptions at all."[10] Only "very few ways of seeing ... that have withstood the tests of group use are worth transmitting from generation to generation. Equally, it is because they have been selected for their success over historic time that we must speak of the experience and knowledge of nature embedded in the stimulus-to-sensation route."[11] So, in spite of the fact that men "who perceive the same situation differently ... speak ... from incommensurable viewpoints" (since what they perceive is mediated by their different theories and paradigms and since, though their stimuli are the same, only theory can affirm that), they do gain knowledge *of nature.*[12]

Here we have a very pretty exhibit of the contemporary problem of realism. For Kuhn wishes to reconcile the thesis (i) that scientific success in puzzle-solving empirically confirms that the body of knowledge thus produced *is* knowledge *of* nature (of the mind-independent world), and (ii) that, historically construed, such knowledge proves to be ontologically relativized, not ontologically convergent. Now, the problem is this: *if* realism holds, in the original sense of a material world's existing independently of mind, then how is it possible to construe ontologically diverging scientific theories as constituting knowledge of the world when such ontologies may be incompatible or the theory-dependent perceptual schemata with which opposing scientists work may constitute "incommensurable viewpoints"? Kuhn wishes to hold that our knowledge is (realistically) *of* the (mind-independent) world but is not knowledge of the world *as* it is mind-independently. He wishes, therefore, to incorporate within a modified realist position what, in an earlier era, had been thought to be part of the opposing idealist thesis. It is fair to say that very possibly all the more recent versions of realism seek to achieve the same sort of reconciliation, however differently they may proceed. But for the moment, we may content ourselves with noting two paradoxes or puzzles of contemporary realism:

(a) that, in spite of the fact that there is no theory-independent way of specifyng mind-independent reality, hence of matching descriptions of reality with reality itself, we can nevertheless validly claim to have knowledge of the real world;

(b) that, in spite of the fact that if there is a real mind-independent world, and that such a world must have a determinate structure of its own, our knowledge of that world can tolerate, diachronically and synchronically, incompatible ontologies and incommensurable perceptual viewpoints.

(It will prove very convenient, as we shall soon see, to reserve one provocative use of the term *"idealist"* for that thesis – Kuhn's, here – that holds that there are divergent, even incompatible, discontinuously generated hypotheses about theoretical entities and processes; and that the relations among such hypotheses, within the activities of science, tend to confirm a holistic sense of realism, without yet yielding any reliable criteria for determining which among such entities and processes must be real.)

Certainly, it is clear that, in Kuhn's account, the "success" of the "very few ways of seeing" that have withstood the test of "historic time" must be construed in a way that is *internal* to the favored paradigms or clusters of such "ways of seeing." Kuhn says that they have "survival value." In effect, then, his realism cannot but rest on a version of pragmatism: baldly put, we know that we must *in some sense* be in touch with the actual world because we survive; and the relevant sense in which we survive corresponds to the paradigms of inquiry by which the successes of science are themselves marked. Kuhn actually says, "In many environments a group that could not tell wolves from dogs could not endure. Nor would a group of nuclear physicists today survive as scientists if unable to recognize the tracks of alpha particles and electrons."[13] (This is a very trimly focused, though entirely implicit, objection to Quine's "inscrutability of reference" thesis, Quine's form of conventionalism, which has so extraordinarily influenced the recent course of disputes about scientific realism.) But, apart from the fact that the race survives remarkably in spite of everything it does, apart from the fact that one can imagine having correct knowledge without the capacity to survive (in fact, that one can imagine having knowledge that we cannot long survive), apart from the fact that what precisely is meant by "survival value" is most unclear, it is not obvious at all that survival value can serve to support a realism opposed to idealism – or, given the general drift of scientific realism toward a holism hovering somewhere between Duhem's and Quine's views, to confirm, within realist accounts, a uniquely correct picture of the structure of "what there is." *Any* theory of knowledge, any claim to know the world – its parts and features – is bound to try to accommodate, in some sense, survival value. The fact remains that (a) and (b) suspiciously resemble positions that idealists have traditionally favored: they seem in fact to be realistically phrased versions of such positions, and they seem in this respect to concede too much to the idealist point of view. In short, they may be fairly construed as elaborations of our alternative (3) formulated above: apparently, we know only the world-as-it-impinges-on-us, or we know the world *an sich* only as it impinges on us; and, in knowing that, we cannot insure the convergence of ontological and perceptual schemata in terms of which the known world is analyzed.

In sum, on the foregoing considerations,

1 we are committed to the existence of a mind-independent world;
2 we are committed to some cognitive access to the structures of that world;
3 we are unable to defend these two commitments in a way that, in cognitively pertinent terms, denies the idealist complication – that is, we cannot sort the world's mind-independent structures from whatever, diachronically, our contingent science imputes as its structures; and
4 we have no antecedent grounds for holding that there must be a single, ideally adequate, convergent description of such imputed structures.

Nevertheless, even at this stage of the argument, the import of the realist–idealist dispute cannot fail to affect the fortunes of the realist–nominalist dispute, cannot in fact fail to yield sufficient evidence for the fatal inadequacy of any strictly nominalist theory *that is taken to be cognitively pertinent* – Nelson Goodman's is perhaps the most heroic version our own time has yet produced. To press the advantage very briefly, in criticizing one of his opponents Goodman remarks (quite characteristically) that "he seems to hold that a predicate applies initially to a property as its name, and then only derivatively to the things that have that property. The nominalist cancels out the property and treats the predicate as bearing a one–many relationship directly to the several things it applies to or denotes."[14] The trouble is that, although this disposes of a platonism opposed to a nominalism regarding entities (that is, a theory or ontology that countenances only individuals – possibly even abstract individuals, in Goodman's usage), the response does not address at all the cognitively pertinent question of *how* the "one–many relationship" could actually work within the spontaneously habituated practices of a living society, unless there were

(i)   some genetic, *species*-wide dispositions to favor selective resemblances among individuals;

(ii)   some culturally emergent conditions for altering, enlarging, even divergently varying such dispositions for selective resemblances within and between *sub*-species-wide practices; and

(iii) some improvisational tolerance of an interpretive sort, congruent with such dispositions, for consensually fixing, even variably fixing, the admissible extension of general terms to hitherto unspecified instances of any *given* "one–many relationship."

Goodman never addresses the question directly.[15]

II

Let us turn now, briefly, to W. V. Quine's views. Speaking of his famous example of the field linguist's disposition to equate the "gavagai" of an observed native's utterance with our term "rabbit," Quine remarks that he takes the linguist's preference to be "sensible" – he "would recommend no other" – but that, nevertheless, the issue to be settled is "objectively indeterminate." He adds at once,

It is philosophically interesting ... that what is indeterminate in this artificial example is not just meaning, but extension; reference. My remarks on indeterminacy began as a challenge to likeness of meaning. ... Of two predicates which are alike in extension, it has never been clear when to say that they are alike in meaning and when not; it is the old matter of featherless bipeds and rational animals, or of equiangular and equilateral triangles. Reference, extension, has been the firm thing; meaning, intension, the infirm. The indeterminacy of translation now confronting us, however, cuts across extension and intension alike. The terms "rabbit." "undetached rabbit part," and "rabbit stage" differ not only in meaning; they are true of different things. Reference itself proves behaviorally inscrutable.[16]

Hence, as Quine puts it, in adopting "a naturalistic view of language and a behavioral view of meaning ... we give up an assurance of determinacy."[17] Ontology becomes "doubly relative. Specifying the universe of a theory makes sense only relative to some background theory, and only relative to some choice of a manual of translation of the one theory into the other."[18] The identification and reidentification of things must invoke some system of reference among alternative such systems; and the equivalence of what we say of them is relativized to some system of equivalent expressions among alternative such systems. Beyond that, says Quine,

The obstacle is only that any one intercultural correlation of words and phrases, and hence of theories, will be just one among various empirically admissible correlations, whether it is suggested by historical gradations or by unaided analogy; *there is nothing for such a correlation to be uniquely right or wrong about.* In saying this I philosophize from the vantage point only of our own provincial conceptual scheme and scientific epoch, true; but I know no better.[19]

It is plain from this that Quine is altogether opposed to speaking of science as acquiring knowledge of the determinate structure of the world as it "really is." Apart from the extravagance of his idiom: "there is nothing ... to be uniquely right or wrong about." In *Word and Object*, Quine had similarly maintained that, regarding our jungle linguist's effort to translate a native speaker's sentences, "the point is not that we cannot be sure whether the analytical hypothesis [on the basis of which we construe the terms and vocabulary of the native as we do] is right, but that there is not even, *as there was in the case of 'Gavagai,'* an objective matter to be right or wrong about."[20] "Rival systems of analytical hypotheses can fit the totality of speech behavior to perfection ... and dispositions to speech behavior as well, and still specify mutually incompatible translations of countless sentences insusceptible of independent control."[21]

Still, Quine attempts in various ways to anchor the entailed relativities in a realist manner. The adjustments remain extremely subtle and signify once again the seeming convergence of realist and idealist pictures of scientific knowledge. In fact, it is difficult to see *how* incompatible accounts could both be realist unless realism and idealism were taken to be indissoluble aspects of the kind of confirming work our principal sciences perform (which, in the order of things as Quine sees matters, is cast *en bloc* in a realist role).[22]

In "Epistemology Naturalized," for instance, Quine offers the following:

> It was sad for epistemologists, Hume and others, to have to acquiesce in the impossibility of strictly deriving the science of the external world from sensory evidence. Two cardinal tenets of empiricism remained unassailable, however, and so remain to this day. One is that whatever evidence there is for science *is* sensory evidence. The other ... is that all inculcation of meanings of words must rest ultimately on sensory evidence. Hence the continuing attractiveness of the idea of a *logischer aufbau* in which the sensory content of discourse would stand forth explicitly.[23]

Here, Quine resists the deducibility, *à la* Carnap, of physical science from original "sensory evidence." He holds, nevertheless, to the realist-motivated thesis that "the stimulation of his sensory receptors is all the evidence anybody has had to go on, ultimately, in arriving at his picture of the world."[24] The trouble is, as we have already noted in Kuhn's account, that only *theory* can affirm that the *stimuli* impinging on different percipients (as distinct from sensations somehow discriminated) are the same. Quine is obliged to equivocate, therefore. He does not make entirely explicit the relationship between his notion of "stimulus meaning" and the cognitive reliance on "sensory evidence." The two, however, cannot be equivalent. The "stimulation of his sensory receptors" cannot be "all the evidence" one has, since fixing such stimulation must itself rest on sensory evidence of a sort *that one can at least report*. In *Word and Object*, Quine sometimes speaks as if there might be a relatively stable order of sensory discrimination – an order at least "closer" to "peripheral" contact with the external world than "collateral information" could provide – that our "analytical hypotheses" *build on* in the alternatively relativized ways already noted. Thus he remarks, "We have been reflecting in a general way on how surface irritations generate, through language, one's knowledge of the world," and, in an apparently sanguine spirit, he signifies that he means to consider "how much of language can be made sense of in terms of its stimulus conditions, and what scope this leaves for empirically unconditioned variation in one's conceptual scheme."[25] In short, there is in Quine a vestigial tendency to favor the cognitive transparency of the world *at some point* (which would obviate the need to admit the indissoluble linkage between contemporary realism and idealism) – at the price of undermining his own radical thesis on the analytic–synthetic distinction, but with the advantage of grounding his extensionalist program; on the other hand, there is also in Quine a more characteristic and robust tendency to favor the ineliminability, *at any point*, of our "analytical hypotheses" (which effectively concedes the realist–idealist linkage) – at the price of precluding a cognitively focused nominalism and of insuring a clear basis for his own extensionalist program, but with the advantage of affording a rationale for tolerating ontological relativity.

The motivation of these remarks is obviously realistic. For either the appeal to "surface irritations" marks (no doubt inconsistently) a range of empirical evidence that is not inscrutable (that is, relativized to theory and conceptual schemata) in the way in which reference and meaning are inscrutable, or it marks at least the minimal constraints on which any putative science may be supposed to yield knowledge of the world. That Quine is drawn in both directions is clear enough: how else to understand such pregnant remarks as "Occasion sentences and stimulus meaning are general coin; terms and reference are local to our conceptual scheme";[26] "Vaguely speaking, what we want of observation sentences is that they be the ones in closest causal proximity to the sensory receptors";[27] "Like all conditioning, or induction, the process [of ostension] will depend ultimately also on one's own inborn propensity to find one stimulation qualitatively more akin to a second stimulation than to a third; otherwise there can never be a selective reinforcement and extension of responses."[28]

Effectively, then, Quine preserves his realism by at least two doctrines that, on inspection, *cannot properly resolve the dispute between realism and idealism*: first, he holds (in effect) that knowledge of the external world rests on sensory evidence; second, he holds that we must be biologically disposed to favor certain sensory elements as more similar than others. But both these doctrines are as congenial to the idealist as they are to the realist. On Quine's own view, there seems to be nothing to appeal to (the indeterminacy issue originally raised) to decide between an epistemologist "who is willing to eke out his austere ontology of sense impressions with ... set-theoretic auxiliaries" and one "who would rather settle for bodies outright than accept all these sets, which amounts, after all, to the whole abstract ontology of mathematics."[29] It is easy to see also that the (entirely reasonable) theory of a biological asymmetry favoring certain sets of sense impressions as "more akin" than others may be used to support the idealist's picture of our knowledge of a mind-dependent world (outflanking any charge of miracle regarding the world's reliability) as much as the realist's picture of remaining in touch with a mind-independent world (even though, as both Kuhn and Quine suggest in different ways, we cannot expect science to provide a progressively and demonstrably more adequate account of the determinate details of *that* world).

In fact, if one takes a very large view of Quine's entire venture, then, on his own conception of ontological relativity, it would seem unlikely (not of course impossible) that an idealist and realist theory of scientific knowledge *would* turn out to be an "invariant" in the very sense in which, in Quine's justly famous claim, "the infinite totality of sentences of any given speaker's language can be so permuted, or mapped onto itself, that (a) the totality of the speaker's dispositions to verbal behavior remains invariant, and yet (b) the mapping is no mere correlation of sentences with *equivalent* sentences, in any plausible sense of equivalence however loose."[30] Notice that the required invariance concerns only the totality of speakers' dispositions *and* that the identity of such dispositions remains, on Quine's (best) view, theory-relative, subject to our analytical hypotheses. Hence, Quine's boldest version of realism is, at best, a coherent but very unlikely fiction.

We may, therefore, capture the realist theme to which both Kuhn and Quine adhere – in spite of the enormous differences between them – by characterizing them both as *interior realists*. That is, they interpret their respective theories of scientific knowledge realistically, *but the evidence that they adduce is supportive of realism only on the assumption of that interpretation itself*. The term "interior" is deliberately selected to permit a comparison, without prejudice, between Kuhn's and Quine's accounts and Hilary Putnam's – for Putnam terms his own theory an "internal realism." Quine, however, provides us with a radical view about the defense of realism on the strength of empirical evidence; for the final sentence of *Word and Object* reads, "True, no experiment may be expected to settle an ontological issue; but this is only because such issues are connected with surface irritations in such multifarious ways, through such a maze of intervening theory."[31] And in the closing sentence of "Ontological Relativity," reflecting on the parallel between "regress in ontology" and "regress in the semantics of truth and kindred notions – satisfaction, naming" (partly in the context of Tarski's work), Quine concludes – because in both cases the resolution of pertinent questions of "referentiality" (as of quantification or of the satisfaction condition of the semantics of truth) demands a background theory of ampler resources – that "both truth and ontology may in a suddenly rather clear and even tolerant sense be said to belong to transcendental metaphysics."[32] The question remains whether that constraint can be overtaken in a straightforwardly empirical way. Obviously not for Quine.

III

Without a doubt, Hilary Putnam's account represents one of the most sustained efforts within recent analytic philosophy to construe realism as confirmed on empirical grounds. (Putnam's view has tended to be, it should be said, a realism inclined toward a Kantian formulation: hence, a realism implicitly bent on accommodating anti-realism – or, idealism. But it appears that, increasingly, Putnam has persuaded himself that more and more of what he took to be in place from an originally sanguine realist view has had to be adjusted under the pressure of necessary anti-realist concessions.) In "Realism and Reason," Putnam specifically contrasts "internal realism with what he terms "metaphysical realism," identifies the first as his own preference (against an earlier conviction), and explicitly characterizes that view as "an empirical theory":

> One of the fact that this theory explains is the fact that scientific theories tend to "converge" in the sense that earlier theories are, very often, limiting cases of later theories (which is why it is possible to regard theoretical terms as preserving their reference across most changes of theory). Another of the facts it explains is the more mundane fact that language-using contributes to getting our goals, achieving satisfaction, or what have you.[33]

His thesis here is explicitly indebted to those views of Richard Boyd's that seek to recover a form of scientific realism,[34] although Putnam himself believes there is a significant body of knowledge ("practical knowledge" – not altogether unrelated to Polanyi's "tacit knowledge") that is not part of science but is presupposed by it.[35] Rightly construed, this adjustment is meant to recover a strongly praxical sense of realism that could not, regardless of the pressures of idealism or anti-realism, be convincingly attenuated or undermined. Hence, despite the putative strength of internal realism as against metaphysical realism, there inevitably remains (for Putnam, somewhat more convincingly than for Dummett) a nagging sense, born of *historical* considerations, that man's cognitive access to the real world cannot satisfactorily decide the realist fate of particular claims, here and now, solely on the strength of the contingent epistemic fortunes of science. One notices already, for instance, in the remark just cited, that Putnam wishes to press, on the strength of the same *empirical* grounds, for a realist reading of distributed claims about theoretical entities and for a pragmatist reading of science as a whole. We shall return to this point of tension shortly.

The main thrust of Putnam's thesis incorporates the following two principles of Boyd's (as Putnam himself summarizes the matter):

(1)   Terms in a mature science typically *refer*.
(2)   The laws of a theory belonging to a mature science are typically approximately *true*.

Boyd, Putnam says, attempts to show "that scientists act as they do because they *believe* (1) and (2) and that their strategy works because (1) and (2) are true."[36] The empirical payoff, apparently, is just that "my knowledge of the truth of (1) and (2) enables me to restrict the class of candidate-theories I have to consider, and thereby increases my chance of success."[37] Part of the charm and persuasiveness of Putnam's (and Boyd's) position is that, *if* (1) and (2) are not themselves construed in a pointedly philosophical sense, what is being claimed is reasonably true; but in that relatively unrefined sense (*not* equivalent to the actual construction Boyd or Putnam put upon the two principles), one supposes that idealists and realists would agree. There is no reason to think idealists are any less "realistic" in the sense of pursuing what seems to work best.

(One must bear in mind, here, that, when he defends the "realist" thesis – the "internal realist" view, which, on the argument presented, amounts to a "scientific realist" view – Putnam means to contrast the thesis with so-called "idealist" views, those particularly of Kuhn and Feyerabend, which he opposes. Nevertheless, in so doing, because he now opposes "metaphysical realism," because he favors "anti-realism" to some extent, and because he regards himself as a Kantian, Putnam's thesis is a realism that ineliminably incorporates idealist elements. There is no way, then, to avoid the strongly equivocal use of the terms "realist" and "idealist" in Putnam's various and changing arguments. Nevertheless, in what follows, it will prove very difficult to keep in mind the distinctions Putnam wishes to press, unless we remember (i) that, when he *opposes* realism and idealism, Putnam means to favor Boyd's theses against Kuhn and Feyerabend; and (ii) that, when he *characterizes* his own view as an internal realism, Putnam means to concede a Kantian-like indissolubility betwen the realist and idealist elements of his position. There is no simple device by which to keep these distinctions clear. The issue is sufficiently muddled to seize this moment to give due warning about Putnam's use of the key terms.)

The problem arises, how to construe the claim represented by Boyd's two principles so as to confirm the *empirical* superiority of realism (in effect, scientific realism) over idealism. For example, on Putnam's view, neither Kuhn nor Paul Feyerabend believes principle (1) *or believes it in the sense in which Putnam intends it*; similarly, Karl Popper certainly does not believe (2) or does not believe it in the sense in which Putnam intends it. Popper explicitly holds that "we must regard *all laws or theories as hypothetical or conjectural*; that is, as guesses."[38] He goes on to explain, "From a rational point of view, we should not 'rely' on any theory, for no theory has been shown to be true, or can be shown to be true ... But we should *prefer* as basis for action the best-tested theory."[39]

There are a number of muddles here that need to be sorted. First of all, Kuhn and Feyerabend are taken to be idealists in a sense opposed to Putnam's realism. Nevertheless, Putnam's *own* (scientific) realism is indissolubly linked with a form of (Kantian) idealism in so far as a realist treatment of theoretical entities depends on evidence internal to an effective science. Secondly, Putnam, Kuhn, and Feyerabend are all realists in an *en bloc* sense loosely linked with Quine's and Duhem's questions. Thirdly, Putnam tends to conflate, without adequate argument, a realist science *en bloc* and his distributively realist view of the theoretical entities of a "successful" science (scientific realism). Finally, Putnam has himself, more recently, treated reference as quite "inscrutable" (in an *en bloc* sense favored by Quine and, more recently, by Davidson) in opposition to what he had earlier supposed[40] – which of course undermines the very thesis at stake (Boyd's thesis). These issues, it should be said, do not depend in a pointed way on favoring anti-realism, in Dummett's sense of the term. (In fact, we should be warned, once again, to bear in mind that, except where he identifies himself as a Kantian or conceds his own near agreement with Dummett, Putnam normally uses "idealist" as a pejorative characterization of Kuhn's and Feyerabend's views; and that his terminological usage and philosophical convictions cannot be given an entirely consistent reading ranging over the various phases of his own pertinent speculations.)

Doubtless, at the stage of reflection here represented, Putnam would urge that one *ought* to subscribe to the realist interpretation of Boyd's argument,[41] but that runs the risk of being question-begging or irrelevant; for, apart from the internal difficulties of particular views – Feyerabend's, say – and apart from arguments about ontological indeterminacy, it may well be false that scientists (or philosophers) act as they do because they *believe* (1) and (2) to be true. The trouble with the two principles, as both Boyd and Putnam understand them, is that they are already formulated in scientific-realist terms; also, it may, in the relevant respects, make no empirical difference to the success of science whether one subscribes to a realist (in particular, Putnam's) interpretation or an idealist (in particular, Kuhn's) interpretation of them (or an idealist analogue of the same). There is no evidence that Putnam is right, and there is a great deal of evidence – witness the rather different views of Kuhn, Feyerabend,[42] and Popper – that internal realism (the favored scientific-realist interpretation of the two principles is not indisputably supported by prominent scientists and philosophers of science. Certainly, *if* the issue between realism and idealism were not empirical or not empirically decidable, then we should have no pertinent reason either to expect the beliefs of scientists and philosophers to favor the realist position or, if they actually did, to judge that their behavior in this regard relevantly bore on the validity of the realist thesis itself. The truth of the matter is that Putnam somehow views "internal realism" as a single thesis having quite a variety of independent targets: in particular, "internal realism" opposes "metaphysical realism" *and* Quine's *en bloc* realism; it favors scientific realism as against Kuhnian and Feyerabendian "idealism" and instrumentalism; it means to reconcile, in a generously Kantian like sense, realism and idealism; and it is prepared to accommodate (to some extent at least) something like Dummett's version of anti-realism. There is obviously no reason to suppose that these objectives can be advanced together. (And Putnam himself has not remained entirely committed to these same objectives as his own account has developed.)

Regarding principle (1), it is reasonably safe to say that, construed realistically, it is not consistent with Quine's conception of ontological indeterminacy. For one thing, Quine holds that we are ontically *committed* by quantificational practice, *not* that we fix the actual entities of the world. Thus he says very plainly, "we have moved ... to the question of checking not on existence, but on imputations of existence: on what a theory says exists."[43] This obviously suits the idealist as well as the realist – possibly, the idealist more. And, for another thing, on Quine's view (as we have seen), ontological relativity itself precludes the notion that there could be – or need be – any fixity of distributive reference in order to save the body of science. But this again, at least on Putnam's own say-so, suits the idealist better than the realist. Here, the simple and crucial point is that Quine advances *his* thesis on formal grounds, although he fully expects it to bear on realist issues; and that Putnam, by contrast, advances his (Boyd's) thesis on grounds allegedly in accord with the actual practices of science, although *he* fully expects it to be compatible with Quine's holism.

In fact, Putnam concedes, with Quine, that "an absolutely 'unrevisable' truth [is] an idealization ... an unattainable 'limit'. Any statement can be 'revised'."[44] But in the context in which he subscribes to ontological relativity, Putnam fails to press the point that, respecting principle (1), terms may be consistently *taken* to refer to the same entities through the changing phases of a science rather than actually *known* to refer to such; and that, on the principle of indeterminacy (the correlative of ontological relativity – in Quine's view at least), the body of science may be preserved despite systematic changes in reference within it. To admit this, however, would be to concede the argument to the "idealists" (Kuhn and Feyerabend). It is also clear that the force of principle (1) is largely conditional on the force of principle (2): if a view like Popper's were adopted, then it would be difficult to see why (1) should be *required* at all; the point of (1) is largely captured by the notion that the preservation of "approximately true" laws through the developing history of a science signifies that the laws hold of just the entities intended in (1). This is why the two principles are already interpreted in terms of a very strong version of scientific realism in Putnam's account (and why scientific realism is wrongly equated with, or wrongly taken to be entailed by, internal realism). There must be some more neutral ("empirical") ground on which to decide the issue if it is to be decided (against Quine) on empirical grounds at all. Clearly, the matter cannot be favorably resolved unless reference (to both observables and theoretical entities) is taken to be relatively independent of shifting theories and conceptual schemes. The advantages to the "idealists" (Kuhn and Feyerabend), then, are these: first, discontinuities of the Kuhnian sort cannot be straightforwardly detected or straightforwardly discounted on empirical grounds, within a Quinean holism; second, if Kuhnian discontinuities be admitted, then ontologies and theoretical entities to which reference may be alleged to obtain may themselves, at least in part, be artifacts of such discontinuities; third, no distributive claims regarding what "there is" – *a fortiori*, no distributive claims regarding theoretical entities or reference to theoretical entities across theory shifts – can be decisively confirmed, within a Quinean holism; and, fourth, no advantages accrue regarding the resolution of these matters by adhering to a Dummett-like anti-realism or to Putnam's own (Kantian-like) internal realism. Put in the strongest terms, Putnam is attempting to hold on to the strong realism that "metaphysical realism" espouses, but without the perceived disadvantages of that doctrine – now that he himself adopts a "Kantian" and anti-realist stance. But he cannot succeed the more he is disposed to think of reality as, at least in part, artifactual (his sympathy for Nelson Goodman) and the more he is disposed to think of questions of distributed truth as arising within a fully-fledged holism (his sympathy for Quine).

Putnam once argued against Feyerabend (ironically, it proves) that meanings could not be strongly theory-dependent.[45] In the present context, he apparently wishes to extend the theory-dependence claim to reference as well. But he attenuates the conceptual basis for the newer claim and increasingly concedes – in the direction of holism – the strong theory-dependence of reference. This is the sense in which Putnam has gradually become an anti-realist (or an idealist) opposed to his former version of (scientific) realism. The important point about internal realism is precisely the point noted earlier in speaking of Quine's and Kuhn's "interior realism": namely, that *any* realist claims of a distributed sort must, once cognitivism or a principled analytic–synthetic distinction is repudiated, be incorporated within an *en bloc* or pragmatist account of realism. But, if so, it then becomes quite impossible to insure, on *empirical* grounds (as Putnam and Boyd pretend to do), that a strong scientific realism (of the sort they favor) could be confirmed from an internal realist vantage. Either they win their claim by construing internal realism (in a question-begging way) as collecting both the beliefs and the actual achievements of scientists, or else they lose their claim by making it quite impossible conceptually (adhering to scientific holism and a pragmatist reading of its realist import) ever to gather decisive evidence in its favor.

The matter is exacerbated (in the present context) by Putnam's appeal to the principle of charity or the principle of benefit of doubt.[46] That principle applies where putative misdescription affects *apparent* or *intended* reference or even what "ought to have been the intended" reference. Thus Putnam holds that it is not enough that a theory T_2, which is to replace "the received theory" T_1 of some branch of physics, imply "most of the 'observation sentences' implied by T_1; it is normally "the *hardest way*" (and the preferred way) to secure that relationship by "making T_2 imply the 'approximate truth' of the *laws* of T_1." Furthermore, we can, by applying the principle of charity, "assign *referents* to the terms of T_1 from the standpoint of T_2" if T_2 satisfies such constraints. For example, Putnam says, "we can assign a referent to 'gravitational field' in Newtonian theory *from the standpoint of* relativity theory (though not to 'ether' or 'phlogiston'); a referent to Mendel's 'gene' from the standpoint of present-day molecular biology; and a referent to Dalton's 'atom' from the standpoint of quantum mechanics."[47] It is clear that Putnam means, here, to subscribe to some form of Saul Kripke's principle of rigid designators.[48] But, if so, the principle of charity must itself already be construed realistically (that is, in scientific–realist terms) and contrary to ontological relativity (contrary to holism and the "inscrutability of reference"); also, there is no reason why a counterpart idealist version of charity could not be formulated, *particularly if Boyd's second principle (or a suitable analogue) were not construed realistically* (or if the theory of rigid designators proved uncompelling or open to an idealist reading or analogue). The difficulty could not fail to be exacerbated by adopting, for instance with Nancy Cartwright, a strongly anti-realist reading of explanatory theories. The *assignment* of referents to T_1 would then count, precisely, as preserving the internal coherence of historically changing theories (on both realist and idealist views). There would be no *need* to fall back to the extreme – and (what Putnam takes to be the) ultimately incoherent – views of Kuhn and Feyerabend regarding reference.[49] But there would also be no necessity – and no clear basis – for advancing Putnam's own very strong scientific–realist interpretation of internal realism. There is certainly no way in which to reconcile a strong reading of Boyd's principles with a strong holism, however realist it may be supposed to be.

Here, the general strategy of idealism obviously lies with matching the internal realist's construction of alleged empirical advantage in order to achieve a stalemate. For, although a stalemate cannot secure an idealist victory (a victory favoring Kuhn or Feyerabend, say), it would restore the dispute (borrowing Quine's term) to its "transcendental" status. Thus seen, the boldness and originality of Putnam's and Boyd's contention cannot be denied. On the other hand, we are led to see the relative modesty of the idealist countermove. Essentially, what Putnam claims is "that science taken at 'face value' *implies* realism."[50] The countermove, therefore, seeks to preserve an "empirical" element in whatever is justified in Putnam's and Boyd's claims and to reach for a "transcendental" stalemate regarding whatever they take to *imply* (scientific) realism. Thus, following Boyd, Putnam places a great deal of emphasis on "*convergence* in scientific knowledge."[51]

Now, it is true that Kuhn and Feyerabend deny convergence, *and* it is true that, in doing so, they deny (in somewhat different ways) that the referents of competing theories are or can be the same. It is also true that, developing the latter thesis, they fail to see "that scientific terms are not synonymous with descriptions."[52] But if, as seems reasonable, we can construe the principle of charity in an idealist manner – in fact, it *must* have a form neutral as between realism and idealism – then convergence itself may be construed neutrally as well. For, for one thing, the ("empirical," neutral) facts of convergence themselves *presuppose a favorable application* of the principle of charity respecting referents marked as only *intended* to be the same through changing and replacement theories. And, for another, the interpretation of the facts of convergence (as favoring realism or idealism) logically depends on the interpretation (realist or idealist) of scientific laws. What this shows, in effect, is the tautologous nature of Putnam's dictum "science taken at 'face value' implies realism"; it *implies* realism simply because, on Putnam's view, to take science at "face value" *is* to construe Boyd's principles, the facts of convergence, *and* the principle of charity realistically. As a matter of fact, as already remarked, Nancy Cartwright has defended a realist view of theoretical entities together with a non-realist view of explanatory laws in physics.[53] Hence, she rejects principle (2), but for reasons that have nothing to do with the historicist arguments of Kuhn and Feyerabend: they concern rather the peculiarities of explanation in physics.[54] On Cartwright's view, the explanatory success of idealized theories (*via* intervening "models") goes hand in hand with their empirical falsity. Again, Bas van Fraassen treats unobservable entities in an anti-realist or instrumentalist manner, but again for reasons remote from those favored by Kuhn and Feyerabend.[55]

Boyd is especially candid about the problem. He concedes that, in assessing the plausibility of competing theories that "have exactly the same observational consequences when taken together with those currently accepted theories with which they are respectively consistent," we might well hold one theory to be implausible because, say, the force it introduces "is dramatically unlike all those forces about which we now know"; hence we could construe the estimate of its implausibility as reflecting *experimental* evidence against [it]." So "the experimental evidence for our current theories of force is indirect experimental evidence that no such force [as is postulated] exists – and that [the theory in question] must be false." But the argument, he acknowledges, requires a principle to the effect that the plausibility of new theories "should, *prima facie*, resemble current theories with respect to their accounts of causal relations among theoretical entities." And *that* principle will be construed as empirically or experimentally decisive "*if and only if* we have already adopted a realistic position with respect to the experimental evidence for the currently accepted body of scientific theories."[56] Here Boyd offers a choice only between ("scientific") realism and "conventionalism" (that is, the doctrine that the differences between competing theories arranged as above are "experimentally indistinguishable").

So formulated, there is no doubt that scientific realism must be favored. But *idealism* represents a much more vigorous antagonist than mere conventionalism. It seeks in effect to provide a relatively complex non-realist or anti-realist account of scientific knowledge (a) by tolerating nonconvergence (of the sort Kuhn reports) where it obtains, and by construing the facts of convergence (of the sort Boyd reports) only in terms of holistic cognitive strategies suited to knowledge of the world-as-it-impinges-on-us; and (b) by conceding conventionalism with respect to distributed ontic commitment.

There is no question that, given these disputes, it becomes increasingly difficult to identify what may be meant by "idealism." The realist, after all, can (as we have already seen) concede an ineliminably idealist (or Kantian-like) dimension to his view – without jeopardizing the sense in which he remains a realist. But (in the present setting) the idealist seems not to be holding a symmetrical position. What threatens the coherence of Putnam's internal-realist account is this: he wishes to hold that, on *empirical* grounds, evidence accrues to confirm the reality of *particular* theoretical entities; yet at the same time he wishes to arrive at his finding by a strategy consistent with subscribing to scientific holism and to something like Quine's "inscrutability of reference." This is just the double purpose of the principle of charity. It is, however, quite imposs-ible to secure the claim without adopting the "metaphysical realist" thesis Putnam means to oppose. In *this* context, the *idealist* (Kuhn or Feyerabend, in particular) merely insists on what holism entails, or on what regarding the incommensurability thesis leads to a similar rejection of a distributed realism with regard to theoretical entities. Hence, ironi-cally, the idealist "reminds" Putnam, in effect, of the implications of his own assumptions.

The idea is that all the "empirical" advantages Boyd very plausibly adduces (that is, advantages reinterpreted neutrally as far as the realist–idealist controversy is concerned) may be retained in order, precisely, to effect the required stalemate. Hence it is *not* decisive to hold that we may assess implausibility (under the conditions sketched) as constituting "experimental evidence," for it is entirely possible to construe such evidence in "idealist" terms (that is, in terms opposed to Putnam's "internal realism") – once one denies knowledge of the world *an sich* as opposed to the world-as-it-impinges-on-us, denies the realist interpret-ation of (certain) scientific laws, denies the distributed realist interpret-ation of the principle of charity, and admits ontological indeterminacy. In short, Boyd's position must, on this reading, be construed as essentially circular. (Of course, the very term "realist" has become nearly intolerably ambiguous. In Putnam's and Boyd's hands, it must be taken to oppose, disjunctively, "conventionalist," "idealist," "instrumentalist," *and* "metaphysical realist." But, once the realist–idealist demarcation is rejected, and once a strong holism is adopted – which *both* internal realists such as Putnam *and* idealists such as Kuhn are disposed to favor – all of these oppositions become increasingly uncertain.)

It may be foolhardy, given Putnam's heady use of terms, to risk at this late point in the discussion an explicit effort at tidying up our classification. But the potential benefits are encouraging. Kuhnian idealism, we may say, is not opposed to realism in the minimal sense we have specified (a mind-independent world and some cognitive access to it). It opposes the strong convergence thesis Putnam and Boyd favor – and, with that, it resists subscribing to their theses (1) and (2) – which is *not to say that it denies in all distributed* cases particular claims of the sort *collectively* considered in (1) and (2). So seen, Putnam's choice of the term "idealism" to describe it is a curious one, both because Kuhn as well as Putnam acknowledges a general Kantian theme coloring his work[57] and because Putnam's own most recent turn of thought has (as we have just seen) veered increasingly in the same direction he had treated as "idealist" in Kuhn and Feyerabend. This is just the point of linking his use of the principle of charity with his favorable reading of Davidson's (and Quine's) view about reference.

On the other hand, having said this much, we may add a further distinction about idealism that is of the utmost importance, though we cannot pursue its full implications here. Apart from such special, eccentric idealisms as platonism, Berkeleyanism, and Hegelianism, there are only two pertinent, large traditions that affect the issue of scientific realism that we have been examining. They are usually not satisfactorily distinguished. One is the theory (or cluster of theories) that may reasonably be termed *representationalism*: that is, the theory that whatever we may claim as knowledge of the world is invariably mediated by some direct, or more direct, awareness of the contents of the would-be cognizing mind – classically, British empiricism and Cartesianism. This is, for instance, the doctrine that Rorty has recently so effectively inveighed against.[58] The other theory (or cluster of theories) is most accurately linked with Kant's revolutionary contribution, though not necessarily with his own particular convictions and claims (since Kant is attracted both to a form of representationalism and to a form of cognitivism). In a fair sense, it is a thesis as nearly globally adopted at the present time – among both Anglo-American and Continental European thinkers – as any that could be formulated. It may, by art, be reasonably termed *textualism*: that is, the theory that our knowledge of the world is an interpretation of whatever we take ourselves to discriminate within an *indissolubly relational condition* in which the actual world is cognitively accessible only through the tacitly organizing concepts of a natural and historically changing *praxis* and language. There are to be sure certain extremely florid versions of the doctrine – for example, those favored in recent years by such figures as Roland Barthes and Jacques Derrida.[59] But the critical difference between the two sorts of idealism is simply that representationalism regains realism only by yielding somewhat in the direction of cognitivism; whereas textualism *is* essentially a form of realism that precludes cognitivism. It admits a kind of mediation, of course: one that does not as such threaten skepticism (of the sort that drives representationalism toward cognitivism); one that does not raise the need for *criteria* of correspondence (which also drive us toward cognitivism); and one that does not suppose that there is a cognitively pertinent sense in which, in principle, our knowledge of the world (of the world-as-it-impinges-on-us) can be *assessed* as approximating the actual structure of the world as it is independent of our inquiries. The latter question never meaningfully arises; but, if it did, it would entail (for instance, as in Popper) some cryptic form of cognitivism again. In a word, it is the generically most viable form of realism itself – just the one in fact that we had identified, at the very beginning of this chapter, as alternative 3. It may be boldly claimed to be *the only form of realism that, in principle, can escape cognitivism or logocentrism*, and it accommodates very nearly all of what is best and most tenable in nearly all of the thinkers we have considered. It is, of course, notably hospitable to the moderate relativism we have been developing. In this sense, Putnam's internal realism is at least partly intended to obviate whatever, in Kuhn's and Feyerabend's "idealism," encourages a threatening relativism. There is a deep irony, therefore, in the latest version of his view.

IV

In effect, all of this is to restore – with a difference – Michael Dummett's emphasis on "the underdetermination of theory" (as well as, if needed, its distinction from Quine's doctrine of "the indeterminacy of translation").[60] Dummett's argument against Quine is to the effect that underdetermination is the only basis Quine offers for the indeterminacy thesis and that it is not sufficient: "If two speakers of a language hold formally inconsistent but empirically equivalent theories," the fact may, unnoticed, affect their interpretation of one another's utterances; but there is no entailment, Dummett thinks, from underdetermination to indeterminacy.[61] Indeterminacy, of course, actually strengthens the idealist alternative (as we have seen). But, apart from that, underdetermination may be softened in a manner mediating Boyd's realism and Dummett's (reasonable) hedging between the alternatives originally posed by Duhem and Hertz – that is, the view (Duhem's) "that physical theory is always underdetermined by the available evidence, in that no falsifying experiment or observation could show conclusively that any single constituent proposition of a theory was false, although it could show that the theory was not correct as a whole," and the opposed view (Hertz's) that that condition is "a defect to be remedied, a defect arising out of the use of a multiplicity of theoretical notions exceeding the multiplicity of the observed facts."[62] Boyd's effort was to demonstrate the untenability of "*radical* underdetermination": that is, that experimental evidence provides at least *indirect* evidence for the truth of a theory still underdetermined in the "direct" respect Dummett explores. The intermediary position, which now seems increasingly reasonable, simply argues that we should construe the indirect evidence Boyd adduces neither in the (scientific) realist's nor in the conventionalist's way. This shows, in effect, that Boyd has rather misgauged the force of his argument: it undermines conventionalism ("radical underdetermination") all right, but is ineffective (as yet) against an idealism that *admits* the bearing of experimental evidence on the appraisal of competing theories that are empirically underdetermined. The experimental evidence itself, as well as the postulation of theoretical entities and forces, remains as "mind-dependent" as ever in respects decisive to the dispute. In effect, distributed realist claims about theoretical entities would have to take a cognitivist form, to be able to escape the limitations of a scientific holism.

No doubt, the realist thesis with which we began, that material objects exist independently of mind, remains difficult to resist. But why should one resist it? The sophisticated idealist (Kuhn) will content himself with restricting his theories to the nature of the world we know: he will leave to the realist – to the "metaphysical realist," in Putnam's phrase – the unknowable world in itself. For Putnam, metaphysical realism is not an empirical theory but, in a sense, a purported model "of the relation of *any* correct theory to all or part of THE WORLD [presumably, the world as it is independent of the knowing mind]." That doctrine, Putnam believes, "is incoherent."[63] But Putnam appears to conclude that the retreat to "internal realism," which is admittedly coherent, plus the defeat of conventionalism *à la* Boyd, is tantamount to a defeat of idealism – which is a palpable *non sequitur*. If there is a viable idealist reading of convergence – which certainly seems facilitated by such views (however diverse) as Quine's indeterminacy thesis and Popper's conception of scientific laws – then the mere defeat of *radical* underdetermination (conventionalism) yields no more than an *empirical* stalemate between "realism" and "idealism". Furthermore, in spite of the polarized way in which realism and idealism are pitted against one another, it may well be, once again in the Kantian spirit, that neither position is entirely satisfactory and that only a theory that combines elements of both in a fresh way – conceding convergence and ontic relativity at least – is likely to be compelling. Alternatively put, it may well be that realism rests not with the *indirect* evidence of convergence but (as Boyd almost concedes, admitting the regress of his own argument) with the ontic import of perceptual knowledge. In that case, it may well be decisive to reconsider the tenability of Quine's radical indeterminacy claims and their bearing on the ontic import of sensory information.

In a curious way, Dummett pinpoints both the indecisiveness of Boyd's and Putnam's arguments *and* the irrelevance (for their issue) of his own brand of anti-realism when he observes that, against the mathematical platonist (and what Putnam calls "the metaphysical realist"), "the question was not whether the reality that rendered our statements true or false was *external*, but whether it was *fully determinate*."[64] Alternatively put, whether Dummett's determinacy or decidability constraints (anti-realism) should be construed in terms of scientific realist or idealist or instrumentalist policies (anti-realism in the rather different sense explored by Cartwright and van Fraassen) *is not at all the same question as* that of whether we should favor Dummett's anti-realism over metaphysical realism. It looks as if the competing views have passed one another in the philosophical night. (That is, Dummett's anti-realist emphasis concerns only the decidability of *any* pertinent claims, *not* the grounds for favoring or disfavoring scientific realism; and Cartwright's and van Fraassen's views on realism and anti-realism are, as such, entirely compatible with moderate views about decidability.)

Now, the most original aspect of Putnam's defense of realism rests with his use of Kant's innovations. Putnam holds that "Whatever else realists say, they typically say that they believe in a 'correspondence theory of truth.'"[65] Before Kant, "almost every philosopher," Putnam holds, subscribed to that theory – namely, that "there is a world out there; and what we say or think is 'true' *when it gets it the way it is* and 'false' when it doesn't correspond to *the way it is*." All this was changed by Kant because, with him, "a new view emerges: the view that truth is radically mind-dependent. It is not that the thinking mind *makes up* the world on Kant's view; but it doesn't just mirror it either."[66] Here, one might not unfairly claim, Putnam has provided the basis for the validity of both the realist and idealist views – as opposed to those of the conventionalist. Basically, there are two currently favored views

of truth: "'realist' views, which interpret truth as some kind of correspondence to what is the case, and 'verificationist' views [in effect,
idealist views], which interpret truth as, for example, what would be
verified under ideal conditions of inquiry [a mere example, one actually
favoring Peirce's version of verificationism]."[67] It is Putnam's intention
to subscribe to *both* (in different regards) and, in doing so, to show that
a correspondence theory" is needed to understand how language works
and how science works" – hence why realism ("internal realism") is
unavoidable.[68]

First of all, Putnam seeks to show that Tarski's semantic conception
of truth, which permits us to construe "true" in terms of its formal
properties, is "amazingly, a philosophically neutral notion." It is just "a
device for 'semantic ascent' – for 'raising' assertions from the 'object
language' to the 'meta-language,' and the device does not commit one
epistemologically or metaphysically."[69] On that view, since Tarski shows
us only the formal properties of the correspondence thesis, accepting his
account does not yet commit us to realism and, therefore, remains
compatible with Kant's constraint. But the "notion of truth" is not
"philosophically neutral"; Tarski's work "requires supplementation"; in
effect, truth as well as reference is "a causal-explanatory notion."[70]

Here, with important caveats, Putnam somewhat favors Hartry Field's
thesis (ultimately failing in another regard, as an objection to Tarski's
account) that truth has a causal-explanatory function, but favors rather
more a thesis (directed against Field's claim) to the effect that the notions
of truth and reference are not mere causal-explanatory notions but serve
a certain expressive purpose under the conditions of human existence
(hence, bear on justifying Tarski's Criterion of Adequacy).[71] On Putnam's view, what is needed in a theory of truth is an account of
speakers' "reliability" – that is, that the sentences they utter "have a high
probability of being true."[72] Given human interests (which, on Putnam's
view, yields a "'transcendental argument' for Tarski's procedure"), we are
led to construe "reference" (effectively, Tarski's "satisfaction" relation) in
a realist way: satisfaction or reference is then construed as "a relation
between words and things" and, as such, exhibits just the sort of explanatory power Putnam found in Boyd's original account.[73] Hence, internal
realism is vindicated.

But what Putnam has shown so far is no more than the formal viability
and coherence of a realist interpretation of the satisfaction relation:
Tarski's original conception, remember, was conceded to be philosophically neutral.[74] Putnam has not yet shown that an "idealist"
interpretation is untenable. Here we come to the very heart of Putnam's
distinctive thesis. Part of its force is somewhat spent, however, since

adopting the extreme dichotomy with which Boyd originally worked leads Putnam (as we have seen) to a *non sequitur*. His summary formulation quite explicitly pits the realist against the conventionalist, but he draws the moral against the "idealist":

> the effect of abandoning realism – that is, abandoning the belief in any describable world of unobservable things, and accepting in its place the belief that all the "unobservable things" (and, possibly, the observable things as well) spoken of in any generation's scientific theories, including our own, are *mere* theoretical conveniences, destined to be replaced and supplanted by quite different and unrelated theoretical constructions in the future – would *not* be a total scrapping of the predicates *true* and *refers* in their *formal* aspects. We could … *keep* formal semantics (including "Tarski-type" truth-definitions); even keep classical logic; and yet *shift* our notion of "truth" over to something approximating "warranted assertibility". And I believe that this shift is what would in fact happen.[75]

The shift involved would eliminate a full-blooded correspondence theory and would replace it with a "verificationist" theory, a theory of "truth within the theory" or "warranted assertibility" or the like – a position Putnam takes (on independent grounds) to have been skeptical of (metaphysical realism) "from Protagoras to Michael Dummett."[76] But there can be no question that, in contesting conventionalism thus, Putnam means to attack "idealism," for it is in precisely the same spirit that he maintains that "the typical realist argument against idealism is that it makes the success of science a miracle."[77] Putnam's point is that conventionalism *seems* plausible because the historical tradition of realism (the antecedents of his own internal realism – including Dummett's anti-realism) has "always" opposed skepticism by appeal to something like "warranted assertibility" (the still-viable discovery of full-blooded verificationism). But this idealist element in internal realism is not to be identified with the "idealist" thesis espoused by Kuhn and Feyerabend (which, of course, Putnam opposes). Nor is Putnam committed, in supporting the mild verficiationism that he here favors (if that is what it is), to supporting the positivist theory of meaning or full-blooded verificiationism.[78]

Our own effort, here, has been to recover an "idealist" (not a conventionalist) interpretation of the very evidence that Putnam draws from Boyd. If the effort is reasonable, then Putnam is caught in the same circle as Boyd. (It may help to remind ourselves once again that "realist" is sometimes opposed to "instrumentalist," "conventionalist," and "idealist" – particularly with regard to unobservable theoretical entities; and sometimes is opposed to "internal realist" – along lines favoring, at least somewhat, Dummett's version of "anti-realism." The "verificationist" attack on "realism" is really an attack on metaphysical realism; but the realist attack on "idealism" (and conventionalism) is really an internal-realist or scientific-realist reading of Boyd's and Putnam's theses (1) and (2) – *not* a symmetrical argument from the metaphysical realist's vantage. Both maneuvers are worth considering, but they are hardly the same. In particular, *whether we should opt for internal realism, in Putnam's and Boyd's sense, is nowhere directly argued.*)

V

We may now draw the argument to a close that may yet have some surprising features. One must remember that Putnam *does* subscribe to a "'verificationist' semantics" – not, to be sure, "a verificationist theory of *meaning*," but a verificationist model of linguistic competence. "Dummett and I agree," he observes, "that you can't treat understanding a sentence (in general) as knowing its truth conditions; because it then becomes unintelligible what *that* knowledge *in turn* consists in. We both *agree* that the theory of understanding has to be done in a verificationist way."[79] What Putnam opposes here is the confusion between meaning and reference and the corollary thesis that "conclusive verificationism [entails that] there must be phenomenal truth conditions for every sentence in every intelligible language."[80] He does, by way of a rhetorical question, concede that "verificationism [is] at bottom a form of idealism"; but, if so, it is, on Putnam's view, a doctrine realists can consistently adopt provided they do not, in doing so – like Reichenbach or Carnap, for instance – treat it as a theory or account of meaning.[81] The idealist element is in a sense incorporated in a stricter correspondence theory of truth. But, now, Putnam argues that a verificationist theory of truth *tout court* (hence idealism) fails to accommodate error in a sense that we require. Thus, assume that we require a causal explanation of the reliability of speakers (in the sense provided above, favoring Boyd's reflections). If so, then, "in the case of seeing what color a rug is, [say,] it is a part of the causal explanation that there is *room for error* – it is *physically* possible that one seems to see a green rug, etc., and the rug *not* be green." "[A] modal statement [is] implied by our theory. But this shows truth *can't* be warranted assertibility!" For any predicate the idealist may substitute for "true" one can find a statement S such that

"S might have property P and still not be *true*."[82]

This is an important finding but hardly decisive against the idealist. It does show that truth cannot be or mean the same thing as warranted assertibility (*or*, warranted assertibility under any merely finite or non-ideal circumstances). And it shows at a stroke that a view such as Gilbert Harman's that treats knowledge as inference to the best explanation[83] must fail for precisely the reason Putnam adduces. But the more serious point is simply that the *falsity* of asserting that the rug is green *must itself wait for the exercise of some verificationist procedure*: the modal statement

(i)   establishes the evidential *relevance* of what proves to be false for what appeared to be true;

(ii) confirms that we are committed to the view that our continuing experience with the world may indeed *warrant* that what we once took to be true may be false; and

(iii) entails that it is *possible*, given the way the world is or the way we come to gain knowledge of the world, that whatever we take ourselves to verify may actually be false.

None of these considerations is incompatible with the idealist thesis. In fact, Dummett, in rejecting a realist conception of truth – that is, a correspondence theory that yields a *criterion* of truth – concedes that "we remain realist *au fond*," in the sense, precisely, that "realism consists in the belief that for any statement there must be something [in the world] in virtue of which either it or its negation is true."[84] Dummett *must*, therefore, allow revisions of earlier verificationist appraisals on the strength of later ones. (Whether an intuitionist model of verificationism is preferable is quite another matter.[85]) Also, as argued earlier (see chapter 1), Dummett's insistence on *tertium non datur* risks exceeding his own anti-realist constraints – at least along lines that a relativistic reading of realism would favor.

One could say, therefore, that idealists *are* realists who insist on the *use* we make of the concepts of truth and reference, and that realists *are* idealists who insist that, whatever that use, there must be *something* in the world in virtue of which we take truths to be truths. But if conventionalists are idealists, then that breed is defeated, in just the same sense that, if the advocates of correspondence criteria of truth are realists, then that breed is defeated. So it is an extremely thin claim that Putnam reserves for the advantage of the realist, if the idealist is willing (as he is) to admit that what he takes to be verified at time *t* he may, for evidential reasons, be willing, at *t'*, to admit to be false. In any case, on the argument offered, Putnam now rests the sole distinction between his own realism and his would-be opponent's "idealism" on a claim that Putnam's own most congenial idealist, Dummett, would either reject or counter.

On Putnam's view, "one does not need to *know* that there is a correspondence between words and extra-linguistic entities to learn one's language. But there is such a correspondence none the less, and it explains the *success* of what one is doing."[86] There is, however, no way to flesh out any putative, determinate correspondence that can be considered in a manner more powerful that the verificationist's: there is no way to say *what* correspondences obtain in the realist's manner except by way of the idealist's devices; and there is no way to say *that* we have verified that the rug is green except by way of the realist's idiom – that *that is* how we find the world to be. But to say that it is *true* that what verification yields corresponds to what is "really there" raises a very subtle conceptual issue. For, *if that* correspondence is to be *true*, then either the force of the original mode of verification will itself be verified within the framework of a more inclusive theory, so that (on the preceding argument) it may be false though it appears to be true; or, since the verificationist picture will lead to a vicious regress, we shall have to construe the metaphysical truth of any such correspondence as "*radically non-epistemic*," that is, that "verified" does not imply "true."[87] The first limb of the dilemma is indecisive; the second is favored by metaphysical realism. Hence, Putnam takes the latter to be incoherent, and he settles for internal realism. Fair enough. But it obliges him to conclude that "in a certain 'contextual' sense, it is an *a priori* truth that 'cow' refers to [or is satisfied by] a determinate class of things (or a more-or-less determinate class of things ...)."[88] To challenge the claim that "cow" refers to cows, demanding, that is, how one knows that it refers "to *one* determinate set of things, as opposed to referring to a determinate set of things in *each admissible interpretation*," is to confuse internal and metaphysical realism. "'Cow' refers to cows" is a "logical truth," given what reference or satisfaction means; remains open to revision in the sense that the theory on which it was introduced may be rejected; cannot be challenged in terms of how the theory should be understood without moving to a theory possessing ampler facilities; and does not meaningfully permit the metaphysical realist's attempt to fix a unique referent.[89] Still, as Putnam himself acknowledges, the truth, the logical truth, the truth that is analytic relative to the theory in acordance with which the reference is taken to hold, would hold "even if internal realism were false."[90] Hence the curious "*synthetic a priori*" truths that Putnam introduces are truths in the purely formal sense in which Tarski provides a formal ("philosophically neutral") account of the correspondence theory of truth.

There is, it must be said, a deep equivocation regarding Tarski's "correspondence" notion: in one sense, it *is* "amazingly" neutral philosophically, but then it has no *cognitive* bearing whatsoever on whether "'Snow is white' is true if and only if snow is white"; in another sense, it has suggested to many that the entirely formal reading of "correspondence" *does* indeed have philosophical import – favoring, for instance, extensionalism or physicalism or the rejection of nominalism, but that is simply a mistake.[91] Putnam's formal truths, therefore, have *nothing* whatever to do with the quarrel between realists and idealists and must (as "neutral") be as compatible with the views of the one as of the other. In particular, these logical truths do not bear at all on the verification of principle (1) of the original thesis – which Putnam attributes to Boyd and which concerns reference in a sense that catches up the actual use and *understanding* of a language. And they cannot serve to explain the realist interpretation of ontological relativity – which does not require that we be able to determine the unique referents of our discourse. Hence their admission has the effect, ironically, of returning us to the finding (not, of course, in the metaphysical realist's sense) that the vindication of realism (or of idealism for that matter) is simply not an empirical issue – or, not an empirical issue in any familiar inductive sense. It is, of course, a transcendental issue.

Notes

1　Particularly in the idiom of Michael Dummett: see his *Truth and Other Enigmas* (Cambridge, Mass.: Harvard University Press, 1978), particularly the Preface and "Realism."

2　Two prominent specimens may be offered: Nelson Goodman, *The Structure of Appearance*, 2nd edn (Indianapolis: Bobbs-Merrill, 1966); and Hartry H. Field, *Science without Numbers* (Princeton, NJ: Princeton University Press, 1980). Field, for example, maintains, "it is not necessary to assume that the mathematics that is applied to the physical world is true, it is necessary to assume little more than that mathematics is consistent. This conclusion is not based on any general instrumentalist strategem: rather, it is based on a very special feature of mathematics that other disciplines do not share" (p. vii). But this of course says nothing about the actual human use of mathematics, nothing about the cognitive capacity to apply general distinctions.

3　Cf. Hilary Putnam, *Meaning and the Moral Sciences* (London: Routledge and Kegan Paul, 1978), particularly "Realism and Reason" (Presidential

Address to the Eastern Division of the American Philosophical Association, Boston, Mass., 29 December 1976).

4 The sense, but not the expression itself (it seems), is perhaps most explicitly favored by Wilfrid Sellars; cf. his "Philosophy and the Scientific Image of Man," "Phenomenalism" and "The Language of Theories," *Science, Perception and Reality* (London: Routledge and Kegan Paul, 1963). Sellars actually holds the most extreme version possible, since he is prepared to deny the existence of "the objects of the observational framework" and to favor the reality of the theoretical entities in order to "explain" the phenomena (pp. 125–6).

5 At the present time, two of the most salient accounts along these lines are developed by Bas C. van Fraassen, in *The Scientific Image* (Oxford: Clarendon Press, 1980), and by Nancy Cartwright, in *How the Laws of Physics Lie* (Oxford: Clarendon Press, 1983). (Van Fraassen and Cartwright hold opposed views, however, on the issues at stake.)

6 For instance by Putnam in "Meaning and Knowledge" (The John Locke Lectures 1976), Lecture III, *Meaning and the Moral Sciences*, p. 37f.

7 Thomas S. Kuhn, *The Structure of Scientific Revolutions*, 2nd, enlarged edn (Chicago: University of Chicago Press, 1970), pp. 206–7.

8 Ibid., p. 201.

9 Cf. Dudley Shapere, "Meaning and Scientific Change," *Mind and Cosmos: Essays in Contemporary Science and Philosophy*, vol. III in the University of Pittsburgh Series in the Philosophy of Science (Pittsburgh: University of Pittsburgh Press, 1966).

10 Kuhn, *The Structure of Scientific Revolutions*, p.195.

11 Ibid., p. 196.

12 Ibid., pp. 195–6.

13 Ibid., pp. 195–6.

14 Nelson Goodman, *On Mind and Other Matters* (Cambridge, Mass.: Harvard University Press, 1984), p. 49.

15 See also Goodman, in Alonzo Church, I. M. Bochenski, and Nelson Goodman, *The Problem of Universals* (Notre Dame, Ind.: University of Notre Dame Press, 1956); "Seven Strictures on Similarity," in Lawrence Foster and J. W. Swanson (eds), *Experience and Theory* (Amherst: University of Massachusetts Press, 1970); and *Languages of Art*, 2nd edn (Indianapolis: Hackett, 1976).

16 W. V. Quine, "Ontological Relativity," *Ontological Relativity and Other Essays* (New York: Columbia University Press, 1969), pp. 34–5.

17 Ibid., p. 28.

18 Ibid., pp. 54–5.

19 Quine, "Speaking of Objects," *Ontological Relativity and Other Essays*, p. 25 (italics added).

20 W. V. Quine, *Word and Object* (Cambridge, Mass.: MIT Press, 1960), p. 73 (italics added).

21 Ibid., p. 72.

22 Cf. George D. Romanos, *Quine and Analytic Philosophy* (Cambridge,

Mass.: MIT Press, 1983), pp. 187–95; and Alex Orenstein, *Willard Van Orman Quine* (Boston, Mass.: Twayne, 1977), pp. 148–54.

23 Quine, "Epistemology Naturalized," *Ontological Relativity and Other Essays*, p. 75.

24 Ibid.

25 Quine, *Word and Object*, p. 26; cf. p. 68.

26 Ibid., p. 53.

27 Quine, "Epistemology Naturalized," *Ontological Relativity and Other Essays*, p. 85.

28 Quine, "Ontological Relativity," ibid., p. 31.

29 Quine, "Epistemology Naturalized," ibid., p. 73.

30 Quine, *Word and Object*, p. 27.

31 Ibid., p. 276.

32 Quine, "Ontological Relativity," *Ontological Relativity and Other Essays*, pp. 67–8.

33 Putnam, "Realism and Reason" *Meaning and the Moral Sciences*, p. 123.

34 Boyd's *Realism and Scientific Epistemology* is apparently forthcoming; cf. Richard N. Boyd, "Realism, Underdetermination, and a Causal Theory of Evidence," *Nous*, VIII (1973).

35 Putnam, "Meaning and Knowledge" Lecture II, *Meaning and the Moral Sciences*, p. 20. See also, in the same collection, "Literature, Science and Reflection," and "Meaning and Knowledge," Lecture VI, pp. 72–3.

36 Putnam, "Meaning and Knowledge," Lecture II, ibid., pp. 20–1.

37 Ibid., p. 21.

38 Karl R. Popper, *Objective Knowledge: An Evolutionary Approach* (Oxford: Clarendon Press, 1972), p. 9. Cf. also Cartwright, *How the Laws of Physics Lie*.

39 Popper, *Objective Knowledge*, pp. 21–2.

40 Cf. Hilary Putnam, "Beyond Historicism," *Philosophical Papers*, vol. 3 (Cambridge: Cambridge University Press, 1983).

41 See Putnam, "Meaning and Knowledge," Lectures III and IV, *Meaning and the Moral Sciences*, pp. 42–3, 47.

42 Paul Feyerabend, *Against Method* (London, New Left Books, 1975).

43 Quine, "Existence and Quantification," *Ontological Relativity and Other Essays*, p. 93.

44 Putnam, "Realism and Reason," *Meaning and the Moral Sciences*, p. 138.

45 Cf. Hilary Putnam, "How not to Talk about Meaning," in Robert S. Cohen and Marx W. Wartofsky (eds), *Boston Studies in the Philosophy of Science*, vol. 2 (New York: Humanities Press, 1965).

46 In *Meaning and the Moral Sciences*, Putnam uses the terms interchangeably; but in "Language and Reality," where he first introduced the issue, he favors the second over the first, which he associates with a principle introduced by N. L. Wilson that is incompatible with his own. See "Language and Reality," *Philosophical Papers*, vol. 2; *Mind, Language and Reality* (Cambridge: Cambridge University Press, 1975) pp. 274–7; also, N. L. Wilson, "Substances without Substrata," *Review of Metaphysics*, XII (1959).

47 Putnam, "Meaning and Knowledge," Lecture II, *Meaning and the Moral Sciences*, pp. 21–2.
48 Ibid., pp. 23–4; also Putnam, "Language and Reality," *Philosophical Papers*, vol. 2, p. 276. Cf. Saul Kripke, "Naming and Necessity," in Donald Davidson and Gilbert Harman (eds), *Semantics of Natural Language* (Dordrecht: D. Reidel, 1971).
49 Putnam, "Meaning and Knowledge," Lecture II, *Meaning and the Moral Sciences*, pp. 22–3.
50 Putnam, "Meaning and Knowledge," Lecture III, ibid., p. 37.
51 Putnam, "Meaning and Knowledge," Lecture II, ibid., p. 20.
52 Ibid., p. 23. Cf. Putnam, "How not to Talk about Meaning," in Cohen and Wartofsky, *Boston Studies in the Philosophy of Science*, vol. 2; and Kripke, "Naming and Necessity," in Davidson and Harman, *Semantics of Natural Language*.
53 Cartwright, *How the Laws of Physics Lie*, Essays 2 and 3.
54 Cf. Richard Feynman, *The Character of Physical Law* (Cambridge, Mass.: MIT Press, 1967); cited by Cartwright.
55 Van Fraassen, *The Scientific Image*, ch. 2.
56 Boyd, "Realism, Underdetermination and a Causal Theory of Evidence," *Nous*, VIII, 5–8.
57 Cf. Thomas S. Kuhn, *The Essential Tension* (Chicago: University of Chicago Press, 1977), p. xv.
58 See Richard Rorty, *Philosophy and the Mirror of Nature* (Princeton, NJ: Princeton University Press, 1979).
59 See for instance Roland Barthes, "From Work to Text," in Josué V. Harari (ed.), *Textual Strategies* (Ithaca, NY: Cornell University Press, 1979); and Jacques Derrida, *Of Grammatology*, tr. Gayatri Spivak Chakravorty (Baltimore: Johns Hopkins University Press, 1976). The more standard Kantian version of textualism, semiotized in fact, appears in Ernst Cassirer, *Language and Myth*, tr. Susanne K. Langer (New York: Dover, 1946), p. 8.
60 Michael Dummett, "The Significance of Quine's Indeterminacy Thesis," *Synthese*, XXVII (1974) 390.
61 Ibid., p. 383; see also Dummett's "Reply to Quine," ibid, p. 414.
62 Dummett, 'The Significance of Quine's Indeterminacy Thesis," ibid., p. 384.
63 Putnam, "Realism and Reason," *Meaning and the Moral Sciences*, pp. 123–4.
64 Dummett, Preface to *Truth and Other Enigmas*, p. xxix.
65 Putnam, "Meaning and Knowledge," Lecture II, *Meaning and the Moral Sciences*, p. 18.
66 Putnam, Introduction, ibid., p. 1.
67 Ibid.
68 Ibid., p. 4; cf. p. 5.
69 Putnam, "Meaning and Knowledge," Lecture I, ibid., p. 10; cf. p. 9.
70 Putnam, Introduction, ibid., p. 4; "Meaning and Knowledge," Lecture I, ibid., p. 17.

71 Ibid., pp. 14–17; Hartry H. Field, "Tarski's 'Theory of Truth'," *Journal of Philosophy*, LXIX (1972).

72 Putnam, "Meaning and Knowledge," Lecture III, *Meaning and the Moral Sciences*, p. 38.

73 Putnam, "Meaning and Knowledge," Lecture II, ibid., pp. 30–2; and Lecture I, ibid., p. 16.

74 See Nicholas Rescher, *The Coherence Theory of Truth* (Oxford: Clarendon Press, 1973).

75 Putnam, "Meaning and Knowledge," Lecture II, *Meaning and the Moral Sciences*, p. 29.

76 Ibid., p. 30; cf. Dummett, "Truth," *Truth and Other Enigmas*.

77 Putnam, "Meaning and Knowledge," Lecture II, *Meaning and the Moral Sciences*, p. 18.

78 See Putnam, "Reference and Understanding," in the same collection.

79 Putnam, "Realism and Reason, ibid., p. 129.

80 Putnam: "Reference and Understanding," ibid., p. 112; "Realism and Reason," ibid., p. 129.

81 Putnam, "Reference and Understanding," ibid., pp. 111–14.

82 Ibid., pp. 108–9; cf. "Meaning and Knowledge," Lecture II, in the same collection.

83 Gilbert Harman, *Thought* (Princeton, NJ: Princeton University Press, 1973).

84 Dummett, "Truth," *Truth and Other Enigmas*, p. 157.

85 See Putnam, "Meaning and Knowledge," Lecture II, *Meaning and the Moral Sciences*.

86 Putnam, "Reference and Understanding," ibid., p. 111.

87 Putnam, "Realism and Reason," ibid., p. 125.

88 Ibid., p. 137.

89 Ibid., pp. 135–6.

90 Ibid., p. 136.

91 See the pertinent observation by Goodman in *Of Mind and Other Matters*, p. 49.

10

Skepticism, Foundationalism, and Pragmatism

Skepticism, G. E. Moore remarks in a well-known essay,[1] "consists in holding, with regard to one particular *sort* of thing, that no human being ever knows with complete certainty anything whatever of that sort"; different forms of skepticism, Moore supposed, concern only the "sorts of things" about which the claim is supposed to hold. Moore took Bertrand Russell to be the arch-advocate of skepticism so construed. He tried to show that Russell's arguments were inconclusive – and many of them clearly are; but Moore also insisted "that I have often known *with complete certainty* things of all these ... sorts" (there are four distinct sorts of "things" Moore considered and that Russell thought impossible to know with certainty), and he supposed that, in demonstrating the inconclusiveness of Russell's arguments, he was somehow showing that he *did* have knowledge with complete certainty of instances of the kinds of things in question. But there are enormous difficulties with Moore's position; and the point of pursuing this otherwise slim issue is just that it introduces us economically to a very wide range of analytic discussions of the nature of knowledge that, by their demonstrable inadequacies, turn us more promisingly in directions that require a broadly pragmatist (or praxicalized) orientation. To anticipate: where they are non-foundationalist, analytic theories tend to restrict themselves to first-order arguments, to favor purely formal or alethic considerations; to press inductively nevertheless for necessary and sufficient conditions of knowledge; and to ignore the history of science, praxical constraints on cognition, questions differentiating particular kinds of claims (for instance, about unobservables, causal processes, natural laws, and the like). Where they are foundationalist (foundationalism being the epistemically most salient form of cognitivism), they tend to present themselves in the guise of a purely formal argument (paradigmatically, as in

Roderick Chisholm's account), simply because of the enormous cognitive power already compressed into the foundationalist thesis itself. The foundationalists are (often) right to believe that, on their own assumption, they have not neglected (but also, that they need not directly address) the kinds of questions nonfoundationalists (as characterized) cannot but have neglected; for either such questions will be favorably and easily accommodated by their theory, resolved by what is entailed by their notably powerful claims, or else they will be largely irrelevant. In particular, puzzles about context, intentionality, historical change, praxical influence, conceptual alternatives and the like tend not to affect the foundationalist's position, once it is granted; but the corresponding pursuit, by nonfoundationalists, of the question of cognition in the same formalist manner developed by their opponents courts almost complete disaster. The rejection of the one opens up questions the other *cannot* ignore.

What, in effect, we shall be tracking, beginning with Moore, is the dawning sense of the peculiar aimlessness of analytic epistemology. Moore's view of skepticism will prove irrelevant to the legitimation of knowledge. The classical skeptical threat will prove remarkably easy to ignore or avoid. Foundationalism will prove unnecessary for knowledge, apart from being uncompelling. The formal analysis of knowledge will prove indifferent to the fortunes and actual practices of science. Correspondence and coherence will prove largely vacuous. Certainty will prove an extravagance. Rehearsing all the hopeless ventures involved with these, we shall find ourselves half-convinced of the fashionable, recent tendency to reject, as pointless and needless, the work of the second-order legitimation of knowledge – that is, epistemology, standard philosophy. But, from another vantage, we shall be retreating two steps in order to advance one step. For we have already reviewed certain of the salient problems of human inquiry and cognition within the setting of the sciences, *praxis*, historical contingency, the divergence of different forms of life, different doubts and guesses about what the world will yield up in the way of knowledge. And, in pursuing those matters, we have persuaded ourselves both of the indissolubility of first- and second-order questions and of the rational (or rationalizing) and directive force of second-order speculations *vis-à-vis* first-order inquiry – under the very circumstances of *not* being blessed with the cognitive transparency of reality (itself a second-order thesis). So the rejection of the dialectic of legitimation is itself the abdication of science, or the pretense that there is no genuine link between the two. This, for instance in the deconstructive reaches of analytic philosophy itself – notably, in Richard Rorty's self-styled pragmatism – is the startlingly popular consequence of confusing the aimless and empty projects (just tallied) with the inherent drive of every sustained practice of social inquiry to determine (as well as possible) the prospects and conditions of its own effective discipline: changing over time, reflective about the significance of its own apparent discoveries, gambling on the reasonableness of construing its own work this way or that.

What follows is, frankly, a detour. But if it yields a certain impatience, a sense of having sidetracked a more promising line of argument, it will have done its work. For by that detour we may confirm again the importance of recovering the tradition of transcendental reasoning (now under heavy fire) as well as of the pointlessness of doing so in that way the deconstructive turn has (let it be said) made quite impossible to defend any longer.

Let us turn then, to the narrative that begins with Moore.

I

In the first place, Moore never explained what he meant by "complete certainty." It looks as if complete certainty must be either a distinct psychological state, which then would bear only a contingent connection with being in a "state" of knowledge, or else a distinct psychological state that qualifies, on some account, as meeting the conditions of knowledge plus further epistemic conditions regarding possible challenges to the justifiability of one's *belief* (belief that is thought to count as knowledge). Secondly, Moore wished to make it very clear that he rejected "the common opinion that doubt is essential to skepticism," which he thought arose "from the mistaken opinion that if a man sincerely believes that a thing is doubtful he must doubt it." Hence Moore supposed that the *doubtfulness* of any of the sorts of "things" that the skeptic was making his claim about had nothing to do with any psychological states at all.

There is, in fact, a serious difficulty in Moore's account of *what* these doubts are about. Moore rejects both facts and propositions and never says what the relevant "that"-clauses designate. But it is clear in context that he simply failed to notice an important equivocation. Thus he says,

> Consider the form of words "That the sun is larger than the moon is a *fact* which nobody knows for certain." Here the proposition "That the sun is larger than the moon is a fact" is logically equivalent to the proposition "The sun is larger than the moon." But the proposition "Nobody knows for certain that the sun is larger

than the moon" is logically equivalent to the proposition "It is possible that the sun is not larger than the moon".

But the second might well be read as, "Though it is a fact (an accepted fact) that the sun is larger than the moon, nobody knows that fact for certain (that is, no one knows that the putative fact, accepted as fact, is a fact for certain." There is a similar quibble that arises with Moore's view of true propositions. But the upshot is that the skeptical position is here unaffected by Moore's maneuvers. So Moore never rightly managed to explain what was meant by "doubtfulness" or what its connection with "complete certainty" might be. But he obviously viewed doubtfulness in terms of the availability of epistemically appropriate challenges to the *truth* of what was claimed. What this means is that, although Moore clearly did not reduce epistemology to psychology, he was disposed to address the question of knowledge (and skepticism) in a distinctly formal way that had absolutely no primary, explicit, or relatively developed linkage with the actual practices of human investigators, in particular of communities of scientists.

Thirdly, Moore does not seem to have sufficiently appreciated the fact that *nothing* that he had to say confirmed that we knew anything with complete certainty. For example, his conclusion against some of Russell's detailed arguments is merely that it is logically possible that knowledge based on "analogical or inductive argument" might be (for all anyone could tell) "certain knowledge"; and that (as an instance) "it seems to me *more* certain that I *do* know that this is a pencil and that you are conscious than that any single one of [Russell's questioned] assumptions is true, let alone all four." But, of course, the defeat of skepticism does not follow from the logical possibility that it might be false; and the fact that certain epistemic claims are *more certain* than Russell's skeptical assumptions does not entail that there are *any* truth claims that can be known with *complete certainty*. Moore also says, incidentally, that "I think I do know *immediately* things about myself." He also seems to hold that "memory is immediate knowledge" and seems to take it that immediate knowledge is known with complete certainty. But he never demonstrates that he actually *has* immediate knowledge; he even concedes that he "thinks" that he does; and he never explains the sense in which memory (even of inner mental states) could be said to be a form of immediate knowledge, in the sense of providing knowledge with complete certainty. Here it seems fair to charge that, in accord with his common-sense orientation, Moore took the question of "certain knowledge" to be a straightforward first-order question: that is, a question entirely restricted to the exercise of would-be native cognitive powers – without the least need for any legitimating argument. The upshot is that Moore's position is utterly inconclusive. For the challenge to skepticism, whatever else it may be taken to be, is a *second*-order challenge, a challenge concerning the *legitimation* of certain first-order claims and findings – hence, to that extent at least, an argument akin to Kantian transcendental arguments, even if *not* (as on grounds not yet supplied) an argument capable of pressing canonically in the direction of the synthetic *a priori*.[2] At best, Moore may have compressed the second-order legitimation of his first-order claims of certainty, on the grounds of the reflexive legitimation of certainty itself – which of course is just the foundationalist's trump.

Here we must be careful. For the sense in which legitimation is a second-order question signifies that it is *not* a "naturalistic" question, in the first-order sense of an empirical science, a matter inadequately addressed by those who assimilate epistemology to psychology (as does Quine[3]) or to sociology (as Barnes and Bloor do[4]) or, in general, by those who advocate straightforwardly causal theories of knowledge.[5] Nevertheless, in so far as second-order questions are themselves "naturalized" – as not addressed to peculiar foundationalist or privileged "higher" cognitive abilities (for instance, contrary to Husserl's persistent search for a phenomenological science capable of drawing apodictically certain truths merely primed by the acknowledged, contingent "facts" of various first-order "naturalistic" or "historicist" disciplines[6]) – second-order arguments cannot but depend on the same cognitive resources (however differently deployed) that are called into play in first-order inquiry. Confusion between these two issues is, it must be admitted, very widespread in both the analytic and Continental European traditions, certainly in positivism and phenomenology. It is in fact the excesses of the foundationalist tradition, at least from Descartes on, that has encouraged the formalism and naturalism of current discussions of knowledge and the increasingly bold dismissal of the pertinence of epistemology itself.[7]

But there is more to the issue, because it may well be that the *kind* of skepticism Moore was attacking is entirely benign – has no untoward consequences for the prospects of knowledge. In fact, Russell's claims are themselves entirely unaffected by certain detailed weaknesses of his own maneuvers that Moore properly uncovers in exploring the prospects of certainty. For instance, Russell seems to have thought that one could remember and yet be mistaken in what one remembered; and that, because one could be led into error in instances of certain kinds of cognitive claims, one could not be completely certain in other instances.[8] But, beyond this, it is useful to note that Keith Lehrer, for one, has actually embraced the kind of skepticism that Moore was attacking. As Lehrer says, "Not only do I doubt that anyone knows for certain that any [contingent] statement[s are] true. I also doubt that the lack of such knowledge is a serious epistemic loss."[9] Indeed, Moore's position is a curious one since he actually allows the skeptic to admit that we have knowledge of the "sorts of things" about which we cannot, on the thesis, have knowledge "with complete certainty" (for instance, knowledge of one's own mental states; memory; knowledge of another's mental states; knowledge of external objects and events). But, if Moore concedes the distinction, then he cannot take his claims against Russell to confirm that we (or he) know(s) anything with complete certainty. For his part, Lehrer embraces the thesis that "the skeptic is correct ... in affirming the chance of error is always genuine."[10] This is to concede Russell's claim (which harks back to Descartes's claim) that error is at least always logically possible. Lehrer's claim, however, goes beyond this minimal concession to argue a stronger *empirical* thesis: roughly, that the world is so disposed that there is a determinate propensity toward error. Hence, Lehrer assigns to the skeptic a more powerful claim than does Moore, in fact a claim that is more familiarly skeptical than is Moore's: "To sustain skepticism, a skeptic must go on to argue that if there is some chance that S is incorrect in his belief that p, then S does not know that p."[11]

The plot thickens considerably, therefore. For one thing, there is every reason to believe that Russell was *not* a skeptic in the clear sense that Lehrer specifies. It is true that Russell believed that, for instance, propositions about material objects could always be doubted; he also believed that, even though propositions about one's beliefs about one's own percepts were "self-evident," they were nevertheless not "cerain" (only less doubtful than any others and the foundation on which other inferentially related propositions depended).[12] In short, Russell only professed a "methodological doubt" in order, precisely, to lead on to some form of foundationalism, somewhat more tentative, it must be said, than Descartes's original view or that of other more recent advocates (for instance, Chisholm).

Moore's sense of "skepticism," then, is neither Russell's nor Lehrer's. But, although his common-sense philosophy is decidedly unorthodox, Moore shares with Anglo-American analysts such as Lehrer, who approach skepticism and other epistemological issues quite differently, a characteristic avoidance of second-order, legitimating concerns and a characteristic avoidance of the usual puzzles of actual professional inquiries. This is the critical double theme that Moore conveniently helps to isolate – by way of failure.

Lehrer's claim is a helpful one, which, though it raises difficulties of its own, serves rather nicely to focus the dialectical importance of skepticism and the options for resisting skepticism. As Lehrer puts it,

> The chance that we are wrong about the truth value of any contingent statement is the probability that we are wrong. The probability that we are wrong is a property, or feature, or propensity of the world that manifests itself in error. This propensity is explained in terms of human conception which continually shifts as a result of our attempt to apply concepts in order to facilitate our goals and objectives.[13]

To locate the strategic point of Lehrer's claim – possibly in a way that he would regard as either too narrow or even not rightly in accord with his intention – one may say that what Lehrer has done is to interpret the skeptical thesis in accord with such views about diachronic changes in our conceptual scheme as have been pressed by Sellars, Kuhn, and Quine,[14] and to test the effective resistance to the force of *this* sort of skepticism afforded by so-called foundationalism (what Lehrer calls the Foundation Theory), most compellingly championed in our own time by Roderick Chisholm.[15]

One difficulty with Lehrer's view is that he wishes to restrict the thesis to contingent statements, to disallow its being applied to logical truths; the trouble is that, if, as he claims, "any concept, even mental ones, or the concept of existence, may be retired from conceptual service and be replaced by other concepts better suited to the job [intended],"[16] then either the cognitively pertinent non-fixity of the analytic–synthetic distinction would undermine the restriction, or else Lehrer would not be able to base his thesis on "standard conceptions of probability" (which would assign logical truths a probability of one), or else a lacuna in the argument remains still to be filled.[17] But, what is more important, although his concession to the skeptic may be generously read in terms of reflections on the history of science and inquiry, Lehrer really restricts his analysis to purely formal (modal) aspects of the conditions of knowledge, separates decisively the theory of knowledge from the theory of the justification of beliefs, and eschews the latter altogether.[18] This is precisely what threatens the peculiar vacancy of analytic theories of knowledge; but, in addition, it lends a seeming plausibility to a kind of philosophical analysis that is second-order all right, but not (pertinently or properly) transcendental. Ironically, it abandons the question of the legitimation of knowledge in pursuing (improbably or impossibly, therefore) its very analysis. There is, then, a double irony in Lehrer's account. First, it appears to promise a measure of attention to the relatively rich cognitive considerations offered by the history of science – but it veers off in a formalistic way; and, second, it most resembles Moore's indifference to the complexities of epistemic justification just in that respect in which it reasonably opposes Moore's own approach to skepticism.

The most important feature of Lehrer's thesis, however, lies in its focusing a confrontation between skepticism and those doctrines that would avoid skepticism – and, because of that, its focusing an even more important confrontation among the varieties of resisting doctrines: in particular, foundationalist and nonfoundationalist solutions. Lehrer, of course, rejects both skepticism *and* foundationalism and advocates instead what he regards as a coherence theory. In short, he advocates "a theory of knowledge without certainty": hence, he embraces the Moorean form of skepticism (pressed in terms of the implications of conceptual change), regards it as benign enough, and concludes that we need not accept "the deep skeptical conclusion of universal ignorance."[19] The upshot is to free, at the level of second-order considerations, any otherwise viable form of realism from the threat of alternative forms of skepticism.

The dialectical possibilities are now clearer. The traditional form of skepticism – universal ignorance (which Russell does not advocate and which Moore does not even formulate as a serious contender) – has been, equally traditionally, offset by some form of foundationalism. Lehrer's characterization is convenient. Foundation theories, usually versions of empiricism, may be said to meet the following conditions: "The first is that a basic statement must be self-justified and must not be justified by any non-basic belief. Second, a basic belief must either be irrefutable, or, if refutable at all, it must only be refutable by other basic beliefs. Third, beliefs must be such that all other beliefs that are justified or refuted are justified or refuted by basic beliefs."[20] Hence, foundationalism requires a demarcation between basic and non-basic beliefs (or basic and non-basic knowledge), where basic beliefs are characterized by cognitive indubitability or infallibility or the like, or where the possibility of error is radically circumscribed in contrast to the fallibility of non-basic beliefs. The details are not important at this point, though it is helpful to notice that Moore's position is somewhat anomalous, since he maintains that we may be certain regarding common-sense beliefs but never explains the full relationship between such beliefs and sense data – with respect to which he seems to hold a foundationalist view.[21]

What is important is this. Foundationalism has appeared as a promising theory, in spite of difficulties about self-evident or "self-presenting" contingent truths, because many theorists have felt that the thesis of universal ignorance would otherwise be irresistible. It is precisely the distinction of Lehrer's account, apart from questions one may wish to raise about its detailed claims, that it attempts to provide what Lehrer terms a coherence alternative to foundationalism – at the same time as Lehrer embraces both what Moore takes skepticism to be and rejects traditional skepticism. That is, traditional skeptics have taken the Moorean sort of concession to lead irresistibly to their own position; Lehrer attempts to demonstrate how to avoid this. But Lehrer's own solution is merely one of a battery of possible alternatives to foundationalism, all of which may be somewhat more compendiously characterized as forms of *pragmatism*. This may seem surprising and even misleading. But the sense of pragmatism here intended is such that it could not be captured by any one familiar figure: it is a philosophical orientation sufficiently resilient to accommodate such diverse thinkers as the following: Charles Sanders Peirce, William James, John Dewey, C. I. Lewis (equivocally at best), W. V. Quine, Wilfrid Sellars, Thomas Kuhn, Paul Feyerabend, Gilbert Ryle, J. L. Austin – even the Wittgenstein of the *Investigations*, and, of course, such more recent authors as Lehrer and Gilbert Harman.[33] It would exclude such thinkers as Moore, Russell, Rudolf Carnap, A. J. Ayer through a number of phases, and (most relevantly in our own time) Chisholm, since all of these thinkers have in one way or another insisted on some form of foundationalism. And, in an attenuated form, it would exclude all those thinkers who, even if they do not directly address foundationalism, support versions of essentialism, correspondence, the cognitive transparency of nature, or the like. But it would also exclude such self-styled pragmatists as Rorty, since pragmatism (as here interpreted) is (and cannot fail to be) hospitable to second-order questions regarding the legitimation of science.

The ulterior benefit and risk of Lehrer's maneuver is easily overlooked. The advantage of foundationalism is simply that it endorses in the strongest possible way a satisfactory cognitive (correspondence or transparency) relation between human inquiry and the real features of the world – and it does this, moreover, in a way that provides *first-order criteria* of such correspondence. The strong tendency for the partisans of foundationalism to speak of "self-evidence," "indubitability," "self-disclosing states," and the like has regularly obscured the fact that the thesis cannot fail to be a second-order claim about a first-order competence: the trick is that the same competence is alleged to disclose that we have certain powers and to be essentially involved in the exercise of those powers. Hence, the need to distinguish between first-order and second-order claims is thought to be obviated. This of course is the strategy of Moore's opposition to skepticism. What, in effect, Lehrer does, then, is to reconcile Moorean skepticism *and* the achievement of human knowledge, by denying any essential conceptual connection between foundationalism and human knowledge. As a result, we are forced to distinguish carefully between first-order and second-order claims. But, once we do *that*, we cannot fail to apply the distinction to Lehrer's own alternative theory. We may, in short, ask whether, once foundationalism is rejected, any substitute proposal of Lehrer's sort could possibly *legitimate* (in a second-order sense) particular interpretations (in realist terms) of the work of our first-order sciences – for example, with as much plausibility as the foundationalist claims for his own thesis. There is reason to think that Lehrer fails to provide suitable support, although the claim that *that's* true need not drive us back to foundationalism – *or*, alternatively, to a strong form of skepticism. What it does lead us to see, somewhat surprisingly, is *why* formal accounts of knowledge of the foundationalist sort seem manageable, whereas formalist accounts of the *non*foundationalist sort – rampant in Anglo-American philosophy – are utterly hopeless in their own terms.

The point is that Lehrer's extremely careful formal account may be taken to betray the conceptual inadequacy of certain large strategies for the philosophical analysis of the nature of knowledge. Foundationalists are, as suggested, able to compress first-order and second-order questions, because of the power of their particular claims; and, in doing that, they may (at least largely) confine themselves to the formal properties of the powers they postulate. Nonfoundationalists of the analytic bent unjustifiably restrict themselves to the would-be formal aspects of knowledge or justification or both; and, in so doing, they inevitably treat their own second-order questions as formally metalinguistic (merely) and disregard the essential issue of the legitimation of knowledge. The irony is that *both* the skeptic's challenge *and* the foundationalist's presumption (which they oppose) are directly addressed to the issue of legitimation. So the impoverishment of analytic epistemology cannot be straightforwardly construed as the cultivation of a distinctive and admirable rigor. In short, once foundationalism is abandoned, the analysis of knowledge and the history of science and informal inquiry *cannot* be separated – any more than can the methodology and history of science.

The curious thing is that it is therefore the (analytic) approach to the problem of knowledge itself that most threatens attempts to formulate a viable theory of science. For at the present time it is generally admitted that to understand the successes of science without reference to the actual historical practices of communities of inquirers is a hopeless task. But contemporary analytic epistemology is decisively committed to certain formal aspects of the definition of knowlecge and hardly at all to the study of the contingencies of actual institutionalized inquiry. The result is that not only our general concern – the reconciliation of realism and relativism – but also detailed questions about the epistemic status of characteristic claims in actual science (for instance, regarding reference to theoretical entities, the confirmation of theoretical laws, the status of inductive and falsifiability strategies, and the like) are extremely difficult to illuminate by reference to the standard epistemological literature. We are therefore obliged to improvise a line of speculation that will at least disclose the essential deficiencies of certain favored forms of analysis. In the process, of course, we may assure ourselves that it is very unlikely that arguments from this quarter could seriously jeopardize the principal thesis we have been pursuing.

II

There are a number of themes that may be termed pragmatic or pragmatist that are not centrally concerned with the present issue, narrowly construed. Nevertheless, it would not be unhelpful, given our deeper purpose, to specify the characteristic pragmatic doctrines, so that one may see how a variety of philosophical inquiries dovetail with our present issue. Of course, doing so will enable us to locate the relatively small technical questions here broached, within the setting of a larger conception of the living inquiries of human beings and human societies; for (as remarked), one can hardly doubt that the analytic Anglo-American account of traditional views of knowledge claims tends to be peculiarly abstracted from nearly all historical, praxical, real-time, or biological considerations regarding the actual careers of human agents. In this respect, there is almost no difference between Moore's and Lehrer's approach to the issue, to their sense of how to debate the issue – which fixes the spirit of pertinent philosophical analysis for the better part of the present century and also signifies, by way of deprivation, the promise of more recent investigative currents attracted at least to the historicity of human existence and to reconciling Anglo-American and Continental European philosophical practices.

The themes in question include the following: first of all, the denial of any foundationalist theory of knowledge, either in terms of self-evident percepts or sensa or the like, or in terms of self-evident truths on which the body of science depends and must depend; secondly, the claim that human inquiry is continuous with, and develops out of, the biological and precognitive interaction between organism and environment and that a theory of science must account for that continuity; thirdly, the affirmation of some form of empirical realism, to the extent at least that human organisms are perceptually in contact with the external world, whatever the internal conditions on which their sentient capacities depend – though of such a sort that contact is inextricably qualified by their conceptual schemes and *vice versa*. In effect, this suggests how a pragmatist account of knowledge concedes the indissoluble linkage of realist and idealist features and, eschewing every form of foundationalism, legitimates science by construing it as continuous with and emergent from the cognitively tacit practices of actually surviving societies. With these distinctions in mind, it is obvious that Lehrer's account is intended to be pragmatist in nature, although its weakness lies in never really availing itself of any conceptual strategy based on such considerations – beyond the rejection of foundationalism itself. Hence it attempts to provide a legitimating schema of a purely formal sort, as if to say that the *formal* structure of the relationship of knowlede claims and their evidentiary grounds *could be* spelled out quite independently of the conditions of actual life. To say this is to draw attention at once to the deeper sense in which Lehrer is not fully committed to a pragmatist undertaking – and to anticipate the reasons why the (rather) standard literature to which Lehrer's effort belongs is so endlessly and hopelessly engaged in adding to or adjusting the would-be necessary and sufficient *formal* conditions of knowledge, every time a *live counterexample* drawn from ordinary experience is recovered.[23]

The ultimate irony is that the very pursuit of a formally adequate *and* substantively pertinent theory of knowledge, relatively independent of – possibly, even logically independent of or prior to – the rich and actual details of the history of human science and the biosocial conditions of human existence itself (for example, along the lines investigated, however disputatiously, by such theorists as Kuhn and Merleau-Ponty[24]), encourages us to suspect Lehrer's account of harboring an attenuated essentialism (or correspondence theory) just at the point Lehrer means to avoid it altogether. There is a parallel to be drawn here between the threatened *reductio* of Lehrer's undertaking and the philosophically unmotivated extensionalism of Quine just at the point at which Quine undermines Carnap's foundationalism. Alternatively and simply put, the limitations seem to be inherent in analytic efforts to free cognition from foundationalist claims; but analytic efforts to legitimate human knowledge, thus freed, lead us inevitably to reconsider the fresh possibilities of transcendental argument. Here we are only considering making the journey, so to say.

It may be thought that Lehrer's theory courts incoherence in so far as it adopts Moorean skepticism on the basis of diachronic conceptual change. But it must be remembered that Lehrer uses the thesis only to insure the impossibility of certainty regarding knowledge, not in a way that threatens the truth and falsity of anything believed to be true. Coherence rightly concerns the latter issue alone.

There are, however, certain interesting limitations in Lehrer's proposal, and these illuminate the strategies available to non-foundationalist opponents of skepticism. Lehrer, as noted, adheres to a coherence theory. The label is easily misunderstood since we are accustomed to speak of coherence and correspondence theories of *truth*. In fact, Lehrer attempts to show that so-called correspondence and coherence theories of truth "must either be rejected as inadequate or else ... reduce to the elimination theory [of truth]."[25] By the elimination theory, he means that the conditions of truth may be specified jointly by the following schemata:

(AT) It is true that p if and only if p

which involves "the absolute conception of truth," in that truth is not relativized to any language; and

(CAm) S is true in L and S means in L that p if and only if S is a sentence in L meaning that p and p

which involves "the semantic conception of truth" since reference to a language L obtains.[26] The theory is an elimination theory because, on the argument, reference to truth may be eliminated by the joint use of the right-hand equivalents. A standard objection to Lehrer's view, apparently, is that "a satisfactory theory of truth is one that tells us *why* a true sentence is true [and] the elimination theory merely tells us when a sentence S is true – crudely, S is true if and only if p – but it does not tell why sentence S is true."[27] But Lehrer demonstrates, on his own view, that "the analysis of knowledge is one thing, and the rules for deciding whether one knows are quite another. The latter are conditions of justification for knowledge claims."[28] In effect, Lehrer retains the condition of truth in his analysis of knowledge but rejects the need to determine when that condition actually obtains. This is perhaps the most telltale feature of his account.

Still, the *point* of the elimination theory invites a closer scrutiny (and therefore something of a detour), because, in a sense, it is (apparently) designed to strengthen *some* form of coherence theory – which Lehrer takes to be sufficient or promising with regard to the development of an adequate theory of knowledge (shorn, now, of foundationalist support). The question remains whether *any* form of coherence theory will be sufficient for a second-order legitimation of science or ordinary knowledge – or for its "analysis." Certainly, it must strike us that the analytic disjoining of knowledge and justification entails, with regard to the "analysis of knowledge," abandoning the very pertinence of the question of legitimating knowledge. The telltale symptom of the bizarre prospects of such a maneuver lies with the overly familiar efforts, among analytic epistemologists, to *complete* the necessary and sufficient *formal* conditions of knowledge so as to obviate so-called Gettier-like problems.[29] But, closer to home, we may anticipate that a purely formal account of coherence cannot satisfy us regarding a correct analysis of knowledge; and that, accordingly, every promising coherence theory (to the extent that it is promising) cannot fail to link the analysis of knowledge with the analysis of the "conditions of justification for knowledge claims." Straight off, the "elimination theory" strongly recalls our objections to the so-called "redundancy theory" of truth as well as to Dummett's use of *tertium non datur* – and, therefore, to the very possibility of *formulating a theory of knowledge without regard to the features of any domain about which we may claim to possess knowledge.* This, of course, is precisely why Lehrer's approach cannot escape the suspicion of having made an antecedent commitment to some form of transparency, correspondence, logocentrism, or the like. How, otherwise, could a purely formal account of knowledge possibly be even pertinent?

Perhaps the most sustained account of the coherence theory of truth is provided by Nicholas Rescher.[30] But Rescher's theory cannot be regarded as an orthodox coherence account, and it explicitly insists on the noneliminability of truth.[31] First of all, pursuing the same issue as Lehrer raises, Rescher emphasizes (correctly) that Tarski's theory provides neither an explicit definition of truth nor a criterion of truth; he stresses that these may reasonably be required and that "any theory of truth – correspondentist or otherwise – can accept the Tarski condition."[32] Secondly, regarding eliminability, particularly with respect to the views of F. P. Ramsey and A. J. Ayer, Rescher observes,

> the thesis that "is true" is *assertively redundant* because "*P* is true" provides the same information as the mere assertion of "*P*" itself cuts both ways. It argues also that declarations are *assertively expansive* with respect to "is true," because the mere declaration

of "*P*" amounts to the declaration of "*P* is true." Thus assertive redundancy, rather than showing "is true" to be inane and dispensable, can be construed to show that it is important because ubiquitous, and represents an omnipresent – if tacit – feature of assertions in general.[33]

Thirdly, Rescher openly concedes that truth cannot be *defined* in terms of coherence; he appears to favor a correspondence theory of truth, which certainly entails the ineliminability of truth and operative truth conditions.[34] He says explicitly that "the position we shall defend supposes that coherence is not the *meaning* of truth in the context of factual claims, but its *arbiter* (to use F. H. Bradley's well-chosen word)."[35]

But, finally, not only does Rescher concede the importance of correspondence elements in an account of truth; he also insists that "the justification of the coherence methodology itself can be neither deductive nor inductive in character ... [but] pragmatic."[36] Here, he rejects classical conceptions of coherence and elaborates the required form of a pragmatic justification of the coherence criterion in a way that makes it extremely difficult to draw a sharp distinction between coherentist and non-coherentist accounts.[37] He characterizes his own thesis as "criterion pragmatism," not "proposition-pragmatism."[38] It is not part of our present concern to examine the force of Rescher's thesis. But it may be noted that his purported justification of coherence depends (1) on the tenability and relevance of distinguishing between cognitive or theoretical concerns (truths and facts) and practical or affective concerns (satisfactory guides to action);[39] and (2) on the tenability and relevance of distinguishing between the practical validation of particular acts and of general rules to which particular acts conform (paralleling the distinction between act- and rule-utilitarianism).[40] But, on the face of it, to confirm that actions are in some sense satisfactory appears to entail that facts regarding their purported satisfactoriness must be independently established, which threatens the proposal with circularity: the theoretical and the practical appear unable to be relevantly distinguished. Secondly, the prospect that the validation of rules guiding action and the validation of particular actions themselves may be collapsed into one another constitutes another genuine threat to the proposal. Rescher himself typically poses the most difficult objections, though he clearly regards his defense as the sketch of a promising strategy.[41] It depends essentially on the tenability of distinguishing questions of truth and presumptiveness or plausibility in a sufficiently strong way;[42] but questions of plausibility may, after all, be parasitic on questions of truth. The admission of a pragmatic justification, therefore, shows at the very least that we must understand coherence in a novel way or that the sufficiency of the coherentist account must be conceded to be as yet quite uncertain. Lehrer's argument fails to come to grips with these difficulties. But failing to do that is tantamount to failing to consider knowledge *as an epistemic achievement* under the actual conditions of human life – which is absurd. Lehrer construes knowledge formally rather than praxically or pragmatically.

Alternatively put, Rescher worries the adequacy of *any* coherence account of truth, precisely because *he* (rightly) construes the issue in an epistemically very strong sense, in just that sense in fact in which the question of legitimation is *not* segregated from the analysis of knowledge. This is the reason why he worries the formalism of Tarski's account, and considers what might serve as the pragmatist *supplement* to coherence – with an eye to insuring a realist interpretation of the latter, pertinent to science and human inquiry. Lehrer's vision of coherence presumes that *any* theory of knowledge assumed to be adequate to realist requirements and not committed to foundationalism *must* conform with the purely formal features of his own account (or another of the same sort), tested piecemeal for possible counterintuitive consequences.

III

The real trouble is that it is not so easy to gain agreement that we can analyze the *nature* of knowledge without, at the same time, providing an account of the *criteria* (on Lehrer's view, "the rules for deciding whether one knows") for proper ascriptions of knowledge or *vice versa*. The reason is instructive. The notions of truth and knowledge are quite different. It is possible in principle to theorize about *what it means* to say that a statement or proposition is true, without supposing that we are in a position to provide the adequate criteria of truth. Presumably, this is precisely what the classical correspondence and coherence theories of truth had attempted to provide (with what success, may be questioned), because standard defenses of such theories (even on Lehrer's view) never attempt to derive criteria of truth from their analyses. In fact, this is normally, though not necessarily convincingly, taken to be a sign of their eliminability or pointlessness (in a sense quite different from Lehrer's). Now, in the more-or-less standard *analysis* of knowledge, admitting the version provisionally advanced by Lehrer –

(i)   If S knows that p, then it is true that p;
(ii) If S knows that p, then S believes that p;

(iii)   If S knows that p, then S is completely justified in believing that p[43]

–, it is clear that (i) alone makes no reference, in the apodosis, to attributes of a cognitive agent. Hence, even if (i) were allowed in the analysis of knowledge, it could never serve to yield *criteria of knowledge* (as the others presumably could) unless we possessed (apart from a theory of the nature of truth) a defensible account of the *criteria of, or the conditions for rightly ascribing, or for testing for the presence of, truth*. Lehrer rightly remarks that a theory which tells us "how we *determine* that a sentence is true or *justify* the claim to know that it is true is not a theory of truth at all but a theory of justification."[44]

Well and good. But then, the elimination theory of truth not only does not (bother to) explain the nature of truth but does not (bother to) provide us with criteria or rules for the *ascription* of truth; and the question remains whether, in spite of the eliminative maneuver, either reference to truth or reference to whatever it is that establishes that p, can fail to be provided in an account of the *justification of ascriptions of knowledge*. For, it may be forcefully argued, the formal meaning of "truth" (say, along Tarski's lines) has as such *no* epistemic import at all; and any putative theory of *knowledge* content with a purely formal account of truth or a formal theory of coherence, or remiss in providing for the justification of ascriptions of knowledge, or remiss in linking (conceptually) an epistemic justification with a formal account or an elimination account of truth, *simply is no theory of knowledge at all*. From this point of view, Lehrer may be said to offer only a coherence theory of belief or, more perspicuously, a coherence theory of the justification of belief: here he *is* concerned with the conditions or criteria on which belief is justified – which is important. As he himself says,

> As a coherence theory, our theory affirms that a man is completely justified in believing that p if and only if the statement that p coheres with a system of kind k. The system of kind k is a system of beliefs. It contains statements describing the beliefs of S which we call a doxastic system of S [that is, the set of statements that describe what S believes, as "S believes that p," "S believes that q"] ... [corrected]. A veracious man seeks to believe only what is true and all that is true. A corrected doxastic system of a veracious man must describe a consistent set of beliefs to make it logically possible for him to avoid erroneous belief.[45]

The trouble is that *this* characterization contains an explicit reference to truth, albeit attenuated: the coherence theory of belief applies only to corrected doxastic systems, but such systems are doxastic systems corrected to conform with the intentions of a veracious man; and, if we lack criteria or rules for *determining* truth or what it is to believe only what is true, there would appear to be no operative basis for distinguishing the veracious man from the ordinary man, except in terms of his mere intentions or say-so – which can hardly be supposed to bear decisively on ascriptions of knowledge. Of course, these remarks do not identify an inadvertence or blunder on Lehrer's part: they accord with his specific intention to provide an "analysis" of knowledge. The fragile finding we are approaching, however, is that he has not succeeded and cannot succeed in this endeavor; *and* that the inevitable failure illuminates our ulterior question.

The formalism of Lehrer's account obscures at least two further fundamental questions regarding epistemic claims: both may be drawn from the same remark – "A veracious man seeks to believe only what is true and all that is true." For one thing, the formulation is entirely indifferent as it stands to various quarrels about realist and anti-realist interpretations of truth claims; and, for another, it fails to consider the possibility of substantive constraints on the global eligibility of bipolar truth values (that is, it fails to consider the bearing of the way the real world is structured *upon* what we may reasonably expect from cognitive inquiries – for instance, along the lines favored by relativistic theories). The objections raised straightforwardly confirm that, regarding knowledge, *alethic characterizations cannot fail to be dependent on epistemic ones and epistemic ones, on praxical ones*: the semantics of "believe" and "know" cannot fail to depend on what we substantively suppose human beings do know, in the exercise of the various forms of rational inquiry. Stated very broadly, then, second-order legitimating theories (so-called transcendental theories) are theories *meant to reconcile the praxical, epistemic, and alethic aspects of cognition.* This is why purely formal coherentist theories (for instance, Lehrer's) are bound to generate an endless need for patching their supposedly adequate conditions of knowledge: they are and must be forever jeopardized by mere contact with the historical, social, informal, tacit, and open-ended nature of the actual human circumstances in which truth claims obtain.

Lehrer enlarges the telltale qualification noted here. Corrected doxastic systems simply involve the intentions of a veracious man and provide for the logical possibility of avoiding erroneous belief – that is, believing what is false. But Lehrer himself admits that "it remains a logical possibility that the beliefs of a man about the world described within his corrected doxastic system could be entirely erroneous";[46] so that "completely justified true belief" that rests on a corrected doxastic system is not knowledge.[47] Actually, Lehrer's final resolution comes to this:

> a man knows that p only if he is completely justified in believing that p in the verific alternative to the corrected doxastic system. The verific alternative to a corrected doxastic system is one in which all statements describing false beliefs in the corrected doxastic alternative are replaced with statements describing true beliefs. If the statement that S believes that it is p is in the corrected doxastic system of S, and it is false that p, then in the verific alternative the statement is replaced with the statement that S believes that it is not the case that p. The verific alternative is, therefore, a description of what S would believe were he to replace each erroneous belief with the contradictory of what he actually believes. If a man is completely justified in believing that p in his corrected doxastic system and he is also completely justified in believing that p in the verific alternative of that system, then his being completely justified does not depend on, nor is it defeated by, any false statement or belief.[48]

But then, clearly, both the corrected doxastic system and the verific alternative can be specified only on the condition that true and false beliefs can be independently specified; in fact, although the verific alternative is formulated in terms of a corrected doxastic system, a corrected doxastic system (if it is to have more than the barest intentional force) can be specified only if the verific alternative can be independently specified.

As already noted, Lehrer correctly observes that the skeptic holds that if there is "some chance" that S is wrong in his belief that p, then S does not know that p. But Lehrer claims that, on the analysis provided (sketched just above), "the premiss is unavailable." "It does not follow," Lehrer says, "from the premiss that there is some chance that S is incorrect in his belief that p, that p is not true, or that S does not believe that p, or that S is not completely justified in believing that p, or that S is not completely justified in believing that p in his verific alternative."[49] True enough. None of these conclusions follow. But, in order to *refute* skepticism (the relevant section is actually titled, "A Refutation of Skepticism"), in order even to *avoid* skepticism, what we need is not only a stalemate regarding the required entailments but a demonstration that the skeptic is unable to interpose any further reasonable or valid premisses from which the skeptical conclusion follows. Lehrer wrongly believes he has succeeded because, apparently, he fails to see that the coherence theory of justification simply does not provide *epistemically* sufficient conditions of knowledge, that its very plausibility rests on reintroducing the distinction between true and false beliefs in a way that, in effect, ignores the skeptic's challenge. For the admission of the corrected doxastic and verific systems presupposes the very knowledge (of how to determine what is true and false) which the skeptic challenges. "We avoid skepticism," Lehrer claims fairly enough, "by construing a theory of justification without a guarantee of truth"[50] But this only shows that knowledge does not entail certainty – once again, against Moore's view (and foundationalism in general).

Nothing that Lehrer has said bears on constructing a theory of justification *without a criterion of or rule for determining truth*: on the contrary, his own theory requires it – as well as the genuine avoidance or refutation of skepticism. *A fortiori*, a theory of knowledge requires some criterion or rule for determining truth. It may therefore be that a viable theory of knowledge avoids foundationalism by giving up certainty *and* avoids but does not refute skepticism by providing an operative criterion of truth. Lehrer, in effect, hobbles his own theory by eliminating a condition necessary to any viable theory of *cognitive* justification. Presumably, the required condition is just what the tradition of transcendental argument, however canonical or deviant, has always pursued and thought necessary to supply.

The short form of the argument, then, is this:

1   skepticism is an epistemically substantive thesis, which cannot, therefore, be subverted by purely formal considerations – we cannot claim to "avoid" skepticism by formal means any more than we can thereby refute it;
2   a theory of knowledge cannot fail to incorporate epistemically pertinent conditions for determining whether knowledge is reasonably taken to obtain – we cannot, unless vacuously, fix the formal conditions of knowledge without attention to conditions (that must be satisfied) that are epistemically pertinent to the way the world is and the way we are cognitively in touch with it.

IV

In effect, this is the point of insisting that an analysis of knowledge is impossible without the provision of adequate criteria of knowledge, and *vice versa*. Chisholm had (we now see, rightly) insisted that there is no way of answering either question ("*What* do we know?," "How are we to decide, in any particular case, *whether* we know?") without the other.[51] The reason is plain: knowledge is a privileged condition of *ourselves* (whereas truth is not). How could we possibly understand what it is to know unless we were in a position to specify the conditions on which knowledge could rightly be ascribed to ourselves? Hence we see why it is that foundationalists both insist on the connection and avoid skepticism by introducing some form of basic or self-evident knowledge.

Chisholm's distinction neatly clarifies, also, the sense in which, although titans or gods may be conceived to know what man can never come to know, it is incoherent to suppose that, in a *cognitively relevant respect* (that is, by the use of their own criteria), humans ever add to *their* knowledge by acquiring the fruits of these greater powers; or intelligibly treat propositions that are (apparently) well-formed grammatically (which, however, *they* cannot judge) as open to ascriptions of standard bipolar truth values by such titans or gods. This is surely an essential part of the objection pressed in Hilary Putnam's attack on "metaphysical realism" and of Michael Dummett's espousal of "anti-realism."[52] It does not, of course, fully vindicate the latter views – if disjunctively linked with "internal realism" and "realism" (respectively.) But it shows the sense in which *some* accommodation of the thrust of intuitionism cannot reasonably be avoided.[53] Again, Chisholm's distinction and his adherence to foundationalism show why a purely formal account of the criteria of knowledge may appear to be adequate to the task: there simply would be no need to attend to any practical or historical considerations *if* one were a foundationalist. Once, however, a foundationalism had been abandoned, *there would no longer be any rationale for a purely formal account of knowledge:* the theory of knowledge could not then fail to be conceptually affected by the perceived contingencies of actual life. Hence, the shift in strategy adumbrates the sense in which transcendental arguments may be (heterodoxly) regarded as empirical arguments of some sort. Also, of course, once historicist and praxical considerations are permitted to bear pertinently on the epistemic status of cognitive claims, foundationalism (and cognitivism) cannot reasonably be taken for granted without some answers to questions regarding the import of contingencies thereby generated. It is not unimportant to remark that Chisholm does not directly address these issues.

It is extremely suggestive that the first paper in Chisholm and Swartz's well-known anthology[54] is Leonard Nelson's "The Impossibility of the 'Theory of Knowledge,'" because that paper introduces in effect the rationale for Chisholm's *Theory of Knowledge*. This is not to say that

Chisholm subscribes to Nelson's arguments regarding so-called "non-intuitive immediate cognition" (or synthetic *a priori* metaphysical judgments) or even the details of Nelson's version of foundationalism. But Nelson raises the spectre of skepticism – that is, the threat of ignorance – precisely in the same way that Chisholm does, by noticing that the questions of the nature and criteria of knowledge cannot be pursued in any way that assigns logical priority to the one or the other. This is the point of Nelson's title. But, of course, we are saved from skepticism, introduced by way of the "theory of knowledge" itself, by acknowledging what Nelson regards as the "psychological facts."[55] Here there is an extraordinary (and, one may almost say, outrageous) similarity to be drawn to Moore's way of proceeding. Moore confutes Russell's skeptical challenge by *announcing* (by doing no more than announcing) that *he* has certain knowledge of certain common-sense matters; and Nelson baldly maintains that the "theory of knowledge" simply "contradicts the facts of inner experience," that we just *have* certain cognitions regarding which there is no "possibility of *error*."[56]

But that is perhaps a quibble. The more important feature of Nelson's argument lies in the clue it inadvertently provides about a distinctive maneuver among foundationalists – which exposes the vulnerability of their essential claim. The following passage repays close attention:

> To convince ourselves of the existence of cognitions that are not judgments, we need only consider any intuition at all, such as an ordinary sensory perception. For example, I have a sensory perception of the sheet of paper that lies here on the table before me. This perception is, first of all, a cognition, not merely a problematic notion. The existential assertion that is an element of this cognition is, however, not a judgment. To be sure, I can also render in a judgment the same circumstances that I here cognize through the perception; but when I judge that a piece of paper is lying before me on the table, that is an altogether different sort of cognition from the perception of this situation. I need concepts for the judgment, e.g., the concept "table," the concept "paper," etc. I connect these concepts in a certain manner and assert that objective reality pertains to this combination of concepts. Perception, on the other hand, has no need of any concepts nor of any problematic notion of its objects whatsoever; rather, it is itself an originally assertoric notion – is, in other words, an immediate cognition.[57]

This is an amazing claim. For one thing, Nelson obviously holds that these "cognitions" have a certain assertoric force (in fact, have the force of a truth claim without making any claim), are not judgments though they have such force, and are valid (as providing knowledge) without the mediation of concepts! For another, such "cognitions" are inner mental states of some sort. Now, it can be fairly argued that no cognition and no mental state that, on a theory, qualifies or counts as knowledge can possibly be relevantly specified except by articulating its content propositionally. Thus, S fears that it will rain; S thinks that today is Tuesday; S sees that there is a piece of paper lying before him. But it is impossible to concede that cognitions are propositionally detailed without also conceding that they count as *judgments* (or involve judgments, if we think of knowledge as a capacity) – that is, acknowledging some "assertoric" force that is the analogue of the illocutionary force of actual speech acts.[58] And it is impossible to concede this without also conceding that cognitions (or judgments that are cognitions) involve the use of *concepts* – that is, the relevant capacity to understand (in some sense, not necessarily linguistically, as with the higher animals) that what may be affirmed by the use of propositions is the case. Notice that to insist thus is *not* to claim that concepts are inherently linguistic. Husserl, for example, championed the apodictic nature of certain self-presenting states while at the same time he treated linguistic formulations of what was thus presented as having a purely recording, otherwise empty (*Zwecklos*), function *vis-à-vis* such disclosures.[59]

The reason this connection is important is simply that, if Lehrer's claim about the "chance" of error be admitted, then the certitude of such basic "cognitions" is effectively undermined. Only if immediate cognitions were not (or did not involve the use of) judgments, did not involve the use of concepts, could the thesis of self-evidence, indubitability, complete certitude, and the rest have any inning at all. Nelson's thesis gives the appearance of a viable foundationalist claim precisely because Nelson himself insists that immediate cognitions are not judgments.[60] They are, as he says, psychological or inner mental states. *But* if they are mere states lacking "assertoric" properties, then there is no prospect that they can be the appropriate analogues of judgments. It is idle, therefore, for Nelson to raise as a puzzle "the possibility of error": the simple reason why Nelson's would-be "cognitions" cannot be in error is that Nelson insists, contradictorily, that they both have "assertoric" force and yet are not (or do not involve) judgments at all. The "chance" of error – in Lehrer's sense – immediately obtains once the correction is made. So the surface plausibility of Nelson's maneuver rests squarely on his having conflated cognition as (or as entailing) a judgment that succeeds in a certain appropriate way (explicit or implicit, linguistically formulated or not so formulated) with "cognition" taken as some sort of psychological state that is not (or does not involve) a judgment. Knowledge, in fact, cannot be straightforwardly regarded as a psychological state, in the manner of belief, and must be analyzed in a way that is utterly different from belief. To put the matter squarely, beliefs are psychological states but knowledge is a certain *status* assigned to beliefs, or beliefs and certain capacities and skills. Moreover – and this is part of the crucial point – the *status* of knowledge requires *the second-order legitimation of first-order claims*. Presumably this is what only transcendental arguments can provide. Furthermore, the recognition of the role of *concepts* is just what leads on to a strongly praxical and historicized grasp of the problem of knowledge. Foundationalism or cognitivism precludes the need to consider such complications in depth; and formalist versions of nonfoundationalism fail to appreciate the complexity of what they themselves acknowledge. The pretty upshot of all of this is that foundationalism does *not* preclude the need to consider the question of second-order legitimation: it merely answers it in its own remarkably compressed way. Hence the rejection of foundationalism does *not* free us from addressing that same question; on the contrary, it makes its contribution more palpable. Also, that double lesson is itself entirely neutral as far as the actual legitimation of foundationalism is concerned.

The foregoing, then, illuminates in an extremely perspicuous way the fundamental difficulty of Chisholm's foundationalism – which, without a doubt, is the most sophisticated version of the doctrine currently available. For in speaking about the "directly evident" – which, on Chisholm's analogue of Nelson's worry about an infinite and vicious regress, provides us (foundationally) with "a proper stopping place" against the Socratic questions of justification – Chisholm offers the following formula:

What justifies me in counting it as evident that *a* is *F* is simply the fact that *a* is *F*.[61]

Chisholm's clarification is instructive. He borrows a term from Meinong and says that "what is directly evident to a man is always some state of affairs that 'presents itself to him.' Thus, my believing that Socrates is mortal is a state of affairs that is 'self-presenting' to me. If I do believe that Socrates is mortal, then, *ipso facto*, it is evident to me that I believe that Socrates is mortal; the state of affairs is 'apprehended through itself'."[62] Chisholm does question Nelson's formula. For he takes it that Nelson has not quite sorted out the distinction between immediate experience and the justification for counting immediate experience as evident.[63] Here he finds Leibniz's formulation more to his liking ("primary truths of fact"). But his point is that, rather in the way Nelson views the matter, the psychological experience – or, more accurately, the fact of having a certain psychological experience – serves to justify my counting it as evident that a is F because "the state of affairs" is "self-presenting" or "directly evident" or (Leibniz's phrase) such that "there is no mediation between the understanding and its objects."[64] Nevertheless, apart from plausible but piecemeal challenges to Chisholm's particular instances or a general attack on self-evidence and indubitability, there can be no question that Chisholm's formulation is open to challenge on the basis of Lehrer's conception of the "chance" of being mistaken – that is, on the basis of the misapplication of a concept or a failure to grasp the significance of diachronic conceptual changes. For either Chisholm adheres to Nelson's view of "cognitions" (which seems not to be the case) or else he construes the apparent cognition as involving a judgment ("What justifies me in counting ... "); but, if he favors the latter alternative, then Lehrer's claim has force. Hence, foundationalism (that is, Chisholm's variety, though not necessarily Russell's) appears to be subject to a serious, potentially fatal, weakness. At the very least, the relevance of the kind of foundationalism Chisholm favors, as far as the inquiries of science are concerned, is open to serious challenge, precisely because the appraisal of scientific knowledge cannot convincingly be separated from the shifting history of the practices of science itself. Needless to say, any theory of knowledge that subscribes to a coherence conception of truth is, to that extent, incompatible with (any form of) foundationalism.[65]

It may be useful to intrude a reminder, here, of the characteristic objection phenomenology raises about foundationalist claims regarding the empirical sciences – since Chisholm's thesis is meant to be taken to be defended in the face of phenomenological views of subjectivity. Merleau-Ponty has put the point as well as any:

> It is essential to the reflective analysis that it start from a *de facto* situation. [That is, it is essential to the "philosophy of reflection," to the analysis of cognition viewed as a part of the natural world about which it is supposed to yield truths, that its capacity to proceed thus be reflexively transparent.] Precisely because it is reflection, re-turn, re-conquest, or re-covery, it cannot flatter itself that it would simply coincide with a constitutive principle already at work in the spectacle of the world, that starting with this spectacle, it would travel the very route that the constitutive principle had followed in the opposite direction. But this is what it

would have to do if it is really a *return*, that is, if its point of arrival were also the starting point – and this exigency is no optional clause, since if it were not fulfilled the regressive analysis ... would be abandoning the pretension to disclose the sources to us and would be nothing more than the technique of a philosophical quietism.[66]

What Merleau-Ponty skilfully brings together is the joint admission that the legitimation of knowledge cannot and need not call into question the *de facto* achievements of empirical science and that, in admitting that, it cannot and need not pretend that legitimation at any point entails restriction to – hence, the reflexive transparency of – such *de facto* accomplishments. Both skepticism and foundationalism are conceptual extremes regarding transparency: skepticism denies the possibility, but insists that that is (or would have been) the only option we have (or had); foundationalism affirms the possibility, but ignores the discrepancy entailed in the (transcendental or "hyper-reflective") "re-turn." That is,

> every effort to comprehend the spectacle of the world from within and from the sources demands that we detach ourselves from the effective unfolding of our perceptions and from our perception of the world, that we cease being one with the concrete flux of our life in order to retrace the total bearing and principal articulations of the world upon which it opens. To reflect is not to coincide with the flux from its source unto its last ramifications; it is to disengage from the things, perceptions, world, and perception of the world, by submitting them to a systematic variation, the intelligible nuclei that resist, and to proceed from one intelligible nucleus to the next in a way that is not belied by experience but gives us only its universal contours.[67]

This clarifies, of course, the phenomenological sense of an "eidetic reduction" at the same time as it pinpoints the conceptual novelty and power of the phenomenological reading of the dictum "there is no *Schein* without an *Erscheinung* ... every *Schein* is the counterpart of an *Erscheinung*" – that is, "what each perception, even if false, verifies, is the belongingness of each experience to the same world, their equal power to manifest it, as *possibilities of the same world*."[68] Merleau-Ponty is frank to acknowledge that "there is no guarantee that the whole of experience can be expressed in essential invariants"[69] – in effect, "invariants" are provisional within one's *Lebenswelt*. In any case, we are led to see that the transparency thesis is not the only accessible and (therefore) inevitable option on which we may pursue epistemology (choosing skepticism or foundationalism); *and* that it is itself reasonably avoidable, once the minimal import of subjectivity is conceded.

There is a further benefit that we may at least collect here, the full force of which we can as yet only anticipate. Once we meet the subjectivity constraint, once we grasp that foundational questions must begin in the middle of an *Erscheinung*, of what appear as the *de facto* achievements of our science, and once we construe both of these conditions in historicist terms (within the horizon of our *Lebenswelt*, as the phenomenologists maintain), then, surprisingly, there is no longer any need to segregate legitimating questions regarding the structures of the world (the Kantian-like aspect of transcendental questions) and legitimating questions regarding the structures of our cognizing capacity (the Husserlian-like aspect of transcendental questions). The two are conceptually symbiotic: we may as well say that, holistically construed, the knower and the known are one; their systematic segregation is, potentially, a variable set of coherent posits legitimated in terms internal to the very achievement of our science, congruent with our historical orientation, favoring apparent necessities and universalities, and (most important) critically tested in terms of what, in a Peircean idiom, is the abductive promise (that is, the inference like envisioning of the fruitfulness[70]) of any modestly extended research programs we may endorse. This, ultimately, is the praxical or pragmatist vindication of transcendental arguments – the pursuit of which the reflexive question of describing human knowledge inevitably generates. But, if we concede that the subject–object distinction is itself not a cognitively pertinent given but a posit that needs to be legitimated within a complexly sedimented body of *Erscheinungen* and that "subjectivity" minimally signifies that ineliminable contingency, then we are entirely free to introduce (for different purposes) an entire range of constructions of subjectivity itself – *le Néant, the ipse, le pour-soi, Dasein, le corps vécu, res cogitans, psyche, der Geist, die Seele,* the generalized other, the person, the self, the transcendental Ego, *Kosmotheoros* – that move in various ways between a completely structureless surd and alternatively structured embodiments of such a surd. The upshot is that, although there is a sense in which Husserl's phenomenology is more fundamental than Kant's idealism, determinate phenomenological claims are and can be no more fundamental than the determinate claims of Kantian transcendental arguments – or, for that matter, no more fundamental than the claims of empiricist, rationalist, intuitionist, objectivist, naturalist, historicist pedigree, provided that the point of minimal subjectivity is honored and all transparency or logocentric presumption is refused.

What we see, finally, bringing these remarks to bear on our earlier argument, is that skepticism may not be demonstrably refuted (or even genuinely avoided) – either by the foundationalist countermove or by that sort of pragmatic maneuver that Lehrer terms a coherence theory of justification. If we concede Moorean skepticism without affirming total ignorance, then it may well be that we can construct a reasonable theory of knowledge that (1) does not require foundationalism; and (2) *does not entail the refutation of skepticism*. We may, therefore, avail ourselves of the point Lehrer correctly presses (without drawing Lehrer's further conclusion about the avoidance or refutation of skepticism): namely, that the skeptic himself has yet to prove that "if there is some chance that S is incorrect in his belief that p, then S does not know that p." We do not have a stalemate here, because the skeptical consequence does not follow from Moorean skepticism; and we do not need a refutation, since the plausibility of ascribing some knowledge is patently linked with every distinctly human effort and strengthened by the very attempt to explore the tenability of the skeptical claim itself. But we *do* need, to "avoid" skepticism, *some* plausible account of determinate knowledge. The point is simply this: the defeat of skepticism and the vindication of the first-order cognitive capacities underlying our sciences are simply different aspects of one and the same transcendental concern. We do not need to *demonstrate* that we have knowledge: that would only lead to Nelson's predicament again; we merely need to *theorize* about the nature and criteria of what we are prepared to count as knowledge – not being obliged to reject it.[71]

Consequently, what we see is that a characteristically powerful theme in contemporary philosophy – that our conceptual scheme changes diachronically – is directly opposed to foundationalism and directly inclined to favor what has here been termed pragmatism. Such theories are, therefore, opposed to skepticism but need not be designed to refute it. They are, however, bound to deny that questions in the theory of knowledge are autonomous or separable from an overview of man's biological and historical aptitudes and practices. The formalism of analytic theories of knowledge is itself hardly more than a vestige of the foundationalist's account – although, ironically, it was the simplicity of the latter (*not* merely formalist at all) that made it appear that purely formal accounts (such as Lehrer's) could be brought to approximate with increasing precision the necessary and sufficient conditions of knowledge. There is every reason, now, to think that that project is profoundly misguided. Its failure, moreover, directs us to an entirely different strategy.

Notes

1 G. E. Moore, "Four Forms of Skepticism" in *Philosophical Papers* (London: George Allen and Unwin, 1959). Further references to Moore are to this paper.

2 This much at least is entirely in the spirit of Barry Stroud's recent compression of the *point* of "transcendental" and "philosophical" investigation. See Barry Stroud, "Die Transzendentalphilosophie und das Problem der Aussenwelt," in Eva Schaper and Wilhelm Vossenkuhl (eds), *Bedingungen der Möglichkeit* (Stuttgart: Klett-Cotta, 1984).

3 See W. V. Quine, "Epistemology Naturalized," *Ontological Relativity and Other Essays* (New York: Columbia University Press, 1969).

4 See Barry Barnes and David Bloor, "Relativism, Rationalism and the Sociology of Knowledge," in Martin Hollis and Steven Lukes (eds), *Rationality and Relativism* (Cambridge, Mass.: MIT Press, 1982).

5 For a sample of fairly recent, not altogether "up-to-date" causal theories of knowledge, see George S. Pappas and Marshall Swain (eds), *Essays on Knowledge and Justification* (Ithaca, NY: Cornell University Press, 1978).

6 For a brief overview of Husserl's general conception – largely, it must be said, as an advertisement rather than a sustained argument – see Edmund Husserl, *Phenomenology and the Crisis of Philosophy*, tr. Quentin Lauer (New York: Harper and Row, 1965), but see also Husserl's *Cartesian Meditations*, tr. Dorion Cairns (The Hague: Martinus Nijhoff, 1960).

7 See Richard Rorty, *Philosophy and the Mirror of Nature* (Princeton, NJ: Princeton University Press, 1979).

8 Moore gives the relevant references.

9 Keith Lehrer, "Skepticism and Conceptual Change" in Roderick M. Chisholm and Robert J. Swartz (eds), *Empirical Knowledge* (Englewood Cliffs, NJ: Prentice-Hall, 1973), p. 47. This seems to be the first appearance of Lehrer's paper. The thrust of the paper conforms quite closely, however, with Lehrer's *Knowledge* (Oxford: Clarendon Press, 1974).

10 Lehrer, *Knowledge*, p. 238.

11 Ibid., p. 238.

12 For instance, in Russell's "Philosophic Doubts," *Philosophy* (New York: W. W. Norton, 1927). This also appeared under the title *An Outline of Philosophy* (London: George Allen and Unwin, 1927). For a full discussion, cf. Roderick M. Chisholm, "Russell on the Foundations of Empirical Knowledge," in Paul Arthur Schilpp (ed.), *The Philosophy of Bertrand Russell* (New York: Tudor, 1951). It is not unimportant to notice Chisholm's connection between the two issues (skepticism and foundationalism), since this is essentially the pivot of his own *Theory of Knowledge* (Englewood Cliffs, NJ: Prentice-Hall, 1966; 2nd edn 1977) as well as the motivation for the structure of the reader *Empirical Knowledge*.

13 Lehrer, "Skepticism and Conceptual Change," in Chisholm and Swartz, *Empirical Knowledge*, p. 50.

14 Cf. Wilfrid Sellars, "Philosophy and the Scientific Image of Man," *Science, Perception and Reality* (London: Routledge and Kegan Paul, 1963); Thomas S. Kuhn, *The Structure of Scientific Revolutions*, 2nd, enlarged edn (Chicago: University of Chicago Press, 1970); W. V. Quine, *Word and Object* (Cambridge, Mass.: MIT Press, 1960).

15 Roderick M. Chisholm: *Perceiving: A Philosophical Study* (Ithaca, NY: Cornell University Press, 1957); *Theory of Knowledge*; *The Foundations of Knowing* (Minneapolis: University of Minnesota Press, 1982), ch. 1.

16 Lehrer, "Skepticism and Conceptual Change," in Chisholm and Swartz, *Empirical Knowledge*, p. 51. Cf. Lehrer, *Knowledge*, p. 81, which is noticeably inconclusive.

17 Actually, Lehrer seems to have confused the probability of logical truths and their contradictories and the probability of one's knowing a logical truth to be a logical truth: cf. ibid., p. 51. Thus, Lehrer wrongly affirms that "one cannot argue that there is always some probability that one is *wrong* no matter what sort of *statement* one thinks is true without abandoning standard conceptions of probability" (italics added).

18 Lehrer, *Knowledge*, p. 48.

19 Ibid., p. 239.

20 Ibid., p. 76.

21 Norman Malcolm's *Knowledge and Certainty* (Englewood Cliffs, NJ: Prentice-Hall, 1963), may be cited also as a Moorean variant of the common-sense view, without foundationalist assumptions.

22 Cf. Gilbert Harman, *Thought* (Princeton, NJ: Princeton University Press, 1973), whose solution to the problem of knowledge Lehrer opposes, but within the framework that I am calling pragmatic.

23 For a sample of recent analytic accounts of knowledge, see Michael D. Roth and Leon Galis (eds), *Knowing: Essays in the Analysis of Knowledge* (New York: Random House, 1970); Pappas and Swain, *Essays on Knowledge and Justification*; Peter A. French et al. (eds), *Midwest Studies in Philosophy*, vol. V (Minneapolis: University of Minnesota Press, 1980).

24 See for example Maurice Merleau-Ponty: *Phenomenology of Perception*, tr. Colin Smith (London: Routledge and Kegan Paul, 1962); *The Structure of Behavior*, tr. Alden L. Fisher (Boston, Mass.: Beacon Press, 1963).

25 Lehrer, *Knowledge*, p. 47.

26 Ibid., ch. 2.

27 Ibid., p. 42.

28 Ibid., p. 48.

29 See Edmund L. Gettier, "Is Justified True Belief Knowledge?" *Analysis*, XXIII (1963); also, Roth and Galis, *Knowing*.

30 Nicholas Rescher, *The Coherence Theory of Truth* (Oxford: Clarendon Press, 1973).

31 Ibid., p. 262.

32 Ibid., p. 19, n. 29.

33   Ibid., p. 17 n. 14.

34   Ibid., pp. 9–10, 12, 16, 23, 27–8, 262.

35   Ibid., p. 12.

36   Ibid., p. 232.

37   Ibid., chs. 2, 10.

38   Ibid., p. 237.

39   Ibid., pp. 239–42.

40   Ibid., pp. 242–44.

41   Ibid., pp. 244–62.

42   Ibid., pp. 249–51, 255–6.

43   Ibid., ch. 1.

44   Ibid., p. 47.

45   Ibid., p. 212.

46   Ibid., p. 213.

47   Ibid., p. 214.

48   Ibid., pp. 234–5.

49   Ibid., p. 238f.

50   Ibid., p. 241.

51   Lehrer, *Theory of Knowledge*, p. 56.

52   Cf. Hilary Putnam, *Meaning and the Moral Sciences* (London: Routledge and Kegan Paul, 1978); Michael Dummett, *Truth and Other Enigmas* (Cambridge, Mass.: Harvard University Press, 1978).

53   Two principal difficulties confront Dummett's anti-realism. First, when intuitionistic constraints are applied to empirical as opposed to mathematical claims, we are not actually provided with a ramified account of how to supply or how to decide that we have supplied suitable and adequate such constraints for determinate claims. Second, Dummett himself does not explain whether the realist–anti-realist disjunction is to be construed as decided once and for all or may allow for *some* diachronic accommodation in the direction of the realist view. The fact is that empirical claims hardly form a formal system and "intuitions" about reasonable constructivist constraints are quite informal and may well be dependent on larger views about the very nature of science and the cognitive powers of man; also, attention to the history of science shows that it would be presumptuous to suppose that, at any time *t*, we *could* (or would need to) formulate suitable constructivist constraints for all would-be empirical claims or that, failing that, we would lack all reasonable grounds *now* for supposing that particular claims may, *in some indefinite future*, be shown to meet our "intuitions." The abuses are compelling enough; but so are the concessions. And what they show is that we need to reject a straightforward disjunction between the realist and the anti-realist. See Ian Hacking, "Language, Truth and Reason," in Hollis and Lukes, *Rationality and Relativism*.

54   Chisholm and Swartz, *Empirical Knowledge*.

55   Leonard Nelson, "The Impossibility of the 'Theory of Knowledge'," ibid., p. 8.

56   Ibid., pp. 8, 9.

57 Ibid., pp. 8–9.
58 Cf. Zeno Vendler, *Res Cogitans* (Ithaca, NY: Cornell University Press, 1972), ch. 3. I have grave reservations about Vendler's general thesis, but not at this point.
59 Edmund Husserl, *Logical Investigations*, tr. J. N. Findlay, 2 vols (New York: Humanities Press, 1970), First Investigation.
60 Here, of course, the views of Moritz Schlick and C. I. Lewis suggest themselves. The relevant papers are reprinted in Chisholm and Swartz, *Empirical Knowledge*.
61 Chisholm, *Theory of Knowledge*, p. 28.
62 Ibid., p. 28. Here he cites in a footnote, apparently approvingly, Meinong, Brentano, Russell, Ledger Wood, and C. J. Ducasse. For more recent developments bearing on certainty, skepticism, and cognitive foundations, see Peter D. Klein, *Certainty: A Refutation of Scepticism* (Minneapolis: University of Minnesota Press, 1980).
63 Chisholm, *Theory of Knowledge*, pp. 27–8.
64 G. W. Leibniz, *New Essays Concerning Human Understanding*, bk. IV, ch. 9 (cited by Chisholm).
65 Cf. Rescher, *The Coherence Theory of Truth*, ch. 13.
66 Maurice Merleau-Ponty, *The Visible and the Invisible*, tr. Alphonso Lingis (Evanston, Ill.: Northwestern University Press, 1968), p. 45.
67 Ibid., pp. 45–6.
68 Ibid., p. 41.
69 Ibid., p. 46.
70 Cf. *Collected Papers of Charles Sanders Peirce*, 8 vols, ed. Charles Hartshorne, Paul Weiss, and Arthur W. Burks (Cambridge, Mass.: Harvard University Press, 1931–58).
71 Rescher comes to a similar conclusion (*The Coherence Theory of Truth*, pp. 330–1).

11

Scientific Realism as a Transcendental Issue

There is a serviceable contrast that Hilary Putnam advances, misleading as it stands but helpful for that very reason in orienting us quickly to certain important questions about the nature and tenability of realism – particularly about what is often characterized as *scientific realism*. Putnam's distinction may be pressed to yield an entire system of linked argumentative maneuvers of a rather large sort not wholly out of sympathy with the purpose for which he originally drew it. His own objective was at least

1 to repudiate the classic opposition between realism and idealism, to confirm their conceptual symbiosis, in the context of providing an adequate theory of the cognitive achievements of the empirical sciences;
2 to repudiate, with respect to the actual practices of science, all forms of foundationalism, essentialism, and related correspondence theories and criteria of truth.

Putnam's intention in this was to preserve a robust sense of objectivity, progress, and realism in science against what he took to be the unnecessarily extreme (and, in any case, untenable) laxity (at the opposite pole) of such views of science as those of Thomas Kuhn and Paul Feyerabend and against his own earlier support of a rather strong correspondence theory.[1]

Putnam introduces two "philosophical points of view" or "philosophical temperaments":

One of these perspectives is the perspective of metaphysical realism. On this perspective, the world consists of some fixed reality of mind-independent objects. There is exactly one true and complete description of "the way the world is." Truth involves some sort of correspondence relation between words or thought-signs and external things and sets of things.

He calls this "the *externalist* perspective," a sort of "God's Eye point of view," to which he contrasts the view he favors, dubbed "the *internalist* perspective, because," as he says

it is characteristic of this view that *what objects does the world consist of?* is a question that it only makes sense to ask *within* a theory or description. Many "internalist" philosophers, though not all, hold further that there is more than one "true" theory or description of the world. "Truth", in an internalist view, is some sort of (idealized) rational acceptability, some sort of ideal coherence of our beliefs with each other and with our experiences as *those experiences are themselves represented in our belief system.* ... [2]

It is easy to suppose that these two "temperaments" form a symmetrical as well as an exclusive pair of views. They certainly seem to be so intended. But such a reading would actually obscure their differences, because they are each compounded of a series of independent claims, because the dominant emphasis of each is quite different from that of the other, and because there are many other possible combinations of their constituent claims that could in some sense be called realist but are versions of neither metaphysical nor internal realism. There is good reason to believe, for instance, that certain paired constituents from the opposed composite views are actually not incompatible. Consider, for example, that it is entirely possible to hold (consistently) both that there are mind-independent objects ("fixed," shall we say, at least as far as the mind's role is concerned, though that term may be construed more powerfully) *and* that the question of what "objects does the world consist of" can only be meaningfully asked "within a theory or description." *Many* hold this view. In fact, Putnam maintains that "Kant is best read as proposing for the first time what I have called the 'internalist' or 'internal realist' view of truth."[3] But can there be any doubt that Kant is an "externalist" as well – at least in so far as he insists on mind-independent things? Putnam says as much: Kant "does not doubt that there is *some* mind-independent reality; for him this is virtually a postulate of reason." He adds (not altogether unequivocally or satisfactorily) that, for Kant, "we can form no real conception of these noumenal things; even the notion of a noumenal world is a kind of limit of thought (*Grenz-Begriff*) rather than a clear concept."[4] But, though we cannot, on Kant's view, have knowledge of noumenal things – hence, trivially, cannot have a conception of actual, particular noumenal things – Kant's transcendental method requires the intelligibility at least of the very notion of noumenal things (after all, concepts without percepts are "empty," not "blind"), and the postulate of noumena is required (Kant thinks) in order to account for science philosophically. Also, what we *have* knowledge of is, for Kant, *not* merely an artifact of our invention.

In fact, Kant's problems about noumena may fairly be tracked to his preference for a form of representationalism (idealism), along the lines already sketched. So that, in the spirit of Kant's account though obviously not in accord with its letter, if one rejected representationalism and favored instead what we have termed textualism (which is precisely what Putnam extracts from Kant), we could, in a non-tendentious sense, reidentify noumena and phenomena – that is, real things and their "appearances" (*Erscheinungen*). This is what, however extravagantly at times and however dubiously linked at times to the advocacy of some form of cognitivism or logocentrism, has been the tendency of post-Kantian reflection – to the extent that it has actually eschewed all forms of representationalism [5] Certainly, at the very least, we must see that there is no difficulty in admitting a mind-independent world while at the same time admitting that our *cognitive* powers extend only to a "textualized" world. Consequently, if, as we usually do, we wish to claim knowledge *of* the mind-independent world (though not as it is mind-independently – as Thomas Kuhn has so very neatly put the matter), we are bound to treat such knowledge as a reasoned artifact of some kind of whatever is possible within the limits of our cognition. But to put the point this way is just to identify the least tendentious characterization of *transcendental* reasoning with respect to science – hence, a way that is more general and more informed than Kant's own characterization, for it is entirely open to novel interpretations as well.

Putnam's own contrast clearly stresses that *his* externalist is initially characterized in ontological terms, and *his* internalist, in epistemological terms. This, of course, can hardly be the whole story, and in any case the ontological and the epistemological are doubtless always closely linked. But there *is* an important difference between them, which colors the entire argument; and there *is* an obvious, even trivial, sense in which one cannot fail to be an internalist along Putnam's initial lines. But it is not similarly obvious that one can fail to be an externalist in the minimal sense Putnam provides (regarding mind-independent objects); and it is not obvious that, in being the sort of internalist mentioned (one who merely concedes that determining what things there are in the world is a question that only arises within some conceptual framework), one is also, necessarily, an "internal realist," *or* opposed to "metaphysical realism," *or* even bound to hold any particular theory at all. Presumably, an internal realist is one who holds that we can favor *over others* "a theory or description" that effectively puts us in cognitive touch with the "objects" of the real world (however affected such objects may be by that theory or description) – in virtue of which our beliefs constitute knowledge of the real world. When Putnam attributes to the *externalist* the view that what he claims to come to know through *his* science is the world as it is in some mind-independent way, he is clearly conflating the "metaphysical realist" with the (mere) externalist who believes (perhaps like Kant) that there is (possibly must be) a mind-independent world. Metaphysical realism may be a viable thesis, as foundationalists, essentialists, correspondence theorists regular affirm; but it is only one of many possible doctrines incorporating the minimal externalist thesis originally mentioned. The ulterior question that lurks in the vicinity of these possibilities is this: "What form of realism best fits the achievement of the sciences?"

I

Here, we may match at least three distinct sorts of externalism with Putnam's own remarks, each progressively richer and each open to alternative but non-equivalent formulations:

(a) externalism$_o$ – *ontic externalism*, the view that "the world consists of some fixed totality of mind-independent objects," or (more moderately) the view (Kant's) that "there is *some* mind-independent reality";

(b) externalism$_a$ – *alethic externalism*, the view that "there is exactly one true and complete description of 'the way the world is,'" or that "truth involves some sort of correspondence relation between words or thought-signs and external things and sets of things" (in the externalist$_o$ sense);[6] and

(c) externalism$_e$ – *epistemic externalism*, the view that external objects (in the externalist$_o$ sense) are also "Self-identifying" to us or (simply) that we are cognitively capable of knowing objects in the externalist$_a$ sense.[7] (Externalism$_e$ seems to be equivalent to, or to entail, cognitivism or foundationalism.)

What Putnam calls "metaphysical realism" entails the conjunction of (a)–(c) but requires *as well* some distinct rationale linking these progressively richer claims. Certainly, (a) does not entail either (b) or (c), nor (b), (c); and, if (as Putnam speculates) there is a God's-eye view, then (b) could still be true when (c) was actually false: a God knowing his own creation would not be a metaphysical realist (in Putnam's sense, strictly speaking, though Putnam himself does not begrudge God the epithet; on the contrary, humans *are* metaphysical realists when they presume to possess a God's-eye view). In fact, metaphysical realism may be attenuated or adjusted – along, say, Peirce's or Karl Popper's lines (with considerable risk of incoherence, it must be admitted) – by treating the correspondence theory of truth as a limit asymptotically approached but never reached by human agents incapable of fulfilling (c). There is, also, some question whether Putnam, as an internal *realist* himself, can actually escape such an attenuated form of, or replacement for, (c): we shall come to the issue shortly. And there is, of course, some question of how "correspondence" should be construed: if it is construed alethically only, no question arises about actual human cognitive faculties competent to satisfy (b) – this is just the point of introducing the God's-eye view, and (also) of taking note of (and rejecting) such different foundationalist doctrines as Brentano's regarding self-disclosing mental states (in opposition to introspection or self-observation) and C. I. Lewis's regarding sense data;[8] but, if correspondence is construed epistemically as well (observationally, in fact, as Putnam sometimes seems inclined to do), then larger questions bearing on the theory of an objective science may be somewhat prejudged by the externalist–internalist schema – which is what the famous quarrel about the methodology of the *Naturwissenschaften* and the *Geisteswissenschaften* preeminently focuses our attention on.

Regarding internalism, a matching triad of claims may be sketched:

(a′)   internalism$_o$ – *ontic internalism*, the view that "'objects' [the things of the real world] themselves are as as much made as discovered, as much products of our conceptual invention as of the 'objective' factor in experience, the factor independent of our will,"[9] or (more moderately) that the question of "'the way the world is' ... only makes sense ... *within* a theory or description" (that is, relative to one conceptual scheme or another);[10]

(b′)   internalism$_a$ – *alethic internalism*, the view that "Truth' ... is some sort of (idealized) rational acceptability – some sort of ideal coherence of our beliefs with each other and with our experiences *as those experiences are themselves represented in our belief system* – and not correspondence with mind-independent or discourse-independent 'states of affairs'," or (more tolerantly) such "an *idealization* of rational acceptability" as would not preclude there being "more than one 'true' theory or description of the world," possibly even "incompatible theories";[11] and

(c') internalism$_e$ – *epistemic internalism*, the view that "the world *does* consist of 'Self-Identifying Objects' – but not [in] a sense available to an externalist$_{[a]}$," or that the world supports even an internalist correspondence theory, for, "Since the objects *and* the signs [of a particular cognitive community] are alike *internal* to the scheme of description, it is possible to say what matches what,"[12] or (more tolerantly) that objectivity in the cognitive sense is only "*objectivity for us*," that "our concepts of coherence and acceptability ... *are* our conceptions ['deeply interwoven with our psychology ... our biology and our culture,' though] they are conceptions of something real."[13]

(b') clearly counts as Putnam's emendation of Peirce's doctrine of the outcome of inquiry in the long run.

What Putnam calls "internal realism" entails the conjunction of (a')–(c'), *as well as* a rationale forging those claims into a single doctrine of distinctive power.[14] Internal realism is obviously open to a great many alternative interpretations, since Putnam cites both Kant and Nelson Goodman as committed to the doctrine, though their theories are plainly incompatible. Kant is committed to some version of externalism$_o$, opposes (in this sense) internalism$_o$ (in at least the first, stronger formulation given); and Goodman explicitly opposes externalism$_o$ and (claiming to be an "irrealist" as well as a "radical relativist") embraces a most extreme formulation of internalism$_o$.[15] There are other difficulties. For one, since Putnam aligns himself with Kant as an internal realist (he also aligns himself with Goodman), and since he explicitly opposes the doctrine that "anything goes" (Feyerabend's notorious maxim, quite uncertain in import),[16] it is clear that Putnam is obliged to reconcile (at least) internalism$_o$ with externalism$_o$, which he does not attempt to do and which (judging from his remarks about Kant) he may not actually believe to be conceptually possible. But anything less would seriously jeopardize *any* robust sense of an objective science; it may even render Putnam open, ironically, to the most extreme charge that "anything goes." (The same problem arises for Goodman's new theory – as is clear from W. V. Quine's well-known review of Goodman's book, which worries the meaning of "world*making*," the very term Putnam features in the strong reading of (a').[17]) Certainly, (a'), at least in the weaker of its formulations, is entirely compatible with (a) and (b) and may, as in Peirce's and Popper's accounts, be compatible even with (c). Even (b') need not be incompatible with (b), as Nicholas Rescher's coherence theory of truth confirms (since it attempts to capture the realist (or externalist$_o$) force of the correspondence theory pragmatically).[18] Certainly, (c') is "not a facile relativism,"[19] though it is also not necessarily opposed to relativism (as Goodman correctly affirms). (c') is, also, oddly reconcilable with (b), as Berkeley's immaterialism demonstrates (a doctrine Putnam discusses but does not link in this particular way).

The real trouble confronting Putnam, however, is, first, that we lack, on his account, any suitably strong reason for construing (c') – the linchpin of "internal realism" – as sufficient or (at least) sufficiently articulated to supply a sense of realism adequate to what modern science requires;[20] and second, that *if* (b') can be said to offer a viable theory of truth fitting scientific practice, then (b) can be shown to do so as well. The point of pressing these distinctions is simply to contrast (Putnam's) *internal realism* and a (sufficiently robust) *realism* suitable for science – probably robust enough to count as one or another version of *scientific realism*. It is worth noticing that Putnam's explicit scientific realism (shared originally with Richard Boyd) is no longer featured in his latest characterizations of internal realism.[21]

What is critical, here, is simply that (b') is frankly admitted by Putnam to be an *idealization* of some sort. That means that it cannot serve as a criterion of truth: it is, rather, an idealization of whatever working criteria the developing practice of science supports, in order (precisely) to treat the effectiveness of *those* criteria (and their attendant findings) *as* realistically grounded. In short, (b') *cannot* have any pertinent realist force of its own, except (dependently) in so far as it is the idealized conclusion of a suitably grounded defense of *whatever the sense* may be in which internal realism is or entails or vindicates, or is a reasonable interpretation of, scientific realism.[22] Now, there is absolutely *no* reason why (b) cannot be construed as an analogous idealization; once foundationalism is rejected, there is simply *no* form of the correspondence theory in which correspondence functions operationally as, or so as to yield, a criterion of truth. In a way, this is just what Peirce and Popper (by rather different strategies) affirm. Of course, one can always construe a strong foundationalist theory (say, Brentano's or Lewis's) as subscribing to (b), but such theories actually preclude the need for independent criteria of any sort – *a fortiori*, for independent criteria of a correspondence sort. No, correspondence theories are always realistically endowed (whether internalist or externalist – the very point of singling out Brentano and Lewis) by their linkage to foundationalism *or* by way of an idealization of the criteria and findings of actual scientific practice (usually, but not necessarily, as Putnam himself affirms, construed in an externalist manner). What this shows is that *neither (b) nor (b') can independently confer realist status on any set of our beliefs strong enough to capture our best intuitions about scientific realism*. Furthermore, (a'), or at least (a') not yet reconciled with (a), cannot possibly add any force to the supposed (scientific) realism of any set of our beliefs offered in the spirit of (c'). In short, there appears to be no way in which to link internal realism to *scientific realism* without reconciling (a) and (a'); and, conceding that possibility, there remains no longer any reason for disallowing (b), or disallowing the compatibility of (b) and (b'), *except in so far as* (b) is construed foundationally – that is to say, in a particular epistemic way and not merely alethically.

Once we dissect internal and metaphysical realism, we cannot fail to see that only (c) and (c') have the least claim about offering directly pertinent grounds for defending a robust sense of realism in science. First of all, only (c) and (c') have any explicit epistemic relevance; secondly, the other claims have a bearing on the argument only in virtue of some doctrinal connection linking them to (c) or (c'), for there are no suitable entailments moving in the direction of the richer claims and (as we have already seen) the possible ways of combining these claims consistently is exceedingly large, almost without regard to the issue of scientific realism; and, thirdly, although metaphysical realism may well be indefensible, the bearing of internal realism on (the varieties of) scientific realism remains entirely unexplained. (In effect, the point at stake catches up the inadequacy of merely formal analyses of knowledge – for instance, along Keith Lehrer's lines.[23])

The truth is that, although Putnam is committed to reconciling realism and idealism – or, more strongly put, to demonstrating that, in the context of science, it is no longer convincing to formulate realism and idealism as alternative, conceptually *independent* interpretations – he does not actually develop the *internalist's* notion of realism in ontological terms, but does so only in alethic terms (even if he pretty well defines realism in the sense of internalism$_o$ as whatever is yielded in accord with the *idealization* provided by internalism$_a$). But that is not enough (as the merest reflection on Peirce's program makes clear). The metaphysical realist *does* commit himself to a notion of realism ontologically strong enough to support a scientific realism *if* only his own cognitive program were also defensible, congruently with his ontological views. But, if the metaphysical realist's adherence to cognitivism and foundationalism – in effect, (c) or the consequences of a strong reading of (c) as embodying (b) (without idealization) – is philosophically untenable, it hardly follows that a relatively strong reading of (a) is also untenable or that it is impossible to defend a doctrine that integrates internal realism with a relatively strong reading of (a): in particular, with a strong reading of (a) *pertinent to the achievements of (c')*. The latter, then, is just what scientific realism (minimally) comes to, *if* metaphysical realism is rejected. Scientific realism must be a unified theory integrating (not merely conjoining) internalism$_e$, internalism$_o$, *and* externalism$_o$. This explains why Putnam's opposition between metaphysical realism and internal realism is so ineffectual while at the same time helping us to see what more is required. Notice, of course, that this way of putting matters applies considerable pressure to the adequacy of Michael Dummett's form of anti-realism – which Putnam similarly questions.[24] (This is not to ignore the charge that we may be characterizing the notion in a heterodox way. But there is an advantage to this reading – which yet does not distort, contrary to what may be feared, the usual disputes about particular scientific realist claims.)

II

Many different theories falling between the extremes of these two realist doctrines may supply an adequate ground for scientific realism; if one such theory can be formulated, there is good reason to believe that there must be indefinitely many others (possibly incompatible) that could be formulated as well. In fact, with a question as complex and variegated as that of realism in science, it is quite likely that there is no single best theory to favor and that, with regard to certain more specialized sub-issues – causality for instance, or laws of nature, or explanation, or theoretical entities – some tolerance of relativistic views of methodology and ontology can hardly be precluded. In this (and only in this) extremely attenuated sense, there is no difference as yet among the views of, for instance, Wilfrid Sellars, Hilary Putnam, Bas van Fraassen, Nancy Cartwright, and Ian Hacking: they are all scientific realists *of some sort* – although, of course, they differ markedly from one another with regard to their own special versions of the doctrine. Nevertheless, there are at least a few salient clues about the prospects of the failure of internal realism – assuming that metaphysical realism is too strong to fit the actual historical development of science and that it is committed to a foundationalism that cannot be philosophically defended. The weakness of Putnam's internalism can be felt at once merely by carefully weighing the import of such phrases as "objectivity for us" (italicized in the text). It is certainly correct that, from an internalist's point of view, we cannot expect to have externalist *grounds* (c) for formulating a workable notion of objectivity; but we still need to know why an internalist interpretation of coherence is also a realist interpretation in a sense that is not deductively or inductively derived as an epistemic instantiation of a merely alethically specified notion of coherence. *The grounds must be internal all right, but the import of the realist claim must be logically stronger than any mere entailment of or induction from what those grounds affirm, in order to vindicate a scientific realism and not merely an internal realism.* But that is to say, precisely, that what is needed is a transcendental argument, an argument that, however confined internally in epistemic terms, proposes and defends what (internally) appear to be the necessary and sufficient *external conditions* (or the best approximation to these that can be offered under the circumstances) in accord with which the realism of science can be sustained as an intelligible and reasonable option.

In short, internal realism cannot but appear circular or vacuous or irrelevant

(α) *if* (*per impossibile*) it cannot avail itself of externalist grounds; or

(β) *if* it treats scientific realism as a mere deductive or inductive issue; or

(γ) *if* it denies the *sui generis* viability of transcendental arguments (not necessarily taken to have the power of a Kantian synthetic *a priori.*)

The metaphysical realist appears to be in a stronger position as far as the form of philosophical debate is concerned, simply because, on his view, we are contingently endowed with certain cognitivist and foundationalist capacities that *insure* a strong scientific realism. He is likely to claim that there are direct cognitive (externalist$_e$) grounds for regarding foundationalist sources *as* foundationalist – that is, as providing a notably reliable, possibly even indubitable, source of *knowledge* on which all other cognitive claims depend.[25] But, if he argued in this way, the metaphysical realist would have ignored the fact that (as already remarked) there is a compelling and trivial sense in which ontic internalism is inescapable (Putnam's most telling point) – which, once conceded, confirms the equally compelling and trivial sense in which transcendental reasoning is similarly inescapable. In short, the strategy mentioned in (α) is inaccessible on the internalist$_o$ hypothesis (as well as on independent grounds); the strategy in (β) is too weak and can lead to no more than an internal realism clearly inadequate, as it stands, to support a robust form of scientific realism; and the strategy in (γ) remains as yet unexplored, though it is apparently the only promising option we have.

Once we grant this much, it is difficult to avoid the conclusion that Putnam has confused and conflated the externalist import of transcendental (necessarily internalist) arguments with the would-be externalist arguments of the metaphysical realist. This may explain, for instance, the noticeable weakness of the phrase "objectivity for us" – that is, that there cannot be any objectivity *sans phrase*, that there can only be objectivity-*for-us*. What Putnam may have missed is that the expression "for us" signifies no more than the internalist's transcendental constraint on "objectivity"; it does *not* (and could not, convincingly) signify only a relativization of objectivity – objectivity merely "for us," say, but not for others – which, after all, would be self-refuting. Exactly the same sort of mistake occurs in trying to reduce the concept of truth to "truth-in-L" or truth-for-us.[26] Terms such as "truth," "objectivity," "validity," "meaning," "knowledge," and "intelligibility" must be assigned a use that is universal in scope, in the sense that, when suitably recognized, all cognitively relevant systems must be supposed to be capable of forming a single coherent system – even when, for a competent agent, parts of that system are actually judged to be incompatible, and even though no *such system can or need be actually realized*. What else could one mean in holding that a competent agent understood such and such incompatible or incommensurable or irreconcilable theories and that he (and all others who entered into debate with him) could possess or share a rich-enough conceptual network on the basis of which such findings could obtain? The trick is that such transcendental reasoning provides only a (second-order) *theory* of the adequacy of theories of truth and coherence and meaning; it does not (and could not) provide higher-order (universal) *criteria* for the proper use of such epistemic terms.[27]

Of course, not all second-order arguments are transcendental arguments – as disputes about grammar, metalogic, and the like confirm; but, in the context sketched, transcendental arguments are fairly construed as *sui generis* empirical arguments, internalist$_e$ but directed to formulating externalist$_o$ proposals exceeding deductive and inductive evidence, affording the best approximation available of at least the necessary conditions accounting for the conceptual possibility of some sector of human experience or knowledge. Clearly, such arguments cannot eliminate a rhetorical or persuasive element reflecting the argumentative convictions and orientation of a particular historical community, or an inevitable informality incorporating the peculiar power of characteristic conclusions, or the real possibility of defending formally incompatible alternative claims. But such features are already not unwelcome to the defenders of internal realism, as Putnam attests; and the essential fault of the metaphysical realist is just that he does not realize that his own theory, which he characterizes as externalist$_e$, cannot but be internalist$_e$ – and, therefore, that cognitivism and foundationalism are untenable.[28] To see this is to see as well that strong internalist arguments are bound to be transcendental in nature – capable, without inconsistency or reliance on the pretensions of metaphysical realism (or foundationalism), of recovering a disciplined basis for speculating on the *externalist* conditions of human knowledge. In fact, this may not unfairly be taken to mark the essential option overlooked in Richard Rorty's well-known rejection of philosophy.[29]

The argument, then, comes to this. Metaphysical realism is untenable, at least because it is committed to foundationalism – that is, the most extreme form of (c); or because (in admitting a God's-eye view) it concedes – inconsistently with (c'), which is taken for granted – the applicability of bipolar truth values for syntactically well-formed propositions that cannot be tested in accord with the constraints of (c'). Put another way, foundationalism need not be committed to (Putnam's version of) metaphysical realism, simply because it need not be opposed to anything like Dummett's version of anti-realism.[30] But, although it is committed to cognitivism or foundationalism *wherever* it supposes science to be cognitively apt in a realist sense, metaphysical realism is also profoundly opposed to the anti-realist's insistence on decidability. This is why metaphysical realism is doubly indefensible in terms of the record of science.

In itself, this does not entail the untenability of any of the various versions of externalism – notably, weakened or attenuated forms of (c). Internal realism is too weak to sustain scientific realism, and all its constituent claims (internalism$_{o,a,e}$) can be interpreted compatibly with suitable interpretations of the constituent claims collected within metaphysical realism. Scientific realism is committed to defending a unified doctrine that combines forms at least of (a), (a'), and (c'). But, if so, then scientific realism must be, or must incorporate, a form of transcendental argument, since there is no deductive or inductive way to derive or infer (c) from (c').

Scientific realism *looks like* metaphysical realism, because, one way or another, it may take an affirmative or realist stance on theoretical entities and causal processes featured in the explanation of observable phenomena. But it is *not* as such, equivalent to, nor does it entail, metaphysical realism – in the straightforward sense (1) that it need not be committed to any form of foundationalism, and (2) that it need not oppose (anything like Dummett's) anti-realism. (2), it must be admitted, is a sensitive and easily misunderstood matter. It is entirely possibly that an interpretation of the actual history of science – for instance a reading of the bearing, on Dummett's decidability issue, of Clerk Maxwell's doubts about the measurability of light and its subsequent actual measurement[31] – might persuade us that either the line of demarcation between metaphysical realism and any internal realism committed to the anti-realist program cannot be drawn in a strongly disjunctive or punctuated way, or else a punctuated anti-realism (decisive once and for all) is simply a false doctrine. If so, then (Dummett's) anti-realism (which is closely linked to the fortunes of internal realism) may have to be construed (it appears, against Dummett's own inclination) in a *diachronically generous way*. One could easily put it that we have no option, once we repudiate all forms of foundationalism. (In fact, one cannot fail to notice, here, an inevitable equivocation on anti-realism itself: for either anti-realism signifies the *idealist* aspect of all current realisms – the *ontological* theme of internal realism, let us say; or it signifies the *decidability* aspect of all viable realisms – the *methodological* theme of internal realism, let us say. Foundationalism is opposed to the first but it need not be opposed to the second.) It may then be no more than a terminological issue to decide whether, on the diachronically generous reading, decidability itself favors anti-realism or metaphysical realism or both or neither.

Furthermore, scientific realism may well be open to alternative, even relativistic, views on theoretical entities, causality, explanation and related issues. For example, van Fraassen, while rejecting (as category mistakes) Grover Maxwell's double denial of a distinction between observation and theory and of observational and theoretical entities (and the mixing of the two),[32] maintains a *scientific-realist* position, simply because he concedes that observable entities may play or be assigned a theoretical role in would-be explanations. Thus, van Fraassen declares, "My view is that physical theories do indeed describe much more than what is observable, but that what matters is empirical adequacy (accounting for what is observable), and not the truth or falsity of how they go beyond the observable phenomena."[33] It is perfectly obvious that alternative conceptions of what we mean by "empirical," "observable," "causal," "theoretical," and the like are bound to affect the form that scientific realism could plausibly take; and there is no antecedently compelling reason to suppose that speculation here can, or is likely to, favor one and only one converging strategy for legitimating science. But we can hardly fail to see that we cannot escape falling back to a second-order effort to legitimate scientific realism itself – what is tantamount to a transcendental defense of the cognitive power of science. And, in doing that, we can hardly fail to consider, dialectically, alternative, nonconverging conceptions of the critical notions – for example, causal explanation. If, for instance, there were good reasons to hold that unobservable entities played a causal role in the production of observables, then van Fraassen's version of scientific realism would have to be rejected or at least stalemated or put into doubt. Van Fraassen is committed, first, to opposing the reality of unobservable entities; and inclined, second, to dissolving questions of causality in terms of contextually variable explanations of observable phenomena: "The description of some account as an explanation of a given fact or event, is incomplete," he claims. "It can only be an explanation with respect to a certain *relevance relation* and a certain *contrast-class*. These are contextual factors, in that they are determined neither by the totality of accepted scientific theories, nor by the event or fact for which an explanation is requested."[34] But van Fraassen does not actually show that there are no causal contexts – for instance, contexts of technological or experimental invention – in terms of which the reality of unobservable entities could be reasonably supproted.[35] Hence, the relevance and essential contribution of transcendental argument is confirmed as well as its potential tolerance for relativistic answers. That is (the point needs to be featured), the reasoned choice of transcendental findings – the play of transcendental dispute itself – *substantively affects the very course of first-order science*. It is no good dismissing transcendental arguments as idle *if* there is no effective demarcation between first-order and second-order questions and *if*, on that condition, the actual direction of scientific practice is itself systematically linked in a deliberate way to our reasoned convictions about such matters as that of the reality of unobservable entities.

III

Of course, we need a much clearer picture of transcendental arguments themselves. So let us remedy things at once.

A transcendental argument is:

1 a *sui generis* empirical argument;
2 internal$_o$ and internal$_e$;
3 not formulable as deductive or inductive or canonically fixed;

4   second-order;
5   concerned with the necessary conditions for some range of human experience or knowledge or capacity to act in a cognitively informed way;
6   construed as providing external (external$_o$) conditions for the conceptual possibility of such experience or knowledge or capacity;
7   (hence) unavoidably rhetorical in some measure, logically informal, open to plural, nonconverging, even incompatible (or relativistic) alternatives;
8   persuasive in accord with the argumentative practices of a historical and historically minded society;
9   extended and disciplined analogically, from salient exemplars drawn from actual, pertinent practices; and
10   (therefore) incapable of being totalized, inherently provisional, and formulated (in that sense) only as an inference to the best explanation.

So seen, transcendental arguments do not provide knowledge *of* the actual external conditions of human knowledge or experience (in any sense favored by the metaphysical realist); they provide knowledge only of what, under internalist constraints, appears to be the most reasonable theory or theories of the external grounds on which such knowledge and experience are conceptually possible. This is the very crux of transcendental arguments: for anything less would give way to the vacuity of internal realism, and anything more would, in effect, constitute, a form of implicit foundationalism.[36] This is *not* to deny that transcendental arguments may be coherently characterized on cognitivist or foundationalist lines. We already have the example of Kant's doctrine to consider. But the interesting question remains, "What would a transcendental argument be like, if it were historicized and denied the advantage of cognitivist resources?" That is a question that seems hardly to have been seriously posed or pursued.[37]

In terms of the obvious importance of Kant's view of the matter, we may say that transcendental arguments are (i) synthetic; (ii) *a priori*; but (iii) incapable of yielding synthetic *a priori* judgments. They are synthetic because, exceeding the formal import of the grounds on which they rest, they cannot be deductively reduced. They are *a priori* because, although they attempt to account for knowledge and experience, rest on empirical grounds, and form a kind of empirical argument, they are not inductive (in the sense that inductive conclusions can in principle be empirically confirmed independently) and they propose instead an inclusive and logically *external* network of concepts or fundamental categories – *not* themselves cognitively accessible in any externalist$_e$ way – in terms of which the phenomena to be explained are first located and interpreted, then rendered conceptually reasonable, and (under the circumstances of historical reflection) assessed as such as effectively as the practice of such arguments can be made to function. They do not yield synthetic *a priori* judgments, simply because, although their conclusions are *a priori*, their mode of reasoning is empirical: we can never know the necessary and sufficient *a priori* conditions of the actual forms of knowledge and experience that we count as such; we can examine and assess only what, relative to our argumentative practice, we find most compelling and convincing and least disputable and contingent in *constructing* external (externalist$_o$) conditions for our internally confined (internalist$_o$ and internalist$_e$) cognitive achievements.[38] Transcendental arguments lack the necessity of deductive and deductive-like arguments, for they are not deductive and are not even characterizable as having a canonical form. They also lack the "necessity" of universalist claims, for they are, however, universalized, initially convincing only within their own historical milieux and only on the strength of the cognitive exemplars they selectively feature there.

But there is no reason for thinking that they are not at least *that*. Even Carnap, with his strong attraction to verificationism and foundationalism (attenuated in part under the influence of Neurath and Schlick) did not really disqualify what we are here calling transcendental issues – which he rather instructively called "external" questions.[39] But Putnam seems to have objected to externalist questions solely because of the impossibility of ever answering such questions completely or decisively or on foundationalist or sub-God's-eye grounds. (It is an irony that Putnam correctly challenges the seeming inflexibility of Dummett's anti-realism – in the direction of a generous diachronic reading; and yet fails to acknowledge the nonfoundationalist reading of transcendental arguments – implicitly compatible with Dummett's anti-realism.) Granting the foregoing argument, what, therefore, we must concede is simply that our adherence to scientific realism commits us to the viability of a form of transcendental argument (the decisive feature of which is still not completely explicit). The argument rests on the fact that the realist–idealist demarcation can no longer be convincingly maintained, that foundationalism is untenable, and that, nevertheless, what scientific realism requires is a rigorous account of *the external conditions of human knowledge*. There seems to be no viable alternative to the strategy suggested.

One somewhat tangential consideration is in order here. *If*, as internal realists or internalists claim, the question of "'the way the world is' ... only makes sense ... *within* a theory or description," or *if*, more radically, "'objects' ... are as much made as discovered ... products of our conceptual invention," then the rejection of the realist–idealist demarcation signifies that scientific realism cannot but remain intensionally constrained in terms of reference, truth, equivalence, validity, and the like. It may be possible, introducing conventions of intertranslatability, that extensional equivalences be specifiable with regard to such canons. But, once externalism$_e$ is rejected,

(i)   extensionality itself cannot but be conceptually *dependent on*, or derivative from, an intensional, holistic, indefinitely open-ended conceptual network;[40] and

(ii)   there can be no independent, extensionally satisfactory way of testing (cognitively) the "adequacy" or "pragmatic" fit of any such network with respect to the body of human experience.

It is an irony of the history of analytic philosophy that the most powerful rejections of the realist–idealist demarcation have also been the most strenuously sustained commitments to various programs of a thoroughly extensional sort. Quine, for example, insists on the "stimulus-equivalence" of alternative conceptual networks fitted to the body of perceptual experience and stimulus-response correlations.[41] And Goodman, insisting on "worldmaking" in the most extreme way possible, nevertheless claims (inconsistently) that such an ontology is fully compatible with his earlier views regarding a realist science resting on cognitively accessible, extensionally equivalent projectibles.[42] In effect, Quine cannot overcome the limitations of (ii), or Goodman, of (i). This is precisely why the demise of foundationalism has been so disastrous to the unity-of-science movement. A suggestive way of putting the point is this: the arguments of Quine and Goodman (and others, such as Davidson) essentially are drawn to conceding, within the analytic idiom, what, in the phenomenological, is meant by "subjectivity";[43] but their strong adherence to extensionalism with respect to the empirical sciences is championed without any explicit consideration of the bearing of phenomenological subjectivity on that very program. The result is a decisive conceptual lacuna or a distinct inclination to restore some version of the transparency thesis.

Two rather obvious supplementary arguments may be drawn from Putnam's own discussion – against certain of his own purposes. They are somewhat interrelated. One concerns the notion of reidentification under the condition of changing theories; the other, the putative philosophical import of the Skolem–Löwenheim theorem. Putnam says flatly that "believing that some correspondence intrinsically just *is* reference (not as a result of our operational and theoretical constraints, or our intentions, but as an *ultimate* metaphysical fact) amounts to a magical theory of reference."[44] Here, he rightly rejects metaphysical realism – in particular, foundationalism. He also plausibly demonstrates that "neither similitude nor causal connection can be the only, or the fundamental, mechanism of reference."[45] And he emphasizes that, for internalists (such as he), the referential use of signs "in a particular way by a particular community of users *can* correspond to particular objects *within the conceptual scheme of those users [and can only thus correspond]*."[46] So, just as he observes that "truth is an *idealization* of rational acceptability,"[47] reference must be an idealization. Hence, reference and reidentification *cannot be determined on grounds independent of the intentions of a cognitive community to use a certain conceptual scheme*, cannot be extensionally determined on grounds neutral as between alternative conceptual schemes.

Here Putnam is inclined to favor Quine's thesis that reference is simply indeterminate.[48] But then, if, as he also says, "it is simply a mistake to think that evolution determines a *unique* correspondence (or even a reasonably narrow range of correspondences) between referring expressions and external objects,"[49] it would be impossible, moving from one theory to another in the evolution of a science, to rely on empirical evidence about sameness of reference regarding theoretical entities in order *to* confirm objective progress in science itself (in the spirit of scientific realism) – for instance, against Kuhn and Feyerabend.[50] This, of course, goes entirely contrary to Putnam's earlier and more sanguine views about reference to theoretical entities under diachronic conditions. The reason, ultimately, depends on Putnam's adherence to Quine's reading of the Skolem–Löwenheim theorem; for, if (interpreting Quine's reading) the range of values for distinct quantified variables is fixed, then, on the theorem, "there is a reinterpretation of [an] entire [natural] language that leaves all sentences unchanged in truth value while permuting the extensions of [the expressions putatively having referential import in that language]."[51] In other words, the indeterminacy cannot but be built into any assessment of progress in the same way in which it is built into reference itself. This is the reason why Putnam's earlier appeal to the "principle of charity" in affirming (from the vantage of internal realism) the (first-order) *empirical* standing of scientific progress is simply question-begging: we cannot, on the internal realist's view, show that our knowledge of *given* theoretical entities is increasing as our theories change diachronically; we can only show the persisting coherence of the body of science as it changes over time.[52]

In fact, on Putnam's reading (essentially, Quine's reading) of the Skolem–Löwenheim theorem,

> Not only may there be correspondence between objects and (what we take to be) incompatible theories (i.e., *the same objects* can be what logicians call a "model" for incompatible theories), but even if we fix the theory *and* fix the objects there are (if the number of objects is infinite) infinitely many *different* ways in which the same objects can be used to make a model for a given theory. This simply states in mathematical language the intuitive fact that to single out a correspondence between two domains *one needs some independent access to both domains*.[53]

But this means, in effect, that, if reference to the entities of two distinct theories is internal to their respective theories, then, if two theories "are incompatible from a metaphysical point of view" (for example, the Maxwell field theory and the retarded potential theory, as Putnam observes), their being "mathematically intertranslatable" cannot be used to *decide* that they are theories about the very same objects: the equiv alence of theories in this respect entails nothing regarding the identity of the paired objects of those theories (Quine's "inscrutability of reference"), and the putative equivalence of actual physical theories presupposes rather than determines the identity of the empirically specified referents shared by those theories. This is the very point of speaking of *applying* the Skolem–Löwenheim theorem *to* empirically provided propositions. It is undoubtedly true that purely formal interpretations of given systems of propositions, preserving truth, could not have been used *originally* to generate the empirically decisive ones.

At the very least, the same entities cannot have incompatible properties. So perhaps (following Quine) "every single physical event could be *described* in two ways" (in terms, say, of "particles acting at a distance, across empty space ... or in terms of particles acting on fields which act on other fields [or other parts of the same field], which finally act 'locally' on other particles").[54] But it would not be possible, essentially on the strength of the Skolem–Löwenheim theorem, to hold (as Putnam and Goodman do) that "'objects' ... are as much *made* as discovered, as much products of our *conceptual* invention."[55] The theorem is entirely formal. The latter doctrine (internalism$_o$) simply obviates the possibility that any seeming "abstract correspondence" (fitted, inevitably, to some finitely specified portion of the infinite domains over which the given theories range) *could* (be counted on to) aid in reidentifying the same objects in those domains. As Putnam himself says, still reflecting on the import of the Skolem–Löwenheim theorem, "there are always infinitely many functions which agree with any given table on any finite set of values, but which diverge on values not listed in the table."[56] What this shows, then, is not merely that internal realism is too weak to support any interesting version of scientific realism, but that, however it may be supplemented in order to be adequate to the task, it cannot be construed (especially with respect to physical nature, where the issue is centered) in the strong sense Putnam and Goodman favor. The thesis that different "worlds" are somehow constructed by *our* conceptual schemes – *not* that *the* world is differently described in accord with such conceptual schemes (or technologically altered) – is essentially inimical to reconciling internalism$_o$ and externalism$_o$.[57] A perspicuous way of pressing the point is this: in Putnam's hands, internal realism characteristically favors alethic considerations – arguments leading to a full epistemic realism are discounted on purely *formal* grounds; but scientific realism pursues transcendental reflections *on* the conditions of human cognition itself – for instance, on the causal import of deliberate human interventions in nature.

This, finally, is the weakness of the alethic internalist thesis: that truth is a kind of ideal coherence of beliefs. *If* (b′) is linked to a strong constructive interpretation of (a′) (ontic internalism), then Putnam can offer no reasons for construing *any or all or selected versions of* the (apparently biologically) viable forms of coherence favored in our "multiple" worlds as supporting a convergent sense of scientific realism ranging over all such worlds.[58] He is, therefore, seriously mistaken in several distinct ways regarding the vindication of scientific realism. First of all, it no longer makes sense to speak of objective progress in science in the context of a strongly constructive view of ontic internalism (just as it no longer makes sense to speak of Goodman's program of *progressively* eliminating pseudo-projectibles in inductive contexts). Secondly, scientific realism cannot be construed as a matter of empirical induction and, assuming a strong interpretation of (a′), can only, when so construed, be question-begging or trivial. And, thirdly, the rejection of a demarcation line between realism and idealism signifies that scientific realism can accommodate (relativistically) the confirmation (or indefeasibility) of divergent, even incompatible, interpretations of empirical data; but it cannot survive the charge that there is no common world that we are trying to understand and interpret through our various theories. In fact, the irony is that, in the context of our present discussion, Putnam's and Goodman's strong speculations about the artifactuality of the world(s) we merely cognize cannot fail to appear to be even more strenuous versions of the incommensurability thesis than could ever reasonably be ascribed to Kuhn.

In Putnam's account, therefore, we find a series of scattered clues – admittedly unintended – that force us step by step to recognize what appear to be the limiting concessions of any viable form of scientific realism. In any case, to resist the finding is still to acknowledge that the dialectical possibilities are arrayed more clearly than before, because of Putnam's defense of internal realism.

IV

One final step remains to be taken. We have argued that scientific realism must, if it is to be defended at all, be construed as the conclusion of a transcendental argument – once we reject foundationalism and a demarcation line between realism and idealism, and once we agree to being confined to epistemic internalism. This is simply the consequence of having considered the prospects of the three strategies that alone appear pertinent:

(α) appeal to externalist$_e$ grounds – in effect, foundationalism or transparency;

(β) appeal to straightforward deductive or inductive grounds within the confines of epistemic internalism; and

(γ) appeal to internalist grounds in support of externalist conditions of cognition.

The first two strategies are indefensible, because (α) is incompatible with the constraint of epistemic internalism, and because (β) can be made to bear relevantly on the issue only by an illicit assumption that the constraint just mentioned is not in place.

Now, then, there are only two lines of counterargument against transcendental reasoning that appear to have attracted strong adherents: one holds that transcendental reasoning (γ) is, or invariably is, or must be, a (disguised) form of (α); the other holds that transcendental arguments are, or invariably are, or must be, committed to (what is usually taken to be) Kant's conception of such reasoning, and that such arguments are (logically) impossible. But these two counterstrategies are, actually, rather easy to discount.

The first is most strenuously pursued by Richard Rorty, and has been used by him to discount the validity of the dominant Western tradition of philosophy.[59] Rorty raises the Kantian *quaestio juris*, the question of how to "justify" or "prove" or "legitimate" the concepts we use in speaking of "the existence of things outside us" in such a way as to defeat the skeptic and to support a vigorous realism.[60] After a good deal of careful analysis, Rorty concludes that standard transcendental arguments, in attempting to *legitimate* realist claims, are simply all foundationalist (or externalist$_e$) in nature. In fact, Rorty divides philosophy into (at least) three camps: one that uses philosophy (transcendentally) to legitimate epistemological realism (notoriously represented by Descartes); one that rejects that (representational or mirror) ideal – in effect, espousing pragmatism – sometimes, most notably in the work of Donald Davidson (on Rorty's view), by employing "a transcendental argument to end all transcendental arguments – one which tears down the scaffolding upon which the standard paradigms of 'realistic' transcendental arguments were mounted";[61] and one that, building on (such) pragmatist arguments, pursues philosophy in a way that "is *not* concerned with the legitimation of knowledge-claims" (here, Rorty mentions Heidegger, Dewey, and the later Wittgenstein, whom he professes to follow).[62]

What Rorty opposes, therefore, are transcendental arguments that are "realist" – that is, that have as their "aim to *guarantee* correspondence of logic, or language, or the practice of rational inquiry to the world." Where such arguments are distinctly Kantian, "our 'legitimating' transcendental knowledge of the necessary truth that content will correspond to scheme [in effect, intuitions to concepts, or the objects of thought to thought, or the world to words], is made possible by the fact that our subjectivity (the scheme) *creates* the content."[63] Viewing matters thus (in effect, following Davidson), Rorty is bound to construe Putnam's attempt to defend internal realism (like Kant's) as vitiated by the underlying "Cartesian notion of privileged access to one's own subjectivity"[64] – in effect, by an illicit foundationalism. (So metaphysical and internal realism come to much the same thing.) Hence, Rorty sees realist transcendental arguments as invariably (and ineluctably) externalist$_e$ (even though, of course, the point of the realist's ultimate appeal is to the reliably self-disclosing nature of the mind itself). This *is* a fair objection, but it is quite easy to offset; it is certainly *not* unavoidable. For, we can either hold that transcendental arguments remain realist, remain constrained in an internalist$_e$ sense, *and* attempt to legitimate knowledge claims in a way that is not illicit; or hold that transcendental arguments do not "legitimate" knowledge claims but legitimate only *the conceptual plausibility of viewing our internalist$_e$ claims as having externalist$_o$ import. How?

The simplest and most obvious way of doing this is to agree with

Rorty that there are *no* circumstances under which we actually possess, at any moment, foundationalist knowledge – whether of the physical world or of our own minds unmediated by our conceptual schemata. This makes it clear once and for all that, whatever they may be supposed to be, transcendental arguments need not be taken to be (thus far at least) disguised versions of (α). Granting that much, we need only hold further that, relative to a tradition of disciplined speculation about such matters, we simply *propose* conceptual schemes linking our intuitions about the best work of science (which Rorty certainly does not wish to threaten in the skeptic's way: he is not denying knowledge, only what Heidegger terms "the onto-theo-logical tradition," and Dewey, "the quest for cerainty" – that is, foundationalism and its cognate doctrines) with coherent, imaginable conditions deemed necessary to the support of scientific realism; and we assess the comparative power of such alternative schemes – we "legitimate" them – by reference to our developing tradition of what is to count as the kind of (logically informal) rigor that such arguments best exhibit.

This catches up very neatly all the features of transcendental arguments (1–10, listed in the previous section). In particular, it enables us to construe transcendental arguments as normative, (yet) empirically cap able of supporting alternative proposals regarding the *quaestio juris* of cognitive claims (not in the externalist, sense), addressed to *a priori* issues, designed to provide the best conjecture regarding the necessary conditions of knowledge and experience, but deliberately confined within the limits of what we take to be our historical horizon. There is absolutely no reason to think that this is an illegitimate or useless intellectual exercise, and there is no reason to deny that it involves a distinctive and plausible interpretation of what a transcendental argument is.

Certainly, one thing that follows from its admission is that Davidson's "third" dogma of empiricism, the false dualism of "scheme and content" (the exposure of which Rorty depends on for the full effect of his own argument), is itself easily avoided – hence, cannot have the decisive force of ending "all transcendental arguments": Davidson's charge is merely a version of the complaint against foundationalism (and, of course, against incommensurability claims that permit the individuation of radically different conceptual schemes); and Rorty's characterization of pragmatism is, derivatively, unnecessarily and altogether too pessimistically restricted. Philosophy has every prospect of flourishing – pragmatically, one may say – by way at least of our revised notion of transcendental reasoning; *for there is no reason to suppose that philosophy – particularly the "legitimation" of scientific realism – must proceed foundationally*: that is, in the foundationalist's way.

To put matters this way leads directly to a *reductio* of Rorty's central thesis. For, if, as argued, first- and second-order questions are conceptually inseparable, then, even if (in agreement with Rorty) questions of legitimation cannot any longer be managed in the foundationalist or logocentric manner, philosophy cannot be merely therapeutic; if it cannot, then appeal to Davidson's "transcendental" argument (or to any similar argument) construed as leading to the rational abandonment of all transcendental argument or transcendental reasoning or philosophy itself must be a *non sequitur*. Rorty's own convenient summary of the principal (therapeutic) arguments against the "mirror" conception, including, now, Davidson's own argument ("against" it), *must* convey more than a merely self-effacing and self-erasing therapeutic function. *It must usher in new options.* In this sense, the *passage* of theories we have been examining regularly neglect at one point or another to make room for the possibility of a conception of philosophy that

1 is committed to pursuing issues of legitimation – transcendental issues;
2 acknowledges the defeat of all versions of cognitive transparency;
3 accepts a pragmatist or holistic defense of realism;
4 opposes anarchism, skepticism, radical incommensurabilism;
5 favors a scientific realism addressed to distributed claims;
6 historicizes and praxicalizes human existence and human inquiry;
7 rejects all forms of traditionalism as cryptic versions of essentialism or cognitive transparency;
8 is hospitable, within limits, to idealism and anti-realism; and
9 espouses a moderate or robust relativism, wherever reasonable.

1–9 are, in fact, the generic features of the philosophical program toward which all of the arguments here assembled distinctly converge. It is tempting to suggest that Rorty's thesis tends more to encourage anarchical and deconstructive tendencies than a sustained recovery of philosophical discipline – unless it is to prompt a mere reaction back to the "mirror" image that, as the somewhat pragmatist and deconstructive critic that he is, Rorty has assisted in demolishing.

The alternative counterargument against the transcendental has been championed by Stephan Körner. Körner holds that a transcendental deduction is "a logically sound demonstration [not necessarily a deductive argument] of the reasons why a particular categorial schema is not only in fact, but also necessarily employed, in differentiating a region of experience"; since at least one of its preconditions "cannot be satisfied ... the impossibility of transcendental deductions follows immediately."[65] Körner's entire argument is designed to show "the impossibility of demonstrating a schema's uniqueness" – that is, that it is "uniquely *a priori*," "the only one possible."[66] The uniqueness claim is taken to be Kantian (though, apparently, Kant never addressed the issue directly), and it is explained in the following way by Körner:

> a method of external differentiation [that is, a method that distinguishes between oneself and the external world *and*, within one's experience, between external objects and their attributes] belongs to a categorial schema ... if, and only if, the attributes employed comprise what may be called respectively ... "constitutive" and "individuating" attributes. An attribute is constitutive (of external objects) if, and only if, it is applicable to external objects and if, in addition, its applicability to an object logically implies, and is logically implied by, the object's being an external object. ... An attribute is individuating (for external objects) if, and only if, it is applicable to every external object and if, in addition, its applicability to an external object logically implies, and is logically implied by, the external object's being distinct from all other objects.[67]

It is clear, therefore, that Körner does not address the issue of realism at all. What he shows, for example, is that, if one concedes some schema of differentiation (in the sense given), then the statement that its attributes are constitutive and individuating will form a mere conjunction about its actual scope and about the required entailments; hence, it will not be able to preclude the possibility of there being some alternative schema that functions similarly. The uniqueness claim will therefore fail: Kant will have been able to produce only "nonuniquely *a priori* statements."[68] (It may of course be disputed whether Körner has represented Kant's view on the uniqueness requirement accurately.)

But we have alrady formulated a viable, non-Kantian conception of transcendental arguments, and Körner's own objections fit that notion very well.[69] The irony, of course, is that our qualification of Körner's view is somewhat in the spirit of his own objection against Kant's. Furthermore, the whole thrust of conceding the constraint of internalism*e* is to be hospitable to alternative, even incompatible, schemata for a given domain – in effect, *to construe transcendental arguments relativistically*. In a way, this is to redeem the alleged import of the Skolem–Löwenheim theorem, but now (very clearly) only on the assumption of *some* effective schema of "prior differentiation," as Körner puts its. But that, precisely, is tantamount to distinguishing between initial, cognitively pertinent findings regarding a given domain and purely formal schemes of alternative "differentiation" *with respect to that domain* thus addressed. In any event, this fits very well with construing transcendental arguments as synthetic and *a priori* but as not synthetic *a priori*. Only if the initial cognitive representation of the domain were foundationalist in some sense could a uniquely *a priori* statement of the sort Körner contests be in place.

Our view of transcendental arguments, then, is fully compatible with construing the question of scientific realism as a transcendental issue *and* with denying the demarcation between realism and idealism – which, in effect, disqualifies both metaphysical and internal realism. It appears to offer a natural solution to a number of puzzles about realist theories. In particular, it affords a way of defending realism and of reconciling relativism and realism – and it shows the reasonableness and conceptual advantage of making the effort.

In effect, to construe transcendental arguments in the way we have is to have assigned logically distinctive properties to the substantive arguments we have been advancing, without intruding any privileged arguments; and to have characterized those arguments thus is to have made provision for substantive possibilities not otherwise eligible. In particular, by rejecting foundationalism and the demarcation between realism and idealism (not by any means equivalent doctrines), we have been able to demonstrate at least that, relative to legitimating the sciences,

1 every viable form of realism must be reconciled with a form of anti-realism (the recoverable import of internal realism);
2 every viable form of anti-realism (as just construed) must be admitted to function in a realist way (the minimal relevance constraint on distributed anti-realist charges);
3 thus characterized, realism and anti-realism address logically independent issues and cannot be expected to function as exclusive and exhaustive alternatives;
4 realism and anti-realism are both complex and generic doctrines the constituents of which may be coherently assembled in various specific ways that defy the usual disjunctive alternatives of metaphysical and internal realism, realism and idealism, realism and instrumentalism, realism and anti-realism;
5 scientific realism cannot be convincingly served by any theory that does not supersede such disjunctions (especially, acknowledging praxical and historical contingencies, by any anti-realism that does not yield some in the direction of metaphysical realism, even where metaphysical realism itself is entirely untenable);

6   anti-realist constraints (relevant to the rejection of foundationalism and of the demarcation between realism and idealism) entail, at least distributively, the provisionality of bivalence itself (in the direction of relativistic truth values for given sectors of inquiry) and the provisionality of any ontological constraints within the scope of scientific realism (for instance, regarding the nature and reality of unobservables and unobservable causes); and, finally,

7   arguments of all these (second-order) sorts are (because of the limited logical force that can be defensibly assigned them) themselves open to a profound form of rhetorical and diachronic contingency – not, however, without their own characteristic rigor – that commits us to an equally deep relativism within philosophical dispute.

In particular, transcendental arguments proceed by way of historically salient exemplars rather than universal rules (in a sense very much akin to Kuhn's sense of "exemplar," though without reference to anything like his various incommensurability theses[70]). These findings return us to the very start of our speculation. But they return us with a larger vision and with suppler strategies.

Notes

1   See Hilary Putnam: *Meaning and the Moral Sciences* (London: Routledge and Kegan Paul, 1978); *Philosophical Papers*, vol. 2 (Cambridge: Cambridge University Press, 1975).

2   Hilary Putnam, "Two Philosophical Perspectives," *Reason, Truth and History* (Cambridge: Cambridge University Press, 1981), pp. 49–50.

3   Ibid., p. 60.

4   Ibid., p. 67.

5   For a recent survey of the reidentification of noumena and phenomena in post-Kantian thought, see Michael Allen Gillespie, *Hegel, Heidegger, and the Ground of History* (Chicago: University of Chicago Press, 1984).

6   Putnam, "Two Philosophical Perspectives," *Reason, Truth and History*, p. 49.

7   Ibid., p. 54.

8   Franz Brentano, "The Distinction between Mental and Physical Phenomena," *Psychology from an Empirical Standpoint*, ed. Oskar Kraus and (English edn) Linda L. McAlister (London: Routledge and Kegan Paul, 1973); and John M. Heaton, "Brentano and Freud," in Barry Smith (ed.), *Structure and Gestalt* (Amsterdam: John Benjamins, 1981); also C. I. Lewis, "Experience and Meaning," *Philosophical Review*, XLIII (1934).

 9   Putnam, "Two Philosophical Perspectives," *Reason, Truth and History*, p. 54.
10   Ibid., pp. 49–50.
11   Ibid., pp. 49, 67, 73.
12   Ibid., pp. 53f, 52.
13   Ibid., p. 55.
14   Cf. Putnam, *Meaning and the Moral Sciences*.
15   Nelson Goodman, Preface to *Ways of Worldmaking* (Indianapolis: Hackett, 1978).
16   Putnam, "Two Philosophical Perspectives," *Reason, Truth and History*, p. 54.
17   Cf. W. V. Quine's review in *New York Review of Books*, 23 November 1978, p. 25.
18   Nicholas Rescher, *The Coherence Theory of Truth* (Oxford: Clarendon Press, 1973).
19   Putnam, "Two Philosophical Perspectives," *Reason, Truth and History*, p. 54.
20   Cf. Richard Boyd, "Realism, Underdetermination, and a Causal Theory of Evidence," *Nous*, VIII (1973) – whose views Putnam had distinctly favored in *Meaning and the Moral Sciencs*.
21   For instance, in *Reason, Truth and History*, and in *Philosophical Papers*, vol. 3 (Cambridge: Cambridge University Press, 1983).
22   Allowance must be made for a variety of scientific realisms: cf. for instance Putnam, *Meaning and the Moral Sciences*; Bas C. van Fraassen, *The Scientific Image* (Oxford: Clarendon Press, 1980); Nancy Cartwright, *How the Laws of Physics Lie* (Oxford: Clarendon Press, 1983); Ian Hacking, *Representing and Intervening* (Cambridge: Cambridge University Press, 1983).
23   See Keith Lehrer, *Knowledge* (Oxford: Clarendon Press, 1974).
24   Putnam, *Philosophical Papers*, vol. 3, pp. xiv–xviii.
25   See Lehrer, *Knowledge*.
26   Cf. W. V. Quine, *Word and Object* (Cambridge, Mass.: Harvard University Press, 1960); and Goodman, *Ways of Worldmaking*, chs. 1, 7.
27   This is, in fact, the fatal flaw of Karl-Otto Apel's and Jürgen Habermas's universalism; also, of Richard Rorty's rejection of a great deal of philosophy – which we shall consider briefly below.
28   This is the point of Putnam's provocative essay "Brains in a Vat," in *Reason, Truth and History*; cf. pp. 49–51.
29   See Richard Rorty, *Philosophy and the Mirror of Nature* (Princeton, NJ: Princeton University Press, 1979).
30   Cf. Michael Dummett, "Realism," *Truth and Other Enigmas* (Cambridge, Mass.: Harvard University Press, 1978).
31   Cf. Hacking, *Representing and Intervening*, ch. 15.
32   Cf. Grover Maxwell, "The Ontological Status of Theoretical Entities," in Herbert Feigl and Grover Maxwell (eds), *Minnesota Studies in the Phil-*

osophy of Science, vol. III (Minneapolis: University of Minnesota Press, 1962).

33 Van Fraassen, *The Scientific Image*, p. 64; cf. p. 14 and also ch. 7.

34 Ibid., p. 130; cf. p. 156 and the whole of ch. 5.

35 An excellent sketch of such possibilities is provided by Hacking in *Representing and Intervening*, ch. 13. Cf. also, Cartwright, *How the Laws of Physics Lie*.

36 The latter is actually the charge Richard Rorty brings against transcendental arguments: see for instance his "Transcendental Arguments, Self-Reference, and Pragmatism," in Peter Bieri et al (eds), *Transcendental Arguments and Science* (Dordrecht: D. Reidel, 1979).

37 One of the most recent, surely one of the best informed, examinations of transcendental reasoning and transcendental argument appears in J. N. Mohanty, *The Possibility of Transcendental Philosophy* (Dordrecht: Martinus Nijhoff, 1985). Nevertheless, Mohanty affirms that "no one – to my knowledge – has shown any satisfactory reason why foundationalism as such should be rejected" (p. xxiii); and in the spirit of this theme he goes on to say, "although transcendental philosophy has to be, by the very nature of its project, foundationalistic, how viable it is depends upon how this foundation is formulated" (p. xxiv). It is not altogether easy to sort out Mohanty's meaning here. For, he also holds that "neither historicism nor relativism logically entails anti-foundationalism" (ibid.), which, on the arguments that have been mustered, is mistaken. He appears to mean, by "foundationalism," the search for necessary foundations (which we here acknowledge); he also speaks of reconciling "a concept of foundation" with both historicism and relativism (ibid.), which really precludes foundationalism; and he admits that "There is a certain contingency in history which transcendental philosophy cannot eliminate" (p. xxix). These concessions substantially temper his own preference for what otherwise appears to be a rather strong foundationalism – in terms of "the self-evidencing, self-illuminating character of consciousness" (see Essay 7). It should be noted that Mohanty's notion of "evidence" (*Evidenz*, "self-evidence₂") is not equivalent to "the notion of apodictic evidence" and does not serve as "a criterion of truth" (pp. 98–9). It is in accord with that notion, apparently, that "transcendental necessity" – concerning the "essential truths" that serve as the "*conditions of the possibility* of empirical facts being what they are" (p. 94) – are "evident." *If* this does really favor the pertinence, for transcendental reasoning, of the contingencies of historicism and relativism, then the view here advanced and Mohanty's converge somewhat. If not, then they do not.

38 These considerations undermine not only Putnam's objections to externalist concerns, but also the need to rely on Kant's view of transcendental arguments (or developments sympathetic to Kant's view), as well as the need to concede the impossibility of transcendental arguments. See for example Stephan Körner: "The Impossibility of Transcendental Deductions," *The*

Monist, LI (1967); "Transcendental Tendencies in Recent Philosophy," *Journal of Philosophy*, LXIII (1966). Also, Jay F. Rosenberg, "Transcendental Arguments Revisited," *Journal of Philosophy*, LXXII (1975).

39 See Rudolf Carnap, "Empiricism, Semantics and Ontology," *Meaning and Necessity*, (Chicago: University of Chicago Press, 1956); and James W. Cornman, *Metaphysics, Reference and Language* (New Haven, Conn.: Yale University Press, 1966).

40 The admission of this problem and a strenuous effort to overcome it (inevitably failed) appear in Donald Davidson, "Mental Events," *Essays on Actions and Events* (Oxford: Clarendon Press, 1980); Cf. also Joseph Margolis, "Prospects for an Extensionalist Psychology of Action," *Journal for the Theory of Social Behavior*, II (1981).

41 Cf. Quine, *Word and Object*; and Joseph Margolis, "Behaviorism and Alien Languages" *Philosophia*, III (1973).

42 Cf. Goodman: *Ways of Worldmaking*; *Fact, Fiction and Forecast*, 2nd edn (Indianapolis: Bobbs-Merrill, 1965).

43 Cf. Edmund Husserl, *The Crisis of European Sciences and Transcendental Phenomenology*, tr. David Carr (Evanston, Ill.: Northwestern University Press, 1970).

44 Putnam, "A Problem about Reference," *Reason, Truth and History*, p. 47.

45 Putnam, "Two Philosophical Perspectives," *Reason, Truth and History*, p. 66.

46 Ibid., p. 52.

47 Ibid., p. 55.

48 Ibid., p. 41.

49 Ibid. (italics added).

50 See Putnam, *Meaning and the Moral Sciences*.

51 Putnam, "A Problem about Reference," *Reason, Truth and History*, p. 44 (cf. also ibid., Appendix; and Quine, *Word and Object*). Putnam quotes, at p. 41, an extremely revealing remark by Quine, which he does not locate. I have been unable to find its source.

52 It is very possible that Quine's reading of the Skolem–Löwenheim theorem has led him (at least at one stage in his reflections on ontology) to the disastrous (and clearly untenable) doctrine that alternative interpretations can be fitted to an entire body of sentences (a science *en bloc*) *without regard to* the fixing of terms *correlative* with the fixing of sentences. But word and sentence are indissolubly connected conceptually, and the theorem is itself entirely formal. It has absolutely no application until some body of empirically promising sentences is actually cognitively supported; and, when it is, terms are fixed at the same time sentences are. This issue is quite different from that of using the theorem reductively – for instance, in a Pythagorean way. Quine opposes such an effort. Cf. Quine: *Word and Object*, especially pp. 27, 53; "Interpretations of Sets of Conditions," *Selected Logic Papers* (New York: Random House, 1966); "On Carnap's Views on Ontology," *The Ways of Paradox*, rev. and enlarged edn (Cambridge,

Mass.: Harvard University Press, 1976), pp. 204–5; "Ontological Reduction and the World of Numbers" in the same volume; and Margolis, "Behaviorism and Alien Languages."

53 Putnam, "Two Philosophical Perspectives," *Reason, Truth and History*, pp. 73–4 (italics added).

54 Ibid., p. 73 (italics added).

55 Ibid. (italics added).

56 Ibid., p. 67.

57 For example, Goodman very clearly states that "We are not speaking in terms of multiple possible alternatives to a single actual world but of multiple actual worlds"; and he links his view to the rejection of foundationalism: "The non-Kantian theme of multiplicity of worlds is closely akin to the Kantian theme of the vacuity of the notion of pure content" (*Ways of Worldmaking*, pp. 2, 6). How "closely akin," one wants to ask? Sufficient for instance, to make the rejection of foundationalism entail the multiple-worlds thesis? Goodman never says which world (or worlds) *we* (as cognitive agents capable of comparing all such worlds) inhabit. Could we, for instance, be multiple selves inhabiting one or another but not all of these worlds? The question suggests the severe risk of incoherence.

58 Cf. Rosenberg, "Transcendental Arguments Revisited," *Journal of Philosophy*, LXXII.

59 Cf. Rorty, *Philosophy and the Mirror of Nature*.

60 Rorty, "Transcendental Arguments, Self Reference, and Pragmatism," in Bieri et al., *Transcendental Arguments and Science*; cf. also, Barry Stroud, "Transcendental Arguments," *Journal of Philosophy*, LXV (1968); and Rüdiger Bubner, "Kant, Transcendental Argument, and the Problem of Deduction," *Review of Metaphysics*, XXVIII (1975).

61 Rorty, "Transcendental Arguments, Self-Reference, and Pragmatism," in Bieri et al., *Transcendental Arguments and Science*, p. 78. See also Donald Davidson, "On the Very Idea of a Conceptual Scheme," *Proceedings and Addresses of the American Philosophical Association*, XLVII (1973)

62 Rorty, "Transcendental Arguments, Self-Reference, and Pragmatism," in Bieri et al., *Transcendental Arguments and Science*, p. 78.

63 Ibid., p. 79 (first italics added). Here Rorty follows Bubner's account in "Kant, Transcendental Argument, and the Problem of Deduction," *Review of Metaphysics*, XXVIII.

64 Rorty, "Transcendental Arguments, Self-Reference, and Pragmatism," in Bieri et al., *Transcendental Arguments and Science*, p. 80.

65 Körner, "The Impossibility of Transcendental Deductions," *The Monist*, LI, 318–19.

66 Ibid., pp. 321, 323.

67 Ibid., p. 317.

68 Ibid., p. 523.

69 I have had the benefit, after having completed this essay, of examining in manuscript Paul Guyer's *Kant and the Claims of Knowledge*, which is to

be published by Cambridge University Press. It affords in an extremely painstaking way a full account of Kant's attempts to formulate a successful transcendental argument, particularly Kant's attempts to defeat skeptical forms of idealism. Guyer's own account makes it very reasonable to conclude both that Kant never succeeded in his various efforts and was himself dissatisfied with these efforts to the end of his life. Furthermore, on the strength of Guyer's search of Kant's *Nachlass* as well as the published texts, it seems fair to conclude that Kant never considered supporting logically weaker forms of "transcendental" thinking than would yield synthetic *a priori* truths – that is, truths synthetic and necessary *de re*. He apparently had nothing to say about historicizing transcendental arguments or relativizing them within less than species-wide constraints. The heterodox conception of transcendental arguments here favored has, therefore, little need for apology in terms of the Kantian canon.

70 See Thomas S. Kuhn, "Second Thoughts on Paradigms," *The Essential Tension* (Chicago: University of Chicago Press, 1977).

Index